Authorship and Publicity Before Print

THE MIDDLE AGES SERIES

Ruth Mazo Karras, Series Editor
Edward Peters, Founding Editor

A complete list of books in the series is available from the publisher.

Authorship and Publicity Before Print

Jean Gerson and the Transformation of Late Medieval Learning

DANIEL HOBBINS

PENN

University of Pennsylvania Press

Philadelphia

Publication of this book has been aided by a grant from The Medieval Academy of America, and by the College of Humanities and the Department of History at the Ohio State University.

Published by
University of Pennsylvania Press
Philadelphia, Pennsylvania 19104–4112

Printed in the United States of America on acid-free paper
10   9   8   7   6   5   4   3   2   1

Library of Congress Cataloging-in-Publication Data

Hobbins, Daniel.
  Authorship and publicity before print : Jean Gerson and the transformation of late medieval learning / Daniel Hobbins.
    p.   cm.— (The Middle Ages series)
  Includes bibliographical references and index.
  ISBN 978-0-8122-4155-6 (alk. paper)
  1. Gerson, Jean, 1363–1429.   2. Authorship—History—To 1500.   3. Gerson, Jean, 1363–1429—Books and reading.   4. Books and reading—Europe—History—To 1500.
I. Title.
  BX4705.G45H63   2009
  282.092—dc22

                                                            2008050860

To my parents

Contents

viii   Contents

Illustrations and Maps

Illustrations

Maps

Preface

Centuries from now, historians of the written word will surely describe this present age as a moment of transition. Not twenty years into the Virtual Age, and Americans are reading fewer books. Some doomsayers announced the end of the printed book prematurely, but does anyone doubt that the world of books and of reading itself has changed in our lifetime? We are sliding, some of us against our wishes, from an age dominated by print into an age of electronic media. The printed book has company now, and everyone appreciates through close experience what scholars have been saying for the past fifty years: that the norms in place since the fifteenth century, all the things we thought we knew about authorship, books, and publishing, are not timeless but historically conditioned and contingent on the printed book.

I would like to exploit this awkward historical moment to consider another period that will challenge our assumptions and force us once again to confront the contingency of our historical situation—and, perhaps, allow us to understand it better. Historians tend to focus on moments or figures of change when a revolution (cultural, intellectual, political) chases the old order away and breaks the world in two. The stirring phrases of transition are embedded in the master narrative of Western history and spring readily to our lips: the "twelfth-century renaissance"; the "print revolution"; the "dawn of the Reformation"; "Après moi le déluge."

This book investigates instead a time before the transition, the world of written culture before print—authorship, books, publishing, writing, reading. Critics of Elizabeth Eisenstein's important book *The Printing Press as an Agent of Change* (1979) sometimes took her to task for failing to understand manuscript culture. A fair criticism: the transformation Eisenstein described was less dramatic than she made it seem, and had deep roots in late medieval written culture. But how many medievalists in 1979 knew more than she did, say, about publishing in a manuscript culture? Even today, wide open spaces of the fifteenth-century landscape remain poorly understood. Yet we shall never fully comprehend the changes brought about by print until we understand the writing and publishing system that preceded it.

We know much more now than in 1979, thanks partly to the controversy generated by Eisenstein. Authorship before print is different from modern authorship. *But it is a form of authorship,* a form different even from earlier medieval forms of authorship as we see it in *The Song of Roland* and the romances of Chrétien de Troyes (fl. 1175). Who is Chrétien? We barely know. Move ahead two hundred years and Christine de Pizan (c. 1364–c. 1430) takes on flesh and blood. Read her books and you cannot escape her: she walks around inside them.

The same point holds with greater force for publication. For centuries we have associated publishing with print, though that meaning is fast being eroded. Yet publishing most certainly did occur before print. It is not even a medieval invention. The idea of publishing a text by circulating or broadcasting it to unknown readers goes back to the ancient world. Clearly, then, premodern publishing means something very different from what it does today.

To recover these lost meanings, this book focuses on a key moment, the fifty years or so before the European invention of movable alphabetic type in the 1450s, and a key figure, arguably the most popular writer of the fifteenth century. This claim for the centrality of Jean Gerson in late medieval culture (see the Introduction) may surprise some medievalists. But this book is not just about rehabilitation. It is partly that, and partly devoted to understanding his writings, his exact place and importance in the fifteenth century. But more important, it uses those writings to recover a world that still remains lost in the shadows of a perceived medieval twilight. It takes one step—not the first or the last—toward rethinking the grand narrative that sees the period from 1100 to 1600 as two mountains, two renaissances of the twelfth and sixteenth centuries, separated by a valley of dry bones. Thanks to scholarship in many fields over the past thirty years, those bones are now coming to life. It remains a strange valley. But that just makes it all the more interesting.

Introduction

In the prologue of a treatise written in 1389, Jean Gerson makes a surprising admission. Years earlier, Petrarch had boasted that "no one looks beyond Italy for orators and poets."[1] His taunt deeply embarrassed French humanists. Gerson simply agrees with Petrarch. "France," he writes in the first sentence, "has hitherto suffered a great famine of worthy and eloquent historians and poets." Distinguished by its warriors and its wise men, France has yet lacked writers to record their accomplishments. What gave such fame to Greece, Rome, and Troy, even in ruin, if not the eloquence of their writers? Even as their walls crumbled, these cities escaped oblivion through the power of writing: "So writings live and endure longer than cities."[2] Gilbert Ouy has pointed to the key word in this passage: "hitherto" (*hactenus*). As if to say, the famine will end as I and others at the University of Paris bring glory to France through our writings.[3] "Long consideration of these matters," Gerson continues, "has moved me to write as truly as possible for the cause of faith that the University of Paris pursues now and of old."[4]

Ouy has seen this text—a tract against the Dominican Juan de Monzon on the Immaculate Conception—as evidence for the early humanist spirit in France.[5] I would like to reorient the discussion toward the real subject of the passage: writing, with its power to foil oblivion and to preserve truth for future ages. This point is so crucial that I could reduce the primary argument of this book to one sentence: the best way to understand Gerson within the context of late medieval culture is to focus on his conviction that the day's pressing need was for people who were self-conscious about the task of writing and skilled in putting it to good use.

Scholars do not usually describe the schoolmen in such terms. Converging on the thirteenth century, they privilege intellectual categories: modes of analysis and logical abstractions in the service of a grand metaphysical program of reconciling authorities. What does any of this have to do with good writing? Alain Boureau recently asked if one can even speak of "scholastic authors."[6] Schoolmen such as Thomas Aquinas, Bonaventure, John Duns Scotus, and William of Ockham may have been authors in the sense that they possessed authority and were known and recognized. But if authorship means more than this, something like individual creation and ownership of texts, then perhaps authorship is not the right word for their activity. When Alexander of Hales died in 1245 leaving unfinished his great summa, the Franciscans commissioned a group of theologians to complete it.[7] Likewise, when Aquinas died in 1274 leaving unfinished works, the Dominicans patched them up with fragments of odd treatises and even memories of his teaching. The true author, says Boureau, is not the person who died in 1274 but the "mind of Thomas" that inspired these works and their continuations.[8]

The opening passage of Gerson's tract communicates a very different sense of authorship from what we see in these examples. Gerson associates authorship with history and poetry, strange pursuits for a schoolman, yet undertaken in the service of something more familiar, "the cause of faith" at Paris. He stresses the need for eloquence in this cause. He imagines writings that outlast empires and bring glory to their native lands. The grave threat is oblivion. France's accomplishments were forgotten because no one wrote them down. Eloquent writing can and will endure; it has permanence (*duratio*); it is "longer-lived" (*longaevior*) than cities. We see here a longing for literary fame that has no dependence upon print.[9]

These comments mark the beginning of a theme that preoccupied Gerson throughout his career. He talked constantly about writing: whether or not to write, the guilt he felt about writing, books that he had written or would write, how to write clearly and how not to, why to write at all. He talked about other authors and their books—stirring books that he had read in a single day, "altogether lovely" books, dangerous and harmful books, books both beautiful and dangerous. And then there is reading: he taught theology students how to read, deplored contemporary reading habits, and compiled reading lists. We can add publishing: he carefully considered the best way to deliver texts to entire categories of people and took advantage of large gatherings to distribute his works. With all this talk about writing and books and reading, no wonder that he wrote the first independent work on scribal practice, *In Praise of Scribes of Healthy Doctrine.*[10] No books without copyists!

We can begin by acknowledging this much as a point of departure: Gerson occupies a more complicated historical space than thirteenth-century schoolmen. His leading role in the great issues of his time once led Étienne Delaruelle to call this period "the century of Gerson"; Gerson was a "mirror of his time."[11] Delaruelle staked his claim on Gerson's wide interests as a theologian. The claim must now go further. Gerson mirrors his world in many ways that Delaruelle did not investigate, and each one requires demonstration. Scholarship on Gerson has become a minor industry. We now have recent studies on many different aspects of his activity and his literary corpus, and Brian Patrick McGuire has provided a helpful biography that combs through much of the literature and organizes the many details of his life around his reforming efforts.[12] Close studies of texts and manuscripts remain essential to moving the field forward. At the same time, such studies tend to look more inside Gerson than outside at the world around him and cannot demonstrate his broad representative value for an understanding of late medieval culture—which is indeed the larger, secondary argument of this book.

Yet an overview of his career shows that Gerson offers nothing less. Born in 1363 in the region of Champagne to a family of modest means, he was granted a fellowship at the College of Navarre, where humanist learning in some form had taken root. He gained early fame as a preacher. By at least 1391, at the age of twenty-seven, he was preaching at court before Charles VI, the year before the king's descent into madness. Gerson's sermons surpassed mere rhetorical display meant to gratify a royal audience and instead tackled the great public issues of the day. In his first published sermon, in January 1391, he called on the king to take a role in ending the Great Schism.[13] For the generation of theologians following the Black Death, the Schism presented the most intractable and pressing problem of the age. Gerson preached and wrote frequently on the subject. When opportunities arose, he cajoled and bullied kings, emperors, and popes to end the breach. He could also sway large crowds. Continuing a tradition going back to the thirteenth century, he preached at Paris churches to ordinary citizens.[14] Sensing that earlier schoolmen had overlooked this important audience, he battered down the wall of prejudice that kept university masters from writing original works in the vernacular.[15]

His reputation as a theological authority soon eclipsed his early fame as a preacher. In December 1392 he finished—ranked first in his class— the marathon of theological studies leading to the magisterial license.[16] In 1395, he succeeded his master Pierre d'Ailly as chancellor of Notre Dame. Chosen by the bishop and cathedral chapter from the regent masters of theology and confirmed by the pope, he now stood (alongside the dean) as the most powerful authority in the theology faculty, at the greatest center of theological learning in Europe. He licensed all candidates in the three higher faculties (theology, medicine, law) and some of those in the arts faculty. He was now charged with the investigation of false teachings. Convinced of the cosmic stakes of this office, Gerson infused it with a restless energy, a sense of deep purpose, and most important, constant public activity.[17]

Historians sometimes emphasize the growth of regional universities in this period. The regionalization of universities does mark one of many sharp breaks between the thirteenth century and the period from 1350 to 1500. But the theology faculty at Paris had lost none of its clout; it could still create tremors in Latin Christendom and needed only a charismatic figure such as Gerson to press its case. He once wrote that it belonged to the chancellor's office to attend to matters of faith, a view he put into action repeatedly over the course of his career.[18]

Famous court preacher, popular orator, and powerful theological authority—Gerson became all of these, both public figure and master of the University of Paris. In this way, his career reveals the porous boundaries between the university and the wider world in this period. Like John Wyclif, who gained the support of the duke of Lancaster, Gerson had protectors in high places.[19] From 1396 to 1400 he spent time at Bruges as dean of the collegiate church of Saint-Donatien, an office he received in 1394 from Philip, duke of Burgundy.[20] At Bruges, he passed through a grave crisis. Like many contemporaries, he sensed that the university encouraged intellectual pride, and he temporarily abandoned the chancellorship in 1400 amid sickness and despair. But later that year he returned to Paris reenergized and began writing as never before. In addition to the Schism, he wrote on many other popular and timely subjects: mystical theology (works in Latin and in French), confession for those sentenced to capital punishment, the ever-popular *Romance of the Rose*, virginity, excommunication, and many more. Tempted by the religious life, he remained a secular clerk but wrote often about its peculiar challenges.

Two great events define Gerson's middle career: the assassination of the king's brother, Louis, duke of Orléans, on 23 November 1407 by agents of John the Fearless, duke of Burgundy, and the Council of Constance from 1414 to 1418. As Charles VI faded from public view, three uncles rose to share power: Philip of Burgundy, Jean of Berry, and Louis of Bourbon. The death of Philip in 1404 left a power vacuum that bred terrible rivalries within the royal family. The assassination of Louis of Orléans set the course of French dynastic politics for the next thirty years and led ultimately to the assassination of John the Fearless himself in the presence of the future Charles VII in 1419. John's son Philip the Good, furious at his father's murder, forged an alliance with the English by the Treaty of Troyes in 1420, putting France in further peril. The political order seemed to be crumbling. In March 1408, the Paris theology master Jean Petit publicly defended the assassination of the duke of Orléans in a four-hour speech.[21] To Gerson, Petit's defense amounted to a justification of murder. Over time (though not initially), the shameless publicity of the defense gnawed at him. He gave speeches to the king in the autumn of 1413 as part of his attack on Petit's *Justification* and engineered its condemnation by an inquisitorial tribunal in February 1414.[22]

The Council of Constance provided Gerson's central stage. He arrived in late February. Just a month later, the Pisan pope, John XXIII, fled in the dark of night, disguised as a stable groom. With the council teetering near collapse and not a single pope present, Gerson preached the most important sermon of his life. Taking his theme from John 12:35, he rallied the participants: "Walk while you have light."[23] In the following months, he dealt forcefully with the accused heretic Jan Hus. Then while others tried to stamp out simony and usury, he worked to have Petit's *Justification* condemned by the plenary council itself, this time unsuccessfully. During the years at Constance, he preached and published sermons (more than any other participant), corrected and distributed old works, and wrote and circulated new ones, in the process fleshing out his conciliar theory of Church government that placed council above pope. In June 1418, just as he was departing from Constance, a calamity struck that darkened the remaining years of his life. Anglo-Burgundian soldiers in Paris carried out massacres that claimed several of his friends. His strong identification with the French royal house prevented him from ever returning to Paris, which remained under Anglo-Burgundian control until 1436. After a short period of wandering in Bavaria and Vienna, he arrived at Lyon; his brother Jean the Celestine would soon become prior of the Celestine house in the city center. At Lyon, Gerson wrote tirelessly for the next ten years while remaining a close supporter of Charles VII—the city's consular registers apparently mention a voyage in 1427 to see the dauphin.[24] Joan of Arc inspired French troops to lift the siege at Orléans in May 1429. Gerson celebrated her victory, wrote to encourage belief in her mission, and died two months later on 12 July 1429.

Even this brief sketch of Gerson's career demonstrates the central place that he occupied in Western Europe for a generation. Counselor of kings and maker of popes, the leading figure at the most important Church council between Fourth Lateran and Trent (Gerson "largely ruled" it, writes a contemporary),[25] he stands at the intersection of nearly every major intellectual, spiritual, and social current of the time. His own master, Pierre d'Ailly, told Jan Hus in a testy exchange that a more illustrious doctor than Gerson could not be found in all Christendom.[26] "Known to all the Christian world" reads his obituary at Notre Dame of Paris. For his student Gérard Machet, he was "the father of many, living and dead."[27] His fame only increased after his death. In German-speaking lands, his name was linked to a tradition that included the brightest stars in the Christian firmament: Jerome, Augustine, John Chrysostom, Basil of Caesarea, Gregory the Great, Bernard of Clairvaux, Bonaventure, and Aquinas.[28] Fifteenth-century readers copied his works in quantity, and by the year 1500 he commanded authority rivaling the

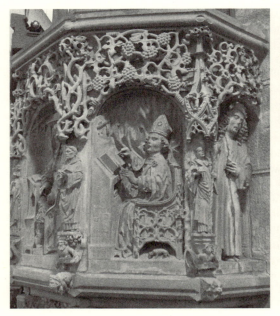

Figure 1. Pulpit of the Five Doctors, Amanduskirche, Bad Urach. Author photographs.

greatest names in the Christian tradition. Any simple accounting of manuscripts puts him among the most popular contemporary authors.[29] Reading him and prizing his words, an entire generation of theologians fell under his spell.[30] In time, even grim Erasmus admired Gerson as the outstanding schoolman of his age.[31]

The late Gothic church of St. Amandus in Bad Urach in Bavaria provides stunning visual evidence of Gerson's meteoric rise to the status of a mighty doctor in fifteenth-century Germany. A papal bull of 1477 had granted the church to the Brethren of the Common Life as a collegiate church. The Brethren never forgot Gerson's intervention for them at the Council of Constance. Around 1501, they commissioned a new pulpit. There, alongside the four antique fathers of the Church stands the great modern doctor, Gerson himself, carved in stone on the pulpit (Figure 1).[32] Admittedly, the image testifies to his special place in the Devout universe as a result of his intervention, but the Brethren would never have dared to exalt Gerson in this way if he did not already command deep respect outside their community. We can and should read this pulpit as the culmination of claims for Gerson's authority that had been gaining ground for nearly a century.[33]

It comes as no surprise, then, that modern scholarship has tackled this complex figure by parsing his thought and activity into compartments: Gerson as theologian, conciliarist, vernacular preacher, protohumanist, pastor, reformer, spiritual guide, poet, and on and on. While this subdivision has served a necessary purpose, it has left Gerson unintelligible as a single, coherent historical actor and made it nearly impossible to imagine the totality of his world. It has done little to bring him to life for nonspecialists and to explain why he matters for an understanding of his times. Despite all these efforts, he remains for many a sour, parochial figure on the margins of medieval history.[34] Yet there is a theme, a single thread, that ties together the parts of this great career and so opens a path to the central features of late medieval culture: writing, the focus of this book. The theme of writing unifies his life and thought, just as it links Gerson to the cultural landscape that produced him. Its priority in Gerson reflects its primary place in late medieval culture. Since the story that I tell depends heavily on this point, I turn now to the claims that scholars have advanced in this area, late medieval written culture, the first of three cultural shifts that provide essential context for this discussion.

The most enduring popular image of scribal culture remains the Benedictine monk copying books in a lonely scriptorium. While this image applies well enough to the early medieval period, written culture changed rapidly along with everything else after the year 1000. We are now coming to recognize a later shift from the high to the late medieval centuries. The scholarship of the past generation has transformed our understanding of late medieval written culture.[35] Changes from the earlier period took hold across society and shaped the world of ideas. The cost of book production declined dramatically. This was partly due to new cursive scripts, which enabled scribes and authors to write more quickly and which had reached a standard form by 1400, but especially to the widespread introduction of paper into most of Europe after 1300.[36] Paper mills spread from Spain and Italy in the late thirteenth century and began operating in northern France by the mid-fourteenth century.[37] The price of paper steadily declined over the next century. A copyist in France could buy four to eight sheets of paper for every sheet of parchment in the fourteenth century, but twenty-five sheets a century later.[38] Paper manuscript volumes soon appeared in large numbers. By the decade of the Council of Constance (1410–1419), about 33 percent of manuscripts were copied on paper in France, but nearly 75 percent in Germany and almost 90 percent in Austria and Switzerland.[39] At the same time, the reading public was expanding. While no one knows exact rates of literacy, we do know that grammar schools became common and that more people could read, including a growing number of women.[40]

Readers needed books. In response to this demand, books multiplied and became widespread as objects of everyday use and part of private libraries.[41] Their layout and appearance changed. Techniques devised in the thirteenth century to facilitate their use—indexes, running titles, and tables of contents, to name a few—became commonplace, as much an expectation of readers as they are today.[42] The shabby books of the fifteenth century—often carelessly written in "bastard" scripts on unlined, cheap paper, objects of use rather than literary trophies—have cast a pall over the period in the history of the book, reinforcing the old and misleading perception of an intellectual and cultural decline.[43] Yet as cultural artifacts, observes Richard Rouse, these volumes appear as distinct as the magnificent codices of the Carolingian Renaissance or the mass-produced university textbooks of the thirteenth century. Rather than a decline, we might see the fourteenth and fifteenth centuries as "a distinguishable epoch in the history of the manuscript book."[44]

For the historian, to evaluate these books solely as cultural artifacts or for their aesthetic value of course misses the basic point that their extravagant abundance was made possible by an upheaval in written forms between 1200 and 1400. Medievalists have long known that book production climbed steadily into the fifteenth century. Uwe Neddermeyer has recently quantified this growth in staggering detail, so providing the best current estimates for survival rates of medieval manuscripts and hence for original manuscript production.[45] He demonstrates that important parts of Europe, especially the Holy Roman Empire and Italy, witnessed an age of mass production of manuscripts from 1370 to 1469, a time when literary texts were duplicated by hand in much greater numbers than ever before. This growth was not incremental but a sustained upward spike in which every decade saw on average a 25 percent increase in book production, all at a time when population growth remained flat due to the heavy and ongoing mortality of the Black Death.

By 1400 book production in the Empire and Italy had recovered to pre-epidemic levels; by the 1460s, it had reached nearly four times the figure for 1400, and more than ten times that for 1250. By contrast, book production stagnated in France and England, bogged down by the costly and devastating campaigns of the Hundred Years' War (1337–1453); in France especially it did not return to the levels it had reached in the glory days of the thirteenth century. But after 1440 production surged in France as well, a threefold increase over the next two decades.[46] Plot these trends on a graph and you get a striking image (Figure 2). This shift to mass production of manuscripts, a shift as revolutionary as print itself, made possible a much more diverse reading public.

The manuscript boom encompassed more than just codex produc-

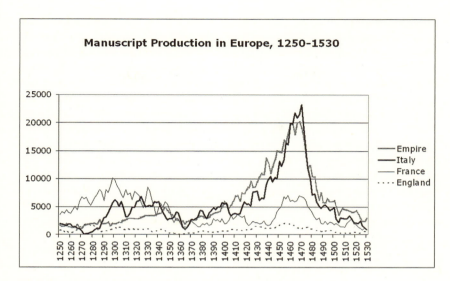

Figure 2. Manuscript production in Europe, 1250–1530.

tion. By the twelfth and thirteenth centuries, papal, state, and local bureaucracies were generating documents in enormous volume— possibly millions of peasants' charters in England alone, for example, and hundreds of thousands of notarial casebooks throughout southern Europe, thousands of which still survive.[47] The cultural impact reached far and wide. Recent scholarship has emphasized the "documentary culture" that formed the emerging vernacular literatures.[48] Ethan Knapp, for instance, has stressed that the poet Thomas Hoccleve (c. 1367– 1426), a clerk at the Privy Seal in London, was shaped in "a world of labor focused solely on the production of textual artifacts."[49] Hoccleve represents a pattern not just for English poets but for French writers such as Guillaume de Machaut, Christine de Pizan, and Alain Chartier; this literature "emerged in the shadow of a chancellor."[50] Similarly, early French humanism drew much of its energy from the papal court at Avignon. Jean de Montreuil, Jean Muret, and Nicolas de Clamanges all spent time there as secretaries.[51] Thinking of Gerson as a schoolman, we overlook his participation as chancellor in a documentary culture. His duties resembled those of the royal chancellor. He kept the seal of the cathedral chapter and oversaw the chapter library.[52] He administered a bureaucracy of notaries and assistants attached to the chancellor's office.[53] Trafficking in documents and running an administration formed part of his everyday experience.

Despite the importance of these written forms, if we are to grasp the full material complexity of Gerson's authorship we must look beyond both books and documents to still more ephemeral forms of written communication. Late medieval society had both a growing appetite for information and a growing capacity to generate and to circulate news and opinions. Research on this point, much of it by literary scholars over the past decade, has now established this claim beyond dispute. Much more than in the twelfth and thirteenth centuries, in this period we can speak of an emerging public opinion that appears clearer than ever by the second half of the Hundred Years' War.[54] The civil war in France in the early fifteenth century witnessed aggressive attempts to channel this public opinion.[55] Supplementing oral forms of delivery such as sermons and town criers, new written forms of communication now swirled about: newsletters, royal ordinances, placards, and especially libels, bills, and "leaflets" (*cedulae* or *schedulae*), single sheets sometimes posted in public places.[56] Wendy Scase has recently investigated the circulation of political poetry in such forms and has emphasized the potential of bill-casting to provide a public channel of communication for those who otherwise would have remained voiceless.[57] This rich field of research, still in its infancy, is modifying our fundamental assumptions about the nature of communication in the fourteenth and fifteenth centuries.

These changes may help us to imagine the written communication of Gerson and his contemporaries. Intellectuals now had to confront a much more chaotic and dynamic literary marketplace. Some were troubled and bewildered by the variety of written forms and the perceived and real challenges to established authority.[58] But they could also enter this public arena and attempt to broadcast their own message. This point underlies one of the central claims of this book and is basic to an understanding of authorship in this culture: Gerson approached writing not as a private, monastic retreat from the world, like a ninth-century monk, or as a pure scholarly occupation, like a thirteenth-century schoolman, but as an entry into a medieval public sphere that brought him into contact with a variety of textual consumers. He now had within his grasp a public much broader and more diverse than that of any schoolman before him.

The manuscript boom is just the first of three major cultural shifts that are crucial for the story and subject of this book. The second is the arrival of a strong new literary current in France in the late fourteenth century. An important body of scholarship over the past fifty years has put forward strong claims on behalf of Gerson as a humanist. Let us define humanism in this case (always a troublesome endeavor) as the tendency of intellectuals to prize the classical tradition, a tendency that manifested itself above all in a greater sensitivity to eloquence and a more classical Latin style, with a special regard for Cicero as a literary model.[59] Since the 1960s, Ouy and his colleagues have followed Franco Simone's lead in tracing the earliest French contacts with Italy at Avignon, and have shown that humanism came to France not in the second half of the fifteenth century as formerly assumed but fifty to seventy-five years earlier.[60] Ouy identified the College of Navarre as the "cradle of humanism" on the basis of the many individuals there whose careers and writings testify to a new attraction for a more eloquent and refined Latin.[61] Petrarch's boast about the superiority of Italian writers stunned and dismayed his younger French contemporaries.[62] Jean de Montreuil took exception to Petrarch's claim and set out to contradict it.[63] Nicolas de Clamanges painstakingly rewrote his letters in a more classical style and provided clearer, more exact citations to classical works.[64] Though Clamanges never admitted Italian influence, Petrarch seems to have swayed his choice of themes and literary forms as well as his style and language.[65] Petrarch profoundly impressed Gerson in his youth. Ouy discovered an eclogue that Gerson wrote in direct imitation of Petrarch's *Bucolicum carmen*.[66] His first surviving sermon borrows heavily from Petrarch's *Remedies for Fortune Fair and Foul* (*De remediis utriusque fortunae*).[67]

Clearly, the argument for early French humanism carries weight in a book about authorship. Why not change the label, then, from Gerson the "author" to Gerson the "humanist"? Because a label that can be stretched in meaning to cover such different figures as Petrarch, Gerson, and Erasmus generates more questions than answers and soon loses any explanatory powers it once had. Even Petrarch scholars have become uneasy with the designation. The great "father of humanism" was best known as a moral writer. His *Remedies for Fortune Fair and Foul,* an encyclopedia of moral advice for every possible turn of fate, survives in all versions in more than two hundred manuscripts and was translated into many European vernaculars.[68] And the differences between Gerson and Erasmus are many, but consider just one: their Latin style. In the treatise against Monzon, Gerson affected a classicizing style, but he soon abandoned it so thoroughly that historians forgot that he ever wrote in such a way. Heinrich Denifle, the great Dominican historian of the University of Paris, refused to consider the work authentic for stylistic reasons despite the clear attribution to Gerson in the manuscript.[69] Erasmus, completely ignorant of the work, thought that Gerson subdivided too much and left the affections of his listeners cold.[70] To suggest that Gerson participated in essentially the same project as Erasmus and Italian humanists may seem to enhance his worth by linking him to our own literary ancestors. In reality, it devalues him by flattening out the many features of his writings that do not fit the humanist template, that make him so interesting as a historical actor, and that are so valuable in a reappraisal of his life and times.

While Ouy has drawn the circle of humanism too large in my view, he recognized something important in Gerson that scholars have yet fully to absorb, namely, that he esteemed writing as a glorious calling and pondered its uses in ways that remove him far from the attitudes of earlier schoolmen. As we shall see, he shared with Petrarch and Erasmus a commitment to rhetoric in literary expression. Likewise, in his reading and handling of books he appears more like the sixteenth-century humanists than the thirteenth-century schoolmen. We must acknowledge the deep and lasting impact on Gerson of his early encounter with letters and literature. He always retained some sense of *duratio*, of eloquent and permanent writing. He requires a new category, one that allows us to break down the rigid scholastic-humanist dichotomy. At different times, he seems to belong to each—or neither. The larger task for us in this discussion, then, is to carve out a new space in our story of transition from the thirteenth to the sixteenth centuries, one that allows us to recognize the late fourteenth and the early fifteenth centuries as a distinct cultural period rather than simply a decline from a golden age of scholasticism or the first stirrings of humanism.

The literary salvo at the opening of this book points to a third cultural change that shaped the world of late medieval authors, Gerson especially. France, he says, has lacked great writers, so linking authorship to national identity. France has avoided heresy so far, he adds farther on, citing a famous passage in Jerome: "France alone has escaped the monster [of heresies]." But it must produce good writers for this to continue.[71] He then locates these new French writers in a French institution, the University of Paris. A *translatio studii* has brought the university from Egypt to Athens to Rome to Paris, where Charlemagne planted it (according to one version of the topos).[72] Gerson moves so fast we may miss the vital link between writing and the university. France needs writers to avoid heresy; the University of Paris produces writers to fight heresy. Writing serves a mighty purpose here, but also one that sets it apart from the conception of writing that we find in the humanists and reminds us that we are dealing with a university chancellor. Writing combats heresy to preserve France's special place in history.

Gerson's strong sense of national identity reflects a general trend that the Hundred Years' War accelerated in France and England. More than any other theologian of the medieval universities, Gerson linked his name to a nation and even a city. Contemporaries and succeeding generations knew him as the chancellor of Paris, his usual designation in the manuscripts and even on the pulpit at Bad Urach. Despite his formal training in Latin and the dismissive attitudes toward the vernacular that clerical culture encouraged, he read deeply in French literature and he mastered and even enjoyed writing in French. Before all other school-men, he wrote extensively in the vernacular. French proverbs flowed from his pen and tongue as easily as Latin phrases. We now find our-selves farther than ever from the world of thirteenth-century masters. Who ever called Thomas Aquinas an Italian theologian?

Gerson's sense of himself as a Frenchman brought with it a growing awareness of threats from outside France, from England above all. Ger-son had at least three reasons to mistrust or fear England. The first was political. The Hundred Years' War approached its pivotal phases in Ger-son's lifetime: the shocking victory of Henry V at Agincourt (1415), news of which reached Gerson at Constance; the subsequent English control of northern France (1416–1419), including the massacres in Paris that took away close friends (June 1418); the assassination of John, duke of Burgundy (1419) on the bridge of Montereau that led to the Anglo-Burgundian alliance ratified at the Treaty of Troyes (1420); and the elec-trifying victories of Joan of Arc that came to him like a longing fulfilled (1429). In a French sermon probably from late 1408, Gerson directly accused the English of desiring civil war in France, and he never forsook this attitude.[73] In a late work, he argued strongly on behalf of Joan and her mission.

Besides this political threat, Gerson sensed a second, theological threat from England. He tells an interesting story that throws this senti-ment into relief. In a 1409 sermon, he claimed to have heard the duke of Lancaster—certainly John of Gaunt, who died in 1399—tell the duke of Burgundy several times that while England had more subtle clerks, those at Paris had "the true and secure theology."[74] I shall have more to say about this traditional indictment of English subtlety and logic. Here, the point is basic: England served as a foil for Gerson in thinking about sound theology.

The spread of heresy represented a third, social threat. By 1413 at the latest, Gerson began raising the alarm that England had exported the Wycliffite heresy not just to Prague but to Scotland and Germany, and was endangering France's special place in history.[75] The heresy spooked Gerson in part because it targeted ecclesiastical possessions, and in this way revived the old Albigensian and Waldensian heresies.[76] In sum, England represented for Gerson the convergence of a triple threat to France, political, theological, and social.

Meanwhile, France compared favorably to England in every way. It could boast political leaders such as Charlemagne, "who decorated all of Christianity, France especially," with wonderful victories, and Louis IX (St. Louis), whose exploits Gerson celebrated in three sermons.[77] France had distinguished theologians at the University of Paris who collectively (in his view) had put theology on a secure footing. And France had suppressed heresy at all times and could boast an unblemished past (again in his view), thanks partly to the University of Paris and partly to great monarchs like St. Louis, the scourge of heretics. Gerson shared this strong sense of national identity with French humanists like Clamanges, who claimed that he was ready to renounce the pope's service if it put him in conflict with the French royal house.[78] When Gerson wrote, he did so not just as a schoolman but as a Frenchman.

Here we have the broad context for this book on authorship and publicity before print: a more humanistic approach to writing and a growing sense of national identity set against the backdrop of fundamental shifts in written culture. Gerson saw writing as a glorious and urgent calling, a view that takes us in a completely different direction from the outlook of earlier schoolmen. He thought of himself as French and Parisian to the point of writing in French and disliking the English. And he lived at a time of rapid expansion in written culture. From a world in which schoolmen viewed writing primarily as an extension of their teaching and saw themselves as Latin schoolmen first and as English, French, or German second, if at all, we now enter a world where books appear less as containers of argument than as literature, and where national universities multiplied and encouraged the growing sense of regional and national identities.

The broad argument of this book depends on a reading of the entire corpus of Gerson's works as edited (1960–1973) by Palémon Glorieux. Whenever possible, I have also drawn on evidence from the manuscripts themselves.[79] Gerson specialists have yet to digest fully the huge secondary literature on Gerson, not just more recent scholarship but even the older studies of Max Lieberman and André Combes, and I have attempted to exploit as much of this literature as possible. Of course, in "authorship and publicity" I have chosen a theme of some breadth—broad enough, I am certain, to raise some eyebrows. I do so with the conviction that Gerson research desperately needs to be drawn into larger conversations that for the most part have excluded him, conversations that will certainly enrich this undertaking and that I hope will benefit from the exchange. These include the histories of reading and the book (including codicology, library history, and publishing history), humanist studies, studies of authorship, and, more specifically, literary studies of the vernacular authors of late medieval Europe, especially French and English authors, and studies of scholarly authors.

Rather than following a narrative thread or adhering to the chronology of Gerson's life, this book develops a double argument—Gerson as writer, Gerson as mirror—through a series of interlocking themes. I begin with the world of books in which Gerson lived and wrote to lay the groundwork for our approach to him as a bookman and man of letters. Aided by the wider availability of books, especially the classic theological textbooks, Gerson developed a sophisticated model of reading that presents a striking contrast to the traditional model of "scholastic" reading, according to which scholars mined old books for arguments and gave little thought to style or historical context. Over time, he identified a select group of writings, a canon of great books that could safely guide theology students in their studies. These works shared a common theological vocabulary that Gerson believed was essential to the preservation of orthodox teaching, a set of formulas that he called the "common school of theological truth." The common school, which Gerson absorbed in his youth, provided a template for the proper way to talk about theological topics. Those troublesome books that failed to conform to the common school, such as Petit's *Justification* and Hus's *On the Church* (*De ecclesia*), should be silenced. In Gerson we see a more humanist approach to books and to reading, but in the service of preserving orthodox teaching.

Chapters 2 and 3 explore the basis for authorship itself, what moved Gerson to write and how he justified doing so. Chapter 2 proceeds from the question: amid so many great books and in a culture that frowned on originality, what task remained for the contemporary writer? Despite his guilt and anxiety over new literary production, Gerson found a plentiful harvest for the theologian in the field of modern morality and its countless individual cases. This particular apology for new writings, though forceful in its claims, had limitations. Permanence and eloquence had no place here. Chapter 3 focuses on a time when Gerson wrote more boldly, as an exile in Lyon (1419–1429), and on a genre in which he put forward stronger claims for writing: his poetry. From the time of his departure from Constance, Gerson saw himself as an exile, a posture familiar to writers since antiquity. This pattern of literary exile gave new vitality to his literary career and reanimated his aspirations as a writer. These aspirations appear clearly in the number, size, and shape of works he wrote at Lyon, and even more clearly in his poetry. But the most striking feature of the late works is that Gerson did not match the scale of these works with his execution of them. They reflect a fluent but sometimes careless writer. This account of Gerson's literary ambitions reveals an extraordinary range of positions, from guilt over his desire to write new works to a celebration of poetic inspiration as part of a divine plan that allowed Christians to grasp truths hidden to pagans. He never doubted that writing should have a central place in a theologian's world, but he also never wrote the enduring works he could have written.

Chapter 4 turns from problems of literary creativity to expression or style. In pursuit of logical demonstration, thirteenth-century schoolmen had ruthlessly purged their works of rhetorical devices or anything that might lend their writing elegance. Even as Gerson celebrated thirteenth-century theologians for consolidating and defining true theology, he sensed that their mechanical efficiency left readers cold. Intensely aware of the broader public for theologians, he blazed a new trail by mostly abandoning scholastic method as a literary device and by calling for a renewed attention to rhetoric, which he called a second logic, capable of demonstration on its own terms. Clarity became both a stylistic and a theological ideal. Just as theological writing should be clear and avoid the jargon of logic and other satellite disciplines, so theology itself should be clear, and theologians should resist confusing terminology by adhering to the teachings of the Church fathers. Clarity thus served as a unifying principle of his approach to writing and to practicing theology.

Gerson embraced rhetoric because he understood the growing public for theologians. Chapter 5 extends this argument by demonstrating the public nature of authorship in this culture. The argument hinges on an important but little understood shift from the classic genres of scholarly production toward the late medieval tract, which allowed schoolmen to treat at any moment any topic that might arise in their daily experience. Gerson seized on the form as an essential part of his strategy of outreach. Authorship before print had this public dimension that distinguishes it from authorship in the thirteenth century, and that justifies a bold new designation of Gerson: the medieval public intellectual.

Chapters 6 and 7 move the discussion of authorship into the material realm of the publishing and circulation of texts. We can best understand publishing in manuscript culture not as a single moment, as in the case of print, but as a series of publishing moments involving both author and readers. Chapter 6 traces the path of Gerson's texts through three of these moments: initial delivery, authorial correction or revision, and reader participation. Fourteenth- and fifteenth-century publishing followed patterns different from those of high medieval practice: autograph composition as standard procedure, swift composition to address contemporary debates and concerns, and authorial participation in the preparation of texts for readers. Chapter 7 turns from the production to the distribution of Gerson's works, from their first delivery to their widest European circulation. The challenge is to explain how, before print, an author succeeded in reaching an international readership. Gerson's many interests allowed him to participate in a wide range of conversations. Securing an international audience, though, required still more. Gerson peculiarly benefited from three distribution circles: the Council of Constance, the Council of Basel, and the European network of Carthusian houses. Soon after his death, with his works reaching many parts of Europe, readers began to collect his works on a massive scale. Collecting gave birth to new reading patterns and networks. But not everywhere. In some places, Gerson had few or no readers. This uneven readership is itself a clue to understanding the rifts in the cultural fabric of fifteenth-century Europe.

His uncertain place in history reflects a more general ambivalence about the historical space that Gerson inhabits, an ambivalence that is written into the master narrative of Western history and appears even in the title of the classic treatment of the period, Johan Huizinga's *Autumn of the Middle Ages*—not the chill of winter, at least, but definitely not spring or summer. Our uncertainty about Gerson and his autumn world results in part from his relation to the past, to the earlier texts and traditions that molded his thought and feeling. While recognizing these debts and influences, we must go beyond the old model of vulgarization, the notion that the men and women of this period simply fed off the carcass of high medieval civilization. Such a perspective fails utterly to appreciate the changed historical landscape of the fourteenth and fifteenth centuries. Gerson may help us to reimagine this world, for not only was he shaped by currents of past and present, he adapted them and in doing so transformed his cultural and intellectual environment. In this book we shall hear many echoes of the past. But if we listen carefully, we shall hear changes in tone and texture. At times they are subtle, at times dramatic. They may sound dark and ominous to some. To my ear, they sound curiously refreshing.

Chapter 1

Gerson as Bookman
Prescribing "the Common School of Theological Truth"

In 1426 a Carthusian monk named Michael Hartrut wrote Gerson asking for advice about books.[1] It was just the kind of question Gerson liked, and he replied with *On Books a Monk Should Read*. At the work's close he speaks adoringly of Bonaventure's *Breviloquium* and *Journey of the Mind to God* (*Itinerarium mentis ad Deum*): "I confess in my foolishness that for thirty years and more I have desired to possess [*habere*] these treatises as my friends, often reading and ruminating upon them, even their words, let alone their meaning. And lo, even at my age and with all my leisure, I have just begun to taste the things which, repeated often, become ever new and pleasant to me, as Horace says of an elegant poem or image: 'It will please though repeated ten times over.'"[2]

While strictly speaking a summary of theology, the *Breviloquium* is also a lyrical masterpiece that moves deductively through the Godhead to creation, sin, the Incarnation, grace, the sacraments, and the Last Judgment. Bonaventure intended this survey as a moral exhortation to help the reader to salvation.[3] *The Journey of the Mind to God*, a meditation on the ways of seeing God, charts a reverse course from the created world to God's being and the mystical union. Specialists are not the only ones who read these works today. Yet even though both have been translated into English several times, I suspect that few medievalists have read a single word of either one.

We cannot therefore comprehend the thrill of reading in this passage. If Gerson were talking about Cicero, perhaps. But Bonaventure tasks our imagination. His description of reading, on the other hand, feels quite familiar. It anticipates Machiavelli's famous description of his encounter with the classics in his letter to Francesco Vettori. Casting off dusty clothing and putting on royal garments, Machiavelli enters "the venerable courts of the ancients . . . unashamed to converse with them."[4] Like the humanists, Gerson speaks of reading as an intimate and personal encounter, rolling the words around in his mind. Like the humanists, he read for pleasure, recommended the reading of whole books in the original, and often considered the historical context of a work. He lived (in Gilbert Ouy's phrase) "surrounded by books."[5]

Gerson talked about them like a connoisseur. Hear him describe them: the "common summa" *On Virtues*, with its "most lovely and profound reasons" why the path of virtues is "more delightful, more sweet, quiet, and pleasant"; *On the Twelve Fruits of Tribulation*, "finely composed"; Augustine's *On Christian Doctrine*, "very useful and elegant"; Boethius's *Consolation of Philosophy*, "choice, compact, and splendid"; *Concerning Dispensation and Precept* of Bernard, *On Friendship* of Cicero, *On True Religion* of Augustine, and *On the Twelve Patriarchs* of Richard of St. Victor, each one "altogether lovely" (*pulcherrimum*).[6] The figures and images in Hugh of St. Victor's *On Ecclesiastes* and Jan van Ruysbroeck's *Spiritual Espousals* struck Gerson for their beauty. He admired the brevity in books like Pseudo-Bonaventure's *Mirror of Love* and Hugh of St. Victor's *On Prayer*. He marveled at the "matchless eloquence" of Cicero in the *Paradoxes*.[7] Someone who talks this way about books is responding not just to their arguments or contents but also to their literary qualities. In this respect, the term *bookman* applies better to Gerson than to Thomas Aquinas.

Problems appear when we try to locate Gerson in the history of reading. Scholars of humanism have made a shift in reading practices central to claims about a new historical consciousness that appeared at the Renaissance. Summarizing the work of Erwin Panofsky, Hans Baron, and Eugenio Garin, Anthony Grafton wrote that medieval scholars "had read a canonical set of authorities . . . in a uniform way. For all their differences of origin and substance, medieval readers considered these texts the components of a single system. Official interpreters made all of them serve as the basis for the system of argument and instruction known as scholasticism. They did so, quite simply, by treating the texts not as the work of individuals who had lived in a particular time and place but as impersonal bodies of propositions."[8] The humanists, by contrast, restored "individual reading to a place of honor" and recommended "direct contact with original works."[9]

This assumption of a sharp break in reading practices should give us pause, if for no other reason, for the stark contrast it draws. Certainly, this model ignores Gerson, and this chapter offers an opportunity to draw him into a larger conversation about the history of reading. For Gerson spoke frequently about books and reading at a transitional moment in reading practices. We should not be surprised to find in him both oral and silent, collective and individual reading. He could skim books or memorize them. In *On the Examination of Teachings* (1423), he encouraged students to memorize Bonaventure. It seems safe to assume that Gerson himself did so. My point here is not to overthrow the schoolman-humanist opposition but to complicate it and to suggest that the standard view moves too rapidly from 1200 to 1500. Beyond our inquiry into Gerson, I would aim to carve out a new historical space in the history of reading, one that allows for more complexity and overlap.

To develop this argument, I explore the different ways in which the label of bookman can be applied to Gerson. I begin with books themselves in the physical world, their presence and absence for a scholar like Gerson. Like other schoolmen of the fourteenth and fifteenth centuries, he possessed a substantial personal library. Though barely a volume survives, he left clues that may help us to understand the material realities of book ownership and authorship in this period. Books were much more abundant than in the thirteenth century, and yet this general abundance masks an unevenness in the availability of books. Certain ones remained scarce, even for a figure like Gerson, located at the heart of European learning.

I turn next to Gerson's anxiety over sources, especially his awareness of problems of authorship in books that he read. He reflects in this a much larger trend, the growing awareness of the author from the twelfth century to the fifteenth. Gerson displayed some care with literary sources, and some impatience with writers—such as Ubertino de Casale—who in his view mishandled those sources.

These two sections of my discussion provide important material context for our central inquiry, Gerson as monitor of books. As chancellor of the University of Paris, charged with overseeing institutional orthodoxy, Gerson evaluated books in a way that distinguishes him from most of his contemporaries. In the rest of the chapter, I investigate Gerson's endorsement of a specific set of books and authors, what we may call a canon of theological authorities for the fifteenth century. In an important letter to the College of Navarre in 1400, he outlined a sophisticated program of reading for theology students and identified a list of great books that in his estimation shared a common way of speaking about theology. Here and in other recommendations, Gerson returned time and again to a set of safe, proven authors who in his view spoke with one common voice on theological and moral matters.

Of course, many authors did not. This notion of a common voice provided Gerson with a principle of exclusion for troublesome books and authors. Early in his student days, he learned that theologians should use a common language to talk about theology, one set of correct theological formulas, what he called the "common school of theological truth." Authors who failed to do so, disregarding Augustine's admonition that Christians must speak according to a "fixed rule," should not be trusted. This idea of a common theological vocabulary shaped Gerson's interaction with books, but it also gave him a principle that he could project onto areas far outside the university's traditional orbit. In this way, our inquiry into Gerson as bookman reaches beyond books themselves and opens wide his dealings with beliefs of all kinds.

Thirteenth-century schoolmen read texts as if they were clusters of formal propositions. I describe instead a theologian who read and handled texts as books belonging to a literary tradition, *as a collection of writings rather than arguments.* Hence my title for this chapter, "Gerson as Bookman." We cannot call Gerson a bookman, though, without first thinking of books in the physical world, their presence and accessibility. I have spoken of a "boom" period of manuscript growth, especially for German-speaking parts of Europe. What were the consequences for a schoolman like Gerson?

Access to Books

Suppose a monk from the great Carolingian house at Fulda, which boasted one of the richest libraries in Western Christendom in the ninth century, somehow found himself transported five hundred years into the future. Of all the changes to the world, the one that might have shocked him most was the widespread individual ownership of books. We have no better indicator of the great shift in written culture after 1350 than the growth of private libraries. Everyone has been told that only the wealthy could afford books in the Middle Ages. For our period, this is true only with strong reservations, and it cannot apply at all to schoolmen, who lived in a world more and more crowded with books.

University legislation had long urged students to possess the book on which the master was lecturing.[10] Before 1350, this was probably wishful thinking for many students.[11] While twelfth- and thirteenth-century schoolmen had some access to books through institutional libraries, few could afford books themselves; contemporary inventories of the possessions of university graduates rarely mention them.[12] In any case, the leading theologians of the thirteenth century were friars, whose books belonged to institutional libraries. The late medieval trend toward secular masters in theology and away from friars took place at the same time that private libraries first appeared in large numbers.[13] Thanks partly to paper, which made books much cheaper, book ownership went from an exception to a rule: though the laity still rarely owned books (especially in France), most fifteenth-century university masters had a personal library of some kind.[14] Books were no longer just tools of the trade, they were personal possessions and could fashion identity just as book ownership can today.

What this means is that Gerson thought of books as physical objects that constituted his library and that he consulted and used every day.

Unfortunately, we have little direct knowledge of his personal library.[15] One lonely volume survives, a Cassian that he gave to the Celestines of Marcoussis.[16] The libraries of his contemporaries can help us to imagine what his library might have been like. A typical student of this period owned six or seven books, and of course each book might have contained many individual works.[17] Graduates could have sizable libraries. The average member of the Parlement of Paris at this time possessed about one hundred volumes—that is, a library as large as some institutional libraries.[18] Among theologians, Jean Courtecuisse, who like Gerson attended the College of Navarre, owned eighty-two volumes at his death in 1423, including many classical authors.[19] Matthew of Cracow (c. 1335–1410), a Prague theologian of a slightly earlier generation, left sixty-eight volumes (including the *Revelations* of Birgitta of Sweden), while Marsilius of Inghen (c. 1340–1396) owned 237 volumes that reflect his broad interests in mathematics, astronomy, law, and medicine.[20]

Gerson's library probably rivaled these contemporary collections. He occasionally referred to books in his possession. In a sermon at the Council of Constance in 1417, he says that he "recently inspected Saint Thomas and Bonaventure," but adds that "I do not have the books of other (theologians) here."[21] This statement is not much to go on, but it suggests two things: that he probably owned the works of Aquinas and Bonaventure and brought them with him to Constance, and that he also owned the works of other theologians, but left them at Paris. We might speculate, then, that Gerson had left behind most of his library, and that, since he never returned to Paris, he probably never saw those books again.[22] We know that he reconstituted a library at Lyon, including his own works, and that he left these volumes to the Celestines of Avignon.[23]

The shift in book ownership from the high to the late Middle Ages has important consequences for how we think about reading practices. Walter Ong generalized that "manuscript cultures remained largely oral-aural even in retrieval of material preserved in texts."[24] Mary Carruthers has deepened our understanding of this "memorial culture."[25] Yet while memorization did remain an important part of university learning into the early modern period, late medieval university masters usually wrote with books at hand and became more precise in their references.[26] Gerson frequently copied long passages from other books into his own works, with citations: two short chapters from Ramon Lull's *Liber de astronomia* that he copied at the close of a letter, to give just one example.[27] Such practice was commonplace. Thomas Netter used a library close at hand to cram his *Doctrinale* with excerpts from the works of John Wyclif, and Denys the Carthusian copied excerpts from books onto wax tablets for later insertion into his compositions.[28] Miniatures showing the author writing rather than dictating first appear in the eleventh century, but sitting in an empty cell. Our image of the writing process should be like the image of Gerson that appears in a copy of the *Imitation of Christ* (ascribed to Gerson in this manuscript): the chancellor in his study, surrounded by books he could and did consult (Figure 3).[29]

What, then, of an author's own works? Until recently, scholars assumed that Gerson usually had copies at hand, despite scattered references showing that at least occasionally he lacked certain ones.[30] A newly discovered letter, written at Lyon in November 1422, records the most striking case we now have of such a situation. In response to requests for his writings, Gerson told his correspondent, Guillaume Minaud (a medical doctor turned Carthusian monk), that he was sending him a copy of *On Mystical Theology* "which I had not seen for many years, nor did I know to be at Lyon."[31] This astounding admission has no parallel in Gerson's writings and exposes the fragile material conditions of his exile at Lyon and even at the Council of Constance. *On Mystical Theology* was among his prized works; he refers to it thirteen times in other writings.[32] Yet this letter suggests that, unlike his friend Nicolas de Clamanges, who cherished and brooded over his own writings, Gerson did not always keep his works close by, he sometimes lacked copies of them, and he even went years without seeing some of them.[33] At Lyon he began a more systematic attempt to collect and to preserve works from throughout his career. Shortly after this letter, Gerson committed *On Mystical Theology* and other writings to the Celestines at Lyon under the care of his brother, the prior.[34] He must surely have felt relieved to have them in a secure library.

The reference to *On Mystical Theology*, then, provides a clue to help us understand an inherent imbalance in medieval book production. An author owned mostly old works and classics. In their early years of circulation, new works such as *On Mystical Theology* had a precarious existence and were difficult to locate. Gerson could always find the classic scholarly texts. If he did not own them, he had access to libraries at the College of Navarre, at the Sorbonne, and at Notre Dame in Paris (the library he oversaw), which contained all of the standard patristic and school texts in many duplicate copies.[35] In 1338, the Sorbonne catalogue listed some 1,720 volumes, including more than three hundred chained volumes.[36] With very few exceptions, this collection had hardly changed from the one that Gerson had access to seventy-five years later.[37]

Thus despite the great increases in book production over the course of the fourteenth and fifteenth centuries and hence the growth in private libraries, certain books eluded readers. The spread of texts in manuscript was uneven and heavily tilted toward older authors. Tracking down new works proved difficult. Book titles and even the names of

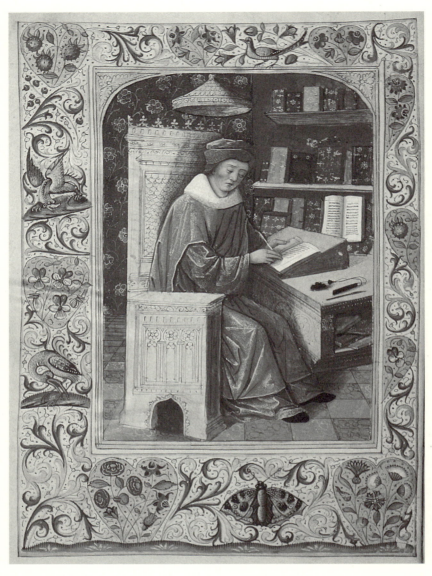

Figure 3. Gerson writing in his study. Paris, Bibliothèque nationale de France, Ms. nouv. acq. lat. 3024, f. 2v. Used by permission.

authors could change from one manuscript to the next. Catalogues were rare. The *Registrum Anglie,* an early fourteenth-century "Franciscan 'Union catalogue' of British libraries" that listed the locations in English houses of about fourteen hundred works by ninety-nine authors, was an impressive but rare exception that was still being used more than a hundred years after its creation.[38] Medieval culture produced no bibliographies as we know them today. From the twelfth century, lists of works by individual authors became more common, and a few enterprising souls attempted to compile more general lists of writers. By the fourteenth century, the first specialized lists appeared—lists of Benedictine or Dominican writers, for example.[39] But the most widely known bibliographical guide before print was still Jerome's *On Famous Men* (*De viris illustribus*), with later amplifications, a work that survives in around 450 manuscripts and went through thirty printed editions following the first in 1470.[40] This was no way to keep up with new literature. For this reason the universities and fifteenth-century councils had a profound impact by providing international communication networks that stimulated the reading and transmission of new works.

Medieval readers, perhaps schoolmen especially, were not content merely to read old textbooks. In fourteenth-century France the trend favored the copying of recent works. A study of the College of Dormans-Beauvais found that for the period 1390 to 1399 every book copied was a recently composed text.[41] Throughout the fourteenth and fifteenth centuries, production of Peter Lombard's *Book of Sentences* and of Bibles swiftly declined. (The old copies on parchment and even the newer ones on rag-based paper could last centuries.) Such works were available everywhere and had flooded the secondhand book market.[42]

How, then, did a medieval author such as Gerson understand and deal with this problem of locating recently written works? Though evidence is scarce on this point, we have enough clues to show that Gerson kept a mental map of their location. In 1415, for instance, he knew that a treatise on tyrannicide—"composed in the year 1388 by the faculty of theology, approved by the University of Paris, and formerly sent to Pope Clement"—was in the possession of a certain cardinal.[43] In 1423, he knew that the Carthusians near Paris (at Vauvert) owned a copy of the works of Ramon Lull (d. c. 1316).[44] (We possess the manuscript of the *Liber contemplationis* that Lull gave to this house in 1298.)[45] And Gerson knew in 1428 that a copy of Pierre d'Ailly's treatise on the calendar could be found at Cambrai with the archdeacon of Hainault or at Berry with a master of theology named Jean de Rouroy (who later translated Frontinus's *Stratagems* into French for Charles VII).[46] The fact that he took care to specify the location of these works proves that he thought they were difficult to find.

Gerson traced his own works in this way, to facilitate general access to them. He especially kept track of those in Celestine monasteries.[47] In 1428 he referred Jean Bassand, provincial of the Celestine order, to Ambert or to Orléans for copies of *On the Passions of the Soul* and *On Distinguishing True Revelations from False.*[48] In 1429, writing to the dauphin's tutor, he recommended his earlier letter-treatise on the consideration of princes, available from the prior of the Celestines at Vichy.[49] And in an earlier letter to a recently named bishop (1408), Gerson recommended a number of texts, mostly classics. He concluded the list with "tracts now found at Paris," including his own *Opus in Three Parts* (c. 1408).[50] The other works were commonly available.[51] But he had completed his *Opus in Three Parts* just within the past few years, and the text could not have been known much outside Paris.

Gerson never caught the fever for classical texts to the same extent as his French contemporaries who had spent time at Avignon. We see the excitement in their letters: Nicolas de Clamanges chasing down a copy of Pliny the Younger or breathlessly awaiting the arrival of Cicero's discourses, Jean de Montreuil lusting after a precious volume of Cicero's orations, tracking it from one owner to the next.[52] Yet, given his bibliographical turn of mind, Gerson must always have been watching for new works or even old works that had never achieved wide circulation. Medieval book hunters experienced a thrill of the chase that modern collectors rarely experience. We know a few of his discoveries, though there must have been many others. In 1409 (or 1413), he replied to a request from Pierre d'Ailly for counsel on the spiritual life with a reading list, including classics like Bernard, Augustine, Gregory, and many more. He concluded with a work recently discovered: "Finally, not long ago there came into my hands the unfinished work of Hugh *On Ecclesiastes.* Greatest God! How concisely has he expounded this whole matter of contemplation using the image of smoke, flame, and coals!"[53] Scholars who have studied this discovery have used it to date certain works of Gerson.[54] This is useful but it overlooks something more basic and interesting. Consider what has happened here: in mid-career, Gerson has finally obtained a major work by one of the greatest writers of the twelfth century. The work was not rare; it survives in sixty manuscripts, twenty-two from France.[55] We do not know if Gerson had never heard of it before, or (what seems more likely) knew of it but had just never found it. In either case, a moment like this drives home for us the circumstances of reading in a world before print: that a writer as centrally placed and as important as Gerson might yet go his entire life without having the chance to read an important and fundamental text.

In such a case we see the bookman in Gerson, delighted at his discovery, but with an interest flowing into a channel different from that of the Italian humanists, toward moral and spiritual concerns. Yet in this as in so much else, he represents contemporary interests much better, certainly north of the Alps. Just 1 percent of codices produced in the Rhineland at this period contained works by contemporary humanists. Instead, literature on moral, spiritual, and devotional themes drove the market.[56] These topics resonated everywhere, at courts, in monastic settings, at universities, even among the judicial elite. Members of the Paris Parlement, all trained lawyers, had a deep interest in such topics and owned numerous works in these categories.[57] And the libraries of fifteenth-century schoolmen normally included such works.[58] The lesson here anticipates a point I develop later in the book: Gerson's works survive in so many copies partly because he wrote the very kinds of works that large portions of the reading public wanted to read.

Gerson lived in a world where books were more abundant than ever before, yet still elusive. Large personal libraries for university masters were now common, and yet sometimes even an author might not have access to his own works. Meanwhile, the search for new works never ended. And when Gerson found a book, a new set of problems might arise, such as a work's authorship. How aware of this problem was he?

Anxiety over Sources

A great deal hangs on this question. Lorenzo Valla's famous exposure of the Donation of Constantine as a forgery (1440) stands as a powerful symbol of the new humanist philology. By contrast, medieval scholars seemingly cared little about the time and place of their authors and texts, and looked only to mine them for propositions. Here again we seem to have stark opposition.

Yet we can already see a growing awareness of the human author centuries before Gerson in high medieval texts. Exploring the tradition of scriptural commentary from 1100 to 1400 through academic prologues to books of the Bible, Alastair Minnis located a shift "from the divine *auctor* to the human *auctor* of Scripture," along with a growing focus on the literal meaning of the text. Scholars engaged in exegesis took a "more literary" interest in their texts.[59] The tradition of commentary on both sacred and secular authors also shaped the way that vernacular authors approached writing.[60] Not surprisingly, Gerson knew (or thought he knew) the historical location of his authors and took this into account in evaluating them.

Theological texts, like revelations, had to be authentic if they were to inform the life of the Church. Gerson frequently spoke of the need for authenticity in various spheres: authentic witnesses (*testes authentici*), authentic books and writings (*scripturae authenticae, libri authentici*), and

authentic histories (*historiae authenticae*).[61] Anyone who works much with
medieval texts faces the problem of spurious attributions. We tend to
think of spectacular cases such as the Donation of Constantine or the
Pseudo-Isidorian Decretals, but there were thousands more. By one
count, Gratian's *Decretum*, the starting point of canon law in the universities, contains at least five hundred apocryphal sources.[62] Medieval manuscripts contain numerous texts spuriously attributed to Gerson himself,
so many that even today we do not have a complete list of his authentic
writings. Even the modern edition (completed in 1973) contains several
texts certainly not by Gerson and others whose attribution remains in
doubt.[63]

A general concern over the authenticity of documents, as opposed to
the authorship of "literary" texts, began long before the fifteenth century.[64] The high medieval papacy put in place a regular system for verify-
ing diplomas. The same concern over authenticity appears in the
procedures for the proof of relics and miracles. Political rulers applied
very high standards of proof to coinage, and harshly penalized counter-
feiters. But disputing the authorship of a text was considered "a very
drastic step," notes Minnis, and medieval scholars usually accepted
"improvable attributions of currently popular works to older and
respected writers."[65] Some twelfth-century writers displayed a critical
attitude toward texts. In his prologue to *Sic et non*, Peter Abelard
observed that many apocryphal works had been attributed to the saints
to lend them more authority, and that scribal mistakes had infiltrated
the Gospels.[66] While Abelard does not seem too troubled by this, Gerson
felt more anxious. By the late Middle Ages, theologians were applying a
critical approach to theological texts. Gerson's anxiety was not properly
philological or literary; rather, it arose from the same need that drove
his quest for the great books: the need to uncover the sources of a safe
and secure theology. While a full investigation of this topic exceeds my
purpose here, a few examples will clarify the issues at stake.

In February 1429, Guillaume de Chalançon, the bishop of Le Puy (a
town near Lyon), consulted Gerson about the teachings of one Matthew
of Fussa, a local preacher and schoolmaster. In *Against Superstition in
Hearing Mass*, Gerson addressed Matthew's claim that certain beliefs
about the power of the mass—the notion that hearing Mass prevents
blindness that day, for example—can be found in writings of the doctors
of the Church. He replies that, even if true, these beliefs should not be
preached to the people but be "reverently glossed." Often some scam is
at work. The leaflets (*schedulae*) that advertise such beliefs are dubious
(*incertus*) and have not been accepted by the Church. Anyone can churn
them out (*fabricare*); often, as with unauthorized prayers that promise
wealth to the one praying them, the motive is greed or even the desire of

authors to give their writings "glory and permanence" (*permanentia*).[67] Gerson betrays a sense of unease not just over the content but over the form and means of distribution as well. The passage seems to describe the practice of selling individual sheets of prayers for profit.

This anxiety over false attributions extended to specific texts. Often, we can see a form of textual criticism in Gerson's attempt to determine authorship. For most of his career, he was ignorant of the author of *The Roads to Zion Mourn*, a great Carthusian treatise on mystical theology. But in a letter in 1428, he correctly identified the author as Hugh of Balma, "as appears in the first part." In this case, he must have discovered the attribution in a manuscript.[68] In 1408 (or 1412), he concluded on the basis of "style and subject matter" that the attribution of a treatise to Thomas Aquinas was incorrect; Bonaventure, he assumed, was the author instead. In fact it was Matthew of Cracow, yet the incident reminds us of the common use of style and content as criteria for establishing authorship, something evident in earlier writers such as Guigo of La Chartreuse in his preface to the letters of Jerome, and in the reception of Gerson's works.[69] It also reminds us of the limitations of such criteria. In the case of the ever-popular *Summa on Vices and Virtues* (more than two hundred manuscripts), Gerson never mentioned the author, William Peraldus (d. after 1260), though by 1423 he knew his identity, possibly from local Dominicans; he correctly describes him as a Dominican of the Lyon house and a near contemporary of William of Auvergne (d. 1249) and Aquinas (d. 1274).[70] In his earliest references to *On the Spirit and the Soul*, he attributed the work to Augustine (the usual attribution in medieval manuscripts) but soon realized the error and after 1400 referred simply to "the author" of that work.[71] In this case, Aquinas had already dismissed the attribution to Augustine.[72] Progress was uneven.

In his critical approach to texts, Gerson represents a general trend toward caution in the use of sources, and this includes authors completely unassociated with the grand humanist narrative. Pierre d'Ailly recognized the spuriousness of the *De vetula*, which had been attributed to Ovid, and Gerson followed him in rejecting the attribution.[73] D'Ailly also criticized Roger Bacon for accepting the work; the real author, he recognized, had written the work many centuries after Christ but had attributed it to Ovid to give the impression that he had foretold the rise of Christianity.[74] Among English scholars, Thomas Netter in the *Doctrinale* (1420s) corrected Wyclif on the authorship of a work entitled *On Divine Offices*, widely attributed to Ambrose. The author was instead a contemporary of Anselm. Netter recalls a debate on this question years earlier at Oxford. At first, some suggested that Ambrose was the author, but others insisted on Isidore. Finally, says Netter, God enlightened the eyes of his servants, and it was discovered—by using the passive voice,

Netter makes the breakthrough anonymous—that the author had written "in the days of Anselm," who had "courteously" attacked him.[75]

Elizabeth Eisenstein gave credit to print for encouraging a new sense of history at the Renaissance.[76] Challenging that claim, Anthony Grafton pointed to "a new interest in historical and philological questions among Italian intellectuals from the very beginning of the fourteenth century."[77] But by the early fifteenth century at the latest, scholars in northern Europe were displaying similar interests. Neither print nor Renaissance humanism explains these incidents. Individual actors made these breakthroughs, aided by an increased commerce and interaction with books, better and larger libraries that allowed for comparison of texts and, perhaps most important, critical methods for reading a text that had originated in a long tradition of academic commentary that climaxed in the universities.

One last example will develop our theme of anxiety over sources in a slightly different direction. The issue in this case was not the attribution of sources but their correct use and citation. In 1426, Gerson wrote a letter from Lyon to Jean Bassand, "one of the most intellectually active Celestines in France" as well as a great advocate of the new stress on observance.[78] Bassand had asked Gerson for his opinion on the *Tree of Life of the Crucified Jesus* of Ubertino de Casale (1259–c. 1329), a work known for its Joachimite tendencies and its arguments in favor of extreme poverty.[79] Gerson's lengthy reply became one of his more popular letters, surviving in at least forty manuscripts. My interest is not the long discussion of the humanity of Christ, which constitutes the bulk of the letter, but the conclusion of the work, where Gerson replies to the rhetorical objection that Ubertino wrote "many good, useful, and devout things." Gerson replies: "He did so, I acknowledge, nay gladly confess it. Would that he had done so in his own style; would that he had conformed to the teachings of those whom he sometimes cites. But he often picks and tears off large sections in his own peculiar way [*in propria forma*], never mentioning the authors' names. Maybe he wants to be like Aesop's crow, decorating himself with other birds' feathers. He frequently uses Bonaventure in the *Breviloquium*, but he hardly ever names him. Many passages that appear as his own words I have read in other none too recent books."[80] Gerson had many criticisms of Ubertino's teachings: his excessive praise for certain holy women and for the Franciscans; his idea that unbaptized children suffer bitter punishment in limbo, which flies in the face of the "common school of all doctors"; and a tendency toward heresy in his teaching on the Eucharist. But this passage blazes a new trail of criticism, not dubious doctrine but mishandling of sources. Plagiarism is not the right word: that implies not only a legal ownership of words but also a general consensus on the acceptable parameters of borrowing from the works of others.[81] Nonetheless, Gerson felt that Ubertino had transgressed, and that there was something almost dishonest in this transgression. Probably in the back of Gerson's mind is a criticism we shall meet soon, of authors who do not speak clearly for themselves but instead burden their works with citations. But the real energy of the attack arises from Gerson's feeling that Ubertino has abused old books, and that in doing so he has even misrepresented himself.

The incident adds one more layer to our portrait of Gerson as bookman, his sense that a good writer notifies the reader of his sources and acknowledges the technical demands of the trade. Gerson himself took great care in his citations, providing incipits in some cases.[82] This precision conforms to the general trend in the period and distances him from earlier schoolmen, who often simply repeated arguments verbatim from earlier sources when it suited their needs.[83] But we can also see in Gerson's criticism his great respect for the sources of a pure and true theology, and his impatience with those who in his view treated them carelessly.

Toward a Canon of Great Books

The portrait I have drawn so far has emphasized the materiality of books in Gerson's world and his awareness of critical problems in the texts themselves. We can now put flesh on this skeleton by exploring how Gerson evaluated and scrutinized books, approving and censuring them throughout his career. While I have anchored this discussion in the material world of books themselves, Gerson's historical importance depends heavily on his commerce and interaction with books as sources of theological authority. It is striking how often others sought his advice about books. Most of the surviving letters have some connection to them. Gerson often suggested titles to his readers. Through these reading lists, we shall now see, he constructed what amounted to a canon of theological books for fifteenth-century readers.

A key text for this investigation is a letter that Gerson wrote in 1400. In that year, as the Great Schism entered its twenty-third year, he endured a great spiritual crisis. He attempted to resign the chancellorship in March, and by July he was so ill in Bruges that he prepared his final will and testament before thirteen witnesses.[84] Amid this turmoil, he wrote from Bruges a series of letters to the College of Navarre. Together, they present a remarkable portrait of a restless, energetic mind. In the second letter (29 April 1400), Gerson roams far and wide over the place and manner of theological education at the University of Paris, the kinds of students and theologians it was producing, and his own standing as a writer.[85] This text provides our point of departure.

In the letter Gerson reflects on his own years of study, his temptation to write new works, and the vices of modern students, especially their clumsy appropriation of old authors. Students come to a university awash with books whose titles they do not even know, and produce writing that lacks force and conviction. This key passage will occupy us later. My focus here is on what follows: the plan of reading that Gerson lays out. He urges students to read old authors and to take the "well-trod path" free of error. We are surrounded by "so many living fountains of wholesome wisdom"; we must embrace the great books, "the more choice and tested books." Here he acknowledges a great challenge. Our reading capacity is not just finite, it is tiny (*perexiguus*), completely insufficient to reckon with the many books that beckon to us.[86] How, then, should a student read and use books? "Browse through some swiftly," he advises, "just so that you are not completely ignorant of them, and then bid them a final farewell. Consult others from time to time, as need or the chance for pleasure [*delectatio*] arises. But call upon a few as your constant companions, and like the most trusted members of your household [*domestici fidelissimi*] keep them continually in the chambers of your heart, as partakers of your close and daily conversations."[87]

And what are these privileged texts that deserve our closest attention and care? In the final section of the letter, Gerson divides them into three categories: "the part of theology that attracts scholars [*scholastici*]," "the part that builds the morals of the reader," and "the part that suits preachers."[88] Recommendations follow. For theology, he suggests authors of questions on the *Sentences*, "especially those doctors who have written more purely and firmly, among whom . . . reverend Bonaventure, Saint Thomas, and Durandus seem to be numbered." (A discrepancy in the manuscripts here will occupy us further below.) Henry of Ghent also excels in his quodlibets. As for "more recent" authors, they excel in many areas, but not when they mix theological language with "purely physical, metaphysical, or, even more shamefully, logical terms."[89]

In the second and third categories, texts useful for morals and for preaching, Gerson suggests sacred histories that commemorate those who "lived uprightly": Gregory's *Dialogues*, two ecclesiastical histories (of Eusebius and Cassiodorus), the *Collations* (John Cassian) and *Lives of the Fathers*, Augustine's *Confessions* and *Meditations* (a popular pseudonymous work)[90] and the meditations of other authors (elsewhere, he recommends those of Pseudo-Anselm and Pseudo-Bernard),[91] William of Auvergne's *Divine Rhetoric*, and legends of the saints "and similar works whose fervent reading deeply spurs us to lay hold on virtuous passions."

"Mystical expositions of Holy Scripture" also fall into this category: Gregory's *Moralia* and *Pastoral Rule*, Bernard's homilies on the Song of Songs, the treatise *On Contemplation and Its Species* and other works of Richard of St. Victor, "which can never be sufficiently admired," and works of William of Auvergne, "who with pleasing art mixed speculative and moral analogies without confusion"—perhaps a reference to his *On Virtues*. Lastly, he recommends pagan writers in a general way for their rich moral stock, for their style, for the skill of their poets and historians, and for "a certain pleasure from a change in reading"—though he thinks that the reader can find as much in Augustine's *City of God*, in Orosius, Jerome, and Lactantius.[92] We sense just a moment of hesitation here, the closest Gerson ever comes to expressing ambiguity about reading the pagan classics.

The strategy of reading proposed here did not follow contemporary practice. Many students in this period encountered authors not through complete copies of their works but through florilegia.[93] Certain collections of quotations became standard and were copied again and again. The most popular florilegium of Aristotle's works, the so-called *Auctoritates Aristotelis*, survives in more than 150 manuscripts and was printed twenty-seven times before 1500.[94] Even Gerson himself, it seems, was introduced to Aristotle through this collection. Just in his short tract on Joan of Arc he quotes from it four times from memory. Most arts students probably memorized it—a revelation that casts a very different light on what it meant to read and to study Aristotle. The popularity of such works affected reading habits. As a result of their success, says Jacqueline Hamesse, "individual book reading tended to disappear," and along with it the experience of hearing and absorbing an author's individual voice and unique style.[95]

Gerson took a different approach. The Navarre letter reveals a thoughtful attempt to craft a strategy of reading to tackle the abundance of inherited literature, then to sift through specific texts to shape a program of theological instruction. Gerson does not advise students to make summaries or compilations. In the Navarre letter, he appears as a sophisticated reader, fully aware of the great demands that books place upon our time, and therefore conscious that reading is a complex activity that can be performed on many levels. The student should skim some books only for coverage and familiarity and never again pick them up, read others more carefully for essential content, and devour a few out of deep and abiding interest. We do not read these last passively, or listen to them being read in lectures, or approach them through glosses; we converse with them in private until they lodge in our souls. The entire discussion presupposes private and silent reading.

In the schools, reading meant lecturing, commenting on a text as part

Figure 4. Grand Seal of the University of Toulouse. Copyright © Archivio
Segreto Vaticano, A.A., Arm. I-XVIII 2201 sigillo recto.

of a curriculum.[96] So central was this practice to university life that it
shaped traditional imagery. Various thirteenth- and fourteenth-century
university seals (Angers, Bordeaux, Bourges, Paris, Toulouse) show a
master reading from a lectern to a class of students holding books of
their own (Figure 4).[97] Gerson provides a model of reading for theologians that depended less on university structures and that echoed the
monastic *ruminatio* or slow "mastication of the Word," the reading practice of monks for centuries before the first universities.[98] It was not the
monastic model, however, but something quite new: reading as a deep
encounter with the entire text and its author, within the context of a
much larger program of reading and study that called for different levels

of engagement with texts and that ultimately led to a theological license. This is reading shaped by its institutional context.

Next, Gerson moves from his reading strategy to those books that the theology student should embrace. We should think of the Navarre reading list not as the sum total or canon of great or approved theological works.[99] Instead, it resembles a syllabus, "a selection of texts for study in a particular institutional context."[100] Gerson is doing here what he does elsewhere, recommending different lists of authors, tailored to his audience—for a newly appointed bishop, for the dauphin, even for a hermit. He often performed such sifting in other contexts, producing what we would call select bibliographies: on the spiritual life (recommending twelve authors), on the contemplative life (seven), on the observance of days (three), on "the praise of tribulation and the deception of prosperity" (five), on the passage from the physical to the spiritual life (four), on the number of the passions (three), on the celestial hierarchy and its three functions of "purging, illuminating, and perfecting" (five), and on reading for monks (five).[101] On a critical topic like contemplation, he drew up a separate list of works (1402–1403) including nine named and five unnamed authors and twenty-eight titles. Later in his career, he continued to expand it.[102]

In these lists, Gerson reduces the tradition to a few, safe authors. The lists contain many duplications of old, approved texts: Gregory's *Moralia* on Job and Bernard's sermons on the Song of Songs (each mentioned six times), various works of Richard of St. Victor (six mentions), Augustine's *Confessions* (four), *City of God* (two), and the pseudonymous *Meditations* (three), Hugh of St. Victor's *On Prayer* (three), *Lives of the Fathers* (three), Boethius's *Consolation of Philosophy* (two), William of Auvergne's *Divine Rhetoric* (two), Chrysostom's *On the Compunction of the Heart* (two), Cassian's *Collations* (two), legends of the saints (two), the standard works of the other great schoolmen Aquinas, Henry of Ghent, Durandus of St. Pourçain, and Nicholas of Lyra, and especially Bonaventure in *The Journey of the Mind to God* (five) and the *Breviloquium* (two).[103]

Gerson stresses the excellence of these works, as one would speak of classics. In the Navarre letter they are the "best books and proven parts" of "those who wrote more purely and firmly." Elsewhere, he refers generally to "the books and teaching of the best masters." Recalling Gerson's words, Jean the Celestine speaks of "the most proven books."[104] These are qualitative, not quantitative judgments. Usually, we are dealing with a small minority of authors. The "more skillful" guides to mystical theology, Gerson observed, instruct both intellect and affections: Augustine, Hugh of St. Victor, Bonaventure, William of Auvergne, Aquinas, "and a very few others," distinguishable by their "rarity."[105] At the Council of Constance, he numbered William of Auxerre, Albert the

Great, Bonaventure, Aquinas, Alexander of Hales, William of Auvergne, and Henry of Ghent among the "great luminaries of the world" at the University of Paris.[106] In a sermon before the king in 1414, Gerson noted that when Philip VI assembled the masters of the University of Paris in an effort to safeguard orthodoxy on the beatific vision, Lyra and Durandus were among them (Durandus was in fact not in attendance). The faculty of theology preserves truth, but Lyra and Durandus excel among theologians.[107] In all of these passages, we are closing in on an elite group of authors.

Stepping back for a moment to consider the wider context, we can see in this turn toward great authorities a pattern much broader than Gerson alone. The need and desire to channel reading through a set of approved and reliable authorities transcended one individual or group. Confronted by an increasingly rich and complex literary tradition, different groups of readers created distinct canons or lists of texts that met their own needs and reflected their own priorities. After 1370, it seems, the trend everywhere led away from "new solutions or new methodologies" and toward engagement with "great thinkers from the past."[108] Shortly after his conversion, Geert Grote compiled a reading list as part of his personal resolutions, a list that later Devout communities adapted for their own purposes.[109] Christine de Pizan looked back to Dante and Boccaccio, and English writers to Chaucer, "this landes verray tresor and richesse," in Thomas Hoccleve's phrase.[110] The Dominican Jean Capreolus (d. 1444), "Prince of Thomists," used his *Sentences* commentary to defend Aquinas against his fourteenth-century critics.[111] Denys the Carthusian commended to Carthusian novices the study of select "devout books," and in a separate work explained to his superior the authors that he had selected for his study.[112] The humanists turned to classical authors and prized those who wrote in eloquent Latin, but they also looked back to Petrarch for guidance and established Dante lectureships in universities.[113] Even in the theological and philosophical schools of the Central European universities, the so-called Albertists, Thomists, and Scotists, and in the conflict between *antiqui* and *moderni*, we see as in Gerson a return to a specific set of thirteenth-century sources.[114]

Contemporaries thus shared a tendency to list approved books for clusters of readers and to privilege those that served their own agendas. To take the next step with Gerson and to speak of a canon of great books rather than a mere list, we must now identify what bound these authors together. The modern literary canon has been defined as "the sum total of works supposed to be 'great,'" selected (in theory) on the basis of a consensus in the community.[115] What process informed Gerson's rationale for selection? If such works as these were superior, why so? Why these authors among so many others? The answer, I think, has partly to do with the status of the University of Paris as the guardian of orthodoxy and even the salvation of France, an idea that had been forming for two centuries and that finds full expression in Gerson's works.[116] In his view, the Paris theologians had set the gold standard for orthodoxy. "No theologian, *especially at Paris,* ever asserted such a damned heresy," he says when speaking of an ecclesiological principle (emphasis mine).[117] Especially after the spread of Wyclif's ideas, Gerson associated England not with healthy theology but with heresy. This idea of a role for France in preserving theology informed the selection of great books, but the selection had still deeper layers.

First among them: Gerson assumed that the best, most reliable authors can only be known over time. In the Navarre letter, before presenting his list, Gerson urged students to attend in their reading to "well-founded" things, to the works of those "holiest and most expert ones who practiced what they taught" rather than to the works of "young fast-talkers" (*loquaces iuvenes*), "contentious dialecticians," or the wicked. Jean Buridan, says Gerson, once admitted "that he never clung to new reasons, however apparent they seemed, because they had often deceived him; but never had the ancients, especially in moral matters." "Let us follow the well-trod path," Gerson continues, "easy and safe from dangerous errors and scandals."[118] The superiority of old authors thus depends in part on the fact that their teaching has been time-tested.

These passages reveal a second layer to Gerson's selection. Gerson emphasizes the holiness and experience of these authors, their character and upright living that conforms to their teaching. He spoke of this combination of piety and learning as the one necessary ingredient in a scholar. His attitude hardened over the course of his life, but he held this position in some form from the start. The seventh and eighth treatises of the late *Compilation on the Magnificat* (1427–1428) describe this ideal balance. In the following passage from the seventh treatise, he imagines the great authors under siege from reprobate schoolmen:

We have known some, alas!, who consider every teaching that mixes piety of faith with speculation as oppressive, annoying, sickening, and burdensome, such that they scorn devout doctors as unlearned men or old women.[119] Such to them are Gregory and Bernard—or with damnable arrogance and madness, Augustine and reverend Bonaventure and the like. "Their doctrine," they say, "is fine for preaching and devotion," as if devotion and erudition cannot stand side by side. . . . Devotion without philosophy or speculative scholastic theology is sufficient unto salvation. . . . But philosophy and theology without devotion "scatter those with proud hearts" [Lk. 1:51], oppress them and lead them astray to become entangled in endless questions.[120]

Later in the eighth treatise, Gerson reserves his greatest praise for the theologian whose teaching unites the intellect and the affections.[121]

Here we have a critical ingredient for Gerson's great books: a blend of learning and piety in the author. This explains his great esteem for Bonaventure, which appears in many works, but most clearly late at Lyon.[122] No longer at the University of Paris, Gerson grew more impatient with authors who lacked piety. He gradually took a much more critical position toward Albert the Great, probably as a result of reading *On the Intellect and the Intelligible*, part of Albert's encyclopedia of the physical sciences that he based on Aristotle.[123] Even Thomas Aquinas could make Gerson uneasy. In the late *Treatise on the Song of Songs* (1429), he notes that the rational power has a double faculty, intellect and will. Theologians like Aquinas, following Aristotle, have preferred the "dignity of the intellect"; others, like Bonaventure, following Augustine and Christian piety, chose the will "for surest reasons."[124] The distinction favors Bonaventure, and one even detects a tone of disapproval toward Aquinas, resurfacing from years earlier. In Gerson's youth, the Dominican Monzon had opposed Pierre d'Ailly and refused to accept the Immaculate Conception, relying on the authority of Aquinas. D'Ailly responded by criticizing Aquinas, just as Gerson did, for mixing terms: "He uses Aristotle's words and mixes his philosophy with the teaching of faith, as is apparent to any observer. This provides the occasion for error."[125] Early in his career, then, Gerson came to understand a potential problem in Aquinas, certainly not enough to undermine his status as a great authority, but a tendency to guard against.

With this in mind, we can now return to the second Navarre letter to consider two different versions of an important passage. The variant appears in Gerson's recommendations for the reading of theology. We saw that the modern edition, based on one of four known manuscripts, has Gerson recommending questions on the *Sentences* by Bonaventure, Aquinas, and Durandus. But two of the other manuscripts add William of Auxerre to the list of those who wrote on the *Sentences*, subtract Aquinas, and then, following the recommendation of Henry of Ghent, add: "Saint Thomas excels especially in the *Secunda-secundae*."[126] The first of these two versions (in the single manuscript) was likely first; the second appears to be a natural modification of it.[127] And though we cannot say with absolute certainty that Gerson himself changed the text, he often revised his texts in just this way. The addition of the *Secunda-secundae*, the part of the *Summa theologiae* where Aquinas treats moral theology, accords well with Gerson's emphasis on applied moral teaching over the course of his career. He also recommended the work to bishops in a letter written around 1408.[128] Finally, we should not overlook an important clue in the new text. Gerson says "*especially* in the *Secunda-secundae*" (emphasis mine). Even though Gerson is recommending books for theology, and really for beginners, he does not recommend the entire

Summa. This is not entirely surprising, since very few manuscripts transmit the entire work, and in fact the *Secunda-secundae* was easily the most popular part of the *Summa.*[129] But of course Gerson did know the entire work, and it was in the *Secunda-secundae* that Aquinas taught best how to think reflectively about ethical questions, which then move the reader closer to affective questions. Though we cannot date Gerson's apparent revision to the letter, we should see this recommendation as part of his growing desire to nudge theologians toward practical rather than speculative theology, toward understanding through the affections rather than through the intellect, a topic to be developed in Chapter 4.[130]

In the same way, Gerson eventually came to see in Bonaventure the best introduction to theology. By the 1420s he has no peers. "Of all the theological doctors," says Gerson of him in *On Books a Monk Should Read,* "he seems especially suitable and safest for enlightening the intellect and for inflaming the affections." In a letter to a Franciscan (1426), he moans that the writings of Bonaventure and Alexander of Hales seem buried, utterly forgotten, while those of others more interested in subtlety are exalted; but the subtle and their followers are taking a path to insanity. Jan Hus and Jerome of Prague among modern masters, Peter Abelard, Berengar of Tours, John Scot Eriugena (in his teaching on theophanies), and Gilbert of Poitiers in former times all erred in this way.[131]

In *On the Examination of Teachings* (1423), Gerson adds other virtues to Bonaventure—his personal holiness and clear terminology. He is "pious, just, and devout," he "resists curiosity to the utmost," and he gives no place to "worldly, dialectical, or philosophical teachings cloaked in theological terms." Instead, "when he seeks to enlighten the intellect, he yields in all things to piety and religious affection.[132] Firm, safe, holy, secure, pious, clear—the ideal model for theology students. Just as students in grammar and logic memorize Donatus and Peter of Spain's *Summulae* even though they may not understand the text at first, "theological disciples" (Gerson is addressing the Carthusians and the Celestines) should memorize the two great works of Bonaventure, the *Breviloquium* and *The Journey of the Mind to God.*[133] In this world full of books, Gerson and his contemporaries still assumed that readers would carry around enormous chunks of literature in their heads. For Gerson, so much the better if they were theological classics.

When we look at intellectual currents in fifteenth-century Europe north of the Alps, we see a world that reflects Gerson's vision for theology and theological training. In his emphasis on piety, he supplied a motive force—arguably *the* motive force—to an entire reform movement that took deep root there and found its voice in the "devout theology" (*Frömmigkeitstheologie*) of that era.[134] In fifteenth-century Oxford, too, theologians preferred the fathers to fourteenth-century speculations and saw dangers in logic.[135] The complaint against theologians who have learning but not devotion—head-knowledge but not heart-knowledge, we might say—resonates as an important theme in the later Middle Ages, inside and outside the university.[136]

Of course, most books never made it onto any list, even old books, even those written by pious authors. Some posed serious problems. Gerson thought deeply about these troubling books and read them carefully. He sometimes devoted entire works to them. We shall now meet a different kind of bookman, one with the weight of orthodoxy on his shoulders.

The Common School of Theological Truth

Besides their praise for authors like Bonaventure, the passages I have been quoting contain rumblings of discontent. *On the Examination of Teachings* chastises those who introduce philosophy or logic into theology. Perhaps the most telling comment in the second Navarre letter is the cutting remark on recent schoolmen and their terminology. They were the only ones singled out in this way. Where exactly were they going wrong?

In the university of his youth, Gerson came to understand that trustworthy theologians spoke with a common voice, that they had formulated a single theological language and terminology: the "common school of theological truth." The great books conformed to this common school; troublesome books deviated from it. The common school thus provides the true key for understanding Gerson's approach to books. We might think of it as the theologian's rulebook. Its authors were the thirteenth-century schoolmen.[137]

To understand the common school and its central place in Gerson's approach to books, we first need to appreciate the sense of unease that pervades so many of his discussions about books. Mostly, it was anxiety over contemporary theological training that provoked the Navarre letters. Gerson had a waking sense that something had gone terribly wrong in the theology of his day. Indeed, he endorsed specific authors in large part because he sensed that theology as a discipline had begun to decline and that only a consensus of authorities could rescue it. He shared this alienation from the theology of his day with many contemporaries, including Richard Fitzralph, John Wyclif, and Thomas Gascoigne among English theologians, Marsilius of Inghen among Dutch, and Guillaume de Salvarvilla among French.[138] During these same years, D'Ailly was closely studying astrology and predicting the imminent arrival of Antichrist.[139] The lingering Schism had something to do with the general gloom, and perhaps the common experience of coming of age in a society racked by plague. Whatever the reasons, a defensive gloominess overshadowed late fourteenth- and early fifteenth-century theology.

Gerson's concern over modern theology cannot be reduced to one tendency. Sometimes, he sensed a dangerous trend toward Platonism.[140] At others, he criticized the schoolmen in general for their lack of piety, as we saw in the discussion of Bonaventure. But the problem that concerns us most here was theological terminology. Theology was in complete chaos, "a Babel of confusion" said Gerson in his second letter on Ruysbroeck's *Spiritual Espousals*.[141] Everyone is talking but no one understands the next person. Zénon Kaluza has shown that Gerson based attacks like these less on what he actually saw around him than on fourteenth-century texts, including those of Thomas Bradwardine, Duns Scotus, Jean of Ripa, William of Ockham, and François de Meyronnes.[142] He had also carefully read the university legislation of the past two centuries and repeated its criticisms of those who introduce logic into theology and strange, sophistical doctrines into classroom teaching.[143] But the important point for us is rather the general sense of malaise that pushed authors like Gerson toward a set of approved, reliable authors. Soon, as the political situation deteriorated with the assassination of Louis of Orléans in 1407, he would have more reasons for concern.[144]

The mixing of terminology especially frustrated Gerson because it was undermining or calling into question what he saw as the greatest achievement of the thirteenth-century schoolmen. In effect, they had stabilized theological terminology by organizing theology into a system, what we would call systematic theology. Yet their true importance surpassed mere organization: using questions, Aquinas, Bonaventure, and "similar ones . . . passed on a supremely safe [*tutissimus*] theology that we might possess it under fixed [*certus*] rules and precise language . . . , reducing all former doctors to a single and secure correctness of speech [*ad unum securamque locutionis proprietatem*]."[145]

Observe three striking features of this passage, again from the second letter on Ruysbroeck. The first is the abundance of words denoting safety or certainty (*tutus, certus, securus*). We see a theologian looking back on the accomplishments of his predecessors in the university, generally pleased with what he saw before the fourteenth century, confident that by reducing variety of speech they had made the world safe for theology. In Bonaventure's day, he once said, "the common and firm teaching thrived at Paris."[146] For Gerson, one vocabulary and style now governs theological discourse. The sense that theology needed precise definition and had a restricted sense had slowly been gaining ground. In a letter to the University of Paris in 1346, Pope Clement VI spoke of a "true theology" that can only be acquired from the Bible and from original writings (*originalia*) and expositions of the saints and doctors.[147] The second feature of the passage quoted above is the language of possession. It is an arresting image: theology is something that we can possess, we theologians do possess it, and therefore we own it. The science of theology, the organization and technical disposition of the field and the production of textbooks—all this belongs to the age of system-building. It has occurred and reached a conclusion. The third feature is the notion of correctness of language or usage, its *proprietas* that reduces earlier authorities to one way of speaking. His notion of proper terminology is nearly Platonic, timeless, even above the fray.

More than all others, the great thirteenth-century masters had established this proper terminology, what Gerson called the "common school of theological truth," the idea that theologians speak in one correct way about theological topics.[148] The common school was not a group of authors, as the phrase might suggest to our ears, but a common, shared, correct theological vocabulary. As such, it gave Gerson a rulebook by which to judge and even to penalize the shortcomings of books of all kinds.

Long before he began listing books, Gerson had come to understand this principle of acceptable terms and formulas for theological discourse. His every discussion of books assumes it. He encountered it first as a student and then absorbed it more deeply as master and especially as chancellor. The development of this idea belongs to a larger story that we can recall briefly here, the growing control of universities over theological debate. William Courtenay and J. M. M. H. Thijssen have shown that with the rise of the universities in the early thirteenth century, masters of theology rather than bishops and popes began to monitor and police academic orthodoxy.[149] Consequently, those who came under scrutiny were advanced students, not masters. Between 1200 and 1285, most of those accused of heresy were no longer masters of theology, as in the earlier period (Abelard springs to mind), but masters of arts or bachelors of theology. After 1280, the mendicants began to oversee cases involving their own members, but this oversight lapsed after 1320. For a time, from 1315 to about 1342, masters of theology and canon law judged cases of academic orthodoxy at the papal court at Avignon, a shift probably encouraged by John XXII and papal bureaucrats. But with the death of Benedict XII in 1342, masters of theology once again oversaw cases of academic orthodoxy internally at Paris.

As time went on, academic censure became ever more routine, like other features of academic life. After 1342 no established master of theology was accused at Paris.[150] Masters policed the views of lecturers in a low-stakes atmosphere. Nothing could be further from Abelard, "the idol of Paris," burning his book on the Trinity in humiliation and anguish before being hustled off to a monastery. Censures took place at appointed times and perhaps only then, as when a student lectured on the *Sentences* or perhaps during debates at his inception as master of theology. These were matters of discipline, not judicial procedure. Censure never wrecked anyone's career. Lists of condemned articles circulated in copies of Lombard's *Sentences* so that student lecturers would know what not to say. They were teaching aids. The Sorbonne library owned ten copies of the *Sentences* with such lists.[151] In sum, we should imagine a "gentle mechanism of regent-master review."[152]

A letter that Gerson wrote in 1426 allows us to witness this oversight in action, to see how Gerson learned to speak correctly about theological topics. In a discussion of articles that the theology faculty had condemned in times past, he comes to the erroneous assertion that the divine essence can be distinguished and separated from the divine intellect and will, "as if divine essence can exist and not be universally perfect, nor understanding, nor willing." Gerson insists that it is better to assert that divine essence, which is singular and wholly simple, contains every perfection in itself. For if we cut away its perfections, what remains is a monstrosity and a confused emptiness. He then tells the following story: "Long ago when I was a young boy [*adolescentulus*], a famous doctor in theology told me something remarkable: 'When someone asks: "If the divine essence is cut off from the divine intellect, what is that essence?" Say that it is God and that it is not God. For it is God, because there is nothing in God that is not God. And yet it is not God, because God is his own intellect, nor can he exist without it.' Implicitly, this is the argument of blessed Bernard against Gilbert [of Poitiers]."[153] We see here an important master of theology communicating to a young student the right and the wrong way to talk about theology. He provides Gerson with a formula, almost as if he is teaching him a catechism of theology. The formula relies for its effect on a logical precision that would presumably confound the person asking the question. This conversation occurred when Gerson was quite young, perhaps around the age of fifteen. Gerson assumes that the young learn best when told what to say by an experienced master. Or told what not to say. In 1400, in his important memoir on the reform of theological instruction, Gerson suggests—he was probably the first to do so—that all former theological errors be put on a list (*schedula*), and that the list be published in the schools with this advice: "These teachings do not please the masters, so from now on abandon them and others like them." Theological instruction has become so routine that common mistakes can be posted on a bulletin board.[154]

This is the fourteenth-century university in which Gerson came of age, a place where senior theologians patrolled and policed bachelors of theology and masters of arts—the junior faculty of the medieval university, if you will—to keep them in line. When Gerson spoke of the "common school of theological truth," he had in mind the correct solutions and formulas and the proper language for theological topics. This was not quite the end of history. Gerson certainly recognized that within the confines of the common school, masters of theology would continue to work out new problems in questions and disputations. But as chancellor, he gave this creative and dynamic process much less thought than the policing function. To avoid trouble, a student need only learn the answers that others long before him had discovered. Gerson invokes the common school on various subjects: the fate of unbaptized children in limbo (attacking Ubertino), the exact meaning of venial sin (it is "not against but outside the commandment"), the goodness of an external act, the supernatural love infused without cognition in mystical theology, and the modes of signifying.[155] In each case, he had one correct formula and solution in mind. These examples can stand for many others, the coordinates of a grid overlaying the science of theology that has now been explored and mapped out—indeed, literally solved—for future generations.

Once we have this principle in view, we see it everywhere in Gerson. He expresses the importance of terminology clearly in *Against the Curiosity of Students* (1402), in a long discussion on the correct words to describe the divine nature: "If, as Augustine says, grammarians are so careful to make their syllables agree [*servare pacta syllabarum*], how careful ought we to be to observe fixed terms [*pacta certa terminorum*] when we speak of divine matters?"[156] At the early councils, he notes, the fathers took great pains to express themselves using exactly the right words, as with the Greek word *homoousion*, which precisely defined Christ's substance.[157]

Translations of Greek works into Latin posed similar problems. Gerson knew that the works of Greek authors such as Aristotle and Pseudo-Dionysius existed in old and new translations. Though it seems he often had to rely on the older translation of the works of Pseudo-Dionysius by John Scot Eriugena (whose translations he twice mentions), he also knew of the translation of Robert Grosseteste, commended for his skill in Greek.[158] Once, he found that Grosseteste's translation solved a difficult passage in another translation, on terms used to describe God the Father.[159] He then proceeded to stress the importance of precision when speaking of divine matters. The comparison of translations served to establish proper theological terminology.

The idea of a common school of theological truth will now help us unpack a critically important passage from *The City of God* that Gerson repeatedly invoked in discussions of troubling books and theological terms: "The philosophers are free in their choice of expressions, and do not fear to offend the ears of the religious when treating difficult subjects. But we [Christians] are duty bound to speak in accordance with a fixed rule" (*certa regula*).[160] We can connect this passage closely to the university context of Gerson's youth. In 1387, the theology faculty had used this exact passage in its condemnation of fourteen articles by Juan de Monzon. Though still a bachelor of theology at the time, at the age of twenty-three, Gerson took part in the decision to refer Monzon to the pope at Avignon.[161] Gerson probably learned this passage not directly from Augustine but from this earlier university condemnation. He cites it again and again, yet he never quotes any of the surrounding text in the original work of Augustine, repeating only these words, which he brandished as a formula, his golden rule for theological expression. When Gerson read and cited this passage, he thought first of university students and the right way to speak about the science of theology. He invoked it in similar contexts for the rest of his career to ensure conformity to orthodoxy. The passage expressed (in Wolfgang Hübener's words) the "fundamental principle of his understanding of the teaching profession."[162]

Peeking into the future, we see by 1500 a fault line forming between schoolmen and humanists, and great battles being waged over this very topic of expression. Defending technical theological language, the schoolmen would suffer heavy losses from humanists under the banner of eloquence.[163] Gerson, as we shall see, thought a union of theology and eloquence was still possible, though he was also aware that some theologians had given up. We thus find ourselves at a pivotal moment in the history of theology before the great split occurs.

Troublesome Books

So far I have linked the common school to the teaching and patrolling of students. But Gerson occupies a prominent place in the fifteenth century in part because he exploited the notion of a common theological vocabulary to justify broad interventions beyond the schools. Always reading and monitoring developments in the wider world, he attempted to project and extend the principle onto a society where discussions about theology and books drew a broader circle of interest than ever before and informed decisions at the highest levels of state. He thus stands at a turning point in the early fifteenth century when university masters strove to exercise greater authority beyond the schools. The policing masters of the late fourteenth century had focused mostly on teaching. Gerson focused his attention on books.[164]

Take his opinion on Ruysbroeck's *Spiritual Espousals*, one of the most original and daring works of late medieval theology. Probably written in the 1330s, the book explores the active life, the interior life, and the contemplative life through the metaphor of marriage.[165] In the third book, Ruysbroeck speaks in rapturous terms of the soul's vision of God and of its absorption into the divine essence. He drives the point home with an exciting metaphor: as a drop of wine fallen into the ocean becomes the ocean itself, so the soul lost in God unites with him.

In 1402, Barthélémy Clautiers, an important official at the Charterhouse of La Chapelle in Herne in the northern Rhineland, submitted the work to Gerson for his opinion.[166] Gerson says in response that he had skimmed the work some time ago, but has now read it more carefully and found in it many good and noble sentiments. He heartily approved of the first two books, which would lead the reader to "saving faith and pure morals."[167] But in the third book, Gerson finds, the author deviates from recognized authorities. This failure to follow the tradition has led him into a catalogue of errors, which Gerson inserts into the letter word for word from the copy of Ruysbroeck that the monk had sent him.[168] The problem is terminology that can lead astray the reader of such works:

Finally, I pray, let us watch that all those insufficiently trained or learned in sacred letters through daily and fervent study take special care not to cling too closely to such strange tracts [*tractatuli insoliti*], although many things in them may be true—for a demon would not teach [*persuadere*] false things without mixing in true. Nor should they presume to investigate theological and difficult matters with novel expressions designed to indulge their own self-worth and feelings. "We are duty bound to speak in accordance with a fixed rule," says Augustine. Otherwise, acting on their own, they will find themselves on an easy path over a precipice.[169]

Ruysbroeck's problem is that he does not conform. Gerson calls his books "tracts," emphasizing not just their brevity but their ephemeral quality, in contrast to the enduring classics. They are "strange." Ruysbroeck's words have no basis in tradition. They do not follow the proper formulas for theological expression. They are instead novel and serve only to indulge his readers and lead them astray. Gerson did admire Ruysbroeck. He included the *Spiritual Espousals* on his list of books that treat contemplation, though warning that the third book is suspect.[170] But these letters communicate a frustration as well, as if to say: we theologians know where the lines are, but you, Ruysbroeck, are changing the way that we talk about theology.

Later in the same letter, Gerson lists other books that fall short: "narrations or rules or particular teachings of certain holy fathers that should be admired rather than imitated"; John Climacus, who (in his

Ladder of Divine Ascent) used the wrong terminology when talking about the virtues—he speaks of them as though they are "free of passion" (*impassibilitates*), an idea with Stoic roots; Cassian on free will; and "other teachings that some have handed down without careful consideration or too rigidly," teachings "that the common school of theological truth rightly does not admit or rejects."[171] We are far from the critiques of the fourteenth-century schoolmen, then, but the problem can be reduced to the same plane of terminology and language. And behind every bad teaching was a bad book.

The two great preoccupations of Gerson's middle career, Jean Petit's defense of tyrannicide and Hus's teachings on the authority of the Church, were both tied directly to books that had transgressed against the common school. Gerson's obsession with tyrannicide crystallized around Petit's *Justification of the Duke of Burgundy* (1408). Petit had actively promoted and circulated the text, and the *Justification* had soon become available both in expensive illuminated copies and soon thereafter in a cheap paper edition.[172] Gerson began his assault in 1413. In November of that year, with royal support, he initiated a consultation of university masters in the episcopal palace. After three months of debate, on 23 February 1414, the bishop condemned the teachings of the *Justification* and had all copies of it gathered and burned two days later in a ceremony in front of Notre Dame. Messengers delivered the same sentence throughout the kingdom.[173]

Likewise, Gerson first attacked Hus on the basis of twenty censured articles drawn from his most famous work, *On the Church*, which repeated some of Wyclif's most violent attacks on the pope and prelates of the Church. In September 1414, Gerson sent these articles to the archbishop of Prague.[174] And before they burned Hus at the stake in July 1415, the authorities at Constance burned all available copies of *On the Church*.[175]

Both Petit and Hus had overlooked what Augustine had said: we theologians must speak "according to a fixed rule."[176] They broke the rules and opened the door to heresy. Our portrait of Gerson as bookman must also make room for this very brutal component. Books were so important that sometimes they had to be burned.

Gerson understood this power of intellectual binding as one of the great purposes of the University of Paris and made no real distinction between internal and external correction. In 1398, he applied the principle of theological terminology to the teaching of the Spanish mystic Ramon Lull, which he and other masters had prevented from being published (*ne doctrina publicetur*) because "it contains terms used by no doctor";[177] or as he says of Lull's teaching in the second letter against Ruysbroeck, it "departs from the manner of speaking of holy doctors and from the doctrinal rule of its tradition as used in the schools."[178] Such interventions punctuate Gerson's entire career. At the Council of Constance, he talked of erroneous articles being condemned at Paris and in the Roman curia, especially those "scandalous to faith and morals, or offensive to pious ears." Absent these condemnations, he thought, "the University of Paris, then the entire kingdom of France, and perhaps a great part of Christendom would have lapsed into numerous errors."[179] Gerson reduces the university to its barest essence and at once dramatizes its entire history as a highly successful story of struggle against heresy. The theologians who patrol internal teaching also preserve orthodoxy beyond the schools. The case of Hus marks a distinct break.[180] By this point, the era of benign correction had come to an end. Yet, considered within the context of Gerson's career, the trial of Hus represents only one forceful example of Gerson's efforts to exercise control beyond the schools.

With these interventions, we arrive at the cusp of a trend much larger than Gerson and one that he himself put in motion. Soon, university theologians would participate in trials such as that of Joan of Arc (1431).[181] English theologians were no different. Though Gerson blamed England for the spread of Wyclif's teachings, he saw eye to eye with English theologians like Netter, who followed events closely at the Council of Constance and later produced the most important written rebuttal of Wyclif's teachings, the monumental *Doctrinale antiquitatum fidei*.[182] These attitudes shaped the very institutions of learning. Lincoln College was founded in 1430 to defend "true theology" against heretics. The founder, Bishop Richard Fleming, left the college his library, including a copy of Netter's *Doctrinale*.[183] Another well-known bishop, William Alnwick, launched a series of trials against Lollards in East Anglia in 1428, then founded Eton College in 1440 to defend against the "sons of Belial who have conspired against our holy mother church of England."[184] "The widespread propagation of orthodox teaching," writes Jeremy Catto, "might have seemed, in the eyes of the masters of 1430, the end to which all studies led."[185]

We can now draw together the threads of the argument. The Navarre list represents Gerson's thinking in terms of the best authors, who are in the minority. Here and in other reading lists, Gerson identified a few authors who belonged to a select group, his theological canon for fifteenth-century theologians. Confronted by the intellectual pride of scholars, he came to believe that the most reliable authors combined learning with piety. Among these, Bonaventure excelled. Behind Gerson's various reading lists there stood the notion of a "common school of theological truth," his primary mental filter through which he sifted and evaluated books. As a young university student, Gerson learned that there was one correct language for theology, one set of formulas in which theology should be expressed. The common school served as a constant point of reference for evaluating troublesome books. Much more concerned than his predecessors with the world beyond the schools, Gerson applied the common school far and wide, to problems well outside the traditional province of masters of theology. This growing awareness of the need for outreach, application, and public involvement reminds us that Gerson stands apart because of his public activity. Now the master of theology monitors not just students but theological discussions in the wider world.

Conclusion

How, then, to characterize the world of books in which Gerson lived and moved? Books have become much more abundant than in the thirteenth century, yet new works remained scarce, even an author's own works. Print would not change this state of affairs immediately, but the time would come when an author like Erasmus could reach a European audience with breathtaking speed. Gerson read silently and consulted books as reference tools; the oral world of disputation and teaching is much less conspicuous in his works. But he also memorized great tracts of literature—more than we shall ever know—and assumed others would do the same. We see a general concern over authenticity, not limited to texts as in the sixteenth-century cry "ad fontes" but extending to everything that informed the life of the Church. We should also note the complete absence of certain features of humanist scholarship in Gerson. Unlike Coluccio Salutati, Gerson never (so far as we know) took the trouble to examine numerous manuscripts of a text, and he never expressed any preference for older manuscripts over newer ones.[186]

We see various canons of literature in this new historical space. The thirteenth-century schoolmen privileged strong arguments; Gerson preferred strong books. Like the humanists, he appreciated books as writings, as literature, but he defined his canon on very different terms. While the humanists found their standard in classical literature, or in the earliest, most authoritative sources of Christian doctrine, Gerson valued works that together constituted a "true" and "safe" theology. We see the importance of language; but whereas earlier schoolmen had mastered a technically precise yet narrow professional language, and whereas the humanists prized elegance and classical syntax, Gerson insisted on correct theological terminology that conformed to the common school. If it was elegant, so much the better. His common school justified a dramatic extension of theological authority to the world beyond the schools.

Our inquiry has also revealed a transitional moment in the history of reading. Robert Darnton expressed the fundamental assumption behind the origins of the field, that "reading itself has changed over time."[187] Clearly, the traditional categories of scholastic and humanist reading, while helpful at identifying certain large tendencies, cannot account for the complexity of the late medieval intellectual world. Gerson read books in a historically specific way that shaped and informed his attitudes to authorship. More than a decade ago, Harvey Graff cautioned against the kind of "great divide" that we see in an easy transition from scholastic (medieval) to humanist (modern) reading, a transition that parallels the break from script to print. If we insist on such dichotomies, then Gerson becomes nothing more than a point of transition on the way to yet one more revolution in the inexorable march toward universal literacy. Yet his reading practices overturn a flat, linear reading of the past and confirm Graff's emphasis on "the fundamental historicity of reading" and on "its refusal to develop linearly."[188]

This investigation into books and reading practices has prepared the way for our study of authorship in the next two chapters. We now have the problem squarely in our sights. Gerson has identified a mighty tradition of theological classics. Where does this leave the modern author? Is there room for one more? In the following chapter we see Gerson trying desperately to justify his profession, racked by guilt over his desire to write but nonetheless carving out space for the modern theologian in the realm of moral theology.

Chapter 2

Justifying Authorship
New Diseases and New Cures

In May 1423, Jean the Celestine wrote a letter to a Carthusian monk named Ambrose who had asked for copies of Gerson's works. Though the request was friendly, something in it struck a nerve. Jean quickly assured Ambrose that his brother never wrote willingly. Asked to write,

he pretended to be deaf, or quickly changed the subject, or rebuked us with hard words: "You know not what you ask! See what great works are at hand for the exercise of devotion, the excellent and most proven books of the holy doctors, which teach wholesomely and with all sufficiency everything needful for the complete perfection of life. Yet we do not heed them. See here are Augustine on the Psalter, Gregory on Job, Cassian in the *Collations* and *Institutes of the Fathers*, Bernard on the Song of Songs, Richard *On the Twelve Patriarchs* and *On the Mystical Ark*, Bernard again *To the Brothers of the Mount of God*, Hugh *On Prayer*, Anselm in the *Meditations*, Augustine again in the *Confessions* and the *Soliloquies*, and besides these the author of the *Summa on Virtues and Vices*, the author of *On the Spirit and Soul*, and many others. What more do you seek? Why, in disdain, do you heap new upon old? There is no end to making books. Abide in these, let your spirit take exercise in these, let your talents sweat in their study, not in curious or needless things which, while feigning subtlety, do not quench the soul but rather inflame itching ears and at last lead away from the truth."[1]

I am arguing for Gerson's centrality to the cultural and intellectual world of the fifteenth century. Yet in such a passage, Gerson appears on the margins of history. The great problem, he frequently says, is no longer the lack of new works but ignorance and neglect of the classics. The old books solved all problems. The saints left out nothing. The fathers penned mighty works, the schoolmen scribble. I can only gather crumbs from their table.[2]

The surest way to misinterpret Gerson's true feelings toward writing is to take these comments literally. Medieval writers shared a sense of indebtedness. Alastair Minnis has traced the sentiment from at least the time of Vincent of Beauvais (d. 1264).[3] The *compilatio* motif—literary composition as nothing more than compilation of older materials—found its way into countless academic prologues to classical and Christian sources. Over time, even vernacular authors invoked it. Chaucer follows in a long tradition when he refuses to receive any praise or blame in *Troilus and Criseyde,* "For as myn auctor seyde, so seye I."[4]

The motif is a topos, then, but also a form of evidence. By his use of it Gerson betrays an acute sense of self-consciousness and guilt. Even in his very last work, the *Treatise on the Song of Songs,* he says that he "long doubted" what he could possibly say that had escaped the great talents. This moment of hesitation offers a clue to his quandary: a longing to write checked by the cold stare of great authors across the centuries. Perhaps Bernard of Clairvaux's great sermons, which he cherished, came to mind. At last, he tells the Carthusians, "trusting to the aid of your prayers, I decided to write something new or at least in a new way."[5] Something "new" is immediately qualified and diminished to something "in a new way."[6] The Navarre letters teem with such anxieties. Gerson admits to loving his works as if they were his children.[7] But he never forgets those books in his study: "I *ought* to prefer that the studious give themselves to the study of old doctors."[8] People *ought* to read the classics, but I want them to read my books too.

Such sentiments reveal with naked clarity an anxiety of influence as profound as anything expressed by poets writing in the shadow of Shakespeare. Indeed, such anxieties recur frequently in Western literary history.[9] But Gerson is more complicated than this, and if we wish to fathom him as an author of more than five hundred works, his sense of place in the theological tradition and his justification for authorship, we must peer further into dark corners of little-read pieces. The dark, haunting passages of the Navarre letters, written at a time of sickness and doubt, reveal just one attitude of many. In a work such as *On Contracts* (1421), for example, written in the prime years at Lyon, Gerson speaks of writing in vigorous, forceful terms: "For living doctors have no less authority to expound Holy Scripture doctrinally or to interpret laws [*jura*] than the dead, and those who have not written have no less authority than those who have. . . . Clearly, some people have too much humility or vanity. For when asked to say what they think about a certain moral case, they at once take refuge in citation after citation and gloss after gloss. . . . We can rightly say to such as these: tell us not what others have written, but what you yourself say or believe."[10] I shall come back to this passage in its context—canon law and canon lawyers. But we can already begin to detect the outlines of a vigorous apology for new writings. Despite his reverence for old authors and his repeated calls for an end to writing new books (he even wrote a poem on the subject),[11] Gerson located a terrain where it was not merely acceptable but incumbent upon the modern theologian to make determinations on the basis of his own authority. For material, the theologian needed only look to cases in moral theology, to consider the circumstances peculiar to each case, and to trust to his experience and judgment, balanced by his deep understanding of the tradition. To fulfill this vision of the theologian's task, to address specific contemporary problems and to offer solutions to different cases, Gerson turned time and again to the tract, which he sharpened with all the rhetorical skills he could muster.

In the next two chapters, I trace this problem of authorial justification through three broad categories of works. In the tracts, we find Gerson's most coherent and consistent defense of new writings. The cases involved were often hotly contested and could easily turn into battlegrounds with canon lawyers. These encounters led Gerson to articulate a core principle of his moral theology, that the theologian should not rely on general rules or legal principles to resolve new moral cases but must instead apply his own experience to resolve each new problem and abandon citation for a clear statement of what he believes. In this model, almost limitless in its application, the theologian diagnoses new moral diseases in the same way that the medical master diagnoses physical diseases.

I turn next to two categories of works from late in Gerson's career, especially from the period of exile at Lyon: what I shall call his "major works" and his poetry (mostly written in this period). Gerson never forsook the tract, but he also never lost sight of permanence or *duratio*, the sense that writings could endure for ages to come. To take our full measure of him as an author, to grasp the truly enormous scale of his corpus, and to understand how he justified his works, we must take things more slowly, like sightseers taking in the features of a foreign landscape. The challenge is to grasp the true dimensions of Gerson's writings. The works of this period are among the most obscure in the entire corpus, yet they allow us to look into Gerson's soul, to see his ambitions, his preoccupations, and the balance he struck between creativity and self-indulgence.

The tracts and the works of exile form important components of a complicated body of work. Before we proceed further, it may therefore be useful to take a whirlwind tour of Gerson's entire literary corpus.

Gerson's Literary Career: A Summary View

One way to appreciate the complexity of Gerson's literary output is to consider Glorieux's eleven-volume modern edition, a snarled tangle of 540 works organized according to principles that change with every volume. After an introductory volume, volume 2 gives the letters. Volume 3 contains "magisterial" works, those that can be tied in some way to teaching. Volume 4 is poetry, volume 5 Latin sermons, volume 6 works on the Schism. Volume 7.1 contains French works, 7.2 French sermons. Volume 8 has pastoral and spiritual writings, volume 9 doctrinal writings, and volume 10 polemical works. This gives us organization by genre (vols. 2, 3, sort of, and 4), by language (7.1), by genre and language (5 and 7), and by content (6, 8, 9, 10), though style is also a factor in volume 10. For works that seem to fit multiple categories, such as French spiritual works, Glorieux sometimes used cross-references. Certain letters circulated in the manuscripts not as letters but as dedications to works edited in other volumes. Likewise, some poems in volume 4 belong to works in other volumes, such as the many poems in *The Consolation of Theology* (vol. 9). The classification of volumes 8 and 9 is almost meaningless.

Glorieux deserves our respect and sympathy. He had an impossible task that needed a team of scholars, and we are better off with his edition than without it. But his organization is of little help here. For our purposes in the next two chapters, we need to grasp the broad strokes of Gerson's literary career. Imagine it, then, in five great overlapping phases, each with some point of emphasis: Gerson the early Latin stylist (1383–1395), the vernacular preacher (1389–1413), the doctrinal and spiritual authority (1400–1415), the Latin orator and international author (1415–1418), and the established author and exiled poet (1418–1429). Then overlay these five phases with a sixth that spans most of the others, Gerson the public intellectual and writer of tracts on moral cases (c. 1395–1429). Consider these phases only as a starting point. Gerson wrote as a spiritual guide at Constance and at Lyon, and he preached Latin sermons before Constance. And finally, complicate everything further with subplots, themes, and digressions: Gerson the "apostle of Church unity" (1395–1417), guide to the religious life (especially 1420–1429), and opponent of John Wyclif, Jan Hus, and Jean Petit (1409–1418).

This overview has its limitations, but it offers a useful sketch to which I can now add texture and depth. The first phase reveals the strong impact of Petrarch, as in the eclogue and the 1393 Latin sermon. But the highlight of this period is the tract against Juan de Monzon, where Gerson writes as a historian. The topic is theological rather than political: "Here are no sounds of arms," he readily admits, "no conquests of cities . . . no fields strewn with dead bodies."[12] In this work, he is an eyewitness to history, but the topic—the Immaculate Conception—reminds us that we are dealing with a theologian. I emphasize this tract again for the insight it gives into his early sense of himself as an author. He moved on to other interests and themes and abandoned an artificial Latin style, but he never stopped writing.

Gerson gained an early reputation for his French sermons, which gave him admission into elite circles. But he soon turned away from court life. Louis Mourin's careful study revealed a shift in focus from sermons at court (1389 to 1397), to sermons in Paris churches (1401 to 1404), to sermons on important political issues (1404 to 1413).[13] It is no exaggeration to say that Gerson's early reputation as a preacher made his career. I shall have more to say in Chapter 6 about this important point.

The shift away from preaching at court owed much to the crisis at Bruges that put Gerson on a trajectory very different from his previous experience. The works of the next fifteen years up to the Council of Constance reflect this new sense of purpose. He now struck out in ten directions at once: criticizing theologians in works such as the lectures *On Two Kinds of Logic* (1401) and *Against the Curiosity of Students* (1402); producing an instant classic on the operation of the Holy Ghost in Christians in *On the Spiritual Life of the Soul* (1402); guiding laity into the spiritual and mystical life in his major vernacular works *La montagne de contemplation* (1400) and *La mendicité spirituelle* (1401); doing the same thing in Latin for clerks in *On Mystical Theology* (1408); compiling and circulating early catechisms such as the *Opus in Three Parts* (c. 1408) to raise the general understanding of the Christian faith; writing guides for the clergy on such topics as confession, visitation, and excommunication; taking the first steps toward suppressing the teachings of Wyclif, Hus, and Petit; and doing all of these things while attempting to end the Schism and to heal growing rifts at court.

Gerson's arrival at Constance in 1415 marked a great passage and saw his star rise as a Latin orator. He sensed great opportunities. We see the first signs of a pattern that will define his late career, the drive to produce lasting works, most evident in the composition of his epic poem the *Josephina* (1414–1418). He spent much of his time pursuing the campaigns against Hus and Petit, contributing to discussions about the reform of clerical behavior, and especially trying to resolve the Schism. These pursuits generated numerous occasional writings.

In May 1418 Gerson left Constance and eventually reached Lyon, the place of his exile. His sense of purpose and the high view of writing evident in his earliest writings returned and gave him the energy to launch great literary enterprises: *On the Consolation of Theology* (1418), his imitation of Boethius; his Gospel harmony the *Monotessaron*; the strange *Treatises on Songs* (c. 1423–c. 1429); the puzzling centiloquies, each a list of one hundred statements (1424–1428); the *Compilation on the Magnificat*, a cavernous literary warehouse for unused and recycled material (1427–1428); and the *Treatise on the Song of Songs* (1429). Throughout these years, following the completion of the *Josephina* in 1418, he wrote numerous poems, many of which he inserted into other works, perhaps in part to ensure their survival.

Soon after he became chancellor in 1395, Gerson mastered the genre that became his trademark: the tract. We may define it as a treatment of a single moral case with some connection to the world outside the university in a form brief enough to be easily distributed.[14] It represents well his brand of applied theology, targeting specific cases and tangling with opponents. Chapter 5 traces the history of this genre and considers what it can teach us about the public nature of theology during this period. Here, our concern remains Gerson's justification of authorship, with our focus first of all on the tracts. We have already seen the anxieties that led Gerson to describe writing as a concession. Yet while guilt-ridden about his desire to write, Gerson found an important role for theologians in the modern world. The tracts represent the battle lines with his opponents or, equally, the medicine bag for the doctor of souls. They were the easiest works to justify.

To understand how the tract became closely linked to Gerson's justification for new writings, we must first step back and try to see the history of theology as Gerson saw it. Modern doctors continued to write and to add to the theological literature. What exact place did their writings have in the modern world? And what authority?

The Place of Modern Doctors in the History of Theology

In terms of the evolution of theology, Gerson saw the Christian era as an unfolding of dispensations. First came the era of the fathers or "ancient doctors" who produced the authoritative works, the guides to the faith. This period began with the apostles and continued to the great authors of the twelfth century. The age of schoolmen followed, the "newest doctors" (*novissimi*), especially those at thirteenth-century Paris when the "scholastic style" reigned and the schoolmen organized theology.[15] Then came the fourteenth-century catastrophe, when "more recent ones" allowed logic to corrupt their teaching and embraced novelty rather than follow the well-trod path.[16] Gerson treats this period as an unfortunate intermediate phase and blames it on English doctors such as Thomas Bradwardine and the "sophists" in the Ockhamist tradition.[17] (Theology masters such as Jean de Maisonneuve and Denys the Carthusian took a similar tone toward the fourteenth century, possibly through Gerson's influence.)[18] Gerson viewed his immediate predecessors more positively, praising Henry of Oyta in particular for bringing the doctors into harmony on certain issues, as well as Henry of Langenstein and of course his master, Pierre d'Ailly.[19]

Before proceeding further, I must stress two features of this version of theological history. First, this is by no means a neutral reading of the past. By regretting and bracketing the fourteenth century, Gerson was doing justice neither to his own tradition nor to one of the richest periods of speculative inquiry in the history of medieval thought. Using Peter Lombard's text as a springboard, fourteenth-century theologians had applied dialectical reasoning far and wide to major problems in the history of natural philosophy. Some commentaries "seem to be works on logic and natural science in disguise," writes Edith Sylla. The schoolmen's healthy curiosity knew few bounds: light, rainbows, astrology, projectile motion, and many other topics came in for investigation.[20] Parts of some commentaries circulated as separate treatises on natural philosophy.[21] The debates over supposition in the mid-fourteenth century (see Chapter 4) dealt with fundamental issues of meaning and language. To further a very specific agenda, Gerson dismissed these major intellectual advances as a deviation from the healthy theology of the thirteenth-century schoolmen. Thinking of Petrarch, who figured his own age as a period of Lethean slumber, we can see here the first steps toward a reappraisal of the past that would take a much harder edge in later humanists.[22] Speaking of Erasmus and Jacques Lefèvre d'Étaples, the powerful Paris theologian Noël Beda (d. 1537) remarked that one sees them holding the fathers, "but never schoolmen like Peter Lombard, Alexander Hales, Albertus, Thomas, Bonaventura, Ockham, and so on."[23] Gerson focused and limited his criticism in ways that later humanists did not. Nonetheless, his chronological criticism targeted an entire generation of schoolmen and opened the door for others to follow.

Second, this version of the history of theology implied a reorientation of the past whereby the thirteenth century first rose to prominence as the great age of classification.[24] Such a scheme went hand in hand with the emergence of canons and classic texts that we saw everywhere in the previous chapter. We are witnessing here a new historical perspective, an awareness that the project of the schools has now entered a different phase. Gerson sensed that he was living at some distance in time from thirteenth-century masters, who—he expressly states—wrote differently, producing works remarkable for their organization.[25] The classic distinction between ancients and moderns had reappeared at various times from the eleventh century onward.[26] It implied an awareness of the distance between the present day and the past, and a comparison that normally favored the ancients. Gerson added further layers to this simple dichotomy by introducing thirteenth- and fourteenth-century theologians into the scheme.

Beyond these two important points, the most remarkable feature of this view of history is the conscious introduction in the early thirteenth century of a new group of professionals licensed "to read, dispute, deliberate and teach." This shift carried profound implications. A phrase such as *ordo doctorum*, formerly reserved for bishops, could now mean university masters of theology.[27] The tradition behind Gerson on this point had tended to place the Church hierarchy—bishops, prelates, and pope—in a class opposite theology masters. Godfrey of Fontaines and William of Ockham had framed the issue in terms of the jurisdiction of prelates on the one hand and the expertise of theologians on the other. In their view, while prelates had authority on their side, theologians had truth itself, which played greatly to their advantage, even challenging the authority of papal teaching in Ockham's case.[28] Faced with the Schism, Gerson would take this notion still further.

Like Ockham, and drawing heavily on his master D'Ailly, Gerson insisted on the corporate authority of theologians and their right to teach and expound scripture.[29] He pondered the issue of teaching and authority in a late work at Lyon, *On the Examination of Teaching*s (1423). There, he explains that every university-licensed theologian is a "doctrinal examiner" of teachings by virtue of the oath he takes: "For the Chancellor says: 'By apostolic authority, I grant you the license to read, to rule, to dispute, and to teach in the holy faculty of theology here and everywhere on earth, in the name of the Father, and the Son, and the Holy Ghost.'" Unlike the prelate, who must teach and preach because these actions belong to his office, the theologian has no obligation to perform these acts "absolutely" and "widely." Yet in the case of heresy, when need demands it, the theologian must indeed preach, teach, or interpret scripture, "or he would seem ungrateful for God's gifts."[30]

Here we see Gerson's sense of the need for oversight beyond the schools, his desire to extend magisterial authority into new domains and to monitor new territories. For Gerson, the authority to write flowed directly from this magisterial authority. Years earlier, in the lectures *On the Spiritual Life of the Soul* (1402), he had explained that while the theology master does not have apostolic authority, he has legitimate authority to expound and interpret Holy Scripture and to produce "a certain magisterial and scholastic declaration" similar in authority to the books of the saints. The Church approves of these, but does not grant them authority equal to that of the Church itself.[31] Just as other fields have their experts, so theology—now more than ever a science—has licensed theologians who have the exclusive right to expound scripture and to make determinations in moral affairs. This principle runs through Gerson's writings: "Trust the expert in his craft," he says again and again, quoting Peter of Spain. Elsewhere, he repeats Horace: "Doctors practice medicine, carpenters handle carpentry tools."[32] By virtue of the complexity of their craft, given the difficulty of their books and of the Christian tradition itself, theologians hold a license that others should acknowledge and respect. Theology is now a profession, and theologians are professionals.

Gerson became even warmer about the role of modern theologians before lay audiences. In a French sermon in defense of the Immaculate Conception (1401), while acknowledging that new doctors might not match the old for holiness, he insisted that their lukewarmness has no bearing on their authority. At all times doctors instructed in scripture may expound and declare its truths, just as prelates have authority equal to prelates of old, even though their holiness has cooled.[33] Gerson affirmed the "common truth" when arguing against the curiosity of the schoolmen, their "sterile variety" and obstinacy in clinging to cherished authorities and doctrines. But when it suited his purpose he also called for new devotions, saints, and doctrines.

Take this very doctrine of the Immaculate Conception. Introduced into England around the year 1000, it had slowly been working its way into popular acceptance, strengthened by growing Marian devotion.[34] Yet every major thirteenth-century theologian rejected it, including Gerson's three favorites: Alexander of Hales, Aquinas, and Bonaventure. But new doctors were not bound by their decisions. In Gerson's lifetime, the Dominicans resisted it so vigorously, adhering to the words of Saint Thomas "too stubbornly," as Gerson put it, that they were expelled from the University of Paris in 1387.[35] In a French sermon, Gerson explains away Bernard of Clairvaux's resistance to it: "Now things are different from the time of Saint Bernard, for the truth is clearer and the solemnity is celebrated nearly everywhere by the entire Roman Church and by others. That is why there is no danger to the conscience of culpable error or of presumption in celebrating this solemnity, but rather much more in not celebrating it."[36] This is just one example of truths revealed late in time. In the same sermon, Gerson observed that many doctrines hidden from our predecessors have been "newly revealed or declared" to recent doctors. He quotes Gregory: Moses knew more than Abraham, the prophets knew more than Moses, the apostles more than they. Then, updating Gregory, he continues: and the doctors have added to the apostles.[37] At one time, the Virgin Mary was not generally supposed to be in paradise in body and soul, as we hold today. Augustine held a view different from ours on the fires of purgatory.[38] The idea of the perpetual virginity of Mary took root slowly among Christians. Devotion to St. Joseph (for which Gerson campaigned) is only the latest example of holy novelty.[39] For good spiritual reasons, Benedict told the parents of a deceased monk to bury a Host with the body, and children three or four years old received the Eucharist; but we should not allow this today because of prevailing custom in the Church and the veneration of the Eucharist.[40]

This idea of preserved magisterial authority and the increase of truth infused Gerson's vision for contemporary masters of theology. While recognizing patristic authority, Gerson jealously guarded the right to expound sacred texts and to determine truths. Without presuming apostolic authority, the schoolmen could supply the need for determinations on moral matters.[41] The faith moves onward under the doctrinal aegis of university theologians.

In conceiving his apology for new writings, then, Gerson focused on contemporary moral theology. At last he seemed to recognize the chasm between old books and modern problems. This recognition, that in the moral sphere the books of the fathers and doctors have limited application, opened the way to a forceful claim for the professional theologian. In his view, this was how university masters should now practice theology, by responding to new problems.

Often, these new problems were moral cases that drew the attention of canon lawyers. Moral theology was a crowded, contested arena. As we shall now see, these confrontations helped to clarify for Gerson the exact purpose of writing in the moral sphere, and allowed him to draw sharp distinctions between theologians and canonists.

Canon Lawyers and the Culture of Citation

In theory, the justification for authorship that I have outlined puts the theologian in a position of great strength. But the reality of Gerson's entry into public debates is that on issue after issue he found himself challenged by canonists.[42] They were formidable opponents, often holding the most powerful offices in Church administration. Since the mid-twelfth century, nearly every significant pope had been a lawyer. Legal training transferred more easily into the world of business that engulfed the medieval papacy. Theologians knew and understood this and resented it. Gerson once remarked that theologians were as rare as can be in the curia, and that there were not two theologians in the whole College of Cardinals.[43] Theologians such as Gerson agreed with St. Bernard—whose classic *On Consideration* they had all read—that the natural order of things had been reversed.[44]

We can see traces of Gerson's conflicts with canon lawyers in the manuscripts themselves. More than half the copies of his tract on Joan of Arc add a rebuttal from an anonymous canon lawyer, bristling with references to legal works and insisting that any defense of Joan directly contravenes canon law and the Catholic faith.[45] *On Contracts* (1421) bears even more traces of confrontation. Gerson wrote at the urging of the Grande Chartreuse and its prior, Guillaume de Mota, who were involved in commercial transactions that appeared usurious from a certain angle.[46] After composing the work, Gerson discovered a diatribe against usurers written by a canon lawyer in Catalonia. (His identity is uncertain.) He then added a section attacking it. In 1429, this exchange came to the attention of the well-known canonist Johannes of Imola at the University of Bologna. After examining the matter *pro et contra*, he agreed with the Catalonian master, while acknowledging the justice of Gerson's position: these contracts were illicit, but not usurious.[47] Gerson replied to works by the canon lawyer and nobleman Guillaume Saignet on clerical celibacy and nobility.[48] He often blasted the practice of frequent excommunication as an abuse of positive (statutory) law. We can hear echoes of his opponents' arguments when he marvels at those who say that excommunication is not a penalty but a medicine. If it is not a penalty, he asks, what is?[49] Such debates illustrate the world theologians were entering. They were now competing with canon lawyers on common ground, writing works on exactly the same topics, and struggling to control the terms of debate.

Gerson sometimes thought the canonists were overstepping their bounds. For their part, remarks John Van Engen, "canonists in their maturity understood themselves as lawyers pursuing supernatural ends."[50] Both theologians and canon lawyers saw themselves as contributors to a healthy spiritual economy and ultimately to individual salvation. At times, Gerson acknowledged the importance of canon lawyers. Addressing the faculty of canon law in 1410, he stated that "the Lord . . . is the first essential foundation of every law and canon," and he further agreed with Ambrose that "the first of all laws is divine will."[51] He saw a historical necessity for canon lawyers after the endowment of the Church and the institution of benefices. He idealized the "ambidextrous" master who can apply himself to both theology and sacred canons, while he criticized those who take sides.[52] Yet amid these measured phrases, he appears stymied and frustrated. He has hard words for "those who want to argue that after the founding of the faculty of canon law, the faculty of theology became unnecessary."[53] Both have their place, and when it comes to matters like judging heretics, theologians should take precedence and judge the case. Canon lawyers should merely determine the appropriate punishment.[54]

We see here a complex set of attitudes toward canon lawyers: respect for their calling, recognition that they perform a historically necessary service, though sometimes subordinate to the task of theologians, and probably some professional jealousy. In the tracts themselves, in open debate with canon lawyers, Gerson expressed himself more frankly. These debates left deep traces in his writings and shaped his attitude to authorship. In particular, they led him to announce his conviction that the writer in the moral sphere must speak with a clear voice on the basis of his professional status and resist the urge to cite authorities—the trademark of the canonists.

Several passages from the tracts themselves may demonstrate this. Gerson wrote the tract against the Hussites (*On the Need for Lay Communion in Both Kinds*) at Constance in August 1417 in response to arguments that masters at the University of Prague had made months earlier in favor of the laity receiving not only the bread but also the wine at Communion. Their open letter from Prague, addressed "to all the faithful of Christ," soon reached Constance. The council fathers then apparently issued a "general warning" on the topic, which moved Gerson to write his tract.[55] He divides it into two sections, each with ten principles (*regulae*), the first set "speculative," the second "practical." Gerson is struggling mightily to circumscribe the interpretation of Holy Scripture, which formed the basis of the arguments put forward by the Prague masters. In the ninth rule of the first section, he insists that authentic interpretation of scripture depends on the authority and approval of the universal Church. This is an absolute first principle of faith. On matters like the sacraments, the custom of the universal Church should have greater authority than that of one doctor, even a saint. Within the context of this vigorous defense of the corporate authority of the Church against the opinion of any single doctor, Gerson launches into a remarkable attack on the undue authority accorded to legal commentators:

> Wherefore those who carefully consider matters marvel when they see that the minute some doctor has produced a single lecture, composition, or gloss upon the *Decretals* or the *Decretum* and has put it in writing, that gloss or lecture earns such respect that it is duly cited in the schools and in the courts. And if that doctor were living, he could not compare to many thousands now alive. And even if an entire university, for example, which has doctors of the highest skill in every faculty, were to pronounce or make a determination upon one exposition of a single passage of Holy Scripture, the *Decretum*, or the *Decretals*, a proof of this kind would scarcely be credited or allowed—as if a dead writing has more authority than living words! And if anyone objects that the judgment of the living is compromised because of the corruption of the will, then why can't we assume that the dead were subject to passions that clouded their judgment when they were alive?[56]

The repeated references to the *Decretals* and the *Decretum*, the great collections of church law, testify to Gerson's sense of his opponents. The passage communicates his deep frustration at the culture of debate with the canonists, who continually cite commentaries as a kind of evidence commanding assent. Elsewhere they are the "text men" (*textuales homines*) who staff the papal curia and craft arguments that prolong the Schism.[57] Their citation of dead legal texts undermines the authority of the living theologian. Gerson's love for the classics traced in the previous chapter had this reverse image, a vigorous belief in the authority of modern doctors to order Christian society and to overrule dissenting voices within the tradition.

Gerson states the case for the modern author even more forcefully in his tract *On Contracts*, cited above. In the section that he added to combat the tract against usurers, Gerson first summarizes the work and then offers ten observations, many of them teeming with citations to canon law and to theological authorities.[58] In the final observation, he recalls a case of possible usury that caused a great deal of commotion. Experts were consulted, "theologians too," in various places and assemblies, including at the Council of Constance itself. Signed opinions were submitted, "and he who witnessed it testified that these and similar contracts are permissible." Gerson continues:

For living doctors have no less authority to expound Holy Scripture doctrinally or to interpret laws [*jura*] than the dead, and those who have not written have no less authority than those who have. And so the multiplication of so many citations is sometimes to no purpose, for as soon as someone writes something, we despise the counsel of the living. Yet quite often they can better attend to the particular circumstances whereby a decision must often be altered. As the most experienced physicians say of healing people, the general rules passed down in theory are scarcely practical without exception. So much more is this true in moral matters, as souls have more alterations [*mutationes*] than bodies. . . . Clearly, some people have too much humility or vanity. For when asked to say what they think about a certain moral case, they at once take refuge in citation after citation and gloss upon gloss, sometimes even setting aside the texts or universal principles that should form the basis of such a decision. They say: "This one thinks this, another thinks that, another agrees with him, and another supports the first." We can rightly say to such as these: tell us not what others have written, but what you yourself say or believe.[59]

Buried deep in the tracts, all but forgotten, these angry, lucid passages paint a vivid picture. Whenever Gerson confronted a jurist, he found himself entangled in citations to commentaries on canon law. The act of comparing and reconciling authorities belonged to the most basic instincts of university-trained scholars. But Gerson understood that this culture of citation could clutter and confuse debate and choke off the voice of the modern theologian, who should write as a modern authority.

Earlier theologians too had pondered the exact place of authorities in constructing arguments, especially in classroom debate, and it is worth pausing briefly to consider this historical development. Aquinas had given the classic statement on the method of magisterial instruction in a quodlibetal question, "Whether theological determinations should be made by authority or by reason." In the case of magisterial disputation, he stated, the master should supply reasons "that search to the root of the truth and show how the thing which is said to be true is actually so.

Otherwise, if the master determines the question by appeal to bare authorities, the listener will have a certainty that the thing is so, but he will have acquired no knowledge or understanding and will go away with an empty mind."[60] The idea of sterile citations, then, stretches back at least to Aquinas. Cool and efficient, the Angelic Doctor barely raises his voice. And of course he is imagining a formal, internal debate among theologians. A veteran of debates in the public forum, Gerson gave the topic an angry new emphasis, deploring the heavy reliance on glosses and stressing the need to clarify the written form of the argument itself for a broader audience, a point to be developed further in Chapter 4.

In coming to this conclusion, Gerson owed something to his master. Earlier in the tract on contracts, he had credited the method of setting aside glosses to D'Ailly, whose advice he recalls: "When truth seems to be under assault from citations to laws, I have found that if I set aside the glosses upon glosses and have recourse to the naked letter of the text, the meaning [*intellectus*] at once becomes clear, and those who are making citations to the contrary will at once acknowledge the point and marvel at it."[61] When determining moral matters, the theologian must speak with his own clear voice. The final sentence of the passage from *On Contracts* quoted above—"Tell us . . . what you yourself . . . believe"— might stand as Gerson's great imperative for theologians, to speak with authority as licensed masters of theology should do.

Here we have one principle that informed Gerson's attitude to authorship on moral topics: the need to abandon glosses and to speak with authority. The passage from *On Contracts* hints at a second principle: the importance of experience in diagnosing moral problems or diseases. In this context, Gerson often applied to theologians the metaphor of the physician as healer of souls. The metaphor was of course extremely ancient, as old as Christianity itself.[62] It was enshrined in canon 21 of the decrees of Fourth Lateran (1215) in reference to priestly confession.[63] Gerson certainly knew of these traditional images, but he applied the metaphor in a new way to masters of theology and supplemented it with his understanding of how doctors actually performed in the faculty of medicine—the third of the higher faculties at Paris.[64] We know that he did in fact communicate firsthand with medical masters at various times.[65] He sometimes observed that medical masters rely not on books alone but on experiential knowledge as well.[66] After being steeped in the learning of the schools, after digesting countless medical authorities, and after receiving his license, the professional physician leaves his study to heal diseases in the wider world.

Increasingly in the later Middle Ages, medical masters were stressing this very point, the need for experience over books in medical practice. Already in the thirteenth century, Guglielmo da Saliceto (d. 1277) drew on his own experience to criticize ancient authorities on matters such as the wisdom of operating on newborns.[67] By around 1300, physicians at Bologna and perhaps Montpellier reintroduced dissection. It did not lead at once to an overthrow of Galen. "Before one could criticize Galen," writes Danielle Jacquart, "one had to reach his level." But those who participated must have sensed some practical value in this procedure, and they soon began to rely on their observations to challenge traditional medical authorities.[68] In the mid-fourteenth century, Gentile of Foligno (d. 1348) introduced the notion of medicine as a labor-intensive and practical field of study (*scientia operativa, practica*).[69] By the late fourteenth century, following their experience with plague, medical masters even began to boast of their achievements, and some, such as John of Burgundy, even claimed a mastery in the art of healing that exceeded that of the ancients. Many others agreed.[70]

On this point, too, the importance of experience, Gerson positioned himself in opposition to canon lawyers. Rather than relying on experience, the canonists (in Gerson's view) were taking principles from legal commentaries and elevating them to general rules. Yet changing circumstances doom this procedure. No branch of knowledge is more difficult than moral theology, he says in *On Guiding the Heart*, owing to the infinite variety of its circumstances. Easy solutions escape us. Even the most talented and experienced discover new things daily in this wide field.[71] The theologian, then, must deal with problems *as they occur*, and *on the basis of experience*, not books. He must accommodate inevitable changes in spiritual appetites, revolutions of taste, personal differences, and shifting circumstances.[72] New cases arise each day that old authors never imagined, and that must be evaluated "as the wise man will judge."[73] "The diversity of human temperament is incomprehensible," says Gerson, "not just in the multitude but in the very same person, and not just over years, months or weeks, but in days, hours, and moments."[74] Everywhere he saw variety and countless personal differences and tastes that demanded a skillful doctor of souls, who would treat moral cases on the basis of his experience.[75]

A good theologian speaks with his own voice and relies on experience—here we have two principles for entering public debates. I turn now to a third principle that would come to define Gerson's legacy in the century after his death: the need to judge each case on its merits, without recourse to general rules or principles.

Doctor Consolatorius

I suppose that the most striking feature of Gerson's treatment of moral theology is that he approached it not systematically like Aquinas in the

Secunda-secundae but as a set of cases. We might have expected something different. For while this thinking in terms of circumstances and cases had its roots in the older literature for confessors, over time it had come to define the outlook not of the theologian but of the canon lawyer, who left the field of speculation and natural law (which yielded concrete cases only with difficulty) to theologians.[76] Leonard Boyle observed that some of the questions in thirteenth-century quodlibets look more like cases in moral theology than like traditional *quaestiones*.[77] Yet these cases are barely visible to the naked eye. To this day, the dominant image of the medieval theologian is the creator of systems built on abstract reasoning.

By contrast, Gerson placed a dramatic new emphasis on cases, even identifying the case approach as necessary to the task of the professional theologian. In this way, it became a central principle of his moral theology and essential to his justification for new writings. If we focus exclusively on his harsh criticisms of canon lawyers, we may overlook the fact that in approaching theology through cases, Gerson had much in common with them. Indeed, this "case" mentality reflects a broad tendency in the theologians of the later Middle Ages toward applied, practical theology.[78] Yet we should also note the differences in Gerson's approach from the canonists. While the canonists traditionally focused on such matters as the sacraments, the dedication of churches, the clerical hierarchy, and penance, Gerson extended the case approach to such areas as revelations, visions, and astrological judgments.[79] In sum, nowhere do we find a better illustration of Gerson's move away from speculative or exegetical toward practical theology than his thinking in terms of specific cases as opposed to what he called "general rules."[80]

The significance of this last point, the inadequacy of general rules to solve moral problems, extends further still, into a sphere where Gerson's historical importance has yet to be gauged: the long history of moral reasoning extending from Aristotle to early modern casuistry.[81] Aristotle supplied the schoolmen with the key concept: *epikeia* or *aequitas* (the term in Roman law), understood as the gentle interpretation of a law.[82] In the *Summa theologiae*, Aquinas stated clearly the underlying principle: no one, including the lawgiver, has the capacity to consider all individual cases. Aquinas therefore allowed that judges who applied a strict law leniently were acting virtuously.[83] Gerson turned this tradition in a sharp new direction by emphasizing the need to relieve the pressure of prescriptive law *on the conscience.*

This principle—that general rules or canons cannot solve moral dilemmas—lies just beneath the surface of case after case that Gerson mentions. Consider four examples taken at random from a much longer list. (1) From the *Rules of the Commandments* (1400–1415), treating confession: someone sins and fears to commit mortal sin by not confessing immediately. He should not fear, "for God grants a space of penance that he knows to be sufficient for our weakness; what that may be in every case, no general rule can say."[84] (2) From *Four Questions Concerning Penance and Slander*, treating whether it is sin to celebrate Mass on broken altars, with priests' belts that have not been blessed, and with mended chasubles: in matters of positive law, you may follow local custom, "the best interpreter of such positive laws." Laws are instituted when they are promulgated, and have the force of law when they take effect in the users. Otherwise, they become a snare and a scandal. Still, "it is no easy matter to come up with a general rule on such things." Custom that has been sufficiently approved and tolerated by superiors may serve as such a rule, especially when it is unclear what pertains only to positive law.[85] (3) From Gerson's Lenten sermon on the life of the clergy (1404), treating simony: in all their actions, clergy should think first of divine honor. Therefore, they may justly desire and acquire temporalities to maintain an appropriate state. But what is "appropriate" (*decens*)? Define it as the wise man judges and resist ambition or greed. Then come all those practices that enraged opponents of simony, like saying masses in return for compensation. For Gerson, it is simply not possible to define all of these areas "under a certain rule," because of the variety of circumstances that produce such variety of law.[86] (4) From the seminal *On the Spiritual Life of the Soul* (1402 or later), treating moral cases in general: our knowledge is uncertain. Yet we turn general principles into strict rules, "especially in doubtful cases." As a result, instead of lifting people from the mire of their sins, we push them deeper into despair. In passing moral judgments, we must consider changing circumstances—and therefore no general rule can be passed down without exceptions for specific cases.[87]

No other principle in Gerson has so many tentacles spread through his works, far too many to trace here. We have just glimpsed in passing other important themes that merit further study: the role of custom in interpreting and even establishing positive law; and the importance of promulgation in the institution of laws, a principle that carries with it an implied attack on laws that are buried and hidden, presumably in legal collections and textbooks. A principle formulated out of frustration with canon law became an intellectual tool to deal with complexity in all its forms. In case after case, Gerson stresses the point that no general rule can be applied to every problem; all rules have exceptions, and what works in one case fails in another; what some do meritoriously, others do at their peril.[88] Astrology, new revelations, public vices such as prostitution and usury, all come under the same heading.[89] Here we begin to see the stakes of his opposition to canon lawyers, the kinds of issues where they might differ, and the sources of their disagreement. Gerson figures his opponents as radical reformers who apply canon law indiscriminately, without considering the consequences.

Gerson's position on the importance of circumstances above general rules represents a major breakthrough in moral theology and provides the key to understanding the nature of his contemporary reputation as a spiritual authority. To demonstrate this point, we need to consider two recurring themes in the passages described above. First, Gerson insists that absolute certainty in moral affairs—mathematical certainty—exceeds human wisdom and leads to unhealthy scrupulosity.[90] Instead, he embraces the idea of "probable and moral conjecture."[91] M. W. F. Stone has skillfully traced this theme of probability in late medieval thought and identified it as an area of great innovation that marks an important departure from the understanding of thirteenth- and fourteenth-century writers. From its purely speculative origins, fifteenth-century theologians such as Gerson, Johannes Nider, and Antoninus of Florence took the concept and applied it to "concrete moral problems."[92]

Consider one example of probability at work in Gerson, taken from *On Contracts*. The doctors say that one must be in a state of grace when celebrating Mass or performing other spiritual tasks. Where *we* see a simple distinction, late medieval men and women saw a dangling sword, threatening their souls' salvation, the source of endless anxiety. With the notion of probability, Gerson set minds at ease: "Probable conjecture suffices for this; for there can be no other certitude without revelation." The priest need not wrack his conscience before Mass. As Aristotle says of moral matters, Gerson continues, certitude must be taken "in general terms and figuratively."[93] Here, Gerson takes a speculative notion from Aristotle and applies it as an ointment to allay scruples and soothe consciences. In his *Declaration of Truths That Require Belief for Salvation*, he even uses the idea of probable truth to open the door to an entire category of marginal beliefs that nourish piety, such as legends and miracles of the saints. In the tract on Joan of Arc, he states that belief in Joan and her mission is permissible, since it falls under "probability or appearance."[94] We begin to see the many possibilities in the application of this concept.

From the use of probable truth to cure scruples, I come now to the second theme in the passages we are considering, still in the moral sphere. Gerson counseled that the opinion of one doctor is insufficient to establish mortal sin. In fact, the doctors often contradict each other. Another passage from *On Contracts* clarifies the issues wonderfully. Gerson has just dismissed the idea that it may be mortal sin to contradict one doctor who has counseled or expressed doubt about something:

On a moral topic, it is best not to assert so glibly that something is a mortal sin when some doctor says not to perform such an act, especially when many others say that it can be done well, or that it is uncertain, as in our case. It is apparent what a tangle [*labyrinthum*] of fearful consciences results if the mere opinion or advice of a doctor can produce doubt. For often, opinions among the doctors are not just different, they conflict with each other due to the passions of souls or shifting circumstances. . . . Hence the adage: "as many opinions as people."[95]

Gerson here strikes a powerful pose as the modern authority, resisting the tradition and making room for the university master, emphasizing the discord rather than the consensus among earlier authorities.

No doubt one of the strongest motives driving Gerson to this position was his frequent experience in confession with tortured souls facing the harsh penalties and threats of a severe tradition. We know that he drew on this experience to answer questions from correspondents.[96] Gilbert Ouy uncovered evidence of a quodlibetal session that Gerson held with his friend Pierre Poquet, probably at the Celestine convent in Paris, where they fielded questions that were true cases of conscience from monks concerned about celebrating the divine office and Mass, and other matters relating to life in a community.[97] Surely it was real-world experiences like these that convinced Gerson of the need for modern doctors who could mediate, interpret, and even silence the threatening language in canon law.

To deepen our understanding of Gerson as an author, we must now grasp that it was in large part this Gerson, the one emphasizing the complexity of the tradition, discouraging scruples, and easing consciences, that gained him so much popularity among fifteenth-century readers. The many copies of works in this general category reveal his reputation as a moral guide: *On Guiding the Heart*, treating intention, more than sixty manuscripts and one or two printings in the early 1470s; *On Preparation for Mass*, treating scruples over nightly emissions, more than a hundred manuscripts and at least eight printings by 1480; the *Moral Rules* or *Rules of the Commandments*, which taught later law students the notion of *epikeia*,[98] more than a hundred manuscripts and at least eight printings before 1480; and the *Treatise on the Anxiety of Clergy*, treating scruples about simony, more than seventy manuscripts and one printing around 1472.[99] Other important works, such as *On the Spiritual Life of the Soul* (more than a hundred manuscripts) included substantial discussions of this theme as well.

We do not have to travel far to find views very different from what we see in Gerson. A recent study of Bernardino of Siena (1380–1444) on the topic of moral reasoning looked for early traces of casuistry, but found instead "a world painted typically in extremes of black and white" and of "absolute moral principles drawn from Scripture and the patristic and canon law authorities." In cases of conscience, Bernardino is "a moral 'geometrician.'" That is to say, he is the complete opposite of his contemporary Gerson. Confronted with the problem of costly female fashions, Bernardino insists with customary bluntness that "we should burn at the stake the woman who dresses in this way, then her mother who allows her to do so, and then afterwards, the dressmaker who provides her with the clothes."[100] In every single case examined by the author of this study, Bernardino had recourse to "an utterly self-confident, mechanistic application of syllogistic logic and universal principles derived from his *auctoritates*" instead of a comparison of cases. Can it be a coincidence that Bernardino had studied canon law before joining the Franciscans?

After Gerson, in the crucible of early modern polemics between Catholics and Protestants, his brand of moral reasoning drew strong criticism for its apparent moral laxity and its evasive techniques, in England especially. "Casuistry destroys . . . all morality," says the great Viscount Bolingbroke, "and effaces the essential difference between right and wrong."[101] The association still appears in some twentieth-century scholarship and of course in the connotations of the word *casuistry* itself.[102] Yet one could just as easily argue that this very criticism reflects a worldview that does not admit enough doubt, especially in the moral sphere. Scholars have recently begun to recognize that a better understanding of this tradition may have important implications for modern ethical dilemmas as well.[103]

To appreciate the importance of Gerson's place in fifteenth-century moral theology, then, we might imagine a best-selling ethicist today with an international reputation on such topics as abortion, genetic research, and just war, topics that matter most in the public sphere. That, I think, is Gerson for his era. Fifteenth-century readers considered him the "Doctor consolatorius," guiding them out of moral dilemmas that imperiled their souls.[104] Geiler of Kaysersberg and many other contemporaries regarded him not as a nominalist theologian but as a spiritual authority and "a veritable father of the church."[105] Denys the Carthusian placed him not among the doctors but among the saints, in a list including (Pseudo-)Dionysius, Augustine, Ambrose, Boethius, Anselm, and Bernard.[106] Jakob Wimpheling (1450–1528) spoke for an entire generation of readers with his description of Gerson in a short biography (1506): "He busied himself in the study of things that seemed useful and necessary to praising God, to strengthening the faith, to planting the Church, to soothing consciences, to consoling the timid, to building morals, and to saving souls."[107]

In these descriptions, we also witness the idealizing tendency that slowly drained the blood from Gerson, the process that turned him from man into marble, the "most Christian Jean Gerson." For a historical understanding of this topic of authorship in its formative stages in Gerson, we must keep in mind the messy arguments with canon lawyers, now often detectable only in the manuscripts, the anger that motivated Gerson to articulate a new strategy for dealing with cases of conscience. Drawing on time-honored wisdom but also on experience, Gerson set the parameters for a new field of study, applied moral theology.

In our search for Gerson the author, so far we have uncovered a theologian racked by guilt and looking over his shoulder at the past, but still capable of producing a bold literary manifesto for masters of theology and blazing trails that would soon transform him into the moral conscience of his age. But Gerson wrote more than tracts. Especially at Lyon, he wrote with a longer view and an eye on posterity. The apology for new writings we have considered so far applies primarily to the tract. But something is missing. We have seen no rationale for longer works or especially for his ventures into poetry. The next chapter extends the problem of writing to these new arenas.

Chapter 3

A Tour of Medieval Authorship
Late Works and Poetry

In 1423, a Carthusian monk asked Gerson if it was permissible to copy books without charge on feast days. Gerson replied with his tract *In Praise of Scribes of Healthy Doctrine*. As the title suggests, he set out to defend copying. But before long he had turned to a theme just beneath the surface of this entire work, authorship itself:

> The writings [*scripta*] of old authors, the kind that our scribe chooses, are quite often more beneficial than the compositions [*dictamina*] of the young. Not that I should blame new writers [*dictatores*] who must continually arise—sometimes because of the fickle change in spiritual taste that desires this meal of the heavenly word one minute, and that meal the next, and then utterly despises everything; and at other times on account of recent doubts over the qualities of individuals, times, and other circumstances, which will never be fully revealed since they vary beyond telling.[1]

Gerson's message is simple: times and tastes change, and people want to read new things, even though they would be better off reading the old. All the forceful claims for the moral theologian in the previous chapter seem to vanish like smoke. The new works do not even deserve the name of writings (*scripta*). They are mere "compositions" (*dictamina*) written by "juveniles" (*novelli*). He had used this meek justification years earlier in the fourth Navarre letter. People are tired of reading the old fare, he says there, so maybe reading the new will do some good. Perhaps the reader will follow the trail of these works back to the ancients, as one would seek for purer sources after drinking from muddied streams.[2]

Writing as a concession—this very justification for new writings reveals its own limitations. Nonetheless, it left the door open just enough for Gerson to write, and we are left with the enormous corpus of his works. To expand our understanding of the works themselves, their great complexity and diversity, this chapter takes a different approach and tempo: a tour through medieval authorship. It is our chance to let Gerson speak on his own terms more than on mine, to let him be our guide. A survey of his entire output is both impossible and unnecessary. Instead, I have chosen one productive and particularly important period of his activity, the time of exile that reveals Gerson as a mature, established author and poet from the moment of his departure from Constance in 1418 to his death in 1429.

Why these works? Because in those few years Gerson wrote a lifetime of literature in forms and genres so diverse that we can begin to understand his complexity as an author. For a picture of medieval authorship in the field that stood at the pinnacle of medieval learning, we can find few better examples than Gerson in exile. There, writing self-consciously as an exiled old man, he wrote the works that he wanted to write, unconstrained by other pressures, and on a scale never before attempted. The author is now out of his prison, at large in the world, writing on the topics closest to his heart, sure in the knowledge that he has a ready audience. The early ideal of permanence, the prospect of lasting writings, seemed within his grasp. Ours is not a tour of the familiar. We shall see strange, foreign things: startlingly ambitious but bizarre and messy works, long on creativity but short on execution, pieced together without much skill, sometimes declining into dull and plodding lists, sometimes so exalted and complex they challenge our understanding. We shall see an author preoccupied by a theory of music that seems to unlock the secrets of the human heart but remains largely a mystery even today. We shall see an established and respected writer adapting dormant genres and inventing new ones. We shall see an author who breathes moral and spiritual life and meaning into every subject he treats. Above all, we shall see a man sensing that his career is at an end, and therefore eager to gather the remaining literary crumbs and to preserve them in strange baskets for future audiences. In the end, this is a story of missed opportunities. Gerson could have written something truly timeless—a real classic that transcended his life and times and would still speak directly to us in the way that so few medieval works really do. What we have instead are works that modern scholarship cannot quite figure out.

Before turning to the works themselves, we first need to describe Gerson's situation in exile. I described this period as a time of great productivity and new ambition. Some scholars have noticed that Gerson found renewed energy at Lyon, but they have not considered why that might be so.[3] What, then, was the source of this great literary strength?

A Career Shaped by Exile

In his letter to Ambrose, Gerson's brother Jean the Celestine eventually came to speak of Gerson's present situation and how he had arrived at Lyon.[4] Jean tells Ambrose of great losses, of "house, country, city, kindred, friends, dignities, and possessions." Gerson's enemies had laid plots for him.[5] Gerson is a second Jeremiah, weeping bitterly over the royal city of Paris, once beautiful, "the joy of all the earth."[6] Then follows a key passage: "Wherefore, rejoicing in the Lord, he has sometimes told me that he now feels within him a spark [*ingenium*] that is brighter and more lively than ever." For Jean the Celestine, this explains Gerson's great productivity. To the world-weary chancellor, exile has become a source of strength and even conquest.

The explanation for this appears to lie in the circumstances of his position at Lyon. Gerson wandered through Bavaria and reached Lyon as an exile from Paris, now under English control. More than just geographical, this exile gave shape and structure to his literary career as well. He thought of his works from this period as in some sense unified by the geography and chronology of exile. Usually, he took care to date them from Lyon, thus reinforcing the sense of exile.[7] Though he lived in the city center, attached in some way to the ancient church of Saint-Paul and later to Saint-Laurent, and within easy walking distance from the Celestine monastery (Figure 5), solitude became a feature of his identity.[8] His brother Jean, who became prior of the Celestine monastery in 1421, was no doubt an important consolation to him there, and soon came to act as his editor.

Gerson's self-appraisal as an exile and outcast of fortune was not imagined or contrived but rooted in historical events. The idea of the wayfaring Christian (*homo viator*) or pilgrim (*peregrinus*) had deep roots in Latin Christian culture, and by Gerson's day was a commonplace even in works of vernacular literature such as Dante's *Divine Comedy*.[9] Yet this conventional image held a deeper meaning for Gerson at this period, as it apparently did for John Wyclif in 1382 following his forced exile from Oxford when he wrote his massive *Trialogus*.[10] Gerson did not choose exile. Soon after his departure from Constance in mid- to late May 1418,[11] the Burgundians entered Paris (28–29 May). In June they began a massacre that lasted until August and claimed the lives of Gerson's friends Jean de Montreuil (12 June), Gontier Col, and possibly Laurent de Premierfait.[12] Charles the dauphin fled from Paris on the night of 29 May and did not see the city for nineteen years.[13] Fresh from a four-year campaign to condemn the articles on tyrannicide supported by the Burgundian duke John the Fearless, Gerson was easily the most famous and visible Armagnac (royalist) theologian in Europe. He lost material possessions in this destruction, maybe even his library. From Constance, he may have initially set out for Paris, but if so, he soon turned and fled in the opposite direction. For the next year and a half, he wandered through the Empire before arriving at Lyon in 1419.[14] His political support for the future Charles VII was strong throughout these years. In

Le Couvent des Célestins au xvi.ᵉ siècle. (Restitution de M. R. Lenail.)

Figure 5. "Le Couvent des Célestins au XVe siècle," as reconstructed by M. R. Lenail for J.-B. Martin, *Histoire des églises et chapelles de Lyon* (Lyon, 1908).

1420, Charles granted him two hundred pounds for his long service and his losses—evidence that his plight was generally known in the highest circles.[15] Despite his return to France, Gerson saw himself as an exile: he was not just French, he was Parisian.

Yet for all the historical reality of his exile, as someone who viewed himself as an author, Gerson could not have escaped patterns of literary exile that were deeply embedded in European culture.[16] He had read some of this exile literature firsthand: the *Consolation* of Boethius, of course, but also Cicero's *Tusculan Disputations*, Ovid's *Odes*, and at least some of Seneca's letters.[17] He read Petrarch, the "eternal pilgrim" (*peregrinus ubique*), more than he admitted.[18] The idea of exile also gripped him because the word *gerson* in Hebrew means "advena" or "peregrinus" in Latin: "pilgrim" or "sojourner," the very words Petrarch had chosen.[19] On 1 January 1417, more than a year before his wanderings, Gerson wrote a letter to Jean the Celestine in which he described his newly devised coat of arms and linked the idea of pilgrimage to a passage from the "heavenly pilgrim," St. Paul: "Our walk [*conversatio*] is in heaven" (Phil. 3:20).[20]

The notion of pilgrimage or wayfaring had this appeal, then, even before the great reverses came. Over the next two years, Gerson endured real physical exile. Spiritual pilgrimage became historical. He must have been on the road for the better part of two years following the council, probably never spending more than a few weeks or months in a single place before reaching Lyon sometime in late 1419. There, he enjoyed the protection of the dauphin and, probably more important, of the archbishop of Lyon, Amadeus of Talaru.[21] To the end of his life, he continued to think of his time in Lyon as exile under a protector.[22] Contemporaries acknowledged and commented on this feature of his identity, which endured into the early editions in the form of a woodcut of Gerson as pilgrim (Figure 6).[23]

Against this backdrop of exile, Gerson wrote without stop until death intervened. The works of this period are among the most poorly understood in the entire corpus—but also in some ways the most revealing of Gerson's ambitions. The following chronological overview will allow us to scale the summit and survey the landscape of fifteenth-century authorship.

The Prose Works of Exile

The works from May 1418 to July 1429 constitute nearly 75 percent of the eighth and ninth volumes in the modern edition—about one thousand out of 1,350 pages. In their structure and scale, they have few precedents. Frequently, they are unlike anything that Gerson had written

Figure 6. Woodcut of Gerson as pilgrim, from the 1488 Strasbourg edition of his works, edited by Geiler von Kaysersberg.

before. He wrote in many different forms and genres—an extraordinary range of voices that reminds us of late medieval stationers who posted specimen sheets illustrating the different scripts available, appropriate to the text: great Gothic letters for service books, elegant cursive for vernacular literature, a documentary script for deeds and charters, a compressed, abbreviated bookhand for scholarly works.[24] By the fifteenth century, the literary traditions and enterprises of the past had come swirling together to create a chaotic mixture that has yet to be fully sorted out. In a work like the *Josephina*, these traditions intersected: classical language, devotional themes, biblical scholarship, magisterial learning, even a liturgical emphasis. In Gerson, we have a stationer who knows all the scripts and sometimes mixes them to create something new, though not always consciously, and not always effectively. To broaden our understanding of Gerson as an author, we must now scrutinize some of these curious scripts.

The first we might imagine as a bold but archaic script—say, a Caroline minuscule in a world of Gothic handwriting—that Gerson used to supplement one of the most popular works of medieval literature. Upon hearing the terrible news from Paris, he responded by writing a work in direct imitation of the masterpiece of exile literature, Boethius's *Consolation of Philosophy*.[25] The parallel of his own situation, the exiled chancellor of the greatest university in Europe, to that of Boethius, who had fallen from the highest Roman office of his day to imprisonment and then execution, proved irresistible. This is not a modest work; as much as anything he wrote, *The Consolation of Theology* reveals Gerson's ambition for permanence.[26] He labored carefully on it, imitating the prosometric form and even the meters employed by Boethius and several by Horace.[27] He did not slavishly imitate his models. Whereas Boethius himself carries on with Lady Philosophy, Gerson appears only as a point of third-person reference, and Lady Theology arrives only at the end to offer consolation, mainly through a long recital of other people's misfortunes: "You're complaining that a lot of people have died in your age? That's nothing new; people die all the time," and so on.[28] He seems to have derived the idea for his two characters, Monicus and Volucer, from Petrarch's eclogues. For Petrarch, Monicus is his brother Gherardo, a Carthusian monk; for Gerson, he is his brother Jean, the Celestine monk.[29] Likewise, Volucer is Petrarch himself, and for Gerson he is a messenger who speaks with Gerson's voice.[30] Here is a pattern we shall see again, Gerson picking up ideas or strategies from things he had read, and plotting them into new forms and contexts.

Volucer and Monicus converse of timeless subjects such as the nature of theology and its superiority to philosophy, divine election and predestination, Christian hope, and the will and the intellect.[31] Eventually—

another recurring theme—they arrive at issues that were debated at Constance: the Hussites and their attacks on the dignity of prelates, the abuse of positive law through excommunication, tyrannicide, and the problems caused by overzealous reformers on issues such as simony. Gerson never let go of topical issues, even in a work that seems designed to put them out of mind. This topicality, while not conducive to long-term success, did not hinder the work's immediate popularity: it survives in about eighty manuscripts.[32]

Soon after completing the *Consolation*, Gerson produced a history in the form of a third-person autobiography, the *Dialogue Apology*.[33] He seems to have considered the work a continuation of the *Consolation*. Volucer launches at once into a discussion with Monicus, as though continuing their discussion. In the 1423 list, Jean the Celestine names it immediately after the *Consolation* and suggests that the two be joined together.[34] Repeating a pattern of literary exiles before him, Gerson defended his role at the Council of Constance.[35] It did not enjoy the popularity of the *Consolation* (Glorieux listed one manuscript), though Gerson composed it with posterity in mind.[36]

It is his *apologia pro vita sua*. Gerson is proud of his role in the condemnation of Wyclif's errors, fully aware that he had failed to condemn the articles on tyrannicide, and therefore defensive and critical of those who opposed him, above all deeply conscious of the verdict of posterity upon his role at the council. For all the council's success in removing the Schism, his failure to have the tyrannicide articles condemned seems to have left Gerson scarred. It is the motive force of the entire work. Now in exile, he felt the need both to record and to justify his actions at the greatest ecclesiastical assembly of his lifetime, an event he probably saw as the climax of his career. His desire to record his feelings at this moment is itself evidence of a sense of great passage, the end of one important phase in his career.

Gerson reached Lyon perhaps a year after completing these two works, sometime in 1419. Before we push ahead to the works he wrote there, it might be helpful for us to survey in one glimpse the scene as I imagine it. Picture, then, a medieval theologian who had once felt the stirrings of a humanist spirit in the Paris of his youth. There, in a city depopulated by plague, he had encountered not just the traditional university curriculum but new currents of thought and feeling, and new authors who fired his mind, encouraging him to think of writing as a high and noble pursuit. All his life he has longed to write for France, and he even harbors ambitions as a poet. After a successful career, he is driven, maybe even pursued, into exile. Eventually, he finds himself in Lyon with plenty of time, sorrowing over losses but energized by his straitened circumstances. His friends now clamor for new works. He happily obliges, writing one after another, summoning all the literary forms he has ever heard of or encountered. He does it to please his readers, but also because he still harbors within him the flame of desire for literary permanence. He writes poems and coyly inserts them into prose works. He strives to present his material in a new way. He writes fast-paced dialogues, he composes works on music, on beauty, and on the beautiful Virgin herself, and he plays to the crowd by quickly turning out a "treatise" on everyone's favorite, the Song of Songs. But he works too fast, and he has leftover bits and pieces. So he takes those on related themes and ties them together with longer works, letting nothing go to waste. And in the end, he writes works that fit no categories at all—not masterpieces by any measure, but odd and sometimes very long works, and collections of works that seem to belong to several genres at once, works that only he could have written. Something like that, I think, is what happened to Gerson at Lyon.

He must have begun writing again soon after his arrival in 1419. We might see in an early work there our next script, Gerson the biblical scholar, an occupation that links him both to the early fathers and to later humanists. The *Monotessaron* (completed in 1420) is a Gospel harmony, a unique Christian genre in which the four biblical accounts of the life of Christ are rewritten as one continuous narrative.[37] In an introductory letter possibly to Jean the Celestine (unaccountably left out of the modern edition), Gerson describes his work as the fruition of an idea that took hold in the early Church with Ammonius of Alexandria (third century).[38] Augustine left us *On the Agreement of the Evangelists* (*De consensu Evangelistarum*), but it is incomplete, stopping with the preaching of John the Baptist. Gerson offers the complement, which he thinks can be preserved "free of corruption" now that Jerome's (Vulgate) translation of the Gospels is widespread.[39]

Considered within the long history of Gospel harmonies, the *Monotessaron* took a step backward in some respects. A problem unique to the genre was that the synoptic Gospels contain duplications. Rather than remove these, Gerson simply repeated them, perhaps fearing to tamper with the text. The resulting narrative thus contains redundancies that other harmonies, such as the great sixth-century *Codex Fuldensis*, had avoided.[40]

But from Gerson's perspective, the work was a scholarly tool in the best sense and might stand as one of the enduring works of the present age. The classic introduction to the Bible in the medieval schools was Peter Comestor's *Historia scholastica*, which departed freely from the biblical text. By contrast, the *Monotessaron* allowed a student to read the events of the life of Christ in the order in which they had actually occurred and in words as close as possible to Jerome's original Vulgate. But more important for Gerson, this text was no commentary. In the first of two prologues, composed perhaps by Jean the Celestine, the author recalls that "a professor of theology" tried to show a new theology student how to begin his studies. But when the professor came to scripture, he found a text burdened by endless commentary: ordinary, interlinear, and marginal glosses, homilies, postils, determinations, compilations, and concordances. "Who can number them?" he asks. Better to let the student study the text on his own.[41] In the text itself, Gerson used abbreviations to signal the source of each passage (he may have recalled the device from other, more recent harmonies).[42] He thus saw himself composing a work that created order from disorder, the confused accounts of the four Gospels, and that directed the reader back to the Gospels themselves.

These concerns reflect Gerson's interest in the sources of a safe and true theology, as we saw in Chapter 1. But we are also seeing the same impulses that would motivate the biblical humanists in their return to scripture and that led Erasmus himself to establish a new Greek text of the New Testament. Gerson did not know Greek, and he displayed no interest in serious textual criticism. Yet Gerson and Erasmus both wanted to guide students past the layers of commentary to the most important original source of Christian doctrine and so to provide a solid foundation for modern theology.[43] In this sphere, at least, Gerson appears very much like the northern humanists.

On the other hand, the architecture of the work does not feel humanist at all. C. S. Lewis referred in passing to its "rather clumsy plan."[44] Gerson organizes it under 151 rubrics divided into three major sections: on the origin of Christ and his entrance (1–11); on the preaching of John and the increase of the preaching of Christ (12–137); and on the outcome of the Passion and Resurrection of Christ (138–51). Marc Vial has suggested that through this scheme of *ingressus* ("entrance"), *progressus* ("advance" or "increase"), and *egressus* ("departure" or "outcome"), Gerson has adapted the Neoplatonic scheme of *exitus/reditus*, a grand cosmic circuit in which the Divine Being is refracted into all things, and all things return to their source. M.-D. Chenu thought—and most scholars have agreed—that Thomas Aquinas structured his *Summa theologiae* along these lines. Almost certainly aware of this, Gerson applied the scheme in an original way to the historical life of Christ. To fit his theme, he reversed the order from departure/arrival to Christ's advent and departure, which frame the *progressus* of Christ through the Gospels.[45] Through these rubrics, Gerson imposed on the Gospels some degree of thematic unity.[46] (In Chapter 6, we shall see how Gerson designed these rubrics with readers in mind, as a device to organize and to contemplate the life of Christ through memorization.)

Though the *Monotessaron* looks ahead in some ways, Gerson seems to have thought of the work in the tradition of the great handbooks of scholastic theology. The author of the first preface links the *Monotessaron* to three great scholastic works that summarized an entire field: Bonaventure's *Breviloquium*, which encompasses all theology; Peter Auriol's *Compendium* on scripture, which reduces the entire Bible to "a few conclusions"; and the *Secunda-secundae* of Aquinas, which embraces all of practical theology.[47] In Gerson's own prologue, he suggests that the work may shed light on the glosses of the doctors, especially Augustine's *On the Agreement of the Evangelists*. He even provides his own marginal glosses—the angel who comforted Christ at Gethsemane was "probably" Gabriel, one of them says[48]—but he warns scribes not to mix them with the text.[49] In some ways this Gospel harmony, now neglected and barely known to modern scholarship (the most recent biography does not mention it), might stand as a symbol of Gerson's own complexity, a Janus-faced production looking backward and forward in one gesture.

The work had some success. About twenty-five manuscripts survive, including a translation into Middle Low German, and it soon became the focus of at least two commentaries.[50] Of course, great changes were coming to biblical scholarship, and the *Monotessaron* eventually faded into obscurity. But not as soon as we might think, and the final chapter in its history is perhaps the most interesting. In 1534 Thomas More—perhaps awaiting execution in the Tower of London—wrote his *Treatise upon the Passion* in the form of a commentary on the *Monotessaron*.[51] Such an unexpected meeting of the English humanist and the Parisian theologian explodes our neat categories, and reinforces the work's fundamental compatibility with the humanist enterprise.

Throughout his years at Lyon, Gerson thought more and more about his literary legacy and how to keep it intact. The clearest evidence for this appears in his attempts to compile his works and to transmit them to posterity in collections. It seems he began to ponder the need for compilation just after leaving the Council of Constance. In the *Dialogue Apology*, Volucer tells Monicus that he will provide him with a list of some of Gerson's works, "for it will be fitting for you or someone else who would enjoy the task to put them into a single compilation [*collectorium*] or into a large gathering."[52] Thus Gerson had already begun to imagine the *collectorium* as a genre for compilation, a device that would go one step beyond merely binding a group of works into the same volume (he was doing that too). At Lyon, he began the assembly process, collecting his works on music into the *Treatises on Songs*, gathering various frag-

ments into the *Compilation on the Magnificat*, bringing the seven centiloquies into the *Compilation of Seven Baskets*, and perhaps compiling a series
of poems into the *Songs on the Magnificat*.[53]

They are, taken together, among the strangest, most difficult works in
the entire corpus—and hence the most ignored. By 1423 at the latest,
Gerson had begun to write about music in a series of works that would
come to be known as the *Treatises on Songs*, a kind of sprawling theological motet.[54] By 1426, he thought of gathering them into one volume.
Gerson himself or possibly Jean the Celestine then assembled them into
the form in which they now survive, in just a few copies that can be
closely linked to the original exemplars.[55]

The construction of the work reveals much about the construction of
authorship itself in this period. The collection contains three books.
Gerson had completed what would become book 2 by May 1423, *On the
Song of the Heart*. He finished *On the Original Reason for Songs*, or book 1,
sometime between May 1423 and April 1426.[56] He divided the third
book into three parts. First, he included a collection of poems or elegies,
personified as "she who sings of the lovers of Lady Theology."[57] Gerson
had already circulated the poems, and he reinserted them here because
of their thematic similarity—and, no doubt, to make them more available to readers. Isabelle Fabre, author of a careful recent study of these
works, reads them as "a kind of fermata offering a meditative pause" or
"aesthetic interlude" following the exposition of the first two books—a
pedal point on the organ, one might say, while the reader absorbs the
lessons of the first two books.[58] To complete the collection, Gerson composed the second and third parts, in fact two lists that together constitute a centiloquy "on songs and on comfort."[59] In company with the
main body of treatises, the manuscripts include still other works and diagrams relating to music that Gerson wished to make available to his
readers—we would call them appendices.[60] At least some of these works
circulated independently before their assembly in the *Treatises on Songs*.

The central theme is the significance of music and its relation to the
music of the soul. The plot moves forward under the impulse of a distinction between sung music and the music of the heart or canticord,
the "audible voice" and the "interior voice."[61] Whereas sung music is
accessible to all, the canticord is secret and accessible directly to God
alone. While sung music can produce polyphony, the music of the heart
cannot. Whereas sung music is subject to the flesh and to sin, the music
of the heart is subject to the spirit of God. And so on. The tradition
looms large in Gerson's understanding of music as a divine art that
offers the soul an ascent to God, an art both encompassing and yet far
excelling the "practical" and earthly music that forms part of one's
everyday experience. Boethius gave the idea its classic formulation in *De*

musica and set the tone for all later theorists.[62] Gerson had more proximate sources as well, traced by Fabre, particularly Augustine.[63] New questions must now be asked, such as whether by his canticord Gerson intended to offer a new model of mystical theology.[64]

We must leave the work there, a faint sketch rather than a detailed map. For our purposes, it reveals the pains Gerson took to establish the category of authorship. Driven by a strong creative impulse, he chose a traditional subject and one close to his heart, which he linked to another subject weighing on people's minds, the mystical ascent. He gave some thought to organization and presentation, but not as much as he should have—another common feature of the late works. Then he did what he could to gather these scattered writings: he added a series of poems that had some bearing on the subject, and he packaged them all as a single collection. It is indeed a collection of works that hang together rather than cohere. The title is *Treatises on Songs*: several treatises, not one.[65]

The strong creative impulse evident here appears in a more shocking form in the diagrams (c. 1423–1424) that Gerson wished to be included with the *Treatises on Songs*. One is a chessboard "at once musical and military," according to the title, "like a chorus of encamped soldiers: for human life on earth is warfare, which music consoles and cheers" (Figure 7).[66] Moralizing the game of chess was not new. Gerson almost certainly knew the *Book of Chess* (*Liber super ludo scacorum*, c. 1300) of Jacques de Cessoles, a popular allegory that was translated into French three times.[67] But Gerson was doing something quite different from Jacques, whose work was a social allegory.[68] By contrast, Gerson's was spiritual—and much more complex. The theme relates to the other diagrams (which originally circulated separately, it seems, though now they appear together in the manuscripts), and the challenge to understanding all of these works is to recognize and to sort through the thick layers of meaning. The chessboard, on the recto side, has an accompanying canon on the verso (in two of three manuscripts) which explains that the game of chess is a figure of spiritual warfare, and that a musical "chekker" (*scaccarium musicale*)—possibly an early clavichord—has been superimposed on this.[69] That is, the figure represents both a chessboard and a musical instrument, and these in turn figure the spiritual warfare within each Christian between the old and the new man. Visually, the instrument appears only in the keys extending from the bottom of the chessboard. When we play the keys of the chekker with the fingers of our meditation, the voices of the affections resonate in harmony. The chessboard carries this spiritual analogy further. The pieces of the spirit, "playing in glory," battle the pieces of the flesh, "raging in malice." Gerson enlarges the analogy to embrace the temporal sphere, each side

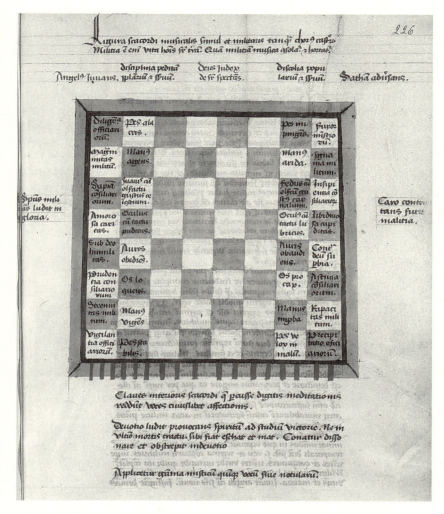

Figure 7. "Figura scacordi musicalis simul et militaris tamquam chorus castrorum" (Figure of a Chessboard at Once Musical and Military, Like a Chorus of Encamped Soldiers). Paris, Bibliothèque nationale de France, Ms. lat. 17487, f. 226r. Used by permission.

representing a kingdom of virtues and vices—a morality play staged on a chessboard. Two opposing knights are called Martial Vigor and Rapacity, for example. The changing colors of the squares signify the reversals of fortune in our present warfare, prosperity and adversity. Angels and saints aid the new man, demons the old, while God watches the contest from on high. The new man will achieve victory if he persists, unless the old man checkmates him at the point of death.

Where to begin? Perhaps with the obvious question: Did anyone really understand this theory? And who read or used the work? We have some evidence for another of the diagrams, the "Ten-Stringed Psalter." One of its intended readers was Charles VII himself, about twenty-one at the time Gerson composed these works. The diagram draws a visual analogy between the Ten Commandments and the ten-stringed psalter or harp of Psalm 143 (144), verse 9—"I will sing a new song to you, O God, on the ten-stringed psalter will I sing praises to you." In his letter of introduction to Jean Cadart, the royal physician, Gerson speaks of the importance of music and its close links to medicine, and the opportunity such a work presented for the king's spiritual improvement, particularly if Cadart were to "adorn" it with skillful words and to accompany it with music.[70] The work begins to sound like a script for performance. Gerson apparently conceived it as a novel courtly entertainment that would instruct the king in that most basic component of Christian belief, the Ten Commandments. We might then imagine a similar noble audience for his moralization of chess, that classic courtly recreation.

In the diagrams especially, Gerson is the pedagogue, searching for new ways to teach essential principles through oral instruction and recognizing the importance of diagrams in education.[71] Diagrams, obscure musical instruments, chessboard and chessmen, virtues and vices, and Gerson's esoteric teaching on the canticord—all came together to form these puzzling works.

So far we have seen Gerson the rival of the fathers in the *Consolation of Theology*, the biblical scholar in the *Monotessaron*, the guide to the mysterious inner workings of the spirit in the *Treatises on Songs*, and the pedagogue in the diagrams. In the centiloquies we see him working at another script, Gerson the university master. At first glance, this script looks much like the script of earlier schoolmen, a highly abbreviated Gothic bookhand used for questions and commentaries. But as we get closer, something seems out of joint.

Gerson wrote the centiloquies (*centilogia*) from 1424 to 1428, around the same time that he was pulling together the *Treatises on Songs*. They cover seven topics: the final cause, which followed the material, formal, and efficient causes in scholastic discussions of causality; the eye, significant because ultimately linked to vision of God; the modes of signifying, or the ways in which language signifies meaning to the mind; concepts, signifying both the abstract "concept" and "conception" or birth; impulses (see below); songs (the last part of the *Treatises on Songs*);

and the doxology, "Glory be to the Father, with the Son and Holy Spirit."[72]

Most of these topics had received some kind of formal treatment in the schools. Vision and the eye, for example, formed a focal point in scholastic questions that distinguished appearance and existence.[73] The genre, though, a list of one hundred statements, takes us some distance from the classroom. Gerson may have taken the idea from the *Centiloquy* of Pseudo-Ptolemy, a collection of one hundred astrological aphorisms that had gained general currency at this period. The work appears in contemporary medieval library catalogues, and Pierre d'Ailly knew and cited it.[74]

.   Around 1428, Gerson decided to gather the centiloquies into a single collection that he sent to the Grande Chartreuse.[75] We see again the ongoing concern to gather the fragments of his works and so to establish his legacy as an author. Reaching for a metaphor, and none too modestly, he compared these works to the fragments left over from Christ's feeding of the multitudes (Mt. 15:37): the "Compilation of seven baskets."[76] This gathering was certainly an afterthought. The works are not thematically related. None has a substantial prologue that explains why Gerson wrote it. Some fall well short of the ideal one hundred statements. He originally called the centiloquy on the eye, written sometime in May 1424, a treatise (its designation in the manuscripts), and it consists of only forty propositions.[77] As I reconstruct the evidence, when the idea for the *Compilation* came to him, to reach one hundred statements he added two other works written in the weeks and months after the treatise on the eye: *On the Agreement of Mystical and Scholastic Theology*, with twelve propositions; and his letter-treatise to Gérard Machet, *On the One Pearl of Great Price*, with forty.[78] But this gave him only ninety-two, lacking eight, which he thought could somehow be supplied from the *Anagogy on the Word and Hymn "Gloria"* (the doxology), another work he later recast as a centiloquy—it has four parts, each with ten "words or considerations," and each consideration with a variable number of propositions, totaling 195.[79] This clumsy collection reflects a familiar pattern of composition at Lyon. It is Gerson sitting at a desk full of papers and sweeping them with one fluid motion into a large, bulky container so that nothing goes to waste.[80]

Each centiloquy follows a peculiar development. The *Centiloquy on Impulses*, for example, takes its cue from the passage in the Magnificat, "He has put down the mighty from their throne and raised up those of low degree" (Lk. 1:52).[81] The text moves forward to explore those impulses "whereby the mighty are put down and the lowly exalted." The discussion fills ten "decades" of ten statements. Each statement of a decade begins with the same word: "impulse" for the first decade, "creature" for the second, "cognition" for the third, and so on. The first decade defines the term *impulse* by listing its various applications: we move from local motions perceived by the senses (statement 1), to violent motions (2), ahead to sudden changes, such as creation (6), and last to the use of impulses by any created being (10). The second decade takes up the thread from the first with created beings and their reception of impulses from God. In the remaining decades Gerson proceeds to human knowledge of moral impulses (3), to the varieties of divine impulses (4), to violent impulses of the demon, using the example of Job (5), to deceitful impulses, which are even more dangerous than violent impulses because hidden (6), to the cunning instigator (*impulsor*) Satan (7), to wicked impulses and their forms, such as blasphemy and violence against women (8), to Satan's transformation into an angel of light and his operations against Christians (9), and at last to the different ways in which the lowly are raised up (10). Gerson ranges widely but never loses sight of the scriptural passage, which he cites throughout the text, and which appears clearly again in the final decade.

These are difficult works for a modern reader. The topics, while familiar to medieval scholars, require great efforts at recovery if we are to imagine once again their significance. They are all the more strange to us because Gerson has abandoned the traditional scholarly genres. Discussions of the modes of signifying usually appeared in treatises, such as that of Thomas of Erfurt, or in questions or even in commentaries.[82] Instead, Gerson gives us a centiloquy—a list.

Something about writing in lists fit Gerson's temperament and style of composition, especially during this period in his life. Like the "consideration," to be discussed in more detail in the next chapter, the list on a single topic allowed him a freedom of development that the syllogism did not. But perhaps even more important—and again, more strange for us—he seems to have liked such lists, especially those that share a common first word, because they were easily memorized. Again, they are teaching texts, guides for the beginner through standard scholarly topics.

From Gerson the university master, we turn to Gerson the dramatist in the *Compilation on the Magnificat*, and to a more flowing, cursive literary script. This long, rambling collection of twelve treatises, each developing a phrase or verse from the passage in Luke 1, verses 46–55, in a dialogue between Master and Disciple (corresponding at some level to Gerson and Jean the Celestine), is today among the least read of Gerson's works. In its breadth of topics as well as in its use of dialogue, it resembles the huge *Trialogus* that Wyclif produced at the end of his life.[83] By my estimate, the work contains about 106,000 words—three-quarters the size of the book you are holding. At 371 pages in the modern edition, it is nearly three times longer than the next longest work, the *Monotessaron* (128 pages).[84]

In a short prologue, Gerson explains his decision to use the dialogue: "I have decided to proceed by dialogue in an instructive fashion [*more didascalico*], the path that Socrates took, and Plato, who introduces Socrates. Our method might be called dramatic, which is (the method) ascribed to the Song of Songs, and is suitable for love songs or poems."[85] Gerson here links the dialogue to a revered tradition, including both sacred and profane authors. He considers it fit for a work in praise of a virgin like Mary. Yet by one calculation, the dialogue between Master and Disciple occupies only 58 percent of the work.[86] The rest is a mishmash of material, some of it already in existence before the composition itself, which occurred between 20 April 1427 and 4 April 1428.[87] He develops much of this material in lists like the centiloquies.

The work is like a medieval wall that incorporates fragments of ruins nearby. Often, the narrative shifts between dialogue and monologue or soliloquy. In the middle of the third treatise, the discussion turns to the beauty (*pulchritudo*) of Mary, and the Master introduces a list of propositions, each beginning with the word *pulchritudo*. The next few pages extend the discussion from natural to intellectual beauty in similar form.[88] The fifth treatise opens in dialogue, which comes to a halt for twelve considerations on the soul of Mary (three pages). The dialogue resumes for a few more pages, until we reach a "part 2" of the treatise (there was no designation of a "part 1"), which is in fact a complete, originally independent treatise on the holy name of God, suggested by the passage in Luke: "And holy is his name." In the seventh treatise, Gerson refers to this treatise on the holy name of God as a separate, independent work.[89] The seventh treatise was itself originally independent, and it contains no dialogue. In the fourth paragraph, Gerson labels the work an *opusculum*, which he entitles *On the Mind of the Heart or On the Dining Room of the Heart*.[90] Dialogue occupies most of the sixth treatise, but toward the end Gerson adds eighteen considerations on the mercy of God (three pages), followed by a short, apparently unfinished section "treating the manner of moral or tropological exposition" of the book of Lamentations.[91] The works that he composed fresh as part of the *Compilation* stay closest to the text of Luke. I take this to be the case with treatises 1–5 (except for treatise 5, part 2), most of treatises 6 and 8, the first part alone of treatise 9 (which has five parts), about half of treatise 10, most of 11, and all of 12.[92]

The substance of the work reveals Gerson's preoccupations during his last years in Lyon. He gravitates toward moral topics, most with a practical application. He traverses the nature of mystical music and the division of soul and spirit (treatise 1), Mary's spiritual exultation and the relation of her song to the Song of Songs (2), the beauty of Mary and therefore the nature of beauty and its relation to the eye (3), the nature of Mary's blessedness and of blessedness itself (4), the movement of her passions and their relation to the soul (5, part 1), the holy name of God (5, part 2), the relation of exultation to mourning and the mercy of God (6), the heart (7), guardian angels and demons (8), the Eucharist (9), the reception of Christ into the soul as distinguished from reception of the Host (10), and the solitary life (11). The twelfth treatise restates the whole. The topics frequently echo the themes of the centiloquies. The first prologue (perhaps by Jean the Celestine) mentions them all, and the text itself refers to four of the seven.[93] Important minor themes also appear, most of them familiar from other texts: the superiority of theology to philosophy, the nature and practice of music, the legitimacy of studying pagan authors, the balance between devotion and learning, the potential and limits of lay spirituality, the pride of the schoolmen and their lack of piety, preachers who attack the clergy for their vices, the link between heresy and Bible-reading, the dangers of misguided speculation, and many more.[94]

Gerson had little concern for structural integrity and symmetry. Instead, as with the *Compilation of Seven Baskets*, he wished only to assemble and to preserve materials in one place, sometimes at the expense of thematic unity. This desire is well expressed in the Latin title *collectorium*, which communicates the original independence of these treatises, here and in the *Compilation of Seven Baskets*. Gerson also used the piece as a guide to his other works. The Master frequently sends the Disciple off to read something of his. The *Compilation on the Magnificat* contains at least twenty-seven references to sixteen different works, plus one instance in the first treatise where Gerson inserts a complete work into the text, his *Twelve Considerations for the Most Summary Understanding of the Song of the Heart* (1424).[95] And this does not count the insertion of the two apparently unpublished treatises *On the Holy Name of God* and *On the Mind of the Heart*.

The work has never received much critical attention or analysis.[96] One might blame its cumbersome and chaotic structure and the lack of precedents—or successors!—in such a genre; the content itself, which appears highly traditional; and perhaps more than anything else, its wallowing length that threatens to swallow the helpless reader. By touching on nearly every important theme in the corpus of his writings, Gerson places a heavy burden on the reader and student of the work. Yet his choice to use dialogue and even his description of the work as a love song suggest a desire to woo readers. He calls his method "dramatic" (*dramaticus*). The dialogue between the Master and the Disciple is in fact a drama, the action of live discourse which animates the text and which readers surely welcomed, just as most readers of novels prefer lively dialogue to long description. In fact, I suppose that if a medieval schoolman had somehow stumbled upon the novel form centuries too soon, the result would look something like the *Compilation on the Magnificat.*

We should not dismiss the content either as entirely traditional. Gerson uses the Magnificat to explore the entire process of how the mind and the heart approach God, and he does so with all the tools of learning at his command, drawing upon the lines of inquiry set forth in many earlier works. The kind of meditation on the Eucharist that he offers in the ninth treatise had long been a feature of Franciscan spirituality, and by the fifteenth century was quite mainstream. In a striking way, he stretched the bounds of this tradition by having the Virgin Mary, the "Mother of the Eucharist" as Gerson calls her, linger in contemplation over her Son who will be eaten by endless generations of future Christians.[97] In the twelfth treatise, Mary recapitulates the previous eleven treatises in a long monologue, and she even prophesies a time when devotion will move some to write the history of the Holy Family—"many things in prose, some things in heroic verse"—and so the *Josephina* will appear.[98] This link to the *Josephina* is more than incidental. To a great extent, the *Compilation on the Magnificat* allowed Gerson to complement his epic poem through a dramatic expansion of the contemplation of Mary, which necessarily had received only summary treatment there. It well illustrates the blend of learning and piety that characterizes Gerson's approach. Despite its apparent drawbacks, medieval readers seem to have enjoyed it. It survives in at least thirty-four manuscripts and was printed twice in the 1470s.[99]

Gerson's last work, the *Treatise on the Song of Songs*, brings us to yet another script, Gerson the biblical commentator. But that designation is somewhat misleading, for this script closely resembles the previous one—the *Treatise* is a work much in the style of the *Compilation on the Magnificat.* Gerson wrote it at the request of the Carthusians and spent nearly two months on the work before leaving it incomplete on 9 July 1429, three days before his death.[100] At the opening, he announces three parts, though he completed only two. The first, a list of twenty considerations on the essence (*quidditas*) of *amor* and its four species, serves as an introduction.[101] The second part begins the commentary proper. In the prologue to this section, Gerson observes that according to Dionysius we can only experience the divine ray in veiled form, through archetypes and symbols. This is why the Song of Songs uses the figure of a marriage. For this reason, Gerson will treat the anagogical or mystical sense in fifty considerations, corresponding to the fifty days of Pentecost.[102] He calls his method rhetorical rather than "scholastic," which is better suited to treat the letter, though he has tried to incorporate some of each method.[103] Offering a mnemonic aid to the reader, he begins with a decade of elegiac verses that summarize the work, and he provides a gloss linking these verses to the text of the Song of Songs.[104] Finally, he organizes the fifty considerations along a pattern of ten strings (as in several of the diagram works), to accord with David's ten-stringed psalter and with the ten verses of Mary's Magnificat.[105]

Gerson felt the weight of traditional commentary even as he wrote. Echoing the first prologue to the *Monotessaron*, he refers to "homilies, sermons, postils, distinctions, and ordinary glosses, alternating through the four senses."[106] Indeed, he could not have chosen a book more laden with commentary. He responded by writing a new kind of commentary, in his own rhetorical style with some mix of scholastic, introduced by another of his poems, and superimposed on one of his favorite devices, the ten-stringed psalter. Far from deterring him, the tradition spurred him on to attempt something bolder than the feats of his predecessors.

We have surveyed a number of prose works that Gerson must have considered an important part of his legacy. They testify to a deep desire to write in creative new ways and to establish his name as an author. They are his most ambitious works—but some are also among the least read, now and then. Given his ambitions, his failure to produce a polished final product is puzzling. The original ideal of permanence also depended on eloquence. Perhaps his blanket justification for authorship—writing as a concession to modern tastes—hindered him at some level. One of his last poems is entitled "Against the Desire to Make Many Books."[107] Deep in the entrails of the *Compilation on the Magnificat*, he defends himself against potential critics who will say that he is just rehashing old ideas in new words and figures. But saying something in a new way makes it less tedious, he replies. And besides, no one is forcing anyone to read the work.[108] Authorship remained a touchy subject. And when he came to a work with layers of commentary like the Song of Songs, the guilt came rushing back. Authorship was a maelstrom of ambition, anxiety, and doubt. But we still have one important script to consider: Gerson the poet. And in the poetry of exile, he justified himself with a clarity that any humanist would have appreciated.

Poetry: Authorship Without Guilt

Gerson had always enjoyed writing verse. But it was late at Constance and at Lyon, at the same time as he penned the works we have been surveying, that he wrote most of his surviving poetry. The modern edition contains about one hundred poems, ranging from simple couplets to a nearly three-thousand-line epic on the Holy Family, the *Josephina*.

What we might take for an eccentricity Gerson took quite seriously. His every comment about poetry stresses its utility or value in some way. The very first passage I quoted in this book, from one of his earliest works, mentions poets favorably. France had lacked great historians *and poets*. Earlier, I mentioned his eclogue written in imitation of Petrarch. Never forgotten and carefully preserved, the poem reappeared twenty years later in a sermon.[109] At the Council of Constance, Gerson composed the *Josephina*, among the most ambitious works of his career. Many poems never took independent form, but found their way into prose works such as the *Treatises on Songs*—a clue to their centrality in his literary production and further evidence that he preserved these works over a long period. The range of meters and forms that he used betrays the care he took with them. His long fascination with Boethius's *Consolation of Philosophy*, which he imitated in the sermon for his master's license in 1393, had much to do with the work's prosometric form.[110] His own *Consolation of Theology* is in this sense not just a theological meditation but an ambitious literary stroke, composed in his maturity, at the time he was correcting the *Josephina*.[111] We cannot talk about Gerson as a writer and man of letters, then, without some discussion of his poetry and some understanding of how he justified poetic production.

According to one model, Gerson the schoolman should never have written any poetry at all. Ernst Robert Curtius can stand for the older view: "Scholasticism," he stated flatly, "is not interested in evaluating poetry. It produced no poetics and no theory of art."[112] Relying on the writings of Albert the Great and Thomas Aquinas, Alastair Minnis has demolished this view. Yet the attitudes of thirteenth-century schoolmen still seem a world apart from Gerson. Here too, then, we must mark out new boundaries and claim a new historical space for Gerson, a schoolman who embraced poetry.

He inherited a complex set of attitudes.[113] Earlier doctors were not encouraging. Confronted by "ancient charges brought against poetry, namely, that it inflames the passions of men, that poets are liars and that poetic writings are full of falsehoods," twelfth-century theologians rescued poetry in scripture by distinguishing it from secular poetry. They stressed that biblical authors expressed themselves differently, sometimes speaking in metaphors.[114] Albert the Great and Aquinas carried on the distinction between sacred and secular poetry, but this hardly amounted to a strong endorsement of poetic production. Because of its "defect of truth," Aquinas classed poetry among studies that cannot be grasped by reason.[115] For Albert, the poetic mode was "the weakest among the modes of philosophy."[116] Poetry may have been defensible, but Aquinas and Albert hardly treasured it. By the early fourteenth century, though, the distinction between sacred and secular poetry seemed less important. Attitudes slowly changed, perhaps influenced (as Minnis suggests) by Arab interpretations of Aristotle's *Poetics*, a work unknown to thirteenth-century writers. This more welcoming attitude appears in authors such as Ulrich of Strasbourg, a student of Albert's, and Peter Auriol in his *Compendium of the Entire Bible*. Petrarch and Boccaccio considered all poets as of a kind, and saw no opposition between theology and poetry.[117]

So Gerson was entering a much larger conversation that had been going on since at least the twelfth century, and that had its roots in the attitudes of the Church fathers toward poetry, Jerome especially, as well as the attitudes of the ancient philosophers. By the late fourteenth century, French and Italian humanists had taken up the challenge, and in these circles the defense of poetry became wedded to a more general defense of classical literature. The controversy over the value of reading and imitating poetry erupted in Italy after 1370 following the publication and spread of Boccaccio's *Genealogy of the Gentile Gods*, a kind of "mythological summa."[118] The most famous exchange occurred in 1405. In that year, the Dominican friar Giovanni Dominici wrote a long book called *The Firefly* (*Lucula noctis*) that attacked secular literature, which he then sent to Coluccio Salutati, the famous humanist and chancellor of Florence. Dominici presented Salutati's arguments in favor of the classics (which he had gathered from a recent letter) and then attempted to refute them, hoping to sway Salutati. The Christian, he stressed, "should devote himself only to those things which lead to blessedness." Poets are even less trustworthy than the ancient philosophers. And it is a rare student who can read poetry without harm.[119] In response, after correcting Dominici's grammar, Salutati insisted that poetry "praises virtue and attacks vice" and therefore may benefit Christians. It is "the greatest of all arts and sciences," "the summation of all," superior even to philosophy.[120]

Paris had no *Firefly*, but poetry was debated there too. In his epistles, Jean de Montreuil complained of jurists and members of the royal chancery who despised poetry.[121] Gerson belonged in the vanguard of the new opinion. In a sermon from 1392, he energetically defended secular learning and poetry against unspecified opponents. Some wish to argue, he says in the sermon, that the books of the infidels should be cast aside. But if so, then Jerome, Augustine, Bernard, St. Paul, Cyprian, and Origen have all erred—not only they, in fact, but all philosophers, legal authorities, and medical doctors. All truth comes from the Holy Ghost, and to say that we should not study the rhetoricians, philosophers, and poets or cite them in sermons is false and damages the reputation of the saints, who frequently consulted secular learning when they wrote holy books. Paul, Augustine, Jerome, and others, the greatest of their kind, mixed poetry, rhetoric, and philosophy with theology, and do so still. He only cautions that these studies must serve as theology's handmaids.[122]

The 1392 sermon shows that early in his career, Gerson knew the terms of the humanist debate over poetry. The phrase "all truth comes from the Holy Ghost, no matter the speaker" was well known, appearing in the first book of Lombard's *Sentences.* But it was a humanist tactic to use it to justify poetry. Salutati had used it to this effect.[123] Montreuil echoes it in his epistles: "The Church embraces all knowledge and all arts." Likewise, Montreuil and Gerson both maintained that the Church fathers had free recourse to pagan learning.[124] Naturally, Gerson knew that poetry had found favor with Christian poets, not just pagans and the authors of scripture: Boethius in the *Consolation* of course, but also Alain de Lille in the *Plaint of Nature*, and other authors.[125]

Gerson frequently defended poetic production in his own verse. G. Matteo Roccati has assembled various passages under this heading, which can be reduced to three themes.[126] First, Gerson finds support for poetry in earlier authors, including biblical authors. A key text here is the poem "In Praise of Spiritual Elegy" (c. 1422–1425) which Gerson probably planned to include in his *Treatises on Songs.*[127] The poem is a kind of dialogue in which Old Age (Senium), speaking for Gerson, defends poetry against an opponent who introduces all the old arguments against it. Old Age points to the Old Testament examples of Jeremiah, Job, David, and Moses, who composed verses of all kinds, and of King Solomon, who wrote five thousand poems. Another poem from the same period, "On the Praise of Music," enlists the support of authorities such as Augustine, who was moved to tears at his baptism by the voices of the church; Cecilia and her organ; and St. Paul, who speaks of "singing with our whole hearts" (Eph. 5:19).[128] We begin to see the important link for Gerson between poetry and music.

Others before Gerson had cited the precedent of biblical authors. Roccati traces the strategy to Isidore, and it is at least implied in the very distinction observed by the schoolmen between sacred and profane poetry.[129] The second theme represents more of a departure from earlier schoolmen. Again in the poem "In Praise of Spiritual Elegy," Gerson emphasizes the advantages that meter itself provides. Like the consideration, it aids organization. It "disciplines the mind" and "lingers in the memory." With serious study, "verses become more meaningful, clearer; their order gives them power."[130] Gerson saw in verse the potential both to harness and to chasten language, to subordinate expression to meaning. A link appears here, more than merely a semantic echo, between chastened language and chastity itself. Proper poetry, indeed, is sexually chaste. For Gerson, secular verse (surely he was think-ing of Ovid) revels in immorality. Poetry should express a "pious love of wisdom," not "filthy desire" (*libido sordida*). Personified, she is a "grave matron," not a "whore, destitute of virtue."[131] Besides its mnemonic value, meter attracted Gerson—a cleric in major orders—as a kind of discipline that reinforced the bonds of chastity.

The third theme takes us to his most ambitious claims for poetry, which he offers in the first lines of the prologue (*exordium*) to the *Joseph-ina*. There, Gerson celebrates the superiority of Christian over pagan inspiration: "Old poets honored the spring sacred to the muses of Par-nassus. . . . But our wisdom has another mountain, a spring and muses with a different voice. The Fountain of Life, the Word of the Lord went forth from highest heavens, flowing down a pure and life-giving course, like unto crystal, pouring from the celestial throne to eternal mountains. It cares not for rustic muses that cry out a mortal strain, that compose harmful songs, that allure only the ears of the body with emptiness."[132]

Gerson develops this theme through thirty-seven lines. The ability of Christians to grasp literal and figurative meanings functions like an exponent in algebra, multiplying hidden truths. Our Fountain reveals much more than does the pagan spring. We see many things through a glass darkly, he says, echoing St. Paul (1 Cor. 13:11). Like mirrors, this Fountain reveals four faces, as Ezekiel saw four animals in his vision. Wis-dom teaches four senses to scripture, which enter the mind "with hid-den sweetness" at once, as four words and as one. The mystical fountain in Eden watered the earth in four rivers even more bountifully than does Paris, the source and mother of studies.

This justification for poetry rivals anything produced by contempo-rary humanists. Gerson may even have gathered ideas from them. In the short treatise *On His Own Ignorance*, Petrarch too had likened classical learning to the river flowing from Parnassus, which he contrasted with the "true and unique source" from heaven that "wells up in eternal life." Gerson may well may have applied the metaphor (whatever his immediate source) specifically to poetic inspiration.[133]

We can now take the argument a step further, beyond the justification of poetry to the act of poetic production itself. The distance between medieval and modern poetry poses a stumbling block. Our own under-standing of poetry, shaped by the Romantics, privileges beauty of images or of expression. Yet it seems that most medieval writers classified poetry as a branch of ethics.[134] Moral themes dominate Gerson's poems. Con-sider their titles: "On the Matter of Indulgences," "On the Sweet Yoke of Christ," "On the Purification of the Inner Senses," "On the Correct Interpretation of Scripture," "Against Physical Beauty," "On Simplify-ing the Heart."[135]

For us, thinking of Gerson as a man of letters, one poem deserves fuller discussion. This is the *Josephina*, a central work that continues to elude historians, though Roccati's new edition may help to rectify matters and Brian Patrick McGuire has also stressed its importance.[136] Gerson clearly considered it an important work and may even have intended to distribute it at the Council of Constance.[137] The work presents a delicate balance between old and new. On the one hand, the poem follows in a long tradition of elaboration upon scriptural or apocryphal accounts of the Holy Family, a tradition that found its highest expression in the *Life of Christ* of Ludolf of Saxony (d. 1377 or 1378) and in the *Meditations of the Life of Christ* of Pseudo-Bonaventure.[138] Yet earlier schoolmen had shunned poetry, and using an epic to tell a story from sacred history was very rare. Gerson understood that his model was classical. Roccati has called the *Josephina* "a Virgilian poem with biblical content."[139] Gerson begins *in medias res* and skillfully balances narrative, description, and dialogue.[140] In the prologue, he dramatizes the moment of composition: God calls upon him at Constance like another Hebrew prophet, telling him to write a poem on the birth and early history of Christ and Joseph's role in these events.[141] We saw Mary prophesy the work in the *Compilation on the Magnificat*. While quoting Virgil, Gerson leaves traces of his scholarly formation. Rather than into cantos or books, he divides the poem into twelve distinctions—a beautiful metaphor for his blending of humanist with scholastic learning.

The *Josephina* is so poorly known and little read today that it may be useful here to suspend analysis for the moment and to outline the basic plot.[142] The action begins with the Holy Family fleeing to Egypt (distinction 1), and then proceeds to the residence of the Holy Family there (2) and the return to Nazareth (3). Then it moves back in time to the Annunciation (4), followed by the virginal marriage of Joseph and Mary (5), the visitation of Mary to her cousin Elizabeth (6), the return to Bethlehem, the birth of Christ, and the shepherds' visit (7), the circumcision of Christ (8), the arrival of the Magi (9), and the offering in the Temple and the massacre of the Innocents (10). Finally, it jumps ahead once more to Christ in the Temple at the age of twelve (11) and the death of Joseph (12). The poem closes with a long prayer to St. Joseph and speculation on his saintly career (he may have arisen at Christ's death to show himself to grieving Mary).

A closer look at one distinction will give the flavor of the work. The second distinction serves the purpose well. In the first, Joseph had been warned in a dream to flee Nazareth, and the Holy Family departed at dead of night. Now approaching Egypt, Joseph has fears because of Mary's beauty, and they decide to claim that she is his daughter. The statues of the false gods have recently fallen down in Egypt as Isaiah had foretold, and Pharaoh, who knows the prophecy, wants answers. The border guard asks all arrivals if they have heard of a virgin giving birth. He sees Mary and marvels at her beauty. They need have no fear, he assures them, for they will soon see the king. He then questions them: Is Joseph Mary's father or husband? And who is the father of this child, whose loveliness betrays his high lineage? Joseph explains only that the father is in a distant land and that an evil fate has driven them into exile. Report of Mary's beauty spreads quickly, and they soon have an audience with the king, who questions them on many subjects, including the rumor of a virgin birth. Joseph recalls Herod's rage and their flight, and asks only for permission to stay and earn an honest living. The king at once grants them shelter but then repeats his question about a virgin birth. Joseph dodges. The rumor comes from Jerusalem, he says, where the scribes have been rereading the prophets; "the time is doubtful, but the expectation is certain." The king gives them suitable lodgings. Joseph and Mary go to work the next morning, Joseph in carpentry, Mary weaving. Time passes. Jesus is now two years old. Struck by a playmate one day, he returns home crying and asks who his father is, if not Joseph. Mary hesitates—Jesus knows all, but experience teaches him certain things as humans learn them, from his mother. And so she tells him the story of salvation, from Satan's fall to his own death. The relation ends in bitter tears. Through these years, both Joseph and Mary tell their neighbors and friends of true religion, what will soon come to pass and what they must believe. It is likely that after the Lord's death, Gerson concludes, many who heard them were inclined to receive the faith.[143]

The narrative is the driving force in this second distinction. Departures from the canonical narrative of the Gospels occur within a space clearly defined as pious speculation or elaboration, deducible from reason.[144] So in the seventh distinction, the shepherds left gifts not of gold like the kings but of honey, milk or butter, wool or woven garments, and tender lambs. And from the scriptural statement that Jesus was subject to God and man, we may assume that he did his chores, fetched water, and fed and watered the donkey.[145]

The poem as a whole is characterized by the blending of this narrative with three other postures. First is the doctrinal posture: the voice of the narrator often becomes the voice of the *magister*. In the eighth distinction, for example, Joseph meditates on what circumcision signifies—and we are led off on an extraordinary journey of two hundred lines to consider its likeness to the intellect, a knife cutting away the phantasms or illusions of our beings. The knife may be blunted by the flesh, but it is sharpened by fervent meditation. Gerson continues to teach. Joseph wishes to learn from Mary—who knows more in these matters—how the soul (*mens*) is transformed through the fire of love. As gold takes on a new shape in the furnace, so the soul, burning with supreme desire, is liquefied, and flows until it rests in the first beloved. The narrative stalls while Gerson compresses some of his favorite doctrines into hexameters.

Second is the exemplary posture. Many events in sacred history become patterns for the modern world. Joseph's parents taught him the Ten Commandments—and so you parents too should teach your children, he implies. Joseph works hard, tells no jokes, plays no games, and prays. He prefers celibacy to marriage, and he obeys the king's bidding and returns to Bethlehem when so ordered.[146] In all cases he serves as a model—a most austere model—for contemporary Christians, and in some cases, such as his obedience to sovereign authority, as a rebuke to those who argue against possession and properly constituted authority. The shepherds also offer a pattern, as they pray to the Holy Family: you should too, says Gerson; they will hear your plea and grant pardon.[147] In this way Gerson praises sober living and celibacy, condemns heresies, and encourages pious devotion.

The third posture appears in the calls to affective meditation, a strategy that Gerson would have absorbed from a rich tradition of late medieval devotional works. The call to experience and to feel Christ's suffering, which owed much to a shift in theological emphasis in the eleventh and twelfth centuries toward Christ's human sacrifice, was the engine of late medieval devotion.[148] Much of this meditation centered on Christ's Passion, as in Gerson's famous Passion sermon in French.[149] In the *Josephina*, the meditation turns to Christ's childhood—a topic of much apocryphal speculation that generated some fantastic stories. When Christ chooses to bear sin's pains on his tender body in circumcision, we see the scene, the mother kissing the baby, their tears mingling: "O heart of adamant," exclaims Gerson, "unmoved by such a pious image!" A hymn follows. Grace gives us the name of Jesus, he exclaims; give him your heart in return.[150]

We should resist the temptation to reduce the *Josephina* to a single motive. Gerson wrote in part to promote the cult of St. Joseph. In the fifth distinction, he calls for a feast in honor of the marriage of Joseph and Mary, and sketches the liturgy that he had drafted years earlier.[151] He notes that a church in Paris has relics of the marriage, golden jeweled rings and the Virgin's girdle.[152] He took this promotion very seriously as a chance to increase devotion toward a safe and secure cult. But the manner in which he chose to go about this brings us back to Gerson the writer, imitating Virgil and perhaps even aware of Petrarch's *Africa*, which seems to have begun circulating in France after 1400.[153] Gerson took himself seriously as a poet, and this needs recognizing in our own estimation of him. His view of writing, infused with national identity, also embraced poetry.

The *Josephina* is a witness to the power of writing to express devotion elegantly in an enduring form. We seem to have moved far from the gigantic, jumbled, patchwork prose collections of Lyon. But even here we begin to see the shortcuts that would soon become common. The distinctions in the poem grow shorter, perhaps because Gerson hoped to distribute it before leaving Constance.[154] In this one work we have a fitting summary of all the tendencies and scripts of exile. Though the genre represents a radical departure from works of earlier schoolmen, the poem does not really stray much from the themes and concerns of his other works. It only abridges them. The contrast with Petrarch's *Africa* is instructive. For Petrarch, the remoteness of the poem's topic (the Second Punic War) increased its charm. For Gerson, the poem's value depended on the topic's relevance. For Petrarch, the form mattered most; for Gerson, both form and content. If the poem ultimately failed as an enduring masterwork, that is partly because it so accurately reflects the kaleidoscope of Gerson's tastes and interests.

Conclusion

Gerson had the skill, the ambition, and the opportunity to write works that might have summarized a grand tradition and earned him a name in the pantheon of authors who transcend time and place. Permanence was within his grasp. He wrote on an impressive scale at Lyon. But few of the late works attracted very wide readership. His enduring legacy remained in other spheres, as a great orator and public figure and as a moral and spiritual guide—not as a poet and author of timeless classics. Sifting through the works of exile, we see nothing that rivals *The Imitation of Christ* in its beauty and power, its lightning thrusts, and its enduring appeal. It is ironic that Gerson was often credited with that work. For though he did not compose it, it aligns so closely with his temper and spirit that plausible arguments can be made (and were) for his authorship. We now know from a recent discovery that he admired the work.[155] The debate over authorship is dead, and a more interesting question now arises: What prevented Gerson from writing a work as permanent as the *Imitation*? Why, in the end, does there have to be a Thomas à Kempis?[156]

This chapter provides one possible answer. The diversity of scripts that holds the secret to Gerson's contemporary success is also a clue to his failure. Gerson wrote with too much facility and too much on his mind. He raced from topic to topic. Finishing one work, he was beginning the next. Writing was not enough of a labor. It is the lesson of the compilations; usually, they are an afterthought. Like the unfinished tower in the Gospel parable, they are a testimony to his lack of forethought and execution, the failure to count the cost. They are above all monuments to individual authorship. Gerson is inescapable, always intruding into the text. He speaks of his reverses, his obsessions, his anxieties, even his other writings. The different "postures" of the *Josephina* betray a mind that never stays put, that wants to do everything at once. Even *The Consolation of Theology* returns to polemics. Scratch the surface and you will find the Hussites. The author of the *Imitation*, by contrast, is lost to us, anonymous enough to generate a scholarly controversy that lasted centuries. He labored on the work for more than twenty years. His theme and execution have struck readers of every generation. The message seems timeless. The work is usually printed without historical notes. *The Consolation of Theology* is so time-bound, it needed glossing within a few years.[157] None of this diminishes Gerson's historical importance. But it does help to explain why a study of Gerson is such an act of recovery.

This chapter and the preceding one have shown us how Gerson justified authorship and have given us some sense of the dimensions of his literary corpus. We now push ahead to the craft of writing itself, language, structure, and organization. Far more than earlier schoolmen, Gerson recognized the importance of rhetoric in demonstration. He urged contemporaries to give more thought to audiences outside the faculty of theology and to consider how jargon was damaging their reputation. This awareness of a public is the kernel of Chapters 5, 6, and 7. Gerson desired to reach his public through effective preaching and writing. The following hinge chapter uncovers the intersection between the author and his public: literary expression.

Chapter 4

Literary Expression
Logic, Rhetoric, and Scholarly Vice

Sometimes a passing phrase unfolds new worlds of meaning. Consider once again this passage from Gerson's second letter on the *Spiritual Espousals* of Jan van Ruysbroeck, now in full:

> Persons of lower rank and learning should therefore bear it patiently if their statements are examined to be brought in line with proper usage rather than widely proclaimed to the detriment of catholic teaching. I suppose that this consideration moved the most recent doctors—Thomas, Bonaventure, and such—when, abandoning all literary adornment, they passed on theology by questions so that we might possess, in fixed rules and precise language, a supremely safe theology in both its practical and speculative forms. [They did so] by reducing all former doctors to a single and secure form of speech.[1]

I have already emphasized Gerson's praise for earlier schoolmen in this key passage. Unifying theological language, they wrote the rulebook and set the stage for the modern possession of theology, the safe, secure world where all terms are defined, all questions answered. Reading carefully, one detects another sentiment here. It is parenthetical, fleeting almost before we register it. In chastening theological language, the schoolmen had sacrificed polish or elegance. They "abandoned all literary ornament" (*omisso omni verborum ornatu*). In this one phrase, a chasm opens between Gerson and the thirteenth century. That was *their* procedure, he implies, not ours. Theologians no longer disregard style.

Here is an important new trail of investigation: expression or the craft of writing, and the demands of rhetoric and theological style. The schools instilled a deeply mannered form of speaking and writing, characterized by rigid organizational patterns and rigorous logical development, "the postulate of clarification for clarification's sake," in the words of Erwin Panofsky.[2] Gerson was thoroughly schooled in this procedure. The power of scholastic method to organize and to solve fascinated him. Yet he also reflected long upon the entire writing process and grew impatient with those who did not. In his treatise against Juan de Monzon, he attacked the Dominican not just for his doctrine but for his style, his "confused and empty speech."[3] Gerson reflects a historical moment when university masters, newly awake to the power of expression in theology and sensitive to a broader audience, came to realize the importance of rhetoric and to ponder their choices as writers.

Yet when we seek to locate this moment in the historiography, we meet instead with grand narratives that threaten to pull our story into their orbit. Discussions of theological language and style tend to gravitate toward the sixteenth-century debates between schoolmen and humanists. Charles Nauert sees in those debates a "yawning chasm between two antithetical conceptions of proper intellectual method" that reflect "two rival cultures." It is a short step to assume that such rivalries always existed "under the surface" of late medieval intellectual currents.[4] The sixteenth century casts its long backward shadow, shaping and obscuring all that comes before it.

Erika Rummel has pushed back the chronology of these debates to the fourteenth and fifteenth centuries by identifying important themes in the early period that lingered on. But Rummel remains focused on the later period: Petrarch and Gerson serve as "paradigms" of the later debate, Petrarch mainly for humanists, Gerson mainly for schoolmen.[5] But neither fits the later mold. Like later humanists, Petrarch attacked Aristotle and scoffed at those who applied dialectic to sacred studies.[6] Unlike theirs, his course of study found meaning in its moral component, which drew from the Bible, Gregory, Hugh of St. Victor, and Bernard.[7] His attack on dialectic featured a "strong mystical element." He had no conception at all of philology in the study of the Bible, which became such a defining feature of the humanist enterprise.[8]

Gerson provides Rummel with an even more perplexing figure. Though "a champion of scholasticism," she writes in a passage that opens up the entire problem for us beautifully, "his views are too complex to serve as a paradigm purely for the scholastic argument." Sixteenth-century schoolmen adopted some of his positions, such as "the distinction between literary and technical language," but he also expressed humanist-sounding critiques of "obscurantism and contentious argumentation." "It is not surprising," she concludes, "to find Gerson quoted on both sides of the debate."[9] Petrarch, Gerson, and other fifteenth-century writers provided arguments for later writers, but in Rummel's account they perform an anticipatory function.

The problem with such views is that they cannot really account for Gerson, a schoolman by training who nonetheless embraced both older and newer forms of expression and new approaches to writing. At least some schoolmen welcomed broader literary currents, even the return to the pagan classics. In an early sermon (1392), Gerson recalled Jerome's famous dream in which he is beaten for reading Cicero at the expense of sacred texts. As we saw in a discussion of this text in the last chapter, Gerson warns against taking this to mean that we should discard pagan authors, "as some wish to conclude falsely." Poetry, rhetoric, and philosophy, he insists, can all be mixed with theology. The greatest authorities drew upon them and do so still.[10] Here as in so much else, Gerson mirrored broader developments. A group of classicizing friars were at work in early fourteenth-century England.[11] The College of Navarre trained a generation of scholars who prized classical texts.[12] And by the mid-fifteenth century in England, a generation of theologians took an interest in humanist learning and the new classical texts, some of which were brought to England as part of Duke Humphrey's famous library, left to Oxford in 1439.[13] As for Gerson, recent scholarship has shown that he was quite aware of what we would call the world of late medieval literature, its authors, its texts, even its underlying theories. Alastair Minnis sees it clearly in the debate over the *Roman de la Rose*.[14] The porous boundaries between theology and "literature" invited cross-fertilization of ideas.

This chapter attempts to map out this peculiar historical landscape of a schoolman unhappy with much about scholarly expression, looking for answers and calling for changes. Gerson recognized the importance of logic and felt drawn to speculation. Nonetheless, he departed from scholarly patterns of writing by developing a less rigid, more personal writing style. As part of this turn, he embraced rhetoric—not Ciceronian rhetorical theory as an end in itself, but a more practical rhetorical emphasis in preaching. Sensitive to the public perception of theologians, he called for greater attention to rhetorical patterns in scripture and to the use of rhetoric in scholarly communication. But unlike the humanists, who wanted to purify the language as part of a backward-looking literary enterprise, Gerson emphasized rhetoric because of its ethical dimension in moral theology, its power to stir the passions. He missed this emphasis in earlier schoolmen. Sadly, they were no sure guides to devotion. In arriving at these positions, Gerson often found opportunities to rebuke the literary and intellectual practices of modern schoolmen. Bad reading practices, he believed, had led to bad writing practices. Meanwhile, academic curiosity had infested the university, scholars giving themselves to arid, fruitless studies. He found a common solution to each of these problems in clarity. The student who strives for clear doctrine will have no need for esoteric teachings and will communicate clearly and effectively.

This chapter therefore describes a dynamic arc, moving from fascination with logic to the renewal of rhetoric to condemnations of scholarly expression. Clearly, we are dealing with someone who felt the winds of every literary movement and carried within him tensions of every kind.

But his most basic instinct drew him to logic, where we begin. And with a challenge: How can we comprehend the mental world of scholars who had mastered a discipline so remote from modern sensibilities?

The Seduction of Logic

Imagine that all scholarly discourse, all lecturing, debating, and writing took place in a technically precise but crabbed language, and that scholars used this language to talk about books adorned with beauties that no translation could hide—books with stories of every color in the spectrum of human experience, in prose and verse, stirring meditations, works of sparkling eloquence in philosophy, rhetoric, history, and theology, sermons, letters, and dialogues. That, I think, is the scholastic method of the high Middle Ages. By the early thirteenth century, the syllogism had come to control the speech and writing of intellectuals. They applied it everywhere. The advantages and effectiveness of syllogistic reasoning, which medieval scholars took over from Aristotle, are generally recognized and need not be restated here, but the effects of such reasoning on literary style were devastating. Admirers of Thomas Aquinas have noted its effects with dismay. M.-D. Chenu finds it "something of an embarrassment" to see him dividing and subdividing an epistle of St. Paul.[15]

To comprehend the fifteenth-century situation, we must imagine familiarity with these patterns from long centuries of exposure, a culture so saturated with logic that even noblemen like John of Gaunt knew its cadences.[16] The university was the intellectual establishment to the end of the fifteenth century and beyond, the only form of truly institutionalized learning until the later humanist academies. Familiarity sometimes turned to weariness and contempt. Those who had mastered the syllogism and the specialized language—like specialists in any field—sometimes reveled in technique and lost sight of application.

Gerson assumed scholastic method as an analytical device. Trained deeply in logic, he marveled at its precision. He had memorized Peter of Spain's textbook, the *Summulae logicales* or "Little Summaries of Logic" (he said that all students do so).[17] He fondly quoted its opening statement: "Dialectic is the art of arts."[18] Through logic, we uncover "many high truths" regarding the Trinity, the secrets of predestination, and future events.[19] Disputation, the framework for logical demonstration, formed a permanent backdrop to Gerson's professional world. In an early sermon, he prefaced the war in heaven with a scholastic debate between Lucifer and Michael, which he then staged for his audience: Michael pleads with Lucifer to remember the source of his gifts; Lucifer, deaf to these arguments, claims that he should have preeminence, since he is wiser, stronger, and more beautiful than the rest.[20] We are not that far off from the debate scene in *Paradise Lost* (though Milton gave Satan far more persuasive arguments).[21]

Gerson treated scholastic method like a clinical procedure. He linked it to the practice of the great schoolmen. Through its precision, they had carved out the "common school of theological truth" and stabilized theological language. Albert the Great and others, Gerson observed, used the scholastic idiom (*mos*) to treat mystical theology in clear and proper terminology.[22] Gerson himself did so in a set of articles against Benedict XIII in 1417 (Benedict had lost nearly all his support by this point).[23] Three conciliar works all treat a single question (*quaeritur utrum*) according to a syllogistic development, with arguments pro and contra (*arguitur sic et non*), followed by a resolution.[24] Such an approach worked best to generate one solution. Logic allows us to separate truth from falsehood and to preserve proper language, Gerson once remarked, and "if anyone casts it aside as useless and not wholly necessary, I will marvel if he does not soon say something false and incorrect, and entangle himself in thousands upon thousands of needless perplexities. . . . We can never speak truly and properly without correct use of logic."[25]

This scholarly way of speaking and writing is the starting point for any study of expression and form in Gerson's works. But formation in the schools wore grooves not only into a scholar's expression but also into his patterns of thought and feeling. For a scholar like Gerson, we must imagine too—and imagination really is paramount here—the thrill of the question: the prospect of learning through questions enticed and fascinated him. He staged little dramas in his Latin sermons that might even have been performed.[26] (At the College of Navarre, he had written a short morality play for the enjoyment and instruction of his fellow scholars.)[27] Characters with names like Swollen Knowledge and Instructing Charity spar and whirl in Boethian dialogues, chastising Gerson for abandoning speculation and neglecting fame or pleading with him to pursue more useful ends.[28]

In these dramas he gave special license to one figure, Earnest Investigator (Studiositas speculatrix).[29] In a 1394 sermon, Gerson tells how she interrupted his thoughts and tried to lure him to an earlier topic, the condition of the saints in glory. She asks eighteen questions, which Gerson patiently answers. Hungry for more, she then desires to know "heavenly secrets, to the point of idle or impertinent curiosity, such as whether joy can be possessed from the Father without the Son." Some line had been crossed, and Gerson finally cuts her off: "There is a time for disputing and a time for instructing; one in school, the other in a sermon."[30] Earnest Investigator reappears in at least eight more Latin sermons over the next twenty-five years, interrupting Gerson's meditations on moral topics with nagging questions.[31] Did Judas become a priest at the Last Supper? Is Christ's circumcised foreskin here on earth "as many believe"? Why and when were the faculties of theology and law divided?[32] Here we see Gerson the schoolman, seduced by a rich field of theological investigation, sometimes resisting these interruptions, more often welcoming them.

We also see the very sorts of questions that later humanists would use to ridicule schoolmen. While speculation and scholarly expression held a powerful grip on Gerson, he recognized that questions served little moral purpose and stirred something in him that needed checking. We might even see in the character Earnest Investigator Gerson indulging a convenient schizophrenia: distancing himself from his lust for questions by projecting them onto an alter ego.

Rethinking Scholarly Style

Despite Gerson's fascination with logic, most of his works employ a more relaxed organization. Even when brandishing scholastic method as a literary technique, Gerson softened its hard edges. Here, then, is the challenge we face in talking about his literary style in a historical way. He retained the scholar's love affair with logic and questions, yet he frequently abandoned traditional organizational features such as the syllogism. Set almost any work of Gerson next to a thirteenth-century scholastic article, and the differences will be unmistakable.

We must be careful not to oversimplify a complex historical development. Scholarly style did not stand still for more than a century. Henry of Ghent wrote differently from Aquinas, and scholars of the mid-fourteenth century had worked out their own structurally complex style. Moreover, all of these writers would have recognized the need for different levels of style, including a more literary approach for sermons and treatises, just as scholars today employ one style for articles and another for oral delivery of a text.[33] Nonetheless, the argument here is that Gerson marks something new and different. My purpose in what follows is neither to identify all of the stylistic devices that Gerson employed nor to trace a development in his style over time. Instead, I propose to explore three features of his style that may help us to locate his place within fifteenth-century culture and so to gauge his distance from both earlier schoolmen and later humanists.

The first feature brings us back to organization. Gerson recognized the great advantage for the reading public of a short work defined by its subject matter in the very title, organized under a few convenient points. To accomplish this, he replaced articles and chapters with "considera-

tions." He used the term *consideratio* much as we use it. "Considerations" were simply ideas that occurred to him on a subject. They appear
everywhere, in tracts, sermons, and letters. Gerson saw them as ideal
organizational devices, not just clear but easily committed to memory—
again we confront memory and its important role.[34] They effectively
freed him from the duress of dialectical reasoning and allowed him to
write in a more leisured and meditative fashion. He associated them with
an "easy and plain style."[35] Without sacrificing basic organization, they
permitted a more fluid text. He thought readers preferred them.
Through considerations, he says at the beginning of *On Mystical Theology*,
the reader will be refreshed at intervals and not wearied with continuous
and confusing discussion.[36] Yet all this is still far from the style of later
humanists.

Gerson hunted far and wide for other organizational devices. Like his
master D'Ailly and in clear imitation of Bonaventure, who (as Gerson
observed) included a meditation on the Passion in his *Tree of Life* using
"twelve fruits and leaves," Gerson found creative ways to organize his
works.[37] In *On Distinguishing True Revelations from False*, he framed the
entire discussion around an analogy likening true and false revelations
to good and bad money, an old metaphor for spiritual discretion, here
applied in a creative new way. Humility gives weight to the spiritual coin,
charity gives it color, and so on.[38] Gerson divided his tract against the
Hussites into two sets of ten rules (*regulae*), ten speculative and ten practical, invoking the parable of the good Samaritan who gave two pennies
to care for the man who had fallen among thieves (Lk. 10:35). In the
Tripartite on Theological Astrology, he treated the subject in thirty propositions, likened to "precious necklaces." He figured the four considerations of his *Proposition to the English* as "a four-cornered building." The
centiloquies reduce a topic to a list of one hundred items. He organized
his *Treatises on Songs* into "parts or tones, notes or little notes" (*per thomos
seu tonos, per notas et notulas*).[39] Such devices may seem puzzling or contrived to modern tastes, but they are evidence of a creative mind at work
striving for new forms of presentation, sometimes by finding alternatives
in old books. In this sphere Gerson represents a broad and deep tradition of creativity in learned Latin culture that is often forgotten or overlooked but that can be recovered merely by translating a few titles of
well-known works: "A Handful of Flowers" (Thomas of Ireland, *Manipu-
lus florum*), "The Clock of Wisdom" (Henry Suso, *Horologium sapientiae*),
"The Work of Ninety Days" (William of Ockham, *Opus nonaginta
dierum*), "The Lily of Medicine" (Bernard of Gordon, *Lilium medicinae*).

Organizational headings and rubrics had another function as well,
which we might easily miss and which becomes at once apparent upon
opening a medieval book. Gerson's considerations aided readers by serv-

ing as markers and signposts that broke up the text on the page. Contemporaries recognized the challenges of navigating the manuscript book, and from the thirteenth century onward, a system of headings, rubrication, marginal notes, content lists, and other readers' aids came into widespread use.[40] I shall have much more to say about this point in Chapter 6.

The second feature of Gerson's writing takes us from organization to his literary strategy to deal with the curse of scholarly debate: citations to authorities. Gerson never really disputed the importance of authorities, but he did abandon the *form* of heaping them in a pile, as in the typical scholastic question, and he streamlined his prose. "I am passing by the proofs," he says in the tract against the Hussites, a perfect motto for his approach.[41] The clearest statement of this strategy appears at the beginning of *On Ecclesiastical Power,* written in 1416 to 1417 at the height of debates at Constance over the relationship between the various orders in the Church.[42] Gerson says here that he intends to provide a clear, readable, and concise treatment of his subject. He explains that in order to purify the intention—here, the intention of deposing and installing popes—he must explore the subject, "dispute or inquire into it": "This thought has moved me to treat of ecclesiastical power under a few considerations, so that a subject that seems somehow endless as normally treated by some, through authorities and citations, may be disentangled [*resolveretur*] to a few certain and clear terms by approaching it in a less complicated way [*resolutive*], through descriptions and divisions, and setting aside confusing citations, which are not hard to find in the doctors."[43] Gerson proposes to offer a clear explanation of a complicated subject, carefully organized under a few clear "terms," designed to be read *as a text in its own right* rather than as a catalogue of authorities. Unlike the canon lawyers—they are probably in the back of his mind here—he will speak with an authorial voice. The most striking feature of this passage to my mind is the consciousness of a shift in approach, the sense that he is climbing out of the worn grooves of scholarly expression for the reader's benefit. Abandoning unnecessary citations and "coming to the point and the heart of the matter as it seems to me," as he says in a French sermon—this direct and personal approach is perhaps the most distinctive trait of Gerson's style.[44]

The third feature of Gerson's style is less easily defined, but links him to broader critiques against the schoolmen. It involves his notion of the end or purpose of writing. Gerson frequently insisted that he was not determining or "proving through argument" but, as in the tract *On Ecclesiastical Power,* exploring or examining a subject in search of truth. In a sermon at Constance in 1417, he again describes the tract as designed "more to examine than to determine, more to shed light on truth than to display vanity [*ostentatio vanitatis*]."[45] The crucial word here is determine (*determinatio*). In a scholarly context, the Latin words *determinare* and *determinatio* originally designated the second phase of a disputation when the master resolved a question that two students had disputed in the first phase.[46] This resolution required expertise and mastery. Such disputations occurred mainly in the higher faculties, especially theology. In time, these technical terms lost their strict association with a formal disputation and took on the idea of settling any question at all in a scholarly setting. The passage from Gerson adds another dimension, the link between determination and display. Scholastic determination, which had always showcased a master's intellectual prowess and hence involved the ego as much as the intellect (Abelard is the classic example), had taken on overtones of vanity and show. In the prologue to her *Mirror of Simple Souls*, Margaret Porette demands humility, not learning, if you would understand her book.[47] "Avoid and abhor every public disputation held simply to score a triumph or to make a good appearance," Geert Grote says to himself in a private resolution, "such as all those disputations of the theologians and artists in Paris."[48]

Gerson would have sympathized. He saw writing, especially when directed to a public problem, as a way to investigate or as a means to an end. He attributed this procedure to the long tradition that came before the schoolmen. This, he says, is why earlier doctors sometimes appear to contradict each other. In a French sermon in 1401, he explains why they occasionally seem to reject the Immaculate Conception, for which he campaigned: "When treating the faith and the Christian religion, the holy doctors always proceeded cautiously, without hastily determining doubtful truths. So they spoke on this subject as searching [*enquerant*] more than determining [*determinant*], which is why they sometimes seem to say things contrary to the faith but do not in fact do so. In such a case, then, we can hold the opposite of their opinion without erring to our peril."[49]

Here we see Gerson reflecting upon traditions other than his own and pondering their success. Surely he owed some of this flexibility to his own formation at the College of Navarre, which put him in touch with the earliest French humanists, and through them, at one remove, with an Italian literary tradition that had little in common with forms of expression commonly used in universities. And of course anyone who had read the fathers or the twelfth-century writers might apprehend the distance between their style and that of later schoolmen. Gerson could see this just as easily as the humanists. Depending on the occasion, he might identify with the schoolmen or with a much older literary tradition. He spoke of thirteenth-century authors as a discrete tradition, "the teachings of the schoolmen" (*de doctrinis scholasticorum*), but there were others before the schoolmen who thought and wrote otherwise.[50] In those other traditions, and even embedded within the university curriculum itself, he discovered an important tool that could persuade where logic failed: rhetoric, the tool that more than any other defines his approach to expression.

Logic, Rhetoric, and Audience

Of course rhetoric belonged to the trivium, but that did not matter much to the schoolmen. By the mid-thirteenth century, the notion of the "liberal arts" was more symbol than substance, and studying at a university meant studying Aristotle. We have little evidence from university manuscripts or statutes at Paris that rhetoric was an important part of arts training. John Ward has argued vigorously that more rhetoric was taught than would appear from university statutes—organized differently from rhetorical training in the Italian universities, perhaps, and focused on Aristotle's *Rhetoric*, but nonetheless drawing on Cicero, Boethius, and Quintilian. Even Aquinas knew Cicero's rhetorical works.[51]

Yet even if we grant Ward's argument about training, the issue here is practical emphasis. And in that sphere, the conclusion seems inescapable that rhetoric was shoved to the margins at the northern universities until the late fifteenth century. Mishtooni Bose observes that scholastic authors almost never spoke of rhetoric "in any context."[52] By contrast, Gerson frequently compared the scholastic style (*scholasticus mos, scholasticus sermo, scholasticus stylus*) to a rhetorical or "polished style."[53] On occasions when he wished to preach "beyond the university" or to teach "outside of ordinary lectures," he chose a "familiar" or "common" manner of speaking rather than a "refined" or "magisterial" one, though he claims that modern schoolmen disdained this style as undignified and even disgusting (*nauseans*).[54] While he never abandoned logic, he realized that scholastic method was not an end in itself, that such scholarly tools could tend toward exaggeration and mannerism, and that theologians had left their flank open to serious criticism by members of other faculties and, more and more, even by persons outside the university.

The topic of rhetoric came to Gerson with a long and complex history. In its classical form, Latin rhetoric depended for its usefulness entirely on the civil life of ancient Rome, where orators wielded it to make pleas in Roman courts. The late antique manuals of Martianus Capellus, Cassiodorus, and Isidore confirmed rhetoric in the standard medieval curriculum, the form in which students encountered it at the universities. Such manuals offered a basic introduction, yet classical rhetoric remained a highly technical subject, transmitted to the medieval West in its full complexity primarily in Cicero's manual *On Invention* and in a second work ascribed to Cicero, *Rhetoric to Herennius.* Gerson had received technical training in rhetoric, probably at the College of Navarre as a teenage boy, and he certainly knew both manuals and Quintilian's *Institutes of Oratory* (*Institutio oratoria*) in its incomplete form, before Poggio's discovery of the complete text at St. Gall in 1416.[55] He occasionally remarks on the value of a figure of speech such as embellishment (*expolitio*), or describing the same opinion in different ways.[56] In what follows, I must stress that his use of these technical devices, while it may deserve further investigation, is entirely secondary to my purpose, and that the great historical importance of this topic derives from his understanding of rhetoric as one form of persuasion in contrast to dialectic.[57] Dialectic produces conviction through proof or demonstration, rhetoric through persuasion and inference.[58]

The distinction between logical and rhetorical persuasion is central to two works that concern us here: *On the Two Kinds of Logic* and *On the Modes of Signifying.* Though neither work reached many readers before print (Glorieux lists three and two copies, respectively), both provide important insight into a topic that came to the center of the humanist-scholastic debates. Gerson wrote *On the Two Kinds of Logic* in perhaps 1401 or 1402 as a lecture on Mark 1:5–6: "And there went out to him [i.e., John the Baptist] all those from Jerusalem, and all the country of Judea, and were baptized."[59] According to pure logic, Gerson observes, such a statement is nonsense. Do we really believe that every single person in Jerusalem and Judea went to see John and was baptized? Rhetoric, on the other hand, "which we call another logic," uses ornaments and figures of speech, as in this passage; the "moral arts" (*scientiae morales*) depend on it. Each logic has its own rules for discriminating true from false. While formal logic (the kind described by Peter of Spain) deals with "interior concepts" and precision arguments, rhetoric persuades through tropes and figures of speech, ornaments and embellishments. Anyone who confuses the two by applying the standards of rhetoric to the speculative arts or those of logic to the practical arts will fall headlong into "the most absurd and silliest of errors." In such passages as this in Mark, the speaker is not following the laws of logic but is instead using a "common manner of speaking."[60]

Gerson then supplies three considerations on the proper use of rhetoric in preaching. I am interested in the third, "against those who, when using moral language, employ a sophistical [*captiosus*] manner of speaking that, while true, is reserved for the first logic"—that is, against those who employ dialectic out of context, especially in preaching. This warning especially applies when such formulations are foreign to the audience—the common people, for example, or the "purely moral, that is, legists or canonists." Modern theologians introduce pure logic, meta-physics, and even mathematics into their discussions before such audi-ences. In doing so, they have earned the reputation of "sophists," "windbags" (*verbosi*), and even "daydreaming fools" (*phantastici*). They have no sense of audience. They speak of the intension of forms, the division of a continuum, priorities, measures, durations, and instants. Instead of edifying their listeners, they expose themselves to mockery and ridicule. This practice often occurs in England and now threatens France.[61]

The passages I have summarized echo concerns discussed earlier. Ger-son is brooding here—over problematic terminology, over England as the source of mischief in the modern university (an idea cemented into university legislation that he knew and read), and over the danger of infection spreading to France. My concern for the moment is the great emphasis on rhetoric, presented here as the pole opposite to formal logic and as linked in some way to the moral arts, a point to which I return below. Gerson's classification had some basis in earlier develop-ments. Following the integration of Aristotle's logical treatises (the Organon) into programs of study in the twelfth century, poetic and rhet-oric were sometimes treated as divisions of logic.[62] This classification still appears in John Buridan (d. c. 1360), who also distinguished between formal logic and a logic appropriate to ethics.[63] Gerson shared this ethi-cal concern, but now logic and rhetoric preside as equals. The great value of Gerson's testimony arises not from the classification itself, how-ever, but from the immediate context of the passage, his sense that mod-ern theologians do not appreciate the correct province and use of logic and rhetoric. He expresses vulnerability and even embarrassment.

For the logician-theologians are twice mistaken, both in their exegesis and in their preaching. First, they subject statements in scripture to logi-cal analysis. Instead, Gerson urges rhetorical analysis to uncover rhetori-cal features of the text itself—a role formerly reserved for grammar but now fully established as a function of rhetoric within the tradition of aca-demic commentary since the twelfth century.[64] Gerson was reacting to a tendency that had first appeared in the mid-fourteenth century among an anonymous group of students and masters in the faculty of arts. Rely-ing on an extreme form of modist logic, they rejected statements incor-porating metaphors and figurative language as "improper supposition." By doing so they also disqualified passages in scripture that incorporate metaphor, such as the passage in Mark that Gerson cites. Their method provoked strong hostility and was at the heart of debates at Paris in the 1330s and 1340s.[65] It was actually condemned in a famous statute in 1340.[66] The issue did not die out. Sometime around 1348–1352, Conrad of Megenberg, a German scholar who had studied at Paris, attacked those who make a hash of grammar, rhetoric, and logic. Among their mistakes, he says, is that they reject metaphorical statements such as the assertion that "winds fly." Apply this approach to scripture, he warns, and you get heresy, for the Bible is rich in metaphorical language.[67] Gerson, then, was resurrecting an older though possibly still relevant complaint.

I sense in Gerson's second complaint a much fresher, possibly more urgent concern: the logician-theologians make a muddle of their preaching. Logic breeds its own technical terminology, and out of context such language is jargon. Gerson's emphasis here on the application of rhetoric to preaching follows in a long though not unbroken tradition. The same emphasis appears in book 4 of Augustine's *On Christian Doctrine*. From there it found strong advocates among Carolingians like Rabanus Maurus. Yet this stress on rhetoric in preaching was by no means universal. Gregory the Great crafted a theory of preaching in his influential *Pastoral Rule* that gave scant treatment to rhetoric.[68] Gerson thus turned to a very old model as a weapon against a very new development, and it is quite possible that he is echoing concerns being expressed by some of the early humanists. These theologians have lost touch with reality and with the ethical application of theology, its great end that Bonaventure understood so clearly. As a result, they have an image problem. The entire discussion takes into account the reputation of theologians among other faculties and audiences outside the schools, the growing public for theological discussion and conversation.

To my knowledge, this intense concern for audience has no precedent among university writers. In his *Sentences* commentary, Bonaventure understood the need to draw on different kinds of syllogisms depending on whether his opponents were pliable or stubborn. And in the *Summa contra Gentiles*, Aquinas had recourse to "probable arguments and authorities" that he adapted to his audience of unbelievers.[69] Gerson takes us into a different world, where schoolmen now give much more attention to outreach. He is responding to critiques against the schoolmen that would only gain momentum. Petrarch had castigated dialectic as "a science that dealt with 'words' rather than 'things,'" a field that "had no connection with life." Its virtue was "intellectual rather than ethical." Scholastic disputation exercises the mind but neglects good morals.[70] This ethical criticism turned to ridicule in later humanists. In *The Praise of Folly*, Erasmus has Folly mock philosophers for claiming "that they can see ideas, universals, separate forms, prime matters, quiddities, ecceities, things which are all so insubstantial that I doubt if even Lynceus [a sharp-eyed Argonaut] could perceive them."[71] For Gerson, the problem is not dialectic itself but its misuse by schoolmen oblivious to their public image who give no thought to presentation and speak as though everyone knows logic. Here he anticipates humanists such as Rudolf Agricola and Juan Luis Vives, who took essentially the same position, that logicians should make themselves intelligible to all, not just to experts.[72]

The late treatise *On the Modes of Signifying* (1426) comes at the topic from a different angle but reaches similar conclusions.[73] By Gerson's day the modes of signifying had a traditional flavor that disguised a long, complex history: the topic emerging into a separate genre (*de modis significandi*) in the twelfth century as a vehicle for teaching modist logic, a curious mixture of grammar, linguistics, and metaphysics (one day Heidegger would fall under its spell); the great fourteenth-century battles at Paris between modist and terminist logic (the new and preferred way to introduce the student to Aristotle's logical treatises), staged around the terminist *Summa logica* of William of Ockham; the modists slowly losing ground into the 1360s; Wyclif anchoring his realism to modist logic; Hussite theology taking shape under the same banner and so provoking the wrath of D'Ailly and Gerson; and this struggle between nominalism (stemming from Ockham) and realism defining the features of the fifteenth-century intellectual landscape in the so-called *Wegestreit*, the battle between rival schools of thought at German universities, the *via antiqua* and the *via moderna*.[74] These topics have generated a massive literature and need not detain us further here, though we shall soon uncover traces of unresolved conflict in Gerson's own treatise.

On the Modes of Signifying follows the form of the other centiloquies, developing its theme—the exact parameters and functions of the three modes of signifying, grammar, logic, and rhetoric—through two lists of fifty propositions, the first explaining the three modes, the second "the agreement of metaphysics with logic." Apparently for the first time in scholarly discussions, Gerson elevated rhetoric to a mode of signifying.[75] In Aristotle, to signify was "to establish an understanding," a phrase that had made its way from the *Auctoritates Aristotelis* into earlier scholarly literature.[76] Gerson defines signifying as "representing something to the intellect" primarily through language.[77] While the grammatical mode of signifying distinguishes between what is suitable and what is unsuitable for speech, and the logical mode between what is true and what is false, the rhetorical mode (now following Cicero) moves to persuade, instructing, delighting, and stirring.[78] As in the lecture *On the Two Kinds of Logic*, he considers it closer than the logical mode to patterns of speech in scripture and therefore as essential to its correct interpretation, especially its moral, historical, and prophetic material. The theologian interpreting such passages must "follow the common and parabolic modes of speaking, the rhetorical and figurative modes."[79]

Gerson does not go much further here into the rhetorical mode. He is concerned mostly to provide clear definitions on a topic that had led to perceived theological errors in the past, as with Jan Hus and Jerome of Prague, both mentioned in the text.[80] To arrive at truth, he insists, the philosopher must respect the province of the three modes and not ignore the boundaries placed by the fathers, "who in setting down terms were great metaphysicians."[81] Here we arrive back in familiar terrain, Gerson's common school of proper formulas, his panacea for every doctrinal deviation, and now everything comes into focus. Gerson is treating major concerns that preoccupied him through these years of struggle against heresy following the confrontation with Hus at Constance.

In these two works, then, Gerson diagnoses a problem in the exegesis and in the expression of contemporary schoolmen. We should mark the significance of this moment. The most important theologian in the faculty of theology at Paris is saying something rooted in earlier developments but still quite unexpected in that space: that logic and eloquence are compatible. No great damage is done to eloquence, Gerson once told the humanist Pierre Col, if we join it to theology.[82] To theologians he says: do not dissect scripture with logic, especially its moral and historical components; improve your public image; stop using jargon before audiences untrained in logic; recognize disciplinary boundaries.

We have now seen Gerson granting a mighty role to rhetoric, which masters the interpretation of scripture and sharpens the moral arts, especially preaching. For Gerson, rhetoric and eloquence never became subordinated to purely literary or oratorical concerns as they did for humanists such as Lorenzo Valla, Agricola, and Vives, who never strayed far from Cicero's triad: instruct, delight, and stir.[83] Instead, as we shall see in what follows, rhetoric served a deep moral purpose: to stir the passions through preaching and writing.

The Vital Link: Rhetoric Stirring the Passions

The link binding rhetoric to the passions is plain enough in *On the Two Kinds of Logic*. Early in the discussion, Gerson explains that rhetoric can move listeners, exciting them to wrath or displeasure, love or hatred. He continues: "Therefore this logic [i.e., rhetoric] is said to be necessary to the moral arts because the first logic is insufficient to stir and produce good passions, or to quiet, check, or remove evil passions. For that [first] logic seeks merely the truth of things as truth is a correspondence of the thing understood to the speculative intellect. But this [second] logic (does so) as a correspondence to the affect or the practical intellect."[84] The key to this passage is the reference to the "moral arts" in the first line. Here we see the stakes of the discussion, that rhetoric plays a crucial role in the moral sphere, while logic leaves the heart cold.

With this discussion of the passions, we thus intersect with a central theme in Gerson, and indeed in the history of Christian mysticism: the delicate interplay between those two great powers of the soul, passions and intellect, loving and knowing, *affectus* and *intellectus*.[85] This classic division forms a fault line separating the two ways of knowing and apprehending God, thus setting the stage elsewhere for Gerson's famous division of theology into its scholastic (or speculative) and mystical (or practical) parts, a division that echoes the distinction above between the speculative and the practical intellect. If we dig a bit further into Gerson, we find that each power, intellect and affect, contains three operations that move the soul: the higher operations (pure intelligence and *synderesis*, respectively) naturally moving the intellect and passions toward God, the middle operations (reason and the rational appetite) moving them through the power of reason, and the lower operations (sensibility and animal desire) moving them through the power of the senses.[86]

Two points of emphasis may help us through this vast, important topic. We should first realize the depth and tenacity of this idea of the passions as a path to God, particularly in the period after 1200 as it joined a mighty current of affective devotion above all to Christ's Passion. Nearly every mystical writer depends on it in some form, though the mystics usually tune it to a much higher pitch than did Gerson. "Know that you will never reach the heights of divinity," Henry of Suso has Christ say, "unless you strive for a certain affect of faith and love through the bitterness of my humanity and passion."[87] "You must let Love and Faith together be your guides," demands Margaret Porette, "to climb where Reason cannot come."[88] Closer in spirit to Gerson, writers among the New Devout, who never spoke of love as a ravishing force ushering them into God's presence, thought that affections governed the heart—evil ones, usually, because of the Fall. Therefore one must nurture good affections such as "desire for God and delight in the good."[89] Gerard Zerbolt van Zutphen (d. 1398), one of the most important spiritual leaders of the New Devout, described devotion as "an inclination sweetly drawing the passions."[90]

The variations on this theme seem endless, and Gerson participated fully in this common affective culture—indeed, he gave it further momentum through his numerous writings, which were then absorbed and refracted once again through writers like Nicholas Kempf (c. 1415–1497).[91] Gerson read deeply in the "affective" school of interpretation of Pseudo-Dionysius, flourishing after 1200 in the commentaries of Thomas Gallus and in the mystical handbook of Hugh of Balma, *The Roads to Zion Mourn*.[92] Bred in the schools, he instinctively understood the pitfalls of a purely intellectual approach to God. We saw in Chapter 1 his preference for authors like Bonaventure who reach and instruct both powers of the soul. In the prologue to the *Journey of the Mind to God*, Bonaventure had beckoned the reader to think more about "exercising the passions than instructing the intellect"—no doubt a passage that struck Gerson (he had probably memorized it) and helped open wide for him the rich and fertile country of late medieval devotional and spiritual literature.[93]

The focus on the passions runs through his works from beginning to end.[94] Gerson often told the story of Arsenius, a lettered Roman patrician who sought out an old, illiterate desert father. After long conversation with him, he sighed and confessed that he had not learned the alphabet of this man's theology "because he had not crossed over into the passions of the heart."[95] Gerson often spoke of the affective turn in this way as a passage or crossing over. To know the secrets of charity, he says in *On the Spiritual Life of the Soul*, "pass over from the theology of intellect to the theology of affections, from learning, that is, to wisdom, from knowledge to devotion." The first and the whole study of the religious life, he tells a Carthusian, is "to cross over into the passions of the heart."[96] Nonetheless, he admires balance. "Do you wish to be and to be called truly wise?" he asks in the first letter on Ruysbroeck's *Spiritual Espousals*. Have both kinds of contemplation, "the *affectus* which gives savor, and the *intellectus* which sheds the light of knowledge, that wisdom may be established, that is, savory knowledge." If you lack one, then have the first, "as it is better to have a humble and devout affect toward God than a cold intellect enlightened only by study." Then, as if remembering the point of the letter, he quickly adds: "But when the issue in question is the truth of faith passed down in Holy Scripture, then you must ask and consult theologians who are reputable in the second contemplation rather than unlearned who are mighty in the first," unless either you have a miracle of revelation in the unlearned or theologians are morally depraved.[97] "Theological investigation," he says in *On the Modes of Signifying*, "should not rest in understanding alone or in the illumination of the intellect, but should fall and melt in the fire of the passions."[98]

Taken together, such passages reflect Gerson's awareness of the dangers of the intellectual approach to God. Yet he never allowed this affective emphasis to compromise the theological authority of university masters. The path of intellect was closed to the unlearned. Ultimately, there were worse things than scholars with lukewarm devotion. The ideal remained the theologian who masters both approaches, "whose doctrine instructs the discrimination of the intellect such that it no less attracts, draws, and leads to the union of the affections."[99] Such oppositions as this—discrimination and union (*discretio, unio*)—abound in Gerson, many of them picked up from earlier literature: speculation and love (*speculatio, dilectio*), learning and devotion (*cognitio, devotio*), knowledge and charity or wisdom (*scientia, caritas, sapientia*).

The second point of emphasis to guide us through this topic concerns the failure of the schoolmen as guides to the passions. In *On the Two Kinds of Logic*, Gerson observes that preachers may use rhetoric to make claims that might not withstand the rules of formal logic, just as scripture does not always observe those rules. They do so in order to "abhor vices and to praise virtues." In *On Guiding the Heart* (1417), he uses the very same language to describe the approach of "holy doctors of old," a crucial passage for us: "Finally, observe . . . that holy doctors of old, who used rhetorical arguments to antagonize vices and to praise virtues, did not hand down a solution to moral matters, or for that matter to speculative matters, unlike more recent doctors who advanced to each part by questions and arguments and through decisions. For this reason, we should devote ourselves to these (latter) teachings to instruct the intellect, though others may be judged better at enkindling the affections."[100] In Chapter 2, I gestured to this passage in the context of a discussion of solutions and circumstances in moral theology. The point here is this comparison of old and new doctors, fathers and schoolmen. Gerson here concedes the advantages of scholastic method in providing solutions and instructing the intellect, but he also recognizes something quite important: the schoolmen may not be the best guides to devotion. Why? Because they overlooked the affections, they focused on theological terminology rather than vice and virtue, and they never learned to practice the rhetorical arts.

Bonaventure and Aquinas, each in his own way, saw morality as the end of theology.[101] Nothing had changed here. But Gerson recognized that to reach and change morals, the theologian had to sway the passions. And to sway the passions, the theologian should call on rhetoric in his preaching and writing. This failure of the schoolmen was by no means their only shortcoming, as we shall now see.

Condemning Scholarly Vices

In this investigation of Gerson's approach to rhetoric and literary style, we have frequently encountered his critiques of the schoolmen. Their shadows fall constantly upon the texts I have been citing. Where exactly did Gerson think that the project of the schools was going wrong? His concern over the schoolmen is a major theme that has received a great deal of attention in the scholarship; I make no claim here to be providing the last word. Nonetheless, the story can be told more clearly than it has, and with an awareness that Gerson found multiple things to criticize in contemporary schoolmen. My argument here is that we cannot separate Gerson's literary critique of scholarly writing and expression from a second critique, an intellectual critique that deplored the schoolmen's habits of mind. I shall take each in turn, but first it may help to trace the lines of this criticism prior to Gerson. For he was hardly the first to criticize the schoolmen.

The term *scholasticus* (with its inflections) had a checkered fate. Riccardo Quinto has traced this history and assembled a variety of texts to show that already by the twelfth century authors such as Walter of St. Victor (d. c. 1180) and Gerhoch of Reichersberg (d. 1169) were using the term as a polemical thrust. Walter deplored the "four labyrinths of France," Abelard, Peter Lombard, Gilbert de la Porrée, and Peter of Poitiers. "Inflated with an Aristotelian spirit," they treat the unspeakable mysteries of the Trinity and the Incarnation "with scholastic levity" and vomit forth heresies. The scholastic dissects holy topics with definitions and arguments.[102] Gerhoch of Reichersberg opposed scholastic reading to "ecclesiastical" reading. Subtle, wise in their own eyes, puffed with learning, the scholastics do not truly understand the things of God.[103] While Aquinas saw no real threat to Christian culture from scholastic learning, Bonaventure warned that "scholastic discipline" without "monastic" or moral discipline does not lead to true wisdom, "for not through hearing alone but through heeding [*observando*] is one made wise."[104] Here we see the crucial link that Gerson inherited, the emphasis on morals that lead to full wisdom beyond mere head knowledge.

Yet Gerson went far beyond Bonaventure in recognizing the literary perils of scholastic method. Moreover, his sense of the need for good writers arose from his belief that the project of the schools was failing to produce them, particularly in his own day. He is already grumbling about scholarly writing in the second Navarre letter. In Chapter 1, I discussed this text for its program of reading for theology students. I revisit it now for its critique of scholarly writing habits.

Gerson's analysis of scholarly style early in the letter deserves quoting at length:

We write, but we give no weight to our sentences, no number and measure to our words.[105] Everything we write is flaccid, coarse, and sluggish. We write not new things but old, and when we try to pass them off as our own by recycling them, we deform them and render them absurd. . . . Terence mentions people like us, who used good Greek comedies to make bad ones in Latin. They make excerpts, or rather mutilate pieces from the best and the proven books, and thereby distend huge volumes. They cast their shadow over complete works [*originalia*], and through their careless reading and writing they render them null and eviscerate them. You see in the lectures on the *Sentences*, when everyone is ashamed to follow his betters, how a sterile variety grows beyond measure.[106]

Instead of following the masters, he continues, in our desire for novelty we seek after new discoveries rather than using things "well founded" (*bene inventa*).[107]

The key to this passage is the close connection between bad reading habits and bad writing habits. Just as students read excerpts and ignore the titles of the books they are reading, so they cannot express themselves properly. They produce not books but enormous compilations, collected rather than written, quotations strung together without being truly absorbed or mastered. Proceeding from no authority in the writer, these compilations produce no conviction in the reader. The schoolmen do not write, they cite. Reading extracts leads to writing extracts.

Gerson's attacks on contemporary schoolmen in his letters to the College of Navarre have been cited as evidence for a decline in teaching practices and been linked to a more general decline of the late medieval university.[108] This is the master narrative driving the interpretation of these texts. Listening to what he is saying, we find that the fundamental issue here is scholarly style, and his critique actually anticipates humanist critiques of scholarly writing. Indeed, Quinto has argued that the attack on scholastic theology should be pushed back one hundred years from the early sixteenth century. Gerson anticipated all of the criticisms of Erasmus and Cornelius Agrippa: the jargon of the schoolmen and their barbarous language, their eagerness for display and their love of argument, and their devotion to schools of thought.[109] Yet we should also mark the differences in the critique of Gerson, who was painfully aware of the vices in his own tradition and tried to correct them. The humanists launched their assaults especially on language, what they considered the inelegant and barbarous terminology of the schools, and on dialectic, the forms of argumentation.[110] As we saw, these things troubled Gerson too when used out of context. But here, Gerson's critique follows a different logic. In the passage above, he is attacking not language but compilation, the cobbling together of earlier texts with no regard for the unity of the resulting product. The image of texts being pulled apart by careless students who take no thought for context or authorship proceeded from a desire for textual integrity, a thinking in terms of whole books from the past instead of the raw materials of the schools—*florilegia*, scraps, glosses, and authorities, torn from their original context, arranged as dicta according to a rigid system, and then subdivided beneath appropriate rubrics. Compilation lacerates a book and tears it to pieces. When Gerson read old texts, he did so not with an eye toward commentary or classification. He thought instead of authors and whole books, their style, thrust, and argument.

Gerson always retained a sensitivity to an author's original style and intent. He thought of texts *as books*, in a manner approaching a more humanist attitude to literature. He was not necessarily original in this respect. Twelfth-century authors such as Peter of Blois, Geoffrey of Auxerre, Ralph Niger, and Stephen Langton all distinguished between extracts and an author's work in its entirety, favoring the latter.[111] Petrarch referred with contempt to the makers of florilegia as "butchers of literature."[112] Contemporary French humanists such as Jean de Montreuil and Nicolas de Clamanges told correspondents to read Cicero himself to gauge the nuances in his style.[113] Gerson was voicing a concern that was gaining ground, then, though it was still not universal even among humanist educators.[114] Yet his letter expresses a deeper frustration, the sense that the practice of excerpting and institutional requirements such as lecturing on the *Sentences* have encouraged bad *writing* habits.

From the literary consequences of "defective" scholastic method, I turn now to its intellectual consequences or the habits of mind that it produced. At first glance, this may seem inconsequential to a literary investigation such as ours, but this important theme relates directly to Gerson's broader agenda for writing. Almost as a matter of course, Gerson assumed that the cardinal sin of the schoolmen was intellectual: curiosity, defined in *Against the Curiosity of Students* (1402) as "a vice whereby a person abandons things that are more useful and turns to the study of things less useful, unattainable, or harmful to himself."[115] Behind this attack lay a long history reaching back to Augustine by way of Bernard of Clairvaux and other monastic writers. Augustine saw vain curiosity as a turn inward, a desire to know truths for the simple joy of knowing them. As such, he argued, it turns men away from the contemplation of God and eternal verities.[116] This understanding of the term was certainly in the back of most people's minds, but Zénon Kaluza has historicized Gerson's understanding of the problem, showing that he linked contemporary sophists and academic curiosity to the English, who in his view of fourteenth-century history had mixed logic and theology in the 1330s and 1340s with evil consequences.[117] His belief in the harmfulness of English logic would have come through university statutes condemning the mixing of theology and logic. Clement VI probably had English logic in mind in his important letter of 1346 when he referred to the "strange and sophistical teachings that are said to be taught in other places of study."[118] Gerson might have found attacks on the English logicians in Petrarch, who reviled them as *barbari britanni*.[119] Leonardi Bruni and Coluccio Salutati described them in similar terms.[120] In any case, the more general and clear implication of Gerson's attacks should not be missed, his belief that the turn of mind that too often results from formation in the schools is fatal to true piety.

The curious schoolman bears certain earmarks. First and more generally, he has a proclivity toward argument for argument's sake. Some masters never stop disputing. The curious schoolman is like a blind man
arguing about colors, or like the master who, with death approaching,
still wants to chop logic.[121] Rather than attempt to bring the doctors into
harmony, the infected student rejoices in attacking them and in willfully
defending one against the rest at the expense of the common truth.[122]
Second and closely related, the curious schoolman discards proven
teachings for unwholesome, "strange" ones (*peregrinae doctrinae*), so
flouting the admonition in Hebrews: "Be not led away with various and
strange doctrines."[123] Some people are always trying to make new discoveries rather than apply themselves to the understanding of proven doctrines.[124]

The scholarship has described Gerson's position on academic curiosity as evidence for his attack on the Ockhamists or Scotists, as support
for an alleged nominalist position linked to Ockham's distinction
between God's ordained and absolute power, or again as a feature of
Gerson's humanist-sounding critique against schoolmen for their intellectual pride and vain questions.[125] While these approaches have their
merits, it may help to bring his attack on curiosity into a unified vision
of Gerson as writer. The same principle informed both his rhetoric and
his theology: his desire for clarity. Just as he strove for a clear and simple
writing style, so in doctrinal matters he wished to avoid the confusion of
tongues that came from mixing the terms of discussion, from seeking
after strange doctrines rather than being satisfied with the proven teachings of the fathers. In *Against the Curiosity of Students*, he links the need
for "clarity in doctrine" and for "clarity of words and writings":

To despise clear and solid doctrines because they seem trifling [*levis*], and to
explore those that are more esoteric [*obscuriores*], is a sign of curiosity and original sin, and contrary to penitence and simple belief. In all doctrine, there is no
greater virtue than clarity, nor is there any clearer proof of a superior and bril-
liant mind than clarity of words and writings. A muddled and confused mind
cannot teach anything clearly and freely. Yet the curiosity of many has so corrupted their judgment (something I suffered from at one time myself, I admit)
that a certain Latin style or form is judged more beautiful insofar as it is more
difficult, and more elegant as it is more inflated—and as a result, more defective—though the reality is far different. For every expression [*oratio*] is lovelier
and worthier of praise just as it is clearer—unless perhaps all taste and correctness have been cast aside, and then it is despised, it lacks energy, and is forgotten.[126]

This concern over clarity surfaced early in his career. In the treatise
against Monzon, he derided his opponent for his "obscure verbal ambi-
guities, intelligible neither to others nor to himself."[127]

The opposition between "clear" and "obscure," which might at first seem vague or traditional, is instead a striking restatement of the language of contemporary debates over style in various fields of study.[128] In his theological *Summa*, for example, Gerard of Bologna (d. 1317) asked "whether [theology] should use clear or obscure language?" His answer: both, according to the listener. Sometimes clear language helps the simple who need to grasp it for salvation, at other times obscure language spurs on the subtle to find hidden truths.[129]

Clearly, theologians were disagreeing about the kind of language they should use. A long, complicated history lay hidden here that I can only sketch in broad outline. Learned understanding of the obscure or esoteric style (*stilus obscurus*) took its start from the reading of Pseudo-Dionysius. "In all his books," Aquinas wrote plainly, "blessed Dionysius used an obscure style." Aquinas then identified this style or "manner of speaking" with the Platonists, whose teachings do not accord with truth.[130] The Platonic style, moreover, had earned a reputation as difficult and obscure thanks to the influential opinion of Averroës, who considered Plato's metaphorical language poor for teaching, and perhaps in part too because of the attribution to Plato of works on magic (*The Book of the Cow*) and on alchemy (*The Book of Quarters*).[131] It makes for a complicated story of misattributions passed from Islamic authors to the West, but the important point here is the circumstantial link in Aquinas between obscurity and theological error. Gerson, closely following Aquinas on this, labeled the style of Pseudo-Dionysius difficult for its brevity and its frequent repetition. In *Against the Curiosity of Students*, he linked this style to the formalists (*formalizantes*), who speak with "a great variety of words, pleasant to new listeners."[132]

This understanding of the difficult language of Pseudo-Dionysius and of the vices of a specific school, the formalists, certainly informed Gerson's understanding of the obscure or esoteric style. Yet the passage quoted above carries with it a more general understanding of obscurity not directly dependent on Pseudo-Dionysius. The terms clarity and obscurity had broader associations beyond the schools. As in so many areas, fifteenth-century authors inherited multiple, sometimes contradictory traditions that they might not clearly distinguish. Literary figures thought of clarity and obscurity as stylistic features. Drawing on Augustine, who freely acknowledged that Holy Scripture was sometimes obscure, Petrarch favored obscurity at one point, particularly in allegory, but moved toward clarity over the course of his life.[133] Following Cicero, Jean de Montreuil exalted *claritas* as the power of eloquence (*vis eloquentiae*).[134] At Avignon, contemporary humanists—who thought little of Pseudo-Dionysius—debated the relative merits of the "obscure" and the "clear" style, sometimes in language remarkably similar to Gerson's in this passage. So Gerson: "For every expression is lovelier and worthier of praise even as it is clearer." And here is Giovannia Moccia, an Italian humanist of a slightly earlier generation, in a letter to Laurent de Premierfait: "Truly, an expression is more beautiful even as it is clearer."[135] The opposition between the *stilus rhetoricus* and the *stilus obscurus* in Italian letter writing, which stretched back at least to the thirteenth century, enriched the association still further.[136] Boccaccio defended obscurity in poetic language in his *Genealogy of the Gentile Gods*, drawing on a host of authorities, including Petrarch.[137]

By no means restricted to the schools or, still less, empty verbiage, these terms informed and shaped literary attitudes in this culture. To grasp Gerson's place in the fifteenth century, we must look at the high theological tradition but also beyond it to grapple with the full complexity of the literary world that he inhabited. Gerson took those terms and applied them in new ways, to the writing style and to the doctrinal interests of contemporary theologians. Rather than a simple or bland feature of his rhetorical method, his emphasis upon clarity characterizes his approach to writing, teaching, and practicing theology. It infused his writing with purpose and moral fervor, and gave him a unified vision of the primary tasks of a theologian.

In his commitment to an accessible Latin style, as Berndt Hamm observed, Gerson anticipated one of the great literary ideals of the fifteenth century. Johannes Hagen, an Erfurt Carthusian, spoke of the need for "simple doctrine in a common and simple style, understandable to all." Jacobus Perez of Valencia strove for a "human and simple manner" of treating theological questions. Johannes von Paltz sought a "simple manner of speech."[138] Konrad Säldner thought that Jerome, Augustine, Gerson, and Henry of Langenstein surpassed the Italian humanist poets because the former used practical rather than skillful language.[139] Later humanists would accuse the schoolmen of disregarding expression. Yet this call for clarity stands as one of the most important trends spearheaded by Gerson within the fifteenth-century university.

Conclusion

Our picture is full of complexities. Gerson thought long and hard about the task of writing, admiring the power of logic, praising eloquence, chastening his prose, defending the authority of schoolmen while rebuking their literary and intellectual practices, exalting clarity to a cardinal literary and theological virtue, considering how his predecessors had succeeded and failed and how contemporaries might do better. This is a story not of declining scholasticism or of nascent humanism, but of challenge and adaptation—and perhaps, taking a very long view, ultimate failure. We can see many of these features in succeeding generations of humanists—and schoolmen too. We rarely see them all in one person. And therein lies one challenge for a broader historical understanding of Gerson's place in fifteenth-century culture. Looking for early patterns of the humanist-scholastic debate, Rummel acknowledged Gerson's complexity. Gerson puzzles us because he represents a path taken but then abandoned—his attempt to harness the learning of the schools, chasten it of its vices, and sharpen it with a new and renewed emphasis on expression tuned to the passions of the soul, all as part of an ambitious program of outreach. It is a case of an insider rebuking his own kind rather than blasting an institution to which he never belonged.

Gerson's message found its warmest reception in Germany among a group of early humanists, including Jakob Wimpheling (d. 1528), a strong admirer and early editor of Gerson.[140] He too valued both logic and rhetoric. The very title of one of his works indicates his bond with Gerson: *Oration in Support of Harmony Between Dialecticians and Orators* (1499). Like Gerson, he criticized university students for their poor literary skills, he praised poetry and classical learning, and he defended theology against its critics. Yet he also succumbed to the polemical battles that scar the early sixteenth-century landscape. Stung by humanist attacks on theologians, he soon took more radical positions, even turning his back on poetry for a time. In one round of polemics, he was driven to defend scholastic disputation and to craft arguments that soon became stock features of later disputes.[141]

In this environment, even Gerson's closest admirers could not close the gap between theology and the *studia humanitatis*, largely because by this period the debate had become institutional. Schoolmen were defending not just a way of writing but the university that had nurtured them. Gerson's program eventually crumbled. After going through many editions and printings from 1483 to 1521, his complete works were not reprinted until 1606, by which time they were being read and studied for very different purposes. The reasons for this collapse of his reputation are complex and poorly understood. Much of it had to do with the rise of new authorities who spoke to present issues much as Gerson had: figures such as the Dominican theologian Pierre Doré (c. 1500–1559), whose twenty-four works appeared in fifty-six editions in the sixteenth century, and of course Jean Calvin himself.[142] But perhaps another reason was that by the time of Wimpheling's death in 1528, with humanists and schoolmen now bitter enemies, Gerson's model began to seem not just remote but contradictory. He had defended *and* attacked the university. Schoolmen such as Jan Dullaert ("The better the grammarian, the worse the theologian and dialectician") might have wondered whose side Gerson was on.[143] Ultimately, even historians forgot about a time when such a model was even possible.

Gerson honed his expression in large part because he knew that the public for scholarly writers had widened. In the following chapter, I situate this development within a much larger context, the move by schoolmen toward greater involvement in the world beyond the schools, and the emergence of the medieval public intellectual.

Chapter 5

The Schoolman as Public Intellectual
Implications of the Late Medieval Tract

A few weeks before Gerson began to pour out his soul to the College of Navarre, he wrote a letter to his master, Pierre d'Ailly (1 April 1400). Still recovering from sickness, he spoke of all that was wrong with the theology students of his day. At the letter's close, he appended a list of remedies. One demands our particular attention. Gerson observed that in the past "the faculty of medicine composed a tract [*tractatulus*] to instruct people in the time of certain pestilences." The faculty of theology, he thought, could use the same strategy to give instruction on the principal points of the Christian faith—especially the Ten Commandments—"to the simple people," whom the learned rarely address, if ever. Or when they do try to reach them, they do it badly.[1]

Gerson must have had in mind the *Compendium* of the Paris medical faculty. First published in October 1348 out of a concern for the public welfare (*utilitas publica*), it famously concluded that a triple conjunction of planets in Aquarius had caused the plague by corrupting the air; in a much longer section, it then offered remedies under the headings of prevention and medicine.[2] The work had enormous impact. French translations appeared almost immediately, and an entire generation of plague tracts borrowed liberally from it. There is evidence to show that the faculty continued to publish it long after 1348; a copy in the British Library says that it was sent from Paris to Milan in 1373 during an outbreak of plague.[3] So the 1348 *Compendium* provided later theologians with a model for how to distribute information. What appealed to Gerson about the plague tract was not its simple language but its portability that allowed for easy distribution. He calls it a *tractatulus* rather than *tractatus*, so emphasizing its brevity. No doubt he was also thinking of expense. He spoke elsewhere of tracts that could be cheaply distributed.[4] I suppose that Gerson would have pounced on the printing press for its capacity to distribute information in a cheap format. To my knowledge, no other contemporary so clearly articulated a desire for something like the printed pamphlet.

Perhaps the most interesting part of this story is Gerson's awareness of a shift in approach from earlier days. Something has changed: the university master now has a nonacademic public, not merely in preaching but also in writing; he has a responsibility to reach them and must adapt his message to them. Earlier schoolmen, he felt, had missed the chance to deepen the roots of the Christian faith. In his awareness of a need for greater outreach to the laity, Gerson reflects a widespread and growing concern in this period, especially in the sphere of religious belief and devotion.[5] In this chapter, we come to terms with this momentous shift by tracing the evolution of academic genres that led to the development of the late medieval tract. In Chapter 2, we saw that Gerson relied heavily on the tract as a feature of his argument for new writings and hence his justification for authorship. The argument here is different: that the genre itself testifies to the public nature of theology in this period, to the broadening of audiences, and to a shift in focus from the interpretation of books to the investigation of moral, social, and spiritual concerns.[6]

The tract evolved out of earlier school genres, but it did something that they could never really do: it permitted an author to treat a current, popular topic in a form easily distributed to a nonacademic audience. Turning to Gerson's contemporaries, we see he exemplifies a much larger trend. Most schoolmen of this period had an enlarged public role, and the tract served many as the primary written vehicle in which they distributed and promulgated their opinions. A publishing world came into being that little resembled the world of thirteenth-century commentaries and classroom debates. Now more than ever, the schoolman became a public figure.[7]

Hence my model: the schoolman as "public intellectual."[8] In a classic study in 1955, Jacques Le Goff called medieval university figures "intellectuals."[9] The designation fits perfectly. Licensed theologians belonged to a guild—the original and enduring meaning of *universitas*. Through their training they mastered a set of Latin texts comprising the sum of learning in the Christian West at this period. They remained life members of the corporation.[10] By the thirteenth century, the *studium* had acquired in some models a typological significance as one of the primary orders of society.[11] Fully conscious of their elite status, and despite the fact that their occupation knew no precedent and invited grave abuse, university theologians articulated their roles in exalted terms as the arbiters of Christian doctrine and, at Paris, even as protectors of the kingdom.[12]

They were intellectuals, then, but after the outbreak of the Black Death in 1347 and 1348 and the Great Schism in 1378, their task acquired a new public dimension. Since Jürgen Habermas the term "public" has acquired a more focused usage through its application to a "public sphere" in eighteenth-century Europe.[13] The appearance of a large reading public, crystallizing in salons, taverns, and coffeehouses and capable of forming "public opinion" as a counterbalance to political authority, has no analogue in the Middle Ages. Yet we certainly can speak of a reading public in earlier periods, even in ancient Rome.[14] The fourteenth and fifteenth centuries witnessed the growth of a reading public and of an increasingly sophisticated media culture. Just as Habermas emphasized the importance of media, especially newspapers, in the formation of the modern public sphere, we should recognize the role of media in forming the late medieval public. The growth in the production of codices and bills or leaflets is just one part of a broad cultural flowering. Michael Camille spoke of a late medieval "image explosion," for instance, resulting from increased lay participation in visual devotion.[15] Focusing on northern European art, and drawing extensively on Gerson, Johan Huizinga recognized the rich texture of late medieval culture, a "luxuriant growth" as he called it, and brought that culture to life for many readers.[16]

We must now acknowledge that Habermas staked his claims for the eighteenth-century public sphere on an old-fashioned understanding of medieval culture—or, as Wendy Scase puts it, on a very powerful myth: that the "feudal society" of the Middle Ages had no public domain separate from private interests.[17] For Habermas, medieval publicity found expression in attributes of lordship such as clothing, seals, publicly staged events, or even bodily carriage and gestures. The lord presented himself publicly as a higher power; publicity meant publicizing one's high status. This "courtly-knightly publicity," says Habermas, "attained its ultimate pure form at the French and Burgundian courts in the fifteenth century."[18] A myth indeed! For in his attempt to identify the essential elements of medieval publicity, Habermas seized on those features of court culture that define medieval society in the popular eye: not writing and books but knights and tournaments. More to the point here, Habermas saw the Middle Ages as a long, continuous, undifferentiated epoch. Like most medievalists when he wrote (1962), he took no account of the increasing sophistication of written culture in the fourteenth and fifteenth centuries or of the growth in the reading public itself. Though it is beyond my purpose here to explore this question further, at the moment it seems clear that the growing complexity of late medieval media and the social consequences of that complexity need to form part of a larger reexamination of the changing nature of the public and of public opinion itself across the whole period from 1300 to 1800.[19]

The key to the argument in this chapter rests upon a fundamental shift within the university. Changes within the school genres between the thirteenth and fifteenth centuries had altered the nature of scholarly discourse. I must now turn back to account for this shift. How is it that a schoolman such as Gerson could write more than five hundred works and entirely ignore traditional scholarly genres? What had become of them?

Thirteenth-Century Academic Genres

When we think of the writings of the schoolmen, we often think of the summa, which seems to typify the medieval intellectual approach. Like the treatise, though, the summa served as an introduction for students. Thomas Aquinas addresses the *Summa theologiae* itself to beginners, who need milk rather than solid food.[20] To understand the literary realities of the thirteenth century, we must look elsewhere. Most thirteenth-century theologians published in very few genres, the most important of which were the quodlibet, the disputed question, and commentaries on the *Sentences* of Peter Lombard (a systematic arrangement and treatment of the "sentences" or opinions of mainly patristic authorities), the Bible, and the works of Aristotle (technically a product of the arts faculty). To appreciate the structure of these written genres, we should remember that each arose out of oral classroom experience. A powerful bond linked classroom and text. The commentary became the classic scholarly genre, but it took form quite literally from teaching a text and then reducing the oral commentary to writing. The quodlibet was public classroom debate at its finest, restricted to the most experienced, an academic free-for-all in which the master displayed his versatility by allowing questions on any topic his audience might choose. And the disputed question allowed the master to treat in more thematic fashion a problem that arose in the course of a class lecture upon a text.[21] A thirteenth-century copy of a commentary by the Greek scholar Eustratius (d. c. 1120) on Aristotle's *Nicomachean Ethics* produced at Paris beautifully illustrates the link between oral performance and the written text. An illustration shows two masters disputing the correct interpretation of Aristotle before a class of tonsured students, who are likewise having their say (Figure 8).[22] Nothing in the text suggested classroom teaching. The author had no connection whatsoever with a university. But readers assumed the oral context from their own experience in classrooms where such works were read and disputed.

The classic genres owed their success in part to their flexibility. The *Sentences* commentary encouraged a bachelor to survey the entire field of theology while permitting philosophical speculation and even discussions of physical science.[23] Areas of practical life that traditionally had been overlooked or that had never been brought within the orbit of

Figure 8. Two masters disputing the correct interpretation of Aristotle. Stockholm, Kungliga Biblioteket, Department of Manuscripts, Ms. Va.3, f. 205v. Used by permission.

Christian teaching—warfare or economics, for instance—now found their place in scholarly discussions.[24] Perhaps more surprisingly, fourteenth-century scriptural commentaries permitted theologians to pursue topics with little connection to the Bible passage.[25] The quodlibet, always popular for treating philosophical issues, was exploited to address more practical questions.[26] The second quodlibets (I–VI) of Aquinas cover such areas as almsgiving, bigamy, crusades and indulgences, hell, and perjury, and they were "known and quoted all over Europe from about 1300" after finding their way into numerous pastoral manuals.[27]

A bachelor or master of theology living in the year 1300 would have written most of his works in these genres. Then they began to fall out of favor. The Parisian statutes of 1366 and 1385 still make nice distinctions among the various forms of disputation. But by then the disputed question had become a teaching tool that held little interest for theologians.[28] The quodlibet fared no better. After 1320, masters stopped collecting them and the written genre practically disappeared at Paris.[29] By 1385, the statutes allow anyone wanting to avoid the required quodlibetal dispute to preach a sermon instead.[30]

The exact stages in this shift are elusive, but this much seems clear: at some point scholars began to use the question as a literary technique, unrelated to classroom setting; the resulting literary production looked increasingly like a short *tractatus*.[31] Sometimes the manuscripts actually label these questions as such.[32] Across the fourteenth century, it becomes ever more difficult to say whether or not a classroom disputation lies behind a given text.[33] The *quaestio*, then, had evolved from an oral to a written form, and by the fourteenth century began to appear as a learned, literary treatise. This, it seems, was a critical moment. The essential link between oral teaching and the written text, a link so strong that medieval readers drew pictures of classrooms in their commentaries, was severed.[34] While oral structures endured in medieval texts to the end of our period and beyond, we must now confront a world in which scholarly authorship had no necessary connection to teaching. Walter Ong spoke of a "strange new mixture of orality (disputations) and textuality (commentaries on written works) in medieval academics." For Ong and others, most medieval authors wrote their works to be read aloud.[35] Such a view does not reckon with the rise of scholarly literary forms in our period that presuppose private reading.[36]

Commentaries on scripture and on the *Sentences* developed along similar lines and further illustrate the changed intellectual environment. While William Courtenay has shown that scriptural commentary survived through long drought into the fifteenth century, these works—as we shall see with *Sentences* commentaries—barely resembled twelfth- and thirteenth-century commentaries.[37] Masters now abandoned exegesis for

more interesting individual questions. Furthermore, the major production of scriptural commentaries, like that of *Sentences* commentaries, had
by the early fifteenth century shifted to the younger Central European
universities, Vienna in particular, as well as Prague and Cracow.[38] Gerson
wrote no true biblical commentaries at all. Glorieux's attempt to credit
him with a series of lectures covering the first three chapters of Mark
over fourteen years (1401–1414) was motivated by a desire to fit his
works into received categories of publication for theologians rather than
by a strict examination of the evidence.[39]

The same pattern applies to the *Sentences* commentary, which by the
late fourteenth century at Paris had seen great changes from the days of
Albert the Great and Aquinas.[40] Rather than bother to treat every question of the *Sentences*, theologians began to choose favorites, often the
same from commentary to commentary, with the result that any notion
of the commentary as an overview of theology was lost—a point that Gerson and others lamented.[41] By the second half of the fourteenth century,
one question was often the focus of a long essay of ten to twelve folios.
The label "*Sentences* commentary" no longer fits, and should be replaced with something like "questions on the *Sentences*."[42] These questions could take the form of small treatises on given subjects, meant to
stretch over several weeks of a class. The theologian Pierre Plaoust organized his lectures (1392–1393) under seven headings, with titles such as
On the Enjoyment of God, On the Trinity, and *On Predestination*.[43] A surviving
student notebook shows how a bachelor could lecture on subjects that
interested him, yet fulfill the university requirement to treat áll four
books of the *Sentences*. At the end of each lecture, Plaoust simply took
the book of Lombard that he was supposed to be teaching and summarized its essential points as "conclusions," which stood in for the entire
distinction.[44] On 22 January, the student's eagerness in copying these
down provoked the smiles of two masters—an incident I take to mean
that they supposed he was overzealous, since he could as easily have consulted the standard commentaries.[45] The notebook even provides dates
that show how Plaoust managed to cover all of Lombard in a single
year.[46] This was now what it meant to "read" the *Sentences*: choose interesting themes, never tarry long, and fulfill the obligation to survey all
four books through token review sessions.[47] In some cases, theologians
did not even go this far but simply cobbled together a commentary from
the barely digested quotations of earlier authorities, or even read
directly from other commentaries, as if loath to waste energy on such a
worn exercise.[48] Under such circumstances, no wonder the late fourteenth century saw a decline in the publishing of *Sentences* commentaries
at Paris.[49]

The trend toward the commentary as an academic exercise, requiring little of what we might call original research (probably not unlike our modern lectures on "Western civilization"), began as early as the 1350s at Paris, when bachelors could read the *Sentences* during summer vacation.[50] The circulated *Sentences* commentary in England, already out of fashion by the 1350s, virtually disappeared for the rest of the century.[51] The genre lasted longer at Paris, yet there too production steadily declined from 1360 to the end of the century, and, as in England, many of these commentaries survive in few manuscripts.[52] Glorieux credited Gerson with a lost *Sentences* commentary, but we have no evidence at all that he ever prepared such a work for publication.[53] After 1400, the *Sentences* commentary seems to have survived only as a formality for most students, who (like Gerson) were merely fulfilling the requirements and did not even pretend to compose a commentary for circulation, or to treat all of the *Sentences*.[54] By 1423 at the latest, instead of devoting a year solely to reading the *Sentences*, every bachelor was combining the requirement with the second of the two required biblical lectures, which were themselves originally supposed to take two years (one year each for a book of the Old and New Testaments).[55] One Martin Berech efficiently managed to do all three—two biblical lectures and the *Sentences*—in a single year.[56]

Masters could still publish *Sentences* commentaries.[57] But Plaoust's lectures, organized around favorite themes and taking the full plan of Lombard's *Sentences* for granted, provides a much better indication of what most bachelors of theology were doing.

The Late Medieval Tract

This is the situation as I have outlined it: by the late fourteenth century, the earlier genres were often disappearing, or were at least far different from what they had been a century earlier, particularly at the English universities and at Paris. The interests of masters were changing as well. The attractive new topics for publication were not expositions of doctrine or commentaries but issues on the margins of the university's traditional domain. To these shifts in genre and in content, we may add a third in the realm of material culture. From around 1250 to 1350 at Paris, scholarly texts were copied and distributed by means of a piece (*pecia*) system of copying, whereby an official university stationer corrected copies of scholarly textbooks for rent and further copying. For reasons that are still obscure, this system had vanished from Paris by the middle of the fourteenth century.[58] Surely part of the explanation for this disappearance must lie in a subtle shift in attitudes toward the usual texts copied under this regime. It cannot be entirely coincidental that these three shifts, in genre, in content, and in material form, followed a similar chronology.

Here we have the context that may help us to understand the rise of what I am calling the "tract" as the most important genre to appear in this later period. Almost every major fifteenth-century theologian relied upon it. Just as the commentary served the needs of an earlier generation, so the tract became the way to respond to new cases that arose across a wide spectrum of issues. The table below offers a sampling of common topics, clearly identifiable by title, addressed by theologians and by canon lawyers in tracts or treatises between 1350 and 1475. I have included canon lawyers to show that these discussions went beyond a single faculty. Whatever the faculty status of these authors, they addressed these common problems from their roles as teachers, advisers, or lawyers. Like the change in genre, this too marked a change from the thirteenth century. The emergence of this broader public space was fundamental in defining the late medieval intellectual world.

All of the explosive issues of the day—the Hussite and Wycliffite heresies, contract law and usury, simony, superstition and magic, and many others—were now being treated primarily in tracts. The tract possessed clear advantages. Earlier genres, especially commentaries, tended to imprison the topic of discussion within a predetermined structure, and could scarcely reach nonuniversity audiences.[59] Thirteenth-century scholarly works were never translated into French or German; their authors never supposed that they would be.[60] The tract was closer to the disputed question, but even more accessible and likely to be read outside the schools. One key reason for this, it seems, and one of its great advantages over earlier genres, was that the tract advertised its topic in the title. Here was a reader-friendly genre defined *by its subject matter*. Finally, the fact that the tract had no necessary connection to teaching meant that schoolmen could use it as a kind of "rapid-response" opinion piece, not unlike our editorial. It could be produced "hastily" (*cursim*) and "on the fly" (*in transcursu*), then quickly copied and circulated.[61] A startling example is Gerson's tract on Joan of Arc, written on 14 May 1429, only six days after her great victory at Orléans, just enough time for the news to reach him at Lyon. Long desiring the recovery of France, Gerson had no doubt considered Joan's claim for some time, and her astonishing victory provided him with an opportunity to distribute his opinion.[62] As much as anything, this capacity for swift composition distinguishes the tract from all earlier genres.

Gerson must have realized the great advantage of a form that invited swift composition. He was not alone. He finished his tract on the Hussites at the Council of Constance on 20 August 1417. Later that year in Prague, on 2 December, the Hussite theologian John of Příbram wrote

	Johannes Calderinus (d. 1365)[a]	John of Dambach (1372)[b]	Nicole Oresme (1382)	John of Lignano (1383)	John Wyclif (1384)[c]	Henry of Langenstein (1397)[b]	Henry Totting of Oyta (1397)	Nicolaus Eymerici (1399)[e]	William Woodford (post 1400)[c]	William Butler (early 15th c.)[c]	Nicholas Radcliffe (by 1401)[c]	Johann Reutter (fl. 1404)[a]	Matthew of Cracow (1410)[d]	Jan Hus (1415)[d]	Pierre d'Ailly (1420)	Dietrich Kerkering (1422)[b]	Richard Ullerston (1423)	Peter of Pulka (1425)[b]
translation of scripture										•							•	
interdict	•			•														
new feasts																		
marriage																		
women's dress																		
ecclesiastical dominion					•				•		•							
nobility																		
Saint Bridget													•					
Wyclif (pro/contra)									•		•			•				
war/just war																		
Joan of Arc																		
discretion of spirits						•	•											
abstention from meat																•		
excommunication	•																	
astrology		•				•		•								•		
tithes				•														
clerical celibacy	•															•		
cult of saints/relics											•					•		•
mortal and venial sins					•	•							•					
Eucharist					•						•		•					
propertied monks		•				•										•		
indulgences		•												•		•		
Immaculate Conception						•		•								•		
simony		•			•		•						•	•	•			
superstition/magic						•		•							•	•		
Hussites																	•	
rents/usury				•		•	•					•	•					

COMMON TOPICS IN LATE MEDIEVAL TRACTS OR TREATISES (CONT.)

Topic	Francis of Retz (1427)[e]	Andreas of Broda (1427)[f]	Henry of Hesse (1427)[d]	Jean Gerson (1429)	Henry of Gorkum (1431)	Kaspar of Maiselstein (1432)[b]	Nicholas of Dinkelsbühl (1433)[b]	Nikolaus Jauer (1435)[b]	Nicolas de Clamanges (1437)[d]	Johannes Nider (1438)[b]	James of Soest (1438/1440)[e]	John of Frankfurt (1440)[b]	Narcissus Herz (1442)	Arnoldus Geilhovenus (1442)[f]	Bernardino of Siena (1444)[f]	Guillaume Saignet (1444)	Job Vener (1447)[b]	Andreas of Escobar (1448)[f]
translation of scripture																		
interdict																		
new feasts				•						•								
marriage																		
women's dress																		
ecclesiastical dominion																		
nobility				•						•						•		
Saint Bridget				•														
Wyclif (pro/contra)				•														
war/just war					•					•								
Joan of Arc				•	•													
discretion of spirits				•														
abstention from meat				•			•	•		•								
excommunication				•														
astrology				•														
tithes					•	•												•
clerical celibacy				•							•					•		
cult of saints/relics				•								•						
mortal and venial sins			•	•														
Eucharist	•			•	•													
propertied monks							•	•		•							•	
indulgences				•										•				
Immaculate Conception	•		•	•						•					•			
simony				•	•				•								•	
superstition/magic				•	•			•	•			•						
Hussites	•	•		•	•			•	•	•		•					•	
rents/usury			•	•			•	•		•		•	•	•	•	•	•	

| Laurentius of Ridolphis (c. 1450)[a] |
| Martinus Laudensis (1453)[a] |
| Guillaume Bont (1454)[a] |
| Alphonso of Madrigal (1455)[f] |
| John of Capistrano (1456)[d] |
| Juan of Segovia (1458) |
| Robert Ciboule (1458) |
| Antoninus of Florence (1459)[f] |
| Heymeric of Campo (1460)[b] |
| Francis of Platea (1460)[a] |
| Ambrose of Vignate (1460?)[a] |
| Jacobus de Paradiso (1465)[b] |
| Antonio Roselli (1466)[f] |
| Marianus Socinus (1467)[g] |
| Johannes Tinctoris (1469)[h] |
| Denys the Carthusian (1471) |
| Gilles Charlier (1472) |

Note: plain text = theologian, *italics* = canon lawyer

Topics treated by the most authors are listed first. Abbreviations next to the date of death refer to the sources used in each case:

a = Johann Friedrich Schulte, *Die Geschichte der Quellen und Literatur des canonischen Rechts von Gratian bis auf die Gegenwart.* Stuttgart, 1875–1880. Vol. 2.

b = *Die deutsche Literatur des Mittelalters: Verfasserlexikon.* Berlin, 1977–.

c = Richard Sharpe, *A Handlist of the Latin Writers of Great Britain and Ireland Before 1540.* Turnhout, 2001.

d = *Dictionnaire de spiritualité ascétique et mystique, doctrine et histoire.* Paris, 1932–1995.

e = Thomas Kaeppeli, *Scriptores ordinis praedicatorum medii aevi.* Rome, 1970–1993.

f = *Compendium auctorum Latinorum Medii Aevi.* Bottai, 2000– .

g = *Dictionnaire de droit canonique.* Paris, 1935–.

h = *Dictionnaire des lettres françaises: Le Moyen Âge.* Paris, 1994.

In many cases I consulted other sources cited in the reference works, and I have not listed these here. For the sources for other writers, see Hobbins, "The Schoolman as Public Intellectual," 1336–37.

a tract "swiftly" (*celeriter*) in response to Gerson.[63] The fact that John of Příbram, Gerson, and others sometimes specified that they had written in haste reflects a recognition that the genre itself invited swift treatment. In this respect, we may compare the tract to the Reformation pamphlet, by definition "a printed item in 'flight,'" as reflected in the French and German terms—*feuille volante* and *Flugblatt*—later coined for the genre.[64] The similarity extends to the physical independence of the printed pamphlet, which was originally unbound.[65] We can define the tract, like the pamphlet, not only by its subject matter—a contemporary issue—but also by its length; its brevity allowed it to circulate as an unbound gathering of sheets, unlike earlier scholarly works such as the commentary, which even at the outset were destined for binding. Likewise, pamphlets were "manifestly not books by design."[66] Neither the pamphlet nor the tract had any necessary link to the bound codex.

But of course tracts were not pamphlets, and it is worth considering some essential differences between them beyond the use of print technology.[67] One difference concerns what we might call the DNA of the tract. Scholarly patterns of expression and thought endured in these works. Even in treating themes with a wider appeal, the authors remained schoolmen who had little conception of a non-Latin-speaking audience. Even Gerson continued to cite Aristotle in his tract on Joan of Arc. His tract on the Hussites illustrates another key difference between the tract and the pamphlet. John of Příbram—who also attacked Nicholas of Dinkelsbühl's tract on the Hussites[68]—circulated his reply by copying it immediately following Gerson's tract, knowing that copies made from this copy would most likely include his reply. All known manuscripts of John of Příbram's reply include Gerson's tract. At least two other works of Gerson demonstrate this phenomenon. The tract on contracts often circulates with a *consilium* of Johannes of Imola, composed years later. But the best example of such textual fusion is the tract on Joan of Arc, which was attacked by a canon lawyer in Paris just a few months after its composition. Eleven of fifteen manuscripts of Gerson's tract contain this reply treatise. The dual circulation of these works stands as a fitting symbol of the contested claims of Joan herself. All three replies discussed here make explicit reference to the tract of Gerson; to be fully comprehensible, such replies had to circulate with the original work. Gerson's name gave life to these replies. Had the anonymous canon lawyer attempted to publish his work independently, his tract probably would not have survived.

The tract benefited from the material changes in written culture that swept Europe in the fourteenth and fifteenth centuries and that form an important backdrop for the argument of this book. Schoolmen too recognized the potential value and impact of works that could circulate in small gatherings (*quaterni*) or booklets. Preaching at a synod in 1404, Gerson said that parish priests might easily learn the Commandments, the articles of faith, and the sacraments by owning "certain tracts" (probably a reference to his own works) that were both easy to understand and cheap to make.[69] His tract on Joan of Arc might originally have filled the four sides of a single folded sheet, the exact layout of the work in some of the surviving manuscripts.

There is every good reason, then, despite its academic genealogy, to associate the tract with more ephemeral forms of literature. Steven Justice has traced some of the early leaflets (which he calls broadsides) in England to John Wyclif and his followers after 1377, and has argued that "broadside publication of vernacular reformist theology formed a part of the cultural project of Wyclif's followers—and indeed of Wyclif himself."[70] Wyclif described one such document that he compiled, a list of thirty-three conclusions on the subject of civil dominion, written both in Latin and in English, which he claimed had appeared throughout Europe.[71] The famous *Twelve Conclusions of the Lollards*, among other tracts, originally circulated as a bill.[72] In Bohemia, Hus's supporters (including Jerome of Prague) posted bills attacking their enemies, sometimes in violent language.[73] But this strategy was by no means restricted to accused heretics. By the fifteenth century, works of orthodox piety such as the *Lay Folks' Catechism* could circulate as unbound quires before being discarded or sewn together in anthologies.[74] Gerson mentions "opuscules" circulating in the wake of the assassination of the duke of Orléans, and others dealing with the controversy between France and England over royal descent through the female line.[75] Some plague tracts originally circulated as *schedulae* as well, including the Latin version of John of Burgundy's popular tract *On Epidemic Disease* (1365).[76] Unfortunately, most copies of such literature that survive in libraries today were produced long after their earliest circulation. In her research into the Lollards, Anne Hudson has found no surviving examples of bills or leaflets and just one of an original quire or gathering.[77] Yet we know from indirect evidence that such physical copies existed at one time, and some may exist still in "composite" manuscripts that were stitched together from preexisting manuscripts.[78]

Thus we should see the tract as part of a constellation of forms that encouraged swift composition and distribution. Gerson's mastery of the genre appears clearly from his choice to write so many tracts, as Table 1 illustrates. More than anyone else, he established this genre as the basic publishing vehicle for theologians. Of course, he did not invent the form. Wyclif (d. 1384) initiated a flurry of tracts toward the end of his career, and soon after 1378 numerous writers wrote about the Schism in short tracts, poems, and longer treatises.[79] If Gerson had models, they were probably two theologians at Paris, Henry of Langenstein and Pierre d'Ailly. In the early work against Juan de Monzon, Gerson referred to two tracts that D'Ailly had written "with flair and eloquence" in an earlier controversy.[80] Other references to their works suggest that he imagined them all participating in a similar project with respect to the publication of these shorter works.[81]

Gerson's contribution, then, was to take a preexisting genre, streamline it, and publish in it so often and so successfully (judging by manuscript distribution) that it soon became a kind of default genre for many theologians, some writing in direct imitation. It is no exaggeration to say that he put his stamp of ownership on it in a way that has never been fully appreciated. In fact, the table cannot do justice to how completely he appropriated the form. He used it to pronounce on all the important issues of the day, and to link his name inseparably to the great controversies of the age. If any previous university theologian had such wide interests, none had tried so consciously to reach an extra-university audience, none had employed the tract, sometimes in the vernacular, to address these issues, and none had been so successful.

Historically, then, the tract effectively symbolizes the nature of theology in this age, the evolution away from system-building at a time when scholars no longer staked their reputations on large commentaries. It served the needs of late medieval theologians better than the commentary. The Dominican theologian Antoninus of Florence (1389–1459), author of an important and enormous summa of moral theology (the *Summa moralis*), illustrates this point well. The complete summa survives in just a few copies. But Antoninus also wrote treatises, some of which enjoyed tremendous popularity. We possess ninety-five copies of *On the Ornament and Attire of Women*, which he incorporated into the *Summa*.[82] The distribution of this work on such a massive scale attests to what drove the written economy of the fifteenth century, what the reading public demanded.

The historical implications go deeper. At some level, this shift away from earlier forms also implied changing attitudes toward the past. Gerson and some others sensed that the production of large commentaries and summas was no longer necessary. As Gerson saw the thirteenth century as the great age of classification, so in practice the earlier *Sentences* commentaries and summas were now being assumed, a few of them serving as "classics." A different task was now called for, the application of magisterial learning to the real world.

The manuscripts themselves reflect this assumption. Focusing on France, Carla Bozzolo and Ezio Ornato counted sixty-nine manuscripts of the *Sentences* of Peter Lombard (d. 1160) from the twelfth and thirteenth centuries, but just three from the entire fourteenth and fifteenth centuries. The same pattern holds even for Bibles: 274 from the thirteenth century, fifty from the fourteenth, and fifteen from the fifteenth.[83] Copying declined not because of lack of interest in these works but because the old copies provided more than enough to meet present demand, especially given the decline in population that followed the outbreak of the Black Death. The Sorbonne library had at least forty-four copies of the *Sentences* and forty Bibles in 1338, and forty and thirty, respectively, one century later, still so many that the college wished to sell some of these to pay for repairs.[84] Even monasteries sometimes had far more copies than they could possibly have needed: during the fourteenth century, St Augustine's in Canterbury owned thirty-five, Christ Church twenty-eight.[85] The new critical edition of the *Historia scholastica* finds a similar decline in the copying of that text everywhere except German-speaking lands, where numerous universities with theology faculties arose in the fourteenth and fifteenth centuries.[86] The *Historia scholastica* was being dislodged by Nicholas of Lyra's *Postilla* on scripture. The Bible and the *Sentences*, on the other hand, were no less central to medieval learning in the fifteenth century than in the thirteenth. But the copying energy—like the energy for new writings—was filling new channels, following the broadening interests of masters. It also seems likely that at some level, the decline or even collapse in copying of the basic textbooks signifies an arrested development in these particular spheres.[87] We can be nearly certain that students at Paris who read the *Sentences* and other classic texts in the fifteenth century had their hands on copies that were at least a century or two old. Thus the very materiality of the classic texts, written in old handwriting and worn with age, reinforced their traditional importance, but maybe too their distance from the contemporary academic world.

Tracts, Treatises, and *Consilia*

Thus far I have argued that the tract was the central and even the defining genre in the works of fifteenth-century schoolmen, and that this was a fundamental change from the earlier period. Foundational genres such as the commentary and the disputed question, while still present, were now largely serving different purposes. I must now meet with a possible objection: that what I have called the "tract" was no different from earlier school treatises.

Earlier university masters did occasionally write systematic expositions of doctrine focused on a single subject, often labeled *tractatus* as well. For convenience's sake, I shall call these "systematic treatises." The systematic treatise was an overview of a single subject, like a summa in that it was designed for beginners as an introduction to a discipline—a kind of expository manual such as Aquinas's *On Being and Essence*, probably the first work that Aquinas wrote.[88] Such a work was nearly incomprehensible outside a university. By contrast, the tract was a further step in the development of the independent question (the form of a question is often retained), now at last free from its immediate classroom origins, and functioning as an independent form. The key distinction here is that the tract addressed or at least drew from a *specific case*, while the systematic treatise provided an impersonal overview of a subject. In theory, we can imagine these categories in direct opposition. In practice, the tract often took on features of the systematic treatise. Gerson wrote his tract on contracts in response to a case submitted to him by the prior and congregation of the Carthusian mother house. In the first section, he listed twenty general "considerations"; in the second, he dealt with the case.[89] So too, in an effort to produce a systematic treatise, an author might take a specific case and strip it of details.[90]

Likewise, earlier treatises sometimes departed from cool exposition and took on a much more polemical tone, and might even respond to a specific case. In some ways, then, we might see the tract as responding to a demand that was present even before it slowly emerged as a popular genre. Studies such as those of Jürgen Miethke have shown that thirteenth- and early fourteenth-century schoolmen took part in debates on papal power.[91] Yet Miethke himself has invited us to see the topic itself as a kind of genre. The common title for many of these works—"On Ecclesiastical Power" (*De potestate ecclesiastica*)—indicates that the topic had *an element of expectation* to it. On a topic such as this, which Gerson also treated, we should expect some continuity of ideas.[92] By contrast, the later tract allowed schoolmen to respond spontaneously to any topic at all. Here the similarity to the pamphlet is crucial because it underlines the different publishing conditions of the tract. Gerson composed his tract on Joan of Arc within hours of the news reaching Lyon, and he gave the work a unique title. As a rule, thirteenth-century schoolmen simply did not compose in this manner, nor in the haste that we see in Gerson. One might compile an even more instructive table than the one above by sampling the unique topics that Gerson alone treated: *Against the Feast of Fools* and *Against the Roman de la Rose* (both in French), *Against Those Who Attack the Carthusians, On Drawing Children to Christ, Against the Sect of Flagellants, Against the Superstitious Observance of Days, On the Teaching of Ramon Lull, Against Superstition in Hearing Mass, Against the Superstition of a Sculptured Lion* (that is, a medical charm). Most of these works might have filled a folded sheet or small quire.[93]

We could wish that schoolmen and scribes would have found another term for my genre of "tract." Many did just that, but no term gained universal acceptance. By far the most common designation is *tractatus*, or *tractatulus*, emphasizing brevity, but there were a host of others.[94] Often the same text receives different designations in different manuscripts. Sometimes these works have no technical designation at all, as in works "On Simony" (*De simonia*), "Against the Jews" (*Contra Judaeos*), "In Support of Clerical Celibacy" (*Pro coelibatu ecclesiasticorum*), and "On the Feat of the Maid" (i.e., Joan of Arc, *Super facto puellae*). The great variety of terminology suggests an implicit awareness that no recognized formal category existed for these works.

To illustrate the structure of a tract, we turn again to Gerson's treatment of Joan of Arc, *On the Feat of the Maid and the Trust That Should Be Placed in Her.*[95] Structurally, it bears signs of hasty composition.[96] While its organization sometimes echoes formal school models, Gerson does not feel hemmed in. He begins with three assumptions drawn from an axiom of Aristotle on probability, adds three further "conditions," then relaxes into a much more discursive style before presenting his conclusion, that it is legitimate to support the maid, whom Gerson never mentions by name. He then elaborates in support of his conclusion, attacking those who speak slightingly of Joan and adducing further circumstances and biblical examples in her favor. Never once does Gerson resort to arguments *pro et contra* in the scholastic manner. Manuscripts of the work show that after the work's completion, he added a short section in defense of Joan's male clothing, the first defense of Joan on this issue.[97] One could find a similarly relaxed scholarly style in other fourteenth- and fifteenth-century writers. Gerson is not exceptional here but representative.

Stepping back to take a broader view, we can see a parallel development in the faculties of law and medicine, where the period after 1350 witnessed the spectacular growth of the most characteristic genre of the age: the *consilium*, essentially a lawyer's advisory brief on a specific case or a physician's report that prescribed treatment "for an individual patient on a specific occasion."[98] In all instances the *consilium* addressed a specific case rather than providing a systematic discussion of an abstract or theoretical topic.[99] Nearly every major late medieval jurist and medical master published in this form.[100] Contemporaries recognized the methodological similarities and sometimes even encouraged "interdisciplinary" cooperation. In one case, the medical master Gentile of Foligno integrated a legal *consilium* with a medical *consilium* and invited jurists to consult "proven *medici*" if questions arose regarding the interpretation of certain laws in the *Corpus iuris civilis*. The key in his view was to treat problems on the basis of both doctrine and experience, anticipating a theme in Gerson.[101]

To reach a larger audience or to develop important themes, lawyers and medical masters could turn to the tract or treatise. Specific events sometimes encouraged this development. Just as the beginning of the Great Schism in 1378 accelerated the trend toward shorter, self-contained treatments among theologians, so the Black Death (1348–1351) led to the publication of numerous plague tracts or "prescriptions" (*regimina*) that often ignored the classic authorities and "launched straight into practical advice and procedures."[102] By the late fourteenth century, the regimen had found a wide market across broad sections of society.[103] Samuel Cohn has estimated that as many as one thousand of these tracts circulated in Europe between 1348 and 1500.[104] Compare this to the period from the ninth to the thirteenth centuries, when not a single medical treatise in the West gave a precise prescription for plague.[105] The trend in theology thus appears as part of a general move across the disciplines toward shorter genres that applied the learning of the schools to specific circumstances.[106] The picture we should imagine of the late medieval university is of a dynamic institution whose faculties were increasingly addressing real-world cases, legal, medical, and moral.

Of course, I am not implying that earlier schoolmen never applied theology to the outside world. John Baldwin has shown that Peter the Chanter and his circle showed "intense interest in practical questions," and "not only formulated ethical theorems, but attempted to apply them to the infinite variety of human behavior."[107] But the question here is audience, and the genres that Peter employed—biblical commentaries, summas, and a long book on ethics—indicate the kind of public he was addressing.[108] However broad their scope, twelfth- and thirteenth-century learned writings targeted a scholarly audience and normally reached nonuniversity audiences only through intermediaries. When Peter Olivi (d. 1298) wrote Latin treatises intended for communities of beguines, he apparently expected others to translate them into the vernacular.[109]

A partial exception to this is the extraordinary physician-theologian Arnau de Vilanova (c. 1240–1311).[110] Arnau draws our attention to a world of learning unlike that of Paris and Oxford, and to a culture oriented toward the Mediterranean basin and the Crown of Aragon. The University of Montpellier, where Arnau taught, granted only medical degrees. There, the production of medical works responded to the demands of nobles, merchants, tradesmen, and practicing physicians.[111] In this environment, learned medical works *were* translated into the vernacular. Guy of Chauliac's *Great Surgery* (*Chirurgia magna*), completed at Montpellier in 1363 and soon translated into many vernaculars, is perhaps the best example of this literature.[112]

It is healthy to keep in mind this alternate world of learning, which drew much of its strength as a great channel for medical knowledge forgotten in the Latin West but then recovered through translations, some by Arnau, from Arabic and Greek. But in pursuing this lead, we have wandered far from Paris and the centers of theological learning. Arnau wanted to think of himself as a theologian and did indeed write a few spiritual works in Catalan. But the fact that he could do so only testifies to his isolation from the traditional centers of theological instruction. He had just a few months of formal training in theology (that is, he was not a licensed theologian at all), he held numerous unorthodox and radical views and only spent enough time at Paris to be accused of heresy, and "his lifestyle suggests full assimilation into the laity." Indeed, he was married.[113] And even on the sunny shores of the Mediterranean, schoolmen like Arnau wrote all of their medical works in Latin. The fact that we have to reach this far to find an exception only strengthens the model.

Scholars have rightly celebrated the quodlibet for its ability to treat practical topics. Ian Wei has pointed to a few manuscripts that demonstrate "considerable interest in quodlibetal questions" by individuals outside the schools.[114] But the authors of these quodlibets had no role in compiling these collections. The great majority of manuscripts containing quodlibetal questions are university manuscripts. The genre could never reach a nonuniversity audience as directly as the tract.

And what of sermons? In their traditional role as preachers, university masters might well address some of the same topics as those in the tracts. And in their oral form, these sermons certainly could reach a wider audience than the other traditional genres.[115] This was especially the case south of the Alps, where the urban context of the Italian city-states encouraged preaching friars such as Bernardino of Siena, Antoninus of Florence, and John of Capistrano.[116] But while the sermon was open to many, the tract became the primary form used by most university masters to address these topics. When Gerson heard the news about Joan, he did not preach a sermon, he wrote a tract.

The Public Intellectual's Public

Gerson's place in the development of fifteenth-century theology now comes into focus. In an age when the commentary seemed downright backward-looking, he represents the coming of a new type, made possible by the shift to the tract: the theologian as controversialist, concerned with issues of public morality, always ready to give his opinion on current popular topics and eager to reach a large audience. He reflects here the growing dominance among theologians of secular masters, a major change from the thirteenth century when friars dominated the ranks.[117] Comparing him to our contemporary public experts, we may think of him as a medieval public intellectual, the licensed expert in moral theology—a field that covered a range of human activity many times broader than the expertise of any modern authority. As chancellor, he held an office that gave him the vision to step outside his own faculty and see developments in others. He regularly addressed the assembled members of other faculties.[118] Court preacher, friend of nobility, the single most important churchman at the Council of Constance, forever moving in exalted circles—Gerson was all this, while still close to "the people," criticizing the political leadership for oppressing them through heavy taxation, conscious of his humble but pious background.[119]

To reach his audience Gerson preached and wrote in Latin and in French. Naturally, he addressed his peers and students at the university. But he also wrote for parish priests, monks and nuns, hermits and popular preachers, and the increasingly literate laity, including women; and for the powerful, for bishops, popes, nobles, and the royal family.[120] Unlike his predecessors, he appealed to these audiences not through intermediaries but directly. To reach the nonliterate, he preached in parish churches and further attempted to shape their world through their social and spiritual advisers and superiors.[121] We saw that Gerson himself sensed something new happening here; he recognized that theologians and other Church leaders had thus far either ignored the "simple people" or addressed them "badly" (*male*), without taking care to communicate their message clearly. His most spectacular success in this regard, judging by distribution—more than two hundred manuscripts—was his *Opus in Three Parts*, a work which Gerson wrote separately in French and in Latin, and which he hoped would ensure universal literacy in the basics of the Christian faith.[122] In an open letter preceding the work, he urged that it be posted on tablets in "common places," churches, schools, hospitals, and "places of religion."[123] We know that the bishop of Thérouanne did in fact post the work "in two large tables" in the choir of his cathedral sometime before his death in 1414.[124] Nicholas of Cusa seems to have been imitating Gerson when he commissioned a large oak board containing the Our Father, the Ave Maria, the Apostle's Creed, and the Ten Commandments in Low German for a church in Hildesheim.[125] As elsewhere, Gerson was desperately attempting to reach his audience, in this case an audience that schoolmen had thus far almost entirely ignored.[126] The work shaped catechetical instruction throughout Europe in the fifteenth century, and was printed twenty-three times in five languages before 1500.[127]

What, then, of Gerson's actual audience? This is an enormous topic that can only be sketched in broadest outline here. Chapters 6 and 7 describe the means Gerson employed to put his works in readers' hands and how he succeeded in reaching an international audience; here, I briefly examine the different audiences of his French and Latin works, focusing on the categories of individuals who read him.

We know more about Gerson's French-reading audience than about his Latin-reading public. Geneviève Hasenohr has used contemporary references to manuscript owners in wills and lists, as well as indications of ownership in the manuscripts themselves to draw a picture of the French-reading public of Gerson's day.[128] We can safely say that already by the end of his life, certain of Gerson's French works were achieving the status of devotional classics, joining a very select and much older group of texts. Copies of his works, bound sometimes in expensive illuminated manuscripts, sometimes in much humbler paper manuscripts, found their way into ducal and other lay libraries. We know for instance that six copies of Gerson's great Passion sermon of 1403 (*Ad Deum vadit*) belonged to ecclesiastical owners, against eleven belonging to lay owners. These lay owners spanned a wide social range: the dukes of Burgundy and Bourbon and the queen of France, lower-ranking nobles and courtiers, a medical master, and two widows, including one Jeanne de Velle, a middle-class widow from Tournai who died in 1434.[129] This general pattern of distribution also holds for Gerson's other popular French works.[130]

We know now that vernacular texts were on the cutting edge. To us, they rightly appear as an emerging market of literature. We must also acknowledge, however, that with few rare exceptions—such as the *Roman de la Rose*, one copy of which was listed among the chained volumes in the 1338 inventory of the Sorbonne library—vernacular literature remained quite marginal to the interests of European intellectuals.[131] Gerson feared the *Roman de la Rose* mostly for its effects on public morals. Most legal, medical, and theological texts were written in Latin. The humanists only increased the bias in its favor. Indeed, nineteenth-century scholars blamed the humanists for retarding the growth of vernacular literature.[132] Latin was the language of nearly all controversial literature (Gerson is a partial exception), of all the debates on the Schism, and still some of the political attacks during the Hundred Years' War. Gerson wrote his tract on the French heroine Joan of Arc in Latin. Looking ahead to the sixteenth century, we still find printed Latin works outnumbering books in all other languages combined. Only at the end of the sixteenth century do vernacular works begin to rival and then to surpass those in Latin.[133]

Thus by choosing sometimes to write in French, Gerson was sacrificing a larger audience for his works. The audience for the Latin works was much more complex than the audience for the French works because it was surely at least ten times larger than that audience.[134] We can speak in general terms of this Latin audience as "clerks," allowing the English word to perform a double task. They were clerics (*clerici*) in a strict legal sense, receiving the tonsure and the protection of the Church; but they were likewise learned clerks or "bookmen," individuals with some book learning who performed a wide variety of tasks as advisers, lawyers, teachers, chaplains, tutors, and religious, tasks that changed and multiplied over time.[135] Yet here too we must allow for some blurring of boundaries. Jacques Verger notes that by the fifteenth century, at southern universities and even at Paris, jurists and medical masters were "largely laicized."[136] Even those who did have clerical status "might have rather loose ties to the church." They could marry, and might even work the land or perform manual labor.[137] Gerson's Latin readers came from this broad university-educated world, less strictly clerical than it had been, but still generating readers who were intensely interested in the writings of theologians. We saw that members of the Parlement in this period, both clerks and laymen, had strong interest in and knowledge of religious matters; their cultural formation had deep roots in the Church and its traditions.[138]

Absent general studies of Gerson's readership, let us look at the early reception of Gerson's tract on Joan of Arc as a suggestive example.[139] Completed at Lyon on 14 May 1429, within weeks the tract had reached Rome, where the Dominican Jean Dupuy copied the work into his continuation of a universal history. As early as the fall of that year, the short version of the work (without the defense of Joan's clothing) surfaced in pro-English territory at Paris, perhaps at the very moment that Joan was leading the siege of the city. There, a canon lawyer read the work and attacked it. The work appeared yet a third time this same year among supporters of Joan at Bruges. On 20 November, the Venetian merchant Pancrazio Giustiniani sent the work from Bruges to his father in Venice, encouraging him to show it to the doge and others who might like to see it. Besides an illustration of how quickly and widely tracts could sometimes circulate, the larger lesson here is how readers responded to texts in different ways. Jean Dupuy found the text useful to buttress his claim that Joan was divinely inspired. The anonymous lawyer may well have thought that she was deluded, but he also sensed the political stakes, perhaps even the urgency of the moment, and felt it necessary to challenge Gerson's opinion publicly. Pancrazio Giustiniani used the work to inform his father and political authorities in Venice not about Joan—the tract almost certainly would have told them little they did not already know—but about "learned public opinion" concerning her, the support she had received from Europe's most important intellectual.

The full story of Gerson's success as a publicist will come in the final chapters. Here, we can say with confidence that Gerson reached a public far different from that of earlier schoolmen. We must be careful not to overstate what was possible in the fifteenth century. The greatest gains in literacy were still to come. Printing made possible the multiplication of works beyond anything scribal culture could muster. But the problem thus far has been that scholars have ignored this success, not overstated it. The public for intellectuals was growing; it was a public that in turn advised, preached, wrote, and informed the rest of society; and more effectively than any previous schoolman, Gerson reached this public.

Conclusion

An aspiring theologian at Paris around the year 1250 would have known that to make a name for himself he would need to publish commentaries or perhaps quodlibets. By 1400, those genres were being assumed and had a traditional feel. The oral exposition of basic texts continued, but on a fairly low level; it could no longer make a scholar's reputation or be used to reach a larger public. Gerson did not publish a single commentary and yet made a name as the greatest schoolman of his age. He did so by entering the public arena as no university master before him, and by attempting to control the terms of debate. Surveying this period from the vantage of the thirteenth century, some scholars have decried the "vulgarization" of theology in the later period.[140] Instead, we should recognize the great historical shift that was occurring here, symbolized by the shift to the tract.

The idea of a public intellectual embraces the new cultural reality of the late medieval schoolman, particularly as applied to Gerson: his mastery of a set of important texts, his stature in the world beyond the university, his wide and varying interests, his many strategies for reaching a wide public and his apparent success in doing so, and his strong political identification with France. Gerson is not alone in these wider interests, but more than others he capitalized on preexisting conditions and set the pattern for others to follow.

We now have in place a model for Gerson's public involvement and a key genre that facilitated his entry into the public forum. We turn next to the mechanisms available for putting works into the hands of readers. Chapter 6 describes a model for understanding the complex publishing world of a medieval schoolman. Chapter 7 maps out the reading networks that allowed Gerson to become the most popular contemporary author of the fifteenth century.

Chapter 6

Publishing Before Print (1)
A Series of Publishing Moments

In January 1417 at the Council of Constance, Gerson preached a sermon in which he mentioned a "recently composed" tract that would soon be published.[1] He was referring to one of the most important statements of conciliar theory ever produced, *On Ecclesiastical Power and the Origin of Laws*, which appeared the following month, on 6 February (the date that appears in most manuscripts). But two Munich copies give an earlier date of completion, thus proving Gerson correct: he *had* composed it recently, on 7 October 1416.[2] The delay in publication is puzzling, though. What was he waiting for?

Piecing together the evidence, I arrive at the following reconstruction of events. The manuscripts that give the later date of completion, 6 February, also specify that the work was "pronounced" (*pronuntiatus*) at Constance.[3] To "pronounce" a work was to have a completed work—not merely one in the author's mind—read to listeners for dictation, a technique that both Gerson and Pierre d'Ailly used several times at the council.[4] Originally a technique of the schools, the *pronunciatio* was soon being used in various contexts to achieve a broader distribution.[5] Those attending the event, it seems, did not just listen but wrote the text down.[6] (Years earlier, Jan Hus had used the same technique to reproduce multiple copies of *On the Church*; Jean Petit had done the same for his *Justification*. Gerson knew of the latter case, and even claimed that copies of the *Justification* were then offered for public sale.)[7] On 1 October 1416, just as Gerson was completing his tract, D'Ailly arranged to have his own tract *On Ecclesiastical Power* pronounced, followed a few weeks later by another tract, *On the Reformation of the Church in the Council of Constance*, which took weeks to finish pronouncing.[8] With the procedure to remove Pope Benedict XIII from office dragging on (he was formally deposed in July 1417), it appears that Gerson waited for the best opportunity to deliver the text to the widest possible audience. In the case of *On Ecclesiastical Power*, the strategy worked: the text survives today in about eighty copies.[9]

This curious example brings into focus a topic that is fundamental to any discussion of medieval authorship: the complex material support system necessary to the production of every text before print. Gerson wrote *On Ecclesiastical Power* in October 1416 and gave it limited release, but waited for just the right moment four months later to broadcast it. He must have advertised the moment of formal publication, the "pronunciation" that occurred at some designated place (perhaps the Dominican convent nearby, where he had pronounced an earlier work). Or how else would anyone know to show up?

The final chapters turn the investigation of authorship in a new direction, to the material realm of the publishing and circulation of texts. We tend to think of publishing as a single moment and to associate it with financial risk because of the investment that it requires.[10] But publishing before print meant something very different: less drama, more complexity and variety, and a much longer time scale. Medievalists have been slow to tackle this topic directly, perhaps out of fear that by applying the category of publication to the world before print, they risk anachronism, or perhaps because of the topic's complexity and the scale of evidence that resists a single, workable model. As recently as 1979 it had still received so little attention (one short article from 1913) that Elizabeth Eisenstein even cast doubt on whether one could speak of publishing before print in a meaningful and consistent way.[11] More recently, from the perspective of New Philology (a more historicist approach to textual criticism, growing out of scholarship in Old French literature), Stephen Nichols frowned on the term *publication* applied to medieval texts because of its "strongly marked semantic associations with the lexicon of printing."[12]

Yet no less than modern writers, ancient and medieval authors published their texts, both orally and in writing. They had a vocabulary for doing so.[13] Gerson frequently speaks of texts being "composed" (*editus*) and "presented to the public" (*prodire in publicum*), and of publication itself (*publicatio*) in the sense of spreading abroad.[14] The January sermon cited above distinguishes clearly between the writing of a text and the act of presenting it to the public. Gerson applied the same distinction elsewhere.[15] Thus although we have come to attach different meanings to it, we must first recognize that *the very notion of publishing is premodern*. Moreover, scribal publication continued long after printing, especially in England, where even newsletters circulated in manuscript.[16] And we can now all too easily imagine a time when the present understanding of publishing as printing and distributing a text for sale will be forgotten, and all publishing will be reduced to electronic impulses.

Medieval publication began at a specific moment when someone—not always the author—presented or sent a work to someone else or

handed an exemplar to a scribe for further copying.[17] This delivery of a
text with the authorization to make copies and to circulate them is the
one and only necessary ingredient to the many kinds of publication.[18]
The central moment that provides the focus of the next two chapters is
publication in this narrow sense, the delivery of a text to a reader or
copyist with the intention for further copying.

Strictly speaking, publication served as the hinge between composition and circulation. The initial writing of a text preceded it, circulation
followed it. Yet this static model fails to describe the dynamic reality of
late medieval publishing conditions in all their complexity for at least
two major reasons. First, an author might continue to modify and distribute a text years after its original delivery. This distribution could take
various forms: an author might send a previously published work to
other correspondents, or direct someone to a place where the work
could be found, or correct faulty copies in circulation, or amplify a text.
Gerson did each one of these things many times. Publication was not a
single moment but *an ongoing process*. To apprehend better the medieval
situation, we should expand our understanding of publishing to
embrace those "publishing moments" when an author personally intervened to spread, to change, or to supplement a text, days, months, or
years after the original delivery.

Second, once a text left the author's control, readers too could add
their own voices to shape the text in ways the author never imagined.
Over the past three decades, a significant scholarly literature has blos-
somed around this most basic point of emphasis, that medieval authors
could not master the meaning of their texts. If we look only at the
printed editions, we shall fail to grasp the fact that authors before print
were severely limited in their control of a text. Even within print culture,
Roger Chartier reminds us, authors are "dependent and constrained."
They cannot control a text's meaning, publishers can disregard their
wishes, and readers can misread their texts.[19] Yet a medieval author had
similar problems plus countless others that arose in recopying.[20] One
reader might constrain reading by adding a gloss that others would
copy, another might abridge a work, or mangle the text, or "improve"
the text, or leave out or supply historical detail, or choose an excerpt to
copy, or simply change the text to say something else, especially in the
case of titles or other secondary material or "paratext" existing outside
the primary text. An artist might supply illuminations that acted as a
countertext. Most of the time, readers could not distinguish between the
author's original text and changes made by later readers—though they
might try, as when they compared different manuscripts of a text, a common practice in the fourteenth and fifteenth centuries. Though it goes
against our instincts to imagine it thus, these reader-copyists were also

participating in publication, and here again we should classify their interventions as publishing moments.

To account for these complexities, I propose a model of medieval publication that allows for its fluid and dynamic character and the ongoing participation of author and readers. Rather than a strict linear progression in stages—write, publish, circulate—we might see a series of publishing moments falling into three separate categories. Before publication, the author composed the text by dictation or by autograph. Writing did not necessarily lead to publication. The printed works of Gerson include various items that might better be thought of as "compositions" rather than publications, since their form suggests that Gerson never intended them for distribution.[21]

The first category of publication itself began with the initial delivery of a text—that is, publication in its narrow sense as understood by medieval authors like Gerson—which might then continue indefinitely. The publication might have an oral component, as in the "pronunciation"; vernacular authors had traditionally performed their works in public. But in general, late medieval writers of all kinds depended less and less on an initial oral delivery of a text as a prelude to publication. The tract had no necessary connection to teaching and could be composed and read in private. Careful reading of the vernacular literature of this period reveals a growing assumption of readership, a trend that authors encouraged.[22] On the whole, the fifteenth-century university and court were more literary places than their thirteenth-century predecessors: more books and libraries, more private reading and personal study.

At this stage, we should also allow for different levels of publication, though a comprehensive taxonomy is probably impossible.[23] Certainly many authors at first gave their works only limited distribution to a small reading circle, and some few never did allow for a more general release. Since the author is not authorizing a general release of the text, we might think of this as limited circulation rather than publication; or perhaps, borrowing a distinction from discussions of early modern publishing, we might speak of "weak" rather than "strong" publication, the text remaining a private possession instead of being publicly available.[24] Petrarch and Boccaccio are the classic fourteenth-century examples, but scribal culture had always allowed this practice.[25] Augustine permitted two monks to read thirteen books of *The City of God* long before the work's completion.[26] Monastic chroniclers often intended their chronicles for domestic consumption, and many of these chronicles survive only in autograph or apograph copies.[27] Gerson once advised the prior of a house of canons not to circulate a collection of visions "generally" (*passim et generaliter*) but to share it with those who had sufficient discretion.[28]

The second category of publication covers the author's correction and/or revision of a text already in circulation. This revision could take many different forms, from simple correction to amplification to everything between. Of course, the changes had no effect on copies in circulation—to the despair of authors like Petrarch.[29]

The third category of publication allows for the participation of bookmakers (scribes, illuminators, and so on) and readers making changes to texts. Readers came in all sizes. Deborah McGrady has distinguished between intermediary readers, who harmonize and satisfy the demands of both author and public, and inventive readers, who "intercept the text" and create "new distinctive writings."[30] The author's name and reputation could matter very much at this stage. An author like Gerson, always described with formal titles in the manuscripts, exerted more pressure on readers both to read the work and to produce a faithful text than did a little-known theologian or vernacular poet or female writer. His titles did not just clarify his identity, they awed the reader. In her recent study of Mechthild of Magdeburg's book of revelations (*The Flowing Light of the Godhead*), Sara Poor found textual instability and anxiety about authorship within the text, due partly to the author's gender.[31] Mechthild does not even sign her name. And why should she? What authority did it have? Why else, indeed, would so many writers attribute their own compositions to great authors of the past or present if not to invest the text with greater authority and to make claims on readers? Literary forgery of this kind is as much as anything a testimony to publishing conditions in manuscript culture, especially the preference for safe, approved authors.

We should resist thinking of these three categories as a strict temporal sequence. Gerson revised *On Mystical Theology* twice, years after its original delivery and after readers had begun to copy and therefore change the text. Moreover, every one of these categories assumes a complex material support system—parchment or paper, ink and quill, rubrication, perhaps painting and decoration, sometimes sewing and binding, the labor to produce these materials and to produce the written artifact (scribes, illuminators, binders). The crucial, essential point that should bring us closer to a historical understanding of medieval publication is the recognition that all three of these categories were publishing moments. While I retain the strict sense of publishing for the moment of initial delivery with consent to broadcast a text, publishing did not begin and end with the author, nor even with the author's lifetime. A scribe who copied Augustine's *Confessions* in the fifteenth century may truly be said to be participating in the publication of that work.

This chapter and the next attempt to untangle this complicated and dynamic process. The present chapter focuses on the role of the author, beginning with the crucial but overlooked moment that preceded publication: the decision to write for an audience. I then investigate the author's involvement in publishing, from composition, to preparation of a text for reading, to revision. Medieval authors could call upon various strategies to control the reception and meaning of a text. A scholar like Gerson had the added advantage of status and theological authority, which doubtless carried some weight in the reception of his works. But readers had voices too. The tract on Joan of Arc illustrates how author and readers both participated in shaping the text for publication. Chapter 7 follows the path of Gerson's texts in circulation. The massive quantity of manuscript evidence offers us the unique opportunity to map out the patterns and networks that turned Gerson into a true medieval authority within the space of a lifetime.

All of this follows from the initial moment of publication. But publication follows from the decision to write. It is a matter easily overlooked, and prompts a question I have not yet asked in this book: When did Gerson begin to think that he had any readers at all?

Awakening to Authorship

From a certain angle, publishing in scribal culture seems deceptively easy. What could be simpler than to deliver a work to a copyist or correspondent and watch it spread? Gerson seems to write and publish at will. Yet every copy of a work required some material outlay and a significant commitment of time and labor. Publishing in the print era required one willing publisher. To attain the distribution of a typical print run before Gutenberg—let us say four hundred copies of a work—required that many willing readers. An author who published a work with the desire to see it replicated was, above all things, a creature of hope. This arrangement might work well if a writer had some sort of status and willing readers. Gerson and other theologians had status. They were licensed professionals whose responsibility was to write, and they could rely on a network of persons who accepted their status, who knew that they were writing, and who wanted to read their works.

Or did they? Readership had to be earned somehow. We easily forget that not every theologian commanded readers—most did not—and we overlook the challenges that an authority like Gerson faced his entire life; even the Lyon works often circulated in just a few copies. It is worth pondering the beginning of this process, that moment when an individual with status first realized the possibility of an audience. It seems obvious if one thinks of it: even Gerson had slowly to awaken to the realization that he could have a reading public. This did not happen instantly. Surely many authors felt hesitation at the brink of authorship, a topic that deserves further study in its own right.

We have here an intriguing historical problem: Gerson's awakening to authorship. One clue suggests a line of inquiry. It comes from the second list of Jean the Celestine, completed shortly after Gerson's death. There, Jean ponders the fate of his brother's academic homilies ("collations"), the earliest works in the list (from the 1390s): "It is uncertain whether they survive and where they may be."[32] These homilies did exist at one time, not merely as compositions but as publications intended for readers—otherwise why mention them? Yet they lacked the necessary readership to give them any meaningful circulation, and in fact they do not survive today. Gerson's earliest works, then, were lost even in his own lifetime. Jean did not even mention other early works such as the tract against Juan de Monzon, which Gerson had published in 1389 and which survives in just two manuscripts, one of them an autograph. One can easily imagine Gerson confronted by the failure of this work. Failure might have led to doubt. He could celebrate the power of writing to outlast empires. But what if no one read?

Gerson's road to professional success began around this time, not through authorship but through preaching at court, then through exercising the chancellorship (1395). The great majority of his surviving works from before 1395 are Latin and French sermons (sixteen in total, versus two lectures, one poem, and the treatise against Monzon), an important clue not just to how others perceived him but to how he saw himself, since he published the sermons. The surest path to fame in this culture was still an oral path, through preaching, not writing. Preaching at court, Gerson participated in a world of splendor and power at a time when court culture in France and Burgundy was blossoming.[33] His early success as a preacher probably led Philip the Bold to make him his almoner and to grant him the deanery of Saint-Donatien's in Bruges in 1393.[34] His sermons attracted large throngs. Some were actually advertised. In August 1393, Gerson distanced himself from posters (*schedulae*) announcing his sermon on St. Louis at the College of Navarre in Paris.[35] Contemporaries marveled at his eloquence. In 1400, Jean de Montreuil claimed that Gerson and Jean Courtecuisse—another Navarre graduate and theologian (d. 1423)—excelled all other preachers in Paris. He wrote in a letter around this time that if Gerson were at Reims to preach on the Passion, he would skip the local scene and hurry there instead.[36] The chronicler at the abbey of St. Denis (Michel Pintoin) also considered Gerson primarily an eloquent preacher, first mentioning him only in 1405 for his famous court sermon urging the reform of the kingdom (*Vivat rex*).[37] Jean, duke of Berry, the famous book collector, was in attendance, possibly with his daughter Marie (1367–1434). Just months later,

Figure 9. Gerson preaching. Valenciennes, Bibliothèque Municipale, Ms. 230, f. 1r. Used by permission.

she possessed a copy of the sermon. (This manuscript survives, decorated with expensive miniatures, including one showing Marie and another woman, perhaps her mother, the duchess, at prayer before the Virgin and Child.)[38] By this time, powerful nobles were requesting copies of Gerson's sermons. The duke of Orléans asked Gerson for a copy of the sermon he gave at Tarascon on 1 January 1404.[39] His reputation as a preacher endured in later manuscript illustrations that show him preaching his famous Passion Sermon to eager, well-dressed listeners (Figure 9). This was the Gerson in France that many knew and remembered: not the solitary author in his study but the public figure surrounded by large crowds.

Slowly, as he gained confidence in the breadth of his audience, Gerson began to find his voice as a writer, but not much before 1400, when he was thirty-six years old. As the years passed he gave less time to publishing French sermons; his latest one dates from 1413, an address to the king on tyrannicide. Besides this, forty-six French sermons survive from before 1405 and perhaps seven from 1405 to 1410. In exile, he even quit publishing Latin sermons—just one survives from after Constance, in a single manuscript.[40] On the other hand, almost every "literary" work of substance dates from 1400 or later. He wrote about the Schism (in a lecture) as early as 1392, a safe and popular subject which attracted many theologians and to which he returned repeatedly. Just one of his early works on the subject—from 1398—survives in more than five manuscripts, and most of them in just one or two.[41] Apart from a stock letter written to beg for a benefice, extant in one manuscript, his earliest surviving letter dates from around 1400.[42] By this time he had begun to secure a strong reputation in university circles and could write knowing that his works might reach unknown readers. He began to experience fame beyond the usual reputation of a scholar. Thieves stole his manuscripts.[43] The period after 1400 saw his reputation steadily increase. Soon messengers were traveling long distances to gather his opinions on delicate matters. In 1413, the religious orders of Basel tracked him down at Paris to deal with a popular and troublesome local preacher.[44] The following year, Gerson counseled the archbishop of Prague on how to deal with the teachings of Hus.[45]

The Council of Constance seems to have enlarged his sense of audience and spurred his ambition. It certainly increased his international stature. By this point, Gerson had recognized the potential scale of his readership. One proof of this is that his works grew even longer. The five longest date from after his departure from Constance. They were soon being recopied in large numbers. Publishing was probably never easier than for a popular author before print.

Once Gerson surmounted the psychological hurdles to authorship, he could think about writing itself. This book treats authorship, yet so far I have only alluded to the material conditions that are basic to any historical understanding of the subject. How are we to imagine the physical act of composition in this period?

Writing "with Unceasing Pen"

Let us begin by conjuring once more the time-traveling monk from Chapter 1. One moment he is copying Augustine in a clear, Caroline minuscule, the next he is whisked ahead to the year 1400. Besides the tremendous growth in the numbers of books and readers, another change would have struck him: most authors now wrote their works by hand.[46] The shift from dictation to autograph composition took centuries. Authors such as Augustine and Jerome had dictated everything to copyists, unless none was available.[47] The high Middle Ages was a period of transition.[48] Thomas Aquinas dictated and wrote, scratching out his text in a hand his own secretaries could barely read. Albert the Great's biographer considered it a mark of humility that Albert wrote his works by hand. But by the fifteenth century, dictation was the exception.[49] Gerson probably wrote most of his works by hand, and no one remarked at all on his humility.[50] This simple fact provides a further layer to our understanding of him as a writer. Autograph composition linked him in a material way to the production of his texts. Hearing news of Gerson's death, his patron the archbishop of Lyon, Amadeus of Talaru, eulogized him as one who wrote "with unceasing pen."[51] Such an image, the author with pen in hand, need not be taken literally, but here we can do so. Gerson wrote his works longhand, and he impressed contemporaries as someone who wrote constantly.

Over the past sixty years, experts have discovered numerous autograph manuscripts of late medieval authors, enriching our understanding of the writing process. Unfortunately, nearly all of Gerson's autographs have perished.[52] Yet they must have been numerous at one time. Gerson frequently refers to letters written in his own hand, and notes in various manuscripts and even a reference in the 1488 edition prove the existence of others.[53] In this respect, he fits the trend of this period: he often wrote by hand.

Before publication, a medieval text might pass through any of several stages: the rarely surviving first draft, an author's initial attempt, sometimes written on wax tablets; the working copy, an intermediate draft falling somewhere between first draft and fair copy; and the fair copy itself, perhaps still in the author's own hand, intended as an exemplar for further copying.[54] A fair copy for Gerson's *Opus in Three Parts* survives. In Gilbert Ouy's estimation, it is a model of legibility, careful punctuation, accuracy, and correct orthography.[55] Ouy has also speculated that a figure named Adam de Baudribosc, an ordained priest, law student, and friend of Simon de Plumetot, might have been Gerson's personal secretary in the early days of his election as chancellor.[56] We also have a few manuscripts copied by Jean the Celestine.[57] Beyond this, it is impossible to say much about the early copying of Gerson's works.[58] Without much evidence from manuscripts or from codicology—without personal letter collections such as we have for Nicolas de Clamanges and Jean de Montreuil, or a book of verse with erasures and scribbled additions as for Petrarch, or autographs of every variety for John Capgrave—we must search in other directions for clues as to how Gerson composed. In general, one trait stands out from the start: Gerson wrote with extraordinary facility and speed.

In just one year at the Council of Constance, for example (1417), besides letters, short poems, memoirs, and unfinished works, Gerson completed from ten to fourteen independent compositions, ranging from one to forty pages in the modern edition.[59] Other theologians—at least those with a ready audience—could write just as swiftly. In the five-year period from 1380 to 1384, for example, John Wyclif wrote fifty-seven Latin works.[60]

Of course, Gerson also wrote lengthy works that required more significant commitments of time and energy. The *Josephina* took him perhaps four years to complete, but those were busy years (1414–1418). This seems to be an exception, and I know of no other work that occupied him this long. He completed *On the Consolation of Theology*, with its complex variety of poetic meters and prosometric form, in a few months.[61] He called the *Monotessaron* (1420) an "exceedingly toilsome" compilation (*compilatio laboriosissima*) and "a labor defying completion," yet it probably took him no more than a year to complete, perhaps much less time.[62] Even the sprawling *Compilation on the Magnificat* required less than one year (though some parts were recycled). In a letter, he told a correspondent that he was composing his *Treatise on the Song of Songs* (seventy-four pages) "with haste beyond measure." He began the work the day after he wrote the tract on Joan, 15 May, and left it incomplete on 9 July, three days before his death.[63]

Gerson wrote most swiftly in the tracts, here following in the steps of his master D'Ailly, who once wrote a work of forty octavo pages in one night.[64] Gerson probably scribbled the tract on Joan of Arc (four pages in Glorieux's edition) within a day or two, perhaps in a single sitting. The dialogue on clerical celibacy (1423), four times as long, took him one day, a lengthy letter to Jean Bassand (1426) just a single morning, and his *Petit livre contre détraction* (probably 1403) an afternoon and a morning. He spent three days at the Council of Constance on a treatise of advice for the dauphin.[65] The *Centiloquy on the Final Cause*, three times as long as the Joan tract, took him two days. He wrote his *Admonition on the Book Called "Climacus on the Thirty Steps of Perfection"* (a work recently rediscovered) on the blank page at the end of a volume of Climacus's *Ladder of Divine Ascent*, probably in one sitting.[66]

This kind of composition sharply distinguishes Gerson from contemporary French and Middle English writers who wrote mostly for patrons, and who normally offered their works in clean presentation copies with elaborate decoration and miniatures. Christine de Pizan, we know, worked closely with the artists who illuminated her works; humanist authors such as Jean Lebègue did the same.[67] But any author who expected a lay patron to give a work wide distribution was bound for disappointment.[68] Christine expected some financial windfall in return for her presentation manuscripts; she did not expect her patrons to spread her works abroad, and it seems they did not.[69] For Gerson and other schoolmen, authorship depended not on the pleasure of patrons but on their magisterial status. The category of swiftly written literature, whether didactic or polemical, reflects different publishing conditions. The "gift economy" of the vernacular poets was a world they could ignore. Gerson did straddle two worlds in a way that most schoolmen did not, preaching at court and addressing and sometimes dedicating works to royalty and nobility or to ecclesiastical dignitaries.[70] But in most cases, he circulated his works with little fanfare and moved on to the next composition, keeping his finger on the pulse of current issues and trends through continuous preaching and writing.[71]

We know that Gerson gave some thought to the visual features of the medium, especially diagrams and spatial elements that could clarify meaning or encourage memorization.[72] Diagrams were common in medieval books.[73] An author like Gerson, faced with the blank page, could draw an image or diagram as easily as the text itself.[74] Eisenstein rightly emphasized the power of print to standardize images, maps, and diagrams.[75] But printers did not always take the trouble to reproduce such elements in their original form. Gerson placed a tree diagram at the end of *On Ecclesiastical Power* to visualize the entire system of human justice. In the copy that belonged to the library at Notre Dame of Paris, the image is clear and recognizable. Reproducing such a diagram in print presented technical difficulties, which the earliest printers solved by not publishing it. To my knowledge, the diagram was not printed until the 1706 edition, which scatters the words across the page in a half-hearted and quite unsuccessful attempt to reproduce the charm of the original diagram (Figure 10). Perhaps an even more telling case is the *Summary Considerations on the Daily Testament of the Pilgrim,* for which Gerson added lines as spatial elements to "map out" the text. Once again, the printed editions disregard these elements and compress the text into something quite different and quite unreadable (Figure 11).

We are just beginning to appreciate the implications of autograph composition such as we see here. Composing and publishing in a manuscript culture also created challenges for the author. Once Gerson had composed a text, he began to think about releasing it to the public. His own voice would soon blend with those of others. Chaos now loomed. How conscious was Gerson of this problem? And what could he do to control it?

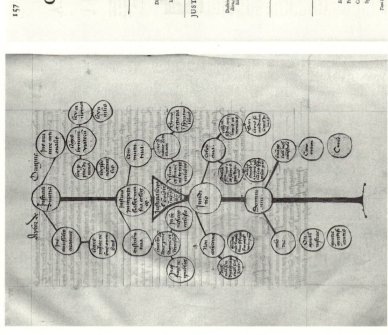

Figure 10. "Arbor de origine juris et legum" (Tree on the Origin of Law and Statutes) in manuscript and print. Paris, Bibliothèque nationale de France, Ms. lat. 17489, f. 20v; *Joannis Gersonii Opera omnia*, ed. L. E. Du Pin (Antwerp, 1706), 2.157–58. Used by permission.

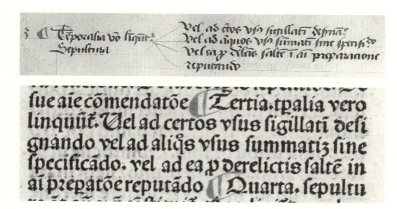

Figure 11. The *Considerationes summariae per quatuor partes super quotidiano peregrini testamento* (Summary Considerations in Four Parts on the Daily Testament of a Pilgrim) in manuscript and print. Paris, Bibliothèque nationale de France, Ms. lat. 18205, f. 143v; Johannes Gerson, *Opera* (Strasbourg, 1488), 2.152a (Y2). Used by permission.

Praising Scribes and Mastering the Medium

Medieval writers released their works to the public much like parents sending their children into the world, hoping they will prosper but fearing the worst. The problem was not just corruption but appropriation and control at all stages of the delivery process. In the vernacular literature of this period, the struggle between author and readers played out in new and creative ways. In her study of the *Voir dit* of Guillaume de Machaut, Deborah McGrady finds within the story itself—a love affair between Guillaume and Toute-Belle—a contest between "a poet who wants his text studied" and "a court culture that would expect an oral performance." The text employs various strategies to constrain readers. Threatened by an increasingly literate and sophisticated audience, Machaut traps them in "a complex literary web" and emerges victorious, his authority only reinforced by the efforts of his readers to resist him.[76]

I cite this particular example not for its direct application to Gerson, whose anxieties flowed into different channels, but as one dramatic example of a larger cultural struggle being played out in the pages of a romance. Most authors worried less about readers than about scribes. Chaucer's warning to Adam the scrivener to "write more true" reflects a general anxiety. This attitude had a long history that has yet to be fully told and that scribal culture fostered at all times. Fearing corruption, the author of the book of Revelation promised dire consequences for those who changed his text. Galen complained about scribal incompetence in the second century and so did later Arabic authors. Maimonides knew the dangers of scribal transmission and therefore designed for himself the layout of his works. When Roger Bacon wanted to present his *Opus maius* to the pope, he worried that the task was beyond the Dominicans, who rarely copied books, but he feared that professional stationers might publish the work without his permission. Here, the problem was not poor but unauthorized copying, even more troubling to authors. Henry of Suso (or perhaps an early editor) pleaded with copyists not to excerpt the *Little Book of Eternal Wisdom,* and threatened those who did with divine punishment.[77]

Writers responded differently to the potential chaos of publication. Some limited the circulation of their own works. Armando Petrucci and Roger Chartier have pointed to Francesco da Barberino and Petrarch as examples of fourteenth-century authors who, frustrated by scribal incompetence, sought to dominate the production and circulation of their works by limiting them to an "author's book" and perhaps a few personal copies.[78] For Petrarch, the author's book offered "perfect textuality," "a guarantee of absolute readability for the reader."[79] Dante, never imagining that he had control over his texts, introduced "readers and writers into the body of the work itself," so providing a model of how or how not to read his text.[80] Middle English and French poets shared the desire for control. Chaucer chose one trusted scribe for years to execute his first fair copies.[81] The fifteenth-century poet Thomas Hoccleve, famous for his worry, went so far as to strive for "total authorization" of his poems, assembling into one or two manuscripts "his poems and only his poems, composed by him, revised by him, edited by him, and manufactured . . . by him."[82]

Though he did not choose this path, Gerson too sensed the hazards of releasing a work to the public. At various times he saw copies of his own works in mangled and truncated versions.[83] He experienced problems of attribution firsthand—he may even have discovered works falsely attributed to himself. He repeated Petrarch's term for illiterate scribes, *pictores,* literally "painters" of words.[84] But while Petrarch reviled scribes, Gerson distinguished word painters from those who understood the text, and he praised the latter, even writing *In Praise of Scribes of Healthy Doctrine* (1423).[85] A writing can endure for a thousand years, he says there, whether "on its own or through the multiplying of exemplars."[86] As in those first lines against Monzon, this is a celebration of writing which here finds life in scribal labor. "Scribes are necessary," he plainly states, and sets out to prove it, "driven to this by the great lack of scribes of useful books that afflicts our age."[87]

This text, the first independent treatment of scribal activity, speaks directly to our investigation here. We saw earlier that Gerson wrote the work at the request of a Carthusian monk who had asked if it was permissible to copy books of devotion on feast days for no charge. He supplies twelve considerations, each one praising the scribe who can grasp the meaning of the text, "at least grammatically or literally."[88] So the good scribe preaches, studies, and bestows good service; he prays, he is afflicted (in place of fasting), he preserves the salt of wisdom for posterity, and so forth. But Gerson does more than just celebrate scribal activity. In the sixth consideration, he also warns the scribe to take care "lest his salt lose its savor . . . if he should spoil it by careless copying. Truly, our age provides many examples of flawed volumes, so many that we would be better off with none rather than such incoherent writings, without rule, meaning, or order. These volumes are of such quality, indeed, that they remain unintelligible to the author himself no matter how carefully he studies them."[89] The fathers, he continues, took more care to see that scribes passed muster and to divide learned from unlearned scribes. They examined them on the formation of the *punctus*, the punctuation "which sheds much light for readers." At the end of their works, ancient doctors like Irenaeus even placed "the awful charge of the divine name" as a threat to ensure the correct copying of their works, now and in the future.[90]

These passages reveal not just a consciousness of the dangers of corruption but also some sense of the possibilities for mastering scribal activity, for immortalizing the written word, and for aiding readers. We turn now from anxieties over scribes to the strategies open to authors to control the reception of a text. Beyond cursing and threatening scribes with unnamed terrors (a strategy that scribes themselves had pioneered), what could an author really do, not merely to master readers but to help them and guide them as they read?

Speaking of printed books, Chartier insisted that physical features such as page layout and textual division should be linked to authorship. Through such features, authors and sometimes publishers "express[ed] intention, orient[ed] reception, and constrain[ed] interpretation."[91] Yet even in the age of manuscripts, especially by our period, many authors participated in the preparation of their texts for readers by supplying apparatus, including devices such as section headings or *tituli* and indexes.[92] In the deep background of all such concern for the spatial arrangement of a text lay the efforts of Origen in the astonishing Hexapla, and especially of Eusebius, "a Christian impresario of the codex" who used tables to synchronize sacred and secular history and to clarify the accounts of the Gospels.[93] By the fourteenth and fifteenth centuries, authors commonly employed rubrication and other spatial devices even in their working drafts.[94] Gerson took this step very seriously, aware of the many hazards readers faced and the difficulty of navigating the contents of a manuscript book. Of course, scribes or readers could also shape the reception of a text by supplying their own apparatus or by changing or removing an author's original apparatus. The problem, then, is twofold. Stated simply, the issues are (1) what apparatus or surrounding material or "paratext" Gerson gave his works, and (2) the extent to which it endured in transmission.[95] The first relates to Gerson's intentions, how he imagined his books being read, the second to how readers actually read his books.

The underlying assumption is that we cannot understand how Gerson intended his works to be read and experienced until we know what apparatus he gave them—the same concern that has occupied scholars of Middle English literature for more than thirty years. In a seminal article written in 1976, Malcolm Parkes explored how the *mise-en-page* or page layout of medieval books had evolved from the twelfth century forward in combination with developments in scholarly method. He focused especially on attempts by readers to make plain a text's organization or *ordinatio* through rubrics and other apparatus designed to facilitate use of the book.[96] This study inspired many others that applied Parkes's notion of *ordinatio* quite broadly, sometimes collapsing the different roles played by authors and scribes in producing a text. Responding in part to Parkes (who was not concerned with agency) and in part to the scholarship, Mary and Richard Rouse have stressed the different agencies involved, and hence the limited control that medieval authors had over the subsequent appearance of their texts. "Literary creation and the physical layout of surviving manuscripts," they stressed, "are not results of the same actions." Authors such as Christine de Pizan and Hoccleve might take steps to control the appearance of their texts and might even succeed in doing so. But control over book production was "severely limited."[97]

Much of the difficulty here follows from the complexity of manuscript production itself. Certainly authors had little control over aspects of *mise-en-page* once the text moved beyond their immediate supervision. The arrangement of margins, the script employed, the number of columns, the size of the writing surface, the writing materials—all extended beyond the author's control in nearly every case. The tract *In Praise of Scribes of Healthy Doctrine* encourages scribes to use parchment, yet most manuscripts of the work (and probably every other work of Gerson's) are paper copies.[98] Yet other components of the text affected layout and reading, such as the organization into parts, headings and subheadings, authorial glosses, and apparatus such as indexes and lists or tables of contents. And these might survive the rough handling of readers quite well.

For once again attitudes to the written page were changing. In a separate study, the Rouses traced the rise of "research tools" such as indexes and concordances to readers of scholarly texts in the thirteenth century, who increasingly incorporated such finding devices into the texts they read. At first, demand from readers drove these changes.[99] But by the fifteenth century, well before print, such apparatus had become commonplace. Fifteenth-century authors, scribes, and editors knew that readers often read selectively, choosing their place, and that in doing so they depended on readers' aids to guide them.[100] Guglielmo da Saliceto, the thirteenth-century author of a book on surgery, reflected general opinion when he remarked that division into parts and chapters helps the reader to find what he wants more easily.[101] While such aids began as readers' inventions, by the fifteenth century they had penetrated the fabric of book production. An author such as Gerson experienced books as mediated and shaped by these readers' aids. Absorbed into the written culture, they had become a common expectation and practice. The same trends are visible in Hebrew manuscripts from the late eleventh century onward: hierarchies of scripts, decorated or rubricated headings and initial words, constant effort to make texts more legible and serviceable.[102] Headings, rubrics, subdivisions—these simplified and aided the difficult task of reading a manuscript book.

We are closing in on a central problem of late medieval publication. Our tendency is to attribute such things as headings, indexes, and tables of contents to scribes or readers. In most cases, Gerson's editor Glorieux cleared away this apparatus like so much scribal rubble accumulated over the centuries and hindering our encounter with the naked text. Yet we can now say with certainty that Gerson sometimes provided such apparatus. A great reader, he included readers' aids in his works because he saw them every time he opened a book. In this, he reflects common practice. Denys the Carthusian probably supplied his works with tables of article titles and carefully divided his texts into "small, easily located units, introduced by pithy, summary headings or authoritative *dicta*."[103] Copies of Richard Rolle's works likewise display "an unusual respect for the structures in the texts." Often, the original structure and layout of his texts—perhaps even the capitalization and rubrication—are preserved in the manuscripts.[104] The forty-plus manuscripts of Hoccleve's *Regiment of Princes* testify to his industry "in safeguarding the accuracy of exemplars and regulating their availability."[105] Hoccleve also glossed this text, as John Gower did the *Confessio amantis* and Gerson the *Monotessaron*. Even the Ellesmere manuscript may contain glosses that originated with Chaucer.[106] This appears even more likely now with the likelihood that Chaucer supervised one scribe over a long period—

Adam Pinkhurst, the very scribe who copied the Ellesmere manuscript.[107]

Obviously, we cannot assume that every copy reflects the author's original disposition of a text, or that every aid to reading originated with the author. Readers such as Jan Hus supplied most of the tools for accessing the works of Wyclif.[108] But authors too could and did supply apparatus.

Gerson's *Monotessaron* provides striking confirmation of this point, and our best example of a work for which Gerson himself provided an elaborate apparatus for the reader. Early editions contain a long list of "rubrics" and "little rubrics" at the beginning of the work that correspond to its different parts. Following each rubric, references indicate which Gospel chapters include the topic. For instance, the rubric "On the fast and temptation of Christ" is followed by the abbreviations for Matthew, chapter 4, Mark, chapter 1, and Luke, chapter 4. These rubrics served both as a table of contents for a reader who wanted to navigate the work and as a synopsis showing common Gospel passages. This lengthy apparatus likewise appears in most of the manuscripts.[109] Not a trace of it remains in the modern edition, though, and we begin to suspect the work of an industrious medieval reader.

Yet Gerson mentions this very apparatus in a letter to Jean Bassand in 1428. There, he observes that some authors have used considerations to comment on the Bible and the Gospels: "Among these, 150 rubrics on the *Monotessaron* were recently composed with little rubrics and suitable quotations. Then all of these were reduced to a few meters and terms, so that a person can run through the entire course of the Gospel from memory when he wishes with perfect ease, even in a moment, resting or walking, and not imagining [*phantasticans*] but grasping the meaning of the points."[110] The passive voice should leave no doubt that Gerson supplied this table of rubrics. He refers to them again in the *Compilation on the Magnificat* in a dialogue, the master taking care to point out again the work's division into rubrics and little rubrics.[111] By the phrase "a few meters and terms" he designates another piece of apparatus: the "Verses on the entire Monotessaron" ("Carmina super totum Monotessaron"), a mnemonic device of twenty-six lines containing a series of words to remind the reader of the basic plot of the Gospel (Figure 12). For example, the first three words—"Verbum, mutus, ave"—recall the prologue to John ("In the beginning was the Word"), the punishment of Zacharias (struck mute by Gabriel), and the angelic salutation to Mary. Above each word appears its number in the list, and above the number the abbreviation of the corresponding Gospel chapter: "Jo 1" for "Verbum," "L 1" for "mutus," and so on. So "mutus," the second word in the series, recalls the story of mute Zacharias found in Luke, chapter 1. Gerson may have taken the idea for these "Verses" from a

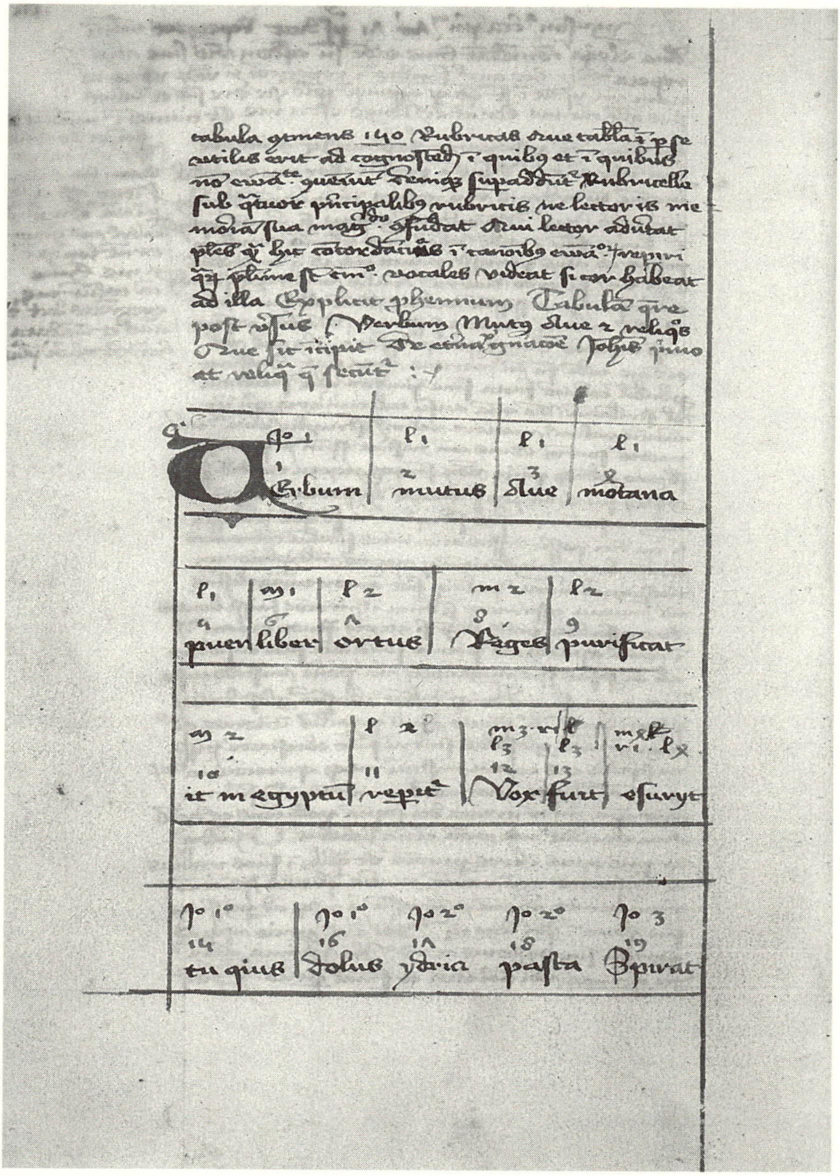

Figure 12. "Carmina super totum Monotessaron" (Verses on the Entire Monotessaron). Vienna, Österreichische Nationalbibliothek, Cod. lat. 4738, f. 18v. Used by permission.

work such as the *Metrical Summary of the Bible* (*Summarium biblicum met-ricum*) attributed to Alexander of Villedieu (d. c. 1250), which per-formed the exact same task for all the chapters of the Bible (so "Sex" for the six days of creation, "prohibet" for the prohibition of the fruit, "peccant" for Adam and Eve's sin, and so forth). We encounter yet another borrowing from the fathomless literary traditions that haunted a late medieval author.[112]

This apparatus of rubrics and verses served at least two purposes. It acted as a table of contents that turned the work into a reference tool; and it reduced the Gospel narrative to a series of key words to be memo-rized and so to aid the reader in contemplating the life of Christ. Just as the *Monotessaron* itself reconciled the complications of the four Gospels, its apparatus facilitated the use of the physical volume and provided an overview of the entire work. The longer a work, the more it needed such apparatus. Most manuscripts of *The Consolation of Theology* contain a table of contents at the beginning of the work, which must have been added very early in the transmission, perhaps by Gerson.[113]

The emphasis on memorization appears in the apparatus of other works and reinforces the continuing orality of a literary world now firmly anchored in the reading and meditation of books. The tree at the end of *On Ecclesiastical Power* summarizes the epilogue of the work, so per-forming a mnemonic function similar to the verses on the Monotes-saron.[114] Toward the beginning of the *Treatise on the Song of Songs*, Gerson provides "a decade of elegiacs" as a kind of summary of the work, here again "as an aid to memory." The rest of the work glosses these verses.[115] Even in the short tract *In Praise of Scribes of Healthy Doctrine* he reduces the twelve considerations to three lines of verse, no doubt once again to aid in memorization. For all his emphasis on books, Gerson apparently thought that something is not truly learned until it is memorized.

Authorizing the Text

As Gerson strove to make his texts more accessible and easier to consult and to remember, he strove to authorize them, to stamp his name on them. Katherine Kerby-Fulton has skillfully mapped out the literary strategies available to an author to reinforce authorship, such as internal references to the author or to the author's previous works, or the inclu-sion of the author as a speaker—all strategies frequently employed by Gerson.[116] My concern here is instead with the medium of manuscript publication and with one of the primary means available *outside* the text to control its reception: the authorial colophon. A thoughtful scribe invented the colophon in the far distant past to specify the details of copying. By Gerson's day, an important shift in colophon usage had occurred. At some point, probably in the twelfth century, whether in conscious or unconscious imitation of scribal practice, authors themselves began to place colophons at the end of their works, thereby indicating their authorship and often the date of completion. The inclusion of a date is a clue to the origin of the author's colophon from the scribal colophon. (Printers would later take over the colophon to supply their addresses.) Sometimes authors might include the place of composition as well. In effect, these were author signatures. This practice gained ground steadily after about 1250. Jean Destrez, who uncovered the pecia system by examining thousands of manuscripts, found in those same manuscripts forty-one different examples of author colophons from the period 1247 to 1364, all but one dated.[117] Yet this was still not general practice. Among the schoolmen, William of Ockham (d. 1347) and Wyclif (d. 1384) rarely dated their works. Chaucer never dated his.[118] The practice gained more general currency in the fifteenth century. Christine de Pizan dated and signed most of her works in colophons, and D'Ailly did so at least sometimes. Just as scribes increasingly supplied colophons to the texts they copied in the later Middle Ages, and as the signature itself became more common among secretaries and even monarchs, so more authors attempted to authorize their texts through this device.[119]

Certain patterns are detectable in Gerson's colophon usage. Early in his career at Paris and at Bruges, he dated few of his works and almost never supplied the place of composition, perhaps because he thought that this could be assumed, that his identity was wrapped up in Paris—or perhaps because he still lacked a clear sense of his own authorial identity. Very few of the French sermons from this period have dates, and their chronology remains in many cases a tangled web of conjecture and controversy. But after around 1401, Gerson often dated his works, and when he left Paris he also supplied the place of composition. This striking change seems to reflect his increasing sense of authorial identity, as well as his sense of dislocation outside Paris. Thanks to this practice we can identify works composed at Tarascon (1404), at Genoa (1407), at Reims (1408), at Constance (1415–1418), at Rattenberg (1418), and at Lyon (1420–1429). Indeed, his practice of signing and dating his works and of supplying the place of composition outside Paris provides much of the evidence for his biography.

The author's colophon followed from the increased participation of writers in the physical production of their works, especially autograph composition. It also testifies to a clear and growing sense of authorship and ownership of these texts. Scholars who stress the great transformation introduced by movable type point out that title pages appeared widely only with printed books.[120] (Many Gerson manuscripts have a list of contents at the front that served a similar purpose.) Yet the colophon allowed the author to supply all the essential information of a title page, and so to provide some means of control over the reception of a text, above all to claim authorship, and sometimes—now going beyond the title page—to localize it within the author's career. Medieval poets often wrote themselves into their works for the same reasons.[121] Long before print, authors sensed their own weakness and sought to control how an audience read and received their works; the author's colophon provided one way to do this.

The tract on Joan of Arc illustrates the range of information that could be included in a colophon to control the text's meaning. Through critical edition, we can also trace the effectiveness of these controls in circulation, how well they endured in the manuscripts. The text has an immediate surprise. The author's colophon actually appears at the beginning of the work, as a kind of introduction or title to the text in its short version (without the section on Joan's male clothing), which survives in twelve manuscripts. Seven of these have the following version of the "title element": "At Lyon, 1429, May 14, the vigil of Pentecost, after the sign received at Orléans by the raising of the English siege. Completed [*actum*] by the most famous and solemn professor of sacred theology, master Jean [Gerson],[122] chancellor of Paris, *On the Feat of the Maid and the Trust That Should Be Placed in Her.*"[123] Besides date and author, we learn the place of composition and the immediate historical context that motivated the work, Joan's victory at Orléans.

But can we really know that Gerson himself supplied this title? Presumably he did not call himself the "most famous and solemn professor of sacred theology." The long version, which survives in three manuscripts (not counting two manuscripts copied from the first edition of 1488), confirms this suspicion. The best manuscript of the group agrees with the title of the short version, but omits the suspect phrase: "A certain (work) compiled *On the Feat of the Maid and the Trust That Should be Placed in Her*, by Jean, chancellor of Paris. At Lyon, the year of the Lord 1429, May 14, the vigil of Pentecost, after the sign received at Orléans by the raising of the English siege."[124] Essentially, we have the same title element in both versions of the text, with the addition of a laudatory phrase describing Gerson in one manuscript family. This agreement between the two families provides very strong evidence that Gerson himself supplied this element. The form of his name in the best of these manuscripts, "Jean, chancellor of Paris," supports the attribution of the title element to Gerson himself. It was his customary signature. This same form (or occasionally "Jean, chancellor of the church of Paris") appears in at least twenty-one letters and in fourteen other works.[125] Besides all this, there is the obvious problem: Who else knew the date, place, and circumstances of the work's composition? We know for a fact that Gerson sometimes did supply long colophons of this kind, as in the following case: "Here ends the *Anagogy on the Word and Hymn 'Gloria in excelsis,'* by Jean, chancellor of Paris, at Lyon, the year 1428. It contains four principal parts, each of which has ten words or considerations, and in each line many little notes or little words with letters of the alphabet, going up to 190. The most reverend father A[madeus] then superintending, archbishop and count of Lyon, primate of Gaul, most benevolent protector of *our* sojourn" (my emphasis).[126] Gerson used the same final six-word phrase at the conclusion of the *Compilation on the Magnificat.*[127] The personal pronoun proves beyond any doubt that Gerson himself wrote those two colophons, and we can safely assume that he supplied them to other texts as well.

In the Joan tract, Gerson may have chosen a long, detailed title rather than a colophon because he wished the reader to understand the critical historical moment that produced this text and he expected it to be read with this in mind. And another attractive possibility presents itself here: that Gerson was sending the work out as a folded sheet, and that he was therefore labeling the physical form of the work for the reader, as one might expect at the beginning of a pamphlet. In any case, we have a real innovation: the turning of an authorial colophon into a title. He had done the same thing, it appears, in at least three other works: *On the Visitation of Prelates* (1408), the *Declaration of Truths That Must Be Believed for Salvation* (1416), and *In Praise of Scribes of Healthy Doctrine.*[128] Guillaume Tuysselet, who copied the Joan tract at St. Victor, disliked this arrangement. He erased the complete title element from the beginning of the text and placed it at the end where he thought it belonged, leaving only the name of the tract at the beginning: *On the Feat of the Maid and the Trust That Should Be Placed in Her.*

Placing controls on a text was one matter. Their "performance" in circulation was another. Authors lost control over a text once it circulated beyond their reach. And it was precisely this kind of title, outside the "official" text, that scribes were most tempted to shorten. The transmission of the title element offers a lesson in the hazards of publishing before print. Let us return to the short version of the text with its twelve manuscripts. Seven manuscripts, we saw, contain the following: "[Mss. ABEIMRT] At Lyon, 1429, May 14, the vigil of Pentecost, after the sign received at Orléans by the raising of the English siege. Completed by the most famous and solemn professor of sacred theology, master Jean [Gerson], chancellor of Paris, *On the Feat of the Maid and the Trust That Should Be Placed in Her.*" The other five manuscripts contain shorter versions:

[W] At Lyon, 1429, May 14, the vigil of Pentecost, after the sign received at Orléans by the raising of the English siege. A treatise of reverend Jean of Gerson, chancellor of Paris, *About the Maid and the Trust That Should Be Put in Her.*

[NN¹] Completed by the most famous and solemn professor of sacred theology, master Jean Cantis,[129] *On the Feat of the Maid and the Trust That Should Be Placed in Her.*

[T¹] A treatise of the outstanding doctor of sacred theology master Jean Gerson, chancellor of Paris, *On the Feat of a Certain Maid and the Trust That Should Be Placed in Her.*

[V] A treatise of master Jean Gerson *On the Feat of the Maid and the Trust That Should Be Placed in Her,* as follows in the raising of the English siege, etc.[130]

Manuscript W, which is very close to the original exemplar (as shown through critical edition), omits the adulatory phrase describing Gerson. Yet it also shortens the title from *On the Feat of the Maid* to *On the Maid,* a significant change in meaning. Two manuscripts (NN¹) corrupt the author's name nearly beyond recognition, four omit the date, and three drop all reference to the victory at Orléans. Three of these manuscripts also classify the work as a *tractatus,* a word that did not appear in the original title element.

The long version of the text tells a more interesting story than simple loss and corruption. Again the best manuscript gives: "[Ms. O] A certain (work) compiled *On the Feat of the Maid and the Trust That Should Be Placed in Her,* by Jean, chancellor of Paris. At Lyon, the year of the Lord 1429, May 14, the vigil of Pentecost, after the sign received at Orléans by the raising of the English siege." But all other manuscripts and the first edition (S) have a dramatic new title:

[L] A certain [work] compiled *On the Wonderful Victory of a Certain Maid, Taken from the Flocks of Sheep to Lead an Army of the King of the French in Battle Against the King of the English,* composed [*editus*] at Lyon by master Jean Gerson in the year of the Lord 1429, May 14, the vigil of Pentecost, after the sign received at Orléans by the raising of the English siege.

[H] [A work] compiled *On the Wonderful Victory of a Certain Maid, Taken from the Flocks of Sheep to Lead an Army of the King of the French in Battle Against the English,* by the chancellor of Paris.

[S] [A work] compiled by master Jean of Gerson *On the Wonderful Victory of a Certain Maid, Taken from the Flocks of Sheep to Lead an Army of the King of the French in Battle Against the English.*[131]

The phrase in LHS "taken from the flocks of sheep" was relocated from the secondary heading that introduces the additional section on

Joan's male attire: "Here follows a threefold truth in justification of the chosen maid, 'taken from the flocks of sheep' [Ps. 77:70], wearing men's clothing." But the rest of the title in LHS is a complete novelty without any support in the text itself. It dramatically changed how the text would be read and received. In this instance, a reader's meddling with the title element surpassed the omission of date and place (except for L) and reached to the title itself, presumably to give it more force. It seems that political pressures played a role. For some readers, saying that Joan had performed a "feat" (*factum*) or simply "accomplished" something was not enough. At some point, an *inventive* reader transformed the feat into a "wonderful victory." Creativity had a part too, probably in this same reader who reworked the psalm to emphasize the dramatic transformation of Joan from simple shepherdess to war captain. This is high theater. The "French" and the "English," whom Gerson had never named in the title or in the text (probably as part of his stated strategy to avoid boasting and partisanship), now appear as great contenders.

Many dangers and pitfalls awaited a text in circulation. Every single item of the original title element—date, place of composition, historical context of the work, even the author's name—was garbled or lost at some point in the transmission. Clearly, many Gerson titles suffered this kind of corruption. Another example is the tract *In Praise of Scribes of Healthy Doctrine*, known merely as *In Praise of Scribes* in all modern scholarly literature. These differences change the meaning in deep and important ways, and this was the hard reality of duplication by hand.

Yet the lesson from the Joan tract is equally the preservation of Gerson's original title in circulation. Eight of fifteen manuscripts, more than half, got everything right, twelve supplied the correct title (a thirteenth came close), and ten correctly supplied the date, place, and occasion.[132] The textual situation in print is instructive. Eisenstein argued that print allowed progress "from the corrupted copy to the improved edition."[133] But the first printed edition of this tract established a text incorrectly titled and lacking the date, place of composition, and all reference to the "sign" at Orléans. This title, supplied by an inventive reader, persevered for more than four hundred years as the correct version of the text and even today remains the most widely known version. The control of scribes over texts was nothing compared to the control of printers, who did not always improve the texts they reproduced.

Each text and colophon will tell a different story. Gerson used colophons to preserve a wide range of information about his texts. The colophon to *On Ecclesiastical Power* states that he published the work "more to inquire into the truth than to determine"—nearly the same phrase he used to describe the work in the January 1417 sermon cited at the beginning of this chapter.[134] A colophon to *On the Pleasure to Be Sought in the Divine Office* (1425) says that Gerson composed the work at the request of Brother Simon, "Bastard of Castellane," of the Celestines of Lyon. The colophon to *Against the Sect of the Flagellants*, finished on 18 July 1417, adds that the work was sent to Vincent Ferrer "around that time."[135] *On the Visitation of Prelates* opens with a title element similar to the Joan tract, specifying that the work is only a "brief and rude instruction . . . gathered from the sermon given at Reims and from different schedules and dicta."[136]

Beyond the date and the author, we see in these examples Gerson telling the reader how the text should be read, at whose request he wrote, where he sent the work, even what sources he used. We learned from the colophon to *On Ecclesiastical Power* how it was originally published. Some manuscripts of *On the Visitation of Prelates* add a colophon stating that the work was corrected at the Council of Constance.[137] This colophon contains another clue about what it meant to publish before print. While the cost equation of print discouraged authorial meddling, scribal culture allowed, even encouraged, an author to correct and change a text at will. Authors like Petrarch, hovering over their private copies, corrected jealously and obsessively. Gerson, with his usual facility, finished his works and sent them on their way. But he sometimes came back to them. I explore now what he did next.

Correcting and Revising

A major advance of twentieth-century scholarship was the recognition that, like most other fourteenth- and fifteenth-century authors, Gerson sometimes revised works that were already circulating. One can see such revision almost everywhere: Gower revising the *Confessio amantis*, Thomas à Kempis developing the *Imitation of Christ*, Christine de Pizan "frequently chang[ing] her mind . . . and recast[ing] her texts."[138] Scholars of vernacular literature have sometimes emphasized the continuous nature of this revision process, the fact that it did not lead to different editions of a text, that instead different versions of a text "leaked" into circulation. "There is no 'first edition,' released for publication by the author," writes Derek Pearsall, "followed after a due interval by a 'second edition' containing his revisions."[139]

This claim may hold as a general principle for vernacular writers, but it has little application for Gerson and other scholarly authors, who nearly always revised in exactly the way that Pearsall says did not happen. We seem to have stumbled onto a fault line separating the publishing practices in two worlds of literature that cries out for further scrutiny.[140] Often, Gerson revised simply by expanding a text, usually at the end, by anything from a few lines to another major section. In such cases, Gerson probably possessed his own original copy, possibly even something like an "author's book," an original autograph copy as we find with Petrarch and the Italian humanists.[141] He did not correct continuously. Instead, he did so at specific moments, then released his text to the public.

The tract on Joan of Arc well illustrates the process. Gerson added to this work not once but twice, and in doing so he left the original text almost completely untouched. First, after he had completed the text but before circulating it, some new proofs of Joan's authenticity occurred to him, which he then supplied—a mere paragraph and little more than an afterthought. (He especially emphasized that she was not looking for personal gain.) He then circulated the tract in this form (twelve of fifteen manuscripts have this early version).[142] At some point, probably in the next day or two, another objection to Joan presented itself: her male clothing. Perhaps an early reader mentioned it to him. So he added a completely new section, preceded by a rubric: "Here follows a threefold truth in justification of the chosen maid, 'taken from the flocks of sheep' [Ps. 77:70], wearing men's clothing."[143] In the course of adding this new section, he may or may not have written out a completely new copy of the text. The manuscripts do not unlock this secret. They do show that he left the original text completely unchanged except for its last two words, *Deus Amen*, which he deleted. This makes perfect sense. Since those words had indicated the end of the work, and since a major new section now followed, they no longer belonged. His revision to the original text apparently extended no further than this minor change.[144]

Gerson performed this kind of expansion quite frequently.[145] Petrucci has identified a similar practice in the "progressive text" of the early Italian humanists.[146] (Such practice has now returned, to an extreme, with the electronic texts that populate the Internet.) Autograph composition encouraged this practice. In the case of the tract on Joan, Gerson must have retained a copy of the text after circulating the first version. Such expansion at the end was easiest, requiring no new copy. The style of the work, a rough shorthand, betrays swiftness in the original composition as well, perhaps even a sense of urgency. Joan had just won a major victory, and he wanted to circulate the tract rather than polish it. He designed it to rally support for Joan at that time, not unlike an editorial today in support of a candidate who has just won an important primary election. Gerson simply added text at the end, perhaps just filling out the page. He was not revising or retracting opinions but supplementing them. Of course, such revision put a second version of the work into circulation. Critical edition has shown that most readers had access only to the short version until the judges at Joan's nullification trial (1456) gave the long version wider currency as part of the trial record.

Another kind of revision involved the simple correction of a text found in circulation. In 1425, for example, Gerson corrected his famous 1408 sermon on the pastoral office (*Bonus pastor*).[147] In one sense, of course, this was not revision at all, since the goal presumably was to provide a copy that reproduced the original words, not to change them. But there was nothing to keep an author from going beyond simple correction of scribal faults to revision of the original words themselves. It was a line easily crossed, and if a legible new fair copy resulted, why resist? In any case, how was an author without an autograph or author's copy at hand to know his original words? Such revision may violate our sense of the permanence of published texts, but it could hardly have disturbed medieval writers.

To illustrate this kind of revision, I return to the newly discovered letter of 1422 discussed in Chapter 1.[148] On 30 October 1422, Gerson wrote a letter-treatise to Guillaume Minaud, a medical doctor who had recently entered the Grande Chartreuse and had asked Gerson whether it was permissible to moderate the strict Carthusian regime in certain cases. Less than two weeks later, Gerson sent a second letter to Guillaume. The letter has just a few lines but includes striking details. Gerson tells Guillaume that he has just found at Lyon a copy of *On Mystical Theology*, which he has not seen "for many years"; that he has corrected it "without [help of] another exemplar"; and that he is sending it to him for further corrections (presumably from copies that Gerson knew, or assumed, existed at the Grande Chartreuse). He encourages Guillaume to return the work and to indicate necessary corrections in this or in his other works, so that he can make the corrections or "compose more carefully." This phrase suggests that Gerson foresaw the possibility of making substantive revisions, it seems, not merely corrections to a faulty text. A critical edition of *On Mystical Theology* has shown that Gerson did in fact correct this text, presumably after receiving a corrected version from Guillaume. But it also shows that (whatever his earlier intention) he apparently limited the corrections to what he considered scribal errors. The reference to correction from an exemplar supplies another important piece of evidence. It suggests that Gerson normally corrected with a second exemplar at hand, but not here. At times in his life, as we saw in Chapter 1, he did not possess copies of his own works. For us, the incident points to one of the great challenges of medieval publishing as authors experienced it: faulty texts circulating beyond their control. Correcting a text was no easy matter. Ideally, an author would possess an authoritative copy as well. In Gerson's case, this was not always possible.

I said that the letter to Guillaume allowed for the possibility of substantive revision beyond the correction of scribal mistakes. We have very little evidence at all that Gerson ever radically modified his works. Most of his revision took the form of his changes to the tract on Joan of Arc, simple expansion at the end, or simple correction. A third kind of revision we may call amplification, the elaboration or fleshing out of a pre-existing passage. One case involves these same two letters to Guillaume. After the first letter was already circulating, Gerson took a paragraph from the second letter and copied it into the first, beneath the closing date—another case of simple expansion. Then he circulated this second version. Still not done, he amplified the same paragraph to make it more suitable for a general audience. This third version then circulated.[149] A brief sample of these amplifications will give their flavor. In the second version, Gerson restates his counsels to Guillaume from the previous letter. Here is the last:

Original version: "I have exhorted you . . . finally, not to omit delivering the special prayers in one's cell that are under the special ordinance of the Church, unless perhaps by counsel of the greater."

Now here is the amplification in the third version:

Amplified version: "I have exhorted you . . . finally, not to omit *offering and* delivering the prayers in one's cell that *fall* under the special ordinance of the Church, unless perhaps *this should happen* by counsel *and permission* of the *superior.*"[150]

A word change here, an extra phrase there, and a clearer text—but no substantial change in meaning.

Another interesting case concerns *Against the Superstitious Observance of Days, Especially Innocents,* originally a letter (which survives in only one manuscript) that Gerson transformed into a tract (which survives in more than eleven manuscripts) by changing the introduction and conclusion. This tract survives in two versions, short and long, though it is unclear whether Gerson himself was responsible for both or whether, for example, he produced only the long version (which contains an additional attack on the observances of the day of St. Paul), which a copyist later truncated.[151] These examples of expansion and amplification could be multiplied, and no doubt more await discovery in the manuscripts.

To sum up: Gerson usually but not always kept his compositions at hand after publishing them; he sometimes added sections at the end, but he seldom modified what he had already written. He probably made additions by hand. As we would expect, his revisions betray his sense of genre, the need to adapt the message to occasion and audience. Like many other writers, he frequently revised and corrected faulty copies. But he rarely bothered with line-by-line revision, he did not pore over old compositions, and he revised his Latin only to make it clearer and more precise, not more Ciceronian. This is all in perfect harmony with his failure to execute great literary projects at Lyon. Instead, he always moved on to other topics. In the end, this must be one of the most striking features of Gerson as a writer—his voracious appetite for new topics and the speed with which he could treat them. But even more important for us now, he exemplifies perhaps better than anyone else the range and possibilities of self-conscious manuscript publication.

Once Gerson had prepared his works for readers and sent them on their way, they took different paths, some to relative obscurity, many to wide readership. The following chapter attempts to uncover the hidden springs and mechanisms that launched one of the greatest manuscript distributions in European history.

Chapter 7

Publishing Before Print (2)
From Coterie Readership to Massive Market

When Étienne Delaruelle described the fifteenth century as "the century of Gerson," he was effectively summarizing claims that could be
found in a century of scholarship. Recent studies have detected Gerson's
long reach in spheres never before imagined. A mystery long surrounded the sixth tapestry of the famous *Lady and the Unicorn* cycle (c.
1480–1500) that now hangs in the Cluny in Paris. Since the 1920s, scholars have agreed that the first five tapestries present an allegory of the
five senses. But the sixth tapestry, with its puzzling motto "A mon seul
desir," does not seem to fit. Jean-Patrice Boudet has recently made a persuasive argument that the solution to this riddle lies in Gerson's notion
of the heart as a sixth sense. For his painting *The Ecstasy of St. Cecilia*,
Raphael drew on Gerson's theories of music, which the great artist had
imbibed from his spiritual adviser, Pietro da Lucca.[1] And the image of
the Holy Family that became so common in European art took inspiration from Gerson, who campaigned at Constance for a feast of the marriage of Mary and Joseph.[2] Surely other examples will surface to confirm
his deep impact on European culture.[3]

Yet despite everything that we have learned, all such claims for Gerson's historical importance have entirely overlooked a category of material evidence that could support them. No study has succeeded in
showing that what distinguishes Gerson as a medieval author is his fantastic success, measured by manuscripts, in reaching a wide and varied
international readership, a process that began while he was still alive. In
retrospect, this must be judged one of the most extraordinary accomplishments of any fifteenth-century writer. Moreover, it challenges current models of medieval communication, which largely stress the
limitations of manuscript culture rather than its possibilities.

To illustrate the problem, let us take the case of Thomas Aquinas,
another university theologian with many readers. The catalogue of the
Leonine Commission, still ongoing, has uncovered more than 2,700 different manuscripts of his works, including 286 of the *Summa theologiae*

alone (mostly partial copies). Many other works soon became academic classics, and by his canonization in 1323 even the Franciscans, his earliest and strongest critics, had become enthusiastic readers. Gerson himself may have contributed to a fifteenth-century revival of interest in Aquinas, which continued to the end of the century.[4]

More than any other medieval author, Aquinas benefited from the pecia system.[5] By the mid-thirteenth century when he wrote, this piece system of copying was just emerging and helped to meet surging demand for his works. Yet herein lies a clue to the limits of his audience. While it made possible an extraordinary circulation, the system catered to a single group, university students and masters. By one calculation, 80 percent of the surviving copies of his *Summa contra Gentiles* stem from a single exemplar produced in the shop of the official university stationer, Guillaume de Sens.[6] Written in heavily abbreviated Gothic script, ruled into double columns, and then rented out in individual quires from official stationers, these exemplars illustrate beautifully the strength of scholarly learning in this period, its formal and material organization, as well as its limitations, particularly the narrowness of the audience. Besides university readers, friars and monks read Aquinas's works, but few others: "relatively few high ecclesiastics," according to J. N. Hillgarth, "and, among the laity . . . some jurists and doctors." For the "intelligent lay person," who did not attend university, he had no appeal at all.[7]

Few schoolmen did. By contrast, to a notable degree Gerson reached lay groups and other audiences beyond the schools. Certain cultural conditions favored him. One factor in his success has to do with the "supply side" of reading, the changes in written culture noted earlier, some of them quite dramatic. Scholars are now beginning to realize that the invention of movable type was only the culmination of technological innovations that transformed the nature of late medieval book production. Print did not create demand, it responded to it. Other changes affected the "demand side," readers themselves.[8] Though exact figures are lacking, we know that more people could read. Primary schools in many cities were now offering basic instruction to urban dwellers.[9] New universities sprang up throughout Europe beginning in 1348, followed by a second wave of foundations after the outbreak of the Schism in 1378: Prague in 1348, Vienna in 1365 (refounded in 1384), Erfurt in 1379 (refounded in 1392), Heidelberg in 1386, Cologne in 1388, Leipzig in 1409. New universities gathered books, together accounting for as much as 20 percent of book production in Germany in the fourteenth century.[10] Among religious orders, the Carthusians earned a reputation as the "book order." Similarly, the Brethren of the Common Life built impressive libraries in the Low Countries and northern Germany.[11]

These changes fostered a broader, more diverse readership and under-lay Gerson's international success.

Yet changes in material and written culture and even in the fabric of society do not explain Gerson's "success," or anyone else's for that matter. The conditions existed for an intellectual to find readers beyond the schools, but Gerson himself capitalized on the opportunity. We must never lose sight of the elementary fact that Gerson became the most popular contemporary writer of the fifteenth century because he had felt the pulse of readers, he knew what many wanted and needed, and he adapted his message to them. It is striking how often Gerson wrote in response to questions. He succeeded because he listened to every one of them. In Chapter 2, I mentioned a quodlibetal session held at the Celestine convent in Paris, where instead of fielding academic questions in an impressive display of learning, he took questions from monks.[12] At Lyon, he responded one by one to a long string of questions over several years from Oswald of Bavaria at the Grande Chartreuse. His answers survive only because the Grande Chartreuse kept them, not because Gerson circulated them.[13] One could argue that no fifteenth-century author knew the fifteenth-century public better than Gerson.

My focus now, however, extends beyond both the cultural matrix that made possible a wide readership and the appeal of the works themselves, to the specific strategies that Gerson employed to find his audience. We who see international reputations made and lost from week to week in the popular media should not underestimate how difficult it was before print to command any kind of general audience beyond a close circle of readers. The challenges facing a medieval author in reaching a diverse international audience were profound and structural, even in a period of great expansion in written culture. Books and new texts spread slowly. General knowledge of a new text sometimes came much later than we would imagine.[14] A reader might hear of a text but never find it. Searches for exemplars could take years; indeed, the difficulty of locating texts probably accounts for the miscellaneous character of many manuscript volumes, rather than any intelligent strategy by the compiler.[15] Nicholas of Dinkelsbühl (d. 1433), the most important Viennese theologian of the fifteenth century, illustrates the great difficulty of reaching across regional boundaries. Of the fourteen hundred manuscripts of his works, only the tiniest fraction circulated outside the Holy Roman Empire. More than four hundred manuscripts survive today in Munich, just three in Paris.[16] Though Nicholas was a colossus in the empire, readers did not know his name anywhere else, and most of his works were never printed.[17]

Medieval authors began with readers in a close circle. Even at the peak of Gerson's fame, with his works being read as far away as Bohemia and even Sweden, he addressed many of his works to monks a short distance away at the Grande Chartreuse. Understanding Gerson's readership means knowing these initial readers, his closest contacts who began the early circulation of his works. But reaching an international audience required more than a painfully slow diffusion through the usual channels. We should start, then, with a basic distinction between these earliest local readers and the networks—I shall call them distribution circles—that opened the way to an international audience. Three distribution circles were crucial for Gerson: the Council of Constance (1414–1418), the Council of Basel (1431–1449), and the network of Carthusian houses in Western Europe.

German scholars have long stressed the importance of the fifteenth-century councils as bookmarkets and centers of diffusion, and have relied on Gerson to make their case. Yet we still have no clear account of how this diffusion occurred, or of its patterns, or of its true impact on Gerson's readership. The councils convened to resolve great crises. But they were likewise great assemblies of intellectuals gathered for years at a stretch, far longer than earlier councils, and at a time of extraordinary growth in book production. The Fourth Lateran Council (1215) and the Councils of Lyon (1245 and 1274), Vienne (1311–1312), and Pisa (1409) lasted weeks or months. The Council of Constance met for three and a half years—long enough, arguably, to create new reading networks that both consumed and inspired new writings. Contemporaries sensed its historical importance and unusual duration. Gerson himself thought that no other council equaled it in length.[18] There, he had a captive audience ready to spread his works to the rest of Europe. This historic opportunity came in the prime of his career. The Council of Basel, which followed Gerson's death by two years and lasted for eighteen, gave his works still greater diffusion.

In one sense, these two councils were fortunate historical accidents for Gerson. The third ingredient, an international monastic order, was always present in some form in medieval society. The Carthusians, however, rose to prominence very late. Founded in the early twelfth century, they still had only thirty-nine monasteries by 1300. Then their great surge began. In Germany they grew from just five houses in 1300 to fifty-three by 1500. We imagine their houses like the Grande Chartreuse, the mother house situated in a remote Alpine valley, the picture of monastic isolation and loneliness. But later medieval foundations took root in urban centers.[19] Copying was central to their way of life. Within a few decades their houses built large and important libraries that the mendicants might have envied. By the fifteenth century, the average collection held 884 volumes and added ten new titles yearly, many through purchase rather than copying.[20] The Carthusians had many authors among

their own ranks, but their favorite author was Gerson, the consoling doctor of souls who answered all their questions and reaped the whirlwind
of this copying energy. Long after Gerson had died, the prior of the
Charterhouse at Basel considered it noteworthy that he had once met
the great Gerson.[21]

The contact with the Grande Chartreuse offers a useful lesson and
starting point. The road to a massive international readership began
locally. Then, through local and international channels, Gerson's readers slowly turned into more than the sum of their parts, a complex international audience. This is the process that I hope to reconstruct.

Coteries, Imagined Readers, and Distribution Circles

Despite Gerson's advantages as a theologian and as chancellor, no
author could circumvent the technological limitations of manuscript
publication—though the use of the *pronuntiatio* shows that they were trying! At first, after coming to believe that they had readers, medieval writers could count only on a clearly defined, close circle of readers, what
Katherine Kerby-Fulton—speaking of Chaucer, Hoccleve, and Langland—has called "coterie readership."[22] Chaucer wrote for a small "literary community," fellow clerks in the royal civil service.[23] Christine de
Pizan dedicated works in expensive presentation copies to powerful
nobles.[24] Boccaccio distributed works through close friends.[25] Such practices extend back to the Roman world and seem to characterize nearly
all publishing before print.[26]

The notion of coterie readership gives us a way to talk about the complexity of Gerson's audience. He reached not one coterie or public but
many, across a broad spectrum. His ability to enter into so many different coteries and conversations is really the key for all preliminary understanding of the circulation and transmission of his works.[27] It seems
there were few circles Gerson could not enter. His tract on the *Roman de
la Rose* took part in a literary and moral debate with the humanists Pierre
and Gontier Col and Jean de Montreuil.[28] Around the same time, Gerson wrote *La mendicité spirituelle* for a pious, elderly virgin named Agnes
of Auxerre.[29] A chronicler tells us that he delivered his famous 1405 sermon on political reform (*Vivat rex*) at the hall of the queen in the presence of the kings of Navarre and Sicily, and the four powerful dukes of
Berry, Burgundy, Orléans, and Bourbon. (The king was suffering from
a bout of madness at the time.)[30] The works on the Schism and Church
polity contributed to a conversation among ecclesiastical lawyers and
schoolmen, and most can be tied to a specific time, place, and discussion.[31] The tracts on magic and "superstition" respond in perhaps every
case to specific incidents and address clearly defined, usually local audi-

ences, sometimes individuals.[32] He addressed *In Praise of Scribes of Healthy Doctrine*, *On the Examination of Teachings*, and many other works of the Lyon period to the Grande Chartreuse and to the Celestines of Lyon.[33] The tract against the Hussites sparked a polemical battle in Bohemia and circulated in manuscripts in Prague, reaching audiences his other works could not; often, this work circulated with other works on the Hussites.[34] Gerson took his campaign for devotion to St. Joseph directly to the duke of Berry.[35] On and on the list could go.

Gerson's introductory letters to works that he sent to readers (what the critical edition calls *lettres d'envoi*) provide crucial evidence of these early coteries because they document the actual delivery of texts to individuals.[36] He sent various works to correspondents in this way: to Charles VII through his tutor-physician Jean Cadart, the dukes of Orléans and Berry, bishops and archbishops such as Guillaume de Chalançon and Amadeus of Talaru, friends like Pierre d'Ailly and Gérard Machet, popular preachers like Vincent Ferrer, Carthusian and Celestine priors and monks, his brothers and sisters, and many more. Sometimes we know of more than one recipient; he sent the *Tripartite on Theological Astrology*, for example, to both D'Ailly and the dauphin.[37] In most cases, Gerson assumed that the recipients would distribute his works. When he wrote his primer on the Ten Commandments that he intended for the laity of France in general, he used bishops to circulate it, and his letter to one of these bishops survives.[38] Gerson also responded to requests for his works. We saw that Louis, duke of Orléans, requested the Latin sermon preached at Tarascon in January 1404 just days after its delivery.[39] At Lyon, Gerson regularly sent works to monks at the Grande Chartreuse who had asked for them. Chapter 1 details other strategies he devised to make his works available to readers, such as compiling lists and depositing copies of his works in Celestine and Carthusian houses.

Given the great numbers of Gerson manuscripts and the apparent demand for his writings, one might have expected to find some evidence of a bespoke trade in his works, if not an outright industry. Aquinas had the pecia system, and the English poets writing in London could oversee the entire production of their manuscripts in Paternoster Row.[40] In fifteenth-century Italian communes such as Florence, *cartolai* or stationers were now producing books in expectation of sales rather than waiting for orders from customers, apparently the first in Europe to do so.[41] By Gerson's day, however, the pecia system had long since vanished from Paris, so utterly that it took heroic feats of scholarship to recall that it ever existed.[42] Commercial scriptoria had appeared in Paris by the early thirteenth century on the Left Bank in the rue Neuve Notre-Dame and around the church of Saint-Séverin. Some works of Gerson could have been copied there, but these scriptoria primarily attracted readers look-

Figure 13. Gerson delivering *La montagne de contemplation* to two female religious. Brussels, Bibliothèque royale, Ms. 9305–6, f. 76r. Used by permission.

ing for vernacular Bibles, chronicles, moral treatises like the *Somme le roi*, and especially romances.[43]

It seems we should imagine the initial distribution of Gerson's works as we see it in a later copy of *La montagne de contemplation*, which shows Gerson delivering the text to two women in religious habit, who then engage in prayer before the crucified Christ. This powerful image captures two essential elements of the market in Gerson's works: the personal delivery of a text to a coterie of nonacademic readers, and the potential impact of the work—hence, why readers wanted to read it in the first place (Figure 13).

The local audience, then, provided the initial readership. Nonetheless, established authors such as Gerson in his maturity knew that their works might reach unknown readers and even future generations. Each of these individual conversations with a historically identifiable audience, the small coterie, thus afforded the chance to address a much larger imagined audience. As with contemporary Middle English poets, we find (in Maura Nolan's phrase) a "narrowing and broadening of the audience" in Gerson's works.[44] We hear him addressing individuals whose names we often know, but the further we read, another audience comes into focus, larger but usually nameless and indeterminate.

The text itself, its theme and content, provides the link from the historical to the imagined audience. By showing the two sisters in an act of devotion, the image from *La montagne de contemplation* may help us to understand why distant, unknown readers might have wanted to read this text. Gerson addresses his sisters in the opening lines of the work, but he clearly understood that this work might speak to a broad and growing readership for devotional texts. We can see the same crossover from real to imagined audience in works on magic, "superstition," and astrology. Gerson sent the *Tripartite on Theological Astrology* to the dauphin in November 1419, partly out of fear that astrologers still had too much sway at court.[45] And he wrote *Against the Superstition of a Sculptured Lion* to criticize the use of an amulet by the dean of the medical faculty at Montpellier.[46] Yet beyond these local circumstances, these and other such works were participating in lively cultural debates about the relationship between astrology and theology and about marginal devotional practices. We begin to understand why each work survives in about twenty to twenty-five manuscripts.[47]

Occasionally, Gerson left traces of his intent to reach both real and potential readers. The first line of *On Conducting Oneself During the Schism*, written at Bruges in 1398, specifies that he is writing *especially*—not only?—for readers in Flanders.[48] A manuscript of his first letter to Guillaume Minaud on religious observance states that, although it was sent to Minaud, it "concerns all religious."[49] The title element to *In Praise of Scribes of Healthy Doctrine* relates that Gerson addressed the work "to the Celestines and Carthusians," but quickly adds "nay rather to all the Church generally"—a marvelous instance of this waking recognition of a broader public even as he addressed specific historical readers.[50] Gerson successfully reached beyond the coterie in every case: each work survives in about fifty copies.[51]

For now, these imaginary audiences must remain shadowy and vague. We have more questions than answers. When Gerson speaks of "the Church," whom exactly does he have in mind? When he imagined his widest possible audience, whom did he picture? How much blending and overlap did he envisage among different categories of readers? Clerks and laypersons both? Elites and the emerging middle class? Would he himself have known the answers to such questions? Two principles seem to apply. First, we should not assume that Gerson always did imagine a wide audience for his works, especially for his local opinion pieces. I suppose that he would have been stunned to see the ultimate scale of readership for a work such as *On Contracts* (more than sixty surviving manuscripts). Second, we should see the imaginary audience as proceeding from the local, historical audience: from known to unknown.

The crossover in the text itself from a historical to an imagined audience might make possible and encourage a general readership, but works that targeted a larger audience still needed conduits or mediating structures to break out of the small coterie. In the fifteenth century, the best way for this to happen was for a work to make its way into what I am calling a "distribution circle."[52] In fact, this strategy seems to belong to any developed manuscript culture. Biblical scholars long puzzled why the author of the book of Revelation addresses himself to "the Seven Churches" in Asia Minor (Ephesus, Smyrna, and so forth). Medieval writers wondered too: "Perhaps [the churches] illustrate the sevenfold spirit," says the Ordinary Gloss on Revelation, chapter 1.[53] Yet there never were just seven churches in Asia, and the author of Revelation overlooked more important ones nearby. Why? In 1905, William Ramsay proposed the solution that is still generally accepted today: each one was located in "a natural center of communication" linked together in "a sort of inner ring circle round the Province" traveled by private messengers.[54] The cities were the nodal points of a provincial postal system.

We can see clear examples of fifteenth-century distribution circles in the reception of Carthusian authors such as Jacobus de Paradiso (1381–1465) and Denys the Carthusian. Denys's manuscripts circulated among the Carthusians, of course, as well as among the Canons Regular, reformed Benedictines and Franciscans, and Croziers. These groups account for all but a tiny fraction of the 294 surviving manuscripts.[55] A study of the reception of Jacobus's works, which survive in an impressive 450 manuscripts, uncovered a similar pattern: distribution mainly to the Carthusians, to reformed Benedictines, to the Windesheim Brethren, and to a group of masters at the University of Erfurt.[56] According to the author of the critical study of Jacobus, the interest of these readers was "fundamentally determined and motivated by [their] group identity."[57] Each author benefited from the fact that the initial coterie, the local Carthusians, also belonged to a distribution circle. The Carthusians, who supported a general reform of the Church, had strong links to the reforming orders, hence to other distribution circles. Motivated by common goals and ideals, these reading networks intersected and shared copies of works that reinforced those ideals. The reformed Benedictines and the Canons Regular participated closely together, even sending joint envoys to the Council of Basel in 1432.[58] Basel seems to mark a meeting place for all of these groups, including the masters of Erfurt, where members of religious orders had always had a prominent role among the faculty.[59] We see, then, a crosshatched pattern, an initial coterie of readers feeding into a distribution circle, which branches out to intersect with other reader networks sharing common interests.[60]

We shall see similar patterns in the reception of Gerson's works, and far more complex ones. Yet to arrive at a historical understanding of his readership and to come to terms with his legacy, we must appreciate both his successes and his failures in this regard. Before turning to the successes, among the failures we must count three works that formed the basis of my investigation in Chapter 4: *On the Two Kinds of Logic* (three manuscripts), *Against the Curiosity of Students* (two), and *On the Modes of Signifying* (two).[61] We cannot blame Jean the Celestine, who mentioned all three works in both of his lists. Why then did they fail to find readers?

The most likely answer, it seems, is not that contemporaries were uninterested in the topics but that the manuscripts never broke out of the close circle around Gerson. All of the surviving copies originated in France, most in Paris. Arsenal Ms. 523, which contains both early lectures, dates from 1408 and is one of the earliest surviving manuscripts of Gerson's works, probably connected in some way to Jean the Celestine.[62] This manuscript and the only other copy of *Against the Curiosity of Students* survived at the College of Navarre. Both copies of *On the Modes of Signifying* likewise have close links to Gerson. One manuscript (Marseille, BM, Ms. 241), which contains works written from 1424 to 1429, belonged to the Charterhouse of Villeneuve near Avignon. It dates from very shortly after Gerson's death, possibly even from the same year, 1429.[63] The copyist of the second manuscript (Paris, BnF, Ms. lat. 17488) had access to original pieces and perhaps autographs.

For all we can tell, these manuscripts bore no fruit. Gerson never sent these works to the Carthusians. They never reached Germany. No one copied them at Constance or Basel, and as a result these works did not share in the formation of Gerson's legacy in Central Europe. It thus happens that certain features of Gerson's indictment of the schoolmen had to await rediscovery until the early sixteenth century. Not one of these works appeared in any of the "complete" fifteenth-century editions of 1483 (Cologne), 1488–1489 (Strasbourg, Nuremberg, Basel), or 1494 (Strasbourg). (In the Low Countries in 1480, *On the Two Kinds of Logic* was printed at Gouda in a small volume together with a few other lectures, but this printing escaped the notice of later editors.)[64] Finally, in 1502, Matthias Schürer and Jakob Wimpheling, searching "the innermost recesses of the school of Paris and various places in France," located these texts and included them in a volume of Gerson's works "not printed before."[65] The humanists then picked them up, read them with glee (for the great Gerson had anticipated them), and cast them like stones at the schoolmen.

The circulation of a medieval work—its "success" or "failure"—owed something to its content and its appeal to readers. But the medieval book trade was never a truly free and open market. How many fifteenth-century readers even knew that Gerson had written these works? Jean the Celestine put them in his lists; but what good would that do a reader in Germany, where most of the lists circulated? In Gerson's case, it seems that a work's "popularity" (measured by surviving manuscripts) depended heavily on its participation in three great distribution circles that I shall now examine in turn: the Council of Constance, the European Charterhouse network, and the Council of Basel.

The First Distribution Circle: The Council of Constance

The first great opportunity for distribution came with the Council of Constance. Convened to resolve the Schism, to suppress heresy, and to institute various reforms, the council gave Gerson the perfect occasion: a multiyear gathering of ecclesiastical dignitaries, of university masters, and of nobles from all over Europe, and, as it turned out, a bookmarket for texts of all kinds. As the weeks turned into months and years, the participants—perhaps 18,000 strong, counting retainers and escorts, in a town of just over 5,000[66]—took time to gather and copy works. New reading patterns emerged. Exchanges between participants from Italy and from northern Europe even led to the creation and spread of a new style of handwriting.[67] Great discoveries were made. The early humanists had been searching desperately for a complete copy of Quintilian's *Institutes of Oratory*, which they knew only in a mutilated version or in a florilegium (the version that Gerson knew). They finally succeeded at Constance when Poggio Bracciolini uncovered one on an excursion to the ancient collection at St. Gall.[68] But the appetite for classics was meager compared to that for theological, legal, and moral works.[69] In sum, the assembly electrified intellectuals, who understood the unique opportunity they had to acquire books they would never have seen otherwise.[70] Gerson shared their enthusiasm. To his great delight, following the council he found a treatise by Matthew of Cracow in Germany (probably *On the Celebration of Mass*) and had it copied.[71]

But Gerson did not collect books, he wrote them, and the council marked a turning point in the circulation of his works. At least a few—probably *On Mystical Theology* and certainly *On Drawing Children to Christ*—had reached the Low Countries before 1415.[72] But we have no evidence at all for circulation in the heart of the Empire before the council. Germany and Italy at this period were experiencing a huge surge in manuscript production. French scriptoria had endured a catastrophic decline in the fourteenth century due to the Hundred Years' War and the Black Death. By the early fifteenth century, with civil war splitting France in two, professional illuminators abandoned Paris, and the book trade ground to a halt. The country limped slowly along and began a slow recovery only after 1450, while England, after losing nearly all of its Continental holdings at the end of the Hundred Years' War (1453), fell headlong into its own thirty-year civil war.[73] The Council of Constance benefited Gerson, then, not just because intellectuals flocked there and many wanted to read and to copy his works, but because it introduced those works into regions that were producing three times as many manuscripts as France was.[74] His works found new audiences and spread to new readers, beginning the transition to a massive market.

Gerson certainly saw the opportunity at hand. At Constance, he seized on the chance to correct and distribute old works, to deliver and publish nine sermons, and to write no fewer than twenty-eight original compositions, sometimes publicly pronouncing them.[75] He was certainly not the only participant who tried to exploit the council in this way. Yet the fate of those attempts is instructive. We saw that a few months before Gerson arranged for the pronunciation of *On Ecclesiastical Power,* D'Ailly had two works pronounced on the very same topic. Yet while Gerson's tract survives in around eighty copies, the two works of D'Ailly survive in perhaps ten each.[76] Other authors did not fare even that well.[77] Dietrich von Niem revised his tract on Church reform (1410) for distribution at the council, but the revision survives in just three copies.[78] The council was an opportunity, not an agency. An author still needed willing readers.

Gerson had tried something like this before, on a much smaller scale. In 1408, he attended a regional synod at Reims. In his famous sermon on the pastoral office (29 April, *Bonus pastor*), he called for the publication of tracts that would instruct clergy in the basic outline of the faith, the Ten Commandments, and the sacraments.[79] The very next day, he compiled a tract *On the Visitation of Prelates and the Spiritual Charge of Priests.* It seems that before leaving he assembled a volume with the sermon, the tract on visitation, his *Opus in Three Parts* (he probably had this in mind in the sermon), his letter-treatise on reserved cases, and the synodal statutes. Gilbert Ouy has suggested that the manuscript is a dossier prepared by Gerson for one of the prelates who attended the synod.[80]

Thus by the time he arrived at Constance, Gerson had some experience in using large assemblies to broadcast his works. He had some help at Constance even before he arrived. In 1414, D'Ailly presented an agenda of issues for the council to address, in the course of which he recommended Gerson's *Opus in Three Parts* and his tract on visitation from the Council of Reims. After being corrected and examined, he suggested, these works should be shared with metropolitans and bishops for publication throughout their dioceses "in word and in writing."[81]

We can get some idea of the importance of the council for the circulation of Gerson's works by comparing three texts on the same theme, the discernment of spirits, one written at Constance, the others at Paris and at Lyon. Gerson wrote the first, *On Distinguishing True Revelations from False*, at Paris in 1401 and sent it to his brother Nicolas, a Celestine monk.[82] He composed the last, *On the Examination of Teachings*, at Lyon in 1423 and addressed it to the Celestines and the Carthusians. He wrote the middle work, *On Testing Spirits*, at Constance in August 1415, following the confirmation in February of the canonization of Birgitta of Sweden.[83] It is the shortest of the three. Gerson probably thought most highly of the first, *On Distinguishing True Revelations from False*, with its coin analogy. He mentions the work five times elsewhere.[84]

The circulation, though, tells a different story. *On Distinguishing True Revelations from False* survives in twenty-two manuscripts, *On the Examination of Teachings* in nineteen, and *On Testing Spirits* in an astonishing 113 copies plus one German translation.[85] This was what the council could accomplish with the right text and author. Perhaps that success also owed something to Birgitta's *Revelations*, which captivated fifteenth-century readers (sixty-nine manuscripts),[86] even theologians, who continued to debate Birgitta through the Council of Basel.[87] Other survival rates support this general conclusion about the important role of the Council of Constance. Gerson's three most popular works relating to Church reform and his three most popular Latin sermons alike were written and circulated at Constance.[88]

Surviving dated manuscripts allow us to see this process unfold. Sometimes we can locate earlier texts being copied at Constance itself. A scribe finished *On Mystical Theology* (1407) there on 30 July 1415, though it seems Gerson may not have brought the work himself and may not even have known of its presence there.[89] *On the Way of Life of the Faithful* (1404), a short collection of rules for twenty-three categories of individuals, from nuns and knights to merchants and shopkeepers, was copied twice at Constance, then again at Freiburg in 1428.[90] Again, we have no certain evidence that Gerson brought it with him to Constance. But we do know that he brought other works with the intention to distribute them. At the time of the Council of Pisa in 1409, Gerson had articulated one of his most dramatic statements on the Schism, *On the Removability of the Spouse from the Church*. The Church, he said there, could remove the pope from office in certain cases. In April 1415, just weeks after his arrival at Constance, Gerson arranged for the work to be pronounced at the Dominican convent.[91] A rare Spanish manuscript of his works, a collection of conciliar texts, plainly states that he published *On the Authority of the Council Representing the Universal Church* (1408–1409) at Constance, while adding that "from its content it's clear that it was produced at the time of the Council of Pisa."[92] Presumably, D'Ailly brought with him both the *Opus in Three Parts* and *On the Visitation of Prelates*, the work written at the synod at Reims. Upon his arrival, Gerson then distributed both works himself. A colophon in a Munich manuscript indicates that Gerson completed (*editus*) the *Opus in Three Parts* at Constance, probably an indication that he corrected and distributed it there.[93] Two surviving copies were made at Constance (one with part 2 only, on examining the conscience), both in 1416.[94] In one, the scribe also copied *On the Visitation of Prelates*, which Gerson had corrected and distributed a year earlier, on 28 August 1415.[95] From Constance the *Opus in Three Parts* spread quickly throughout Germany and Austria. Dated copies survive from an unknown German city (1420), from Vienna (1422), from Herzogenburg (1424), from Cologne (1425), and from the region of Saxony or Bohemia (c. 1430).[96] By 1423 it had already been translated into German. Its impact in German-speaking lands through the end of the sixteenth century is almost beyond calculation.[97]

Other works that Gerson wrote prior to 1415 circulated in German-speaking lands in the years that followed—almost certain evidence that the works were copied at Constance. Such is the case with at least two texts: *On the Art of Hearing Confessions* (c. 1406), copied around 1420 in Heidelberg by a student in arts, and again in 1426 at Basel;[98] and *Remedies for Timidity* (1405), copied twice in Cologne, it appears, during the 1420s.[99]

Of course, works that Gerson composed at Constance spread quickly as well. The tract against the Hussites, composed in August 1417, had reached Prague by December and soon spread to southern Germany; *On Testing Spirits* surfaced at Basel in 1426.[100] The great sermon on the departure of the emperor Sigismund in July 1415, *On Ecclesiastical Power*, and the popular letter-treatise on prayer all survive in early, dated copies from the Empire or from Constance itself.[101]

These manuscripts represent just small traces of the great copying efforts during these years. Yet they give us a much clearer picture of Gerson's rise to prominence as Europe's most popular fifteenth-century author. The Council of Constance secured him an international readership during his lifetime in places his works would otherwise have reached only after many years and with great difficulty, if at all. Some of these texts reached Scandinavia in a direct line of transmission from Constance and found a receptive audience. His tract on the art of dying (the third section of the *Opus in Three Parts*) was translated into Swedish by the mid-fifteenth century, and his *Traité des diverses tentations de l'ennemi* became the first book in Swedish to be printed in Sweden (1495).[102]

The Second Distribution Circle: The Carthusian Empire

With his works finding readers in Central Europe, Gerson made his way from Vienna to Lyon. He now began to think more carefully about providing access to the works that he was producing so rapidly. To help with this task, he turned to the Carthusians and the Celestines. He had strong connections with these orders from early on.[103] He was apparently close friends with the prior of the Celestine convent in Paris, Pierre Poquet. According to historians of the Celestine order, Gerson summoned Poquet to what he thought was his deathbed in 1400.[104] Two of his brothers, Nicolas (b. 1382) and Jean (1385–1434), joined the Celestines, and already by 1413 Gerson was giving manuscripts to Celestine houses.[105] His connection to the Carthusians can be documented from 1401 (though it extended back even earlier) when he wrote his treatise *On Abstention from Meat Among the Carthusians* and sent it to Jean de Gonnant, a knight who had entered the order years earlier. Gerson's friendship with the order led to further compositions during the Paris years: the letters to Barthélémy Clautiers on the *Spiritual Espousals* in 1402 and 1408, a scholarly determination in 1410 about a knight who had entered the Carthusians and broken his vows, a letter to the Carthusians of Basel in 1413 concerning a troublesome Servite preacher in that city, and a defense of the order against the charge that its members perform no miracles, written sometime before 1415.[106]

Long before his death, then, some privileged houses had copies of Gerson's works. Most of these early copies have perished.[107] But the Grande Chartreuse and the Celestines of Lyon held the great collections. The 1423 list of Jean the Celestine mentions five volumes that may well have belonged to the Celestine house in Lyon: three sermon collections (Constance, university, and French sermons), one collection of writings on tyrannicide, and one collection of short moral works.[108] Jean also lists about sixty other works, though he says that some of these cannot be found and may have perished.[109] After 1420, Gerson regularly sent works to the Grande Chartreuse and recommended that they be copied for further distribution.[110] The fifteenth-century catalogue lists ten manuscript volumes of Gerson's works, a collection that must have rivaled the Celestine collection at Lyon.[111] These volumes have all perished, probably consumed in a fire that destroyed the library in 1473.[112] Finally, in early 1429 Gerson gave to the Celestines of Avignon his personal library, including copies of his own writings.[113]

I have referred often to Jean the Celestine, and here we should pause to consider him more carefully. Summing up a lifetime's work, Ouy has demonstrated Jean's important role in the earliest distribution of Gerson's works.[114] Ouy contends that it is thanks to Jean that nearly all of Gerson's works were preserved for posterity.[115] He was indeed critically important for the works at Lyon, especially Gerson's final works, including his last poems and especially the incomplete *Treatise on the Song of Songs*, to which Jean supplied a short note communicating news of Gerson's death. Most manuscripts transmit this note, and we can reasonably conclude that Jean the Celestine edited and circulated the work. He seems to have composed certain colophons and notes that survive in various manuscripts.[116] He supplied an epitaph that circulated with Gerson's last works. Both the *Compilation on the Magnificat* and the *Monotessaron* contain prefaces that he may have written.[117]

Clearly, then, Jean the Celestine deeply shaped Gerson's reception. But this point can be overstated. The transmission of Gerson's works passed through many different channels that Jean had no part in at all. In his letter to the monk Anselm in 1423, Jean describes receiving "excellent works" from his brother. "When he shared them with me recently," he writes, "I read them through so greedily that I became intoxicated with their doctrine as with purest wine."[118] The sense of discovery here is that of a reader, not a copyist. Before 1421, when Jean became prior, we have no solid evidence that he was part of Gerson's immediate circle, nor much evidence of his role in distributing Gerson's works.[119] (He might have lived with Gerson for a time in Paris before 1408, but that is conjecture.) He had nothing to do with Constance or Basel. Gerson enjoyed the help of personal secretaries such as the elusive Jacques de Cerisy.[120] But, unlike Aquinas, he did not have a Guillaume de Sens, the Dominicans' personal publisher.[121] In my view, we should see Jean the Celestine as having a very important role in the shaping and distribution of Gerson's works. But he was just one part of a very large and complicated network.

Gerson's death in 1429 led to a new phase in circulation, the direct diffusion of his works from the Grande Chartreuse to its daughter houses, and possibly from Jean the Celestine as well. The full scale of this diffusion has never been appreciated.[122] Using fifteenth-century catalogues when they survive, existing manuscripts, and references to lost manuscripts, I show on Map 1 every fifteenth-century Carthusian and Celestine house known to possess at least one Gerson text in its library.[123] This map must be used with caution. Certainly many of these houses had much larger collections than I can now recover, and other houses not shown had collections that have vanished without a trace. But the general pattern is clear. The Charterhouses in the Empire had by far the greatest collections, especially those linked by the great ship-

Map 1. Gerson manuscripts in Carthusian and Celestine houses. © David Mengel and Daniel Hobbins.

ping channels: Cologne, Trier, Mainz, and Basel along the Rhine and the Mosel, Buxheim and Aggsbach along the Danube and its tributaries. Probably aided by reform efforts at the city's university, the Charterhouse at Erfurt (Salvatorberg) also had a substantial collection.

We might look at this evidence and conclude that Gerson's readers were mostly monks sitting in lonely cells. Such a view would overlook at least four features of Carthusian intellectual life in the fifteenth century. First, many monasteries acquired manuscripts not just through copying but also through purchase or bequest. At Basel, the only house for which a close study is available, at least six or seven of the sixteen manuscripts were donated—by a local dean, by a parish chaplain, and by a medical master.[124] This reinforces a point to be developed below, that the Council of Basel unleashed a frenzy of copying activity not confined to monastic readers, but now largely hidden from view. Who knows how many other manuscripts never made it into monastic collections? Second, the monks who did read Gerson were often university graduates. For the Charterhouse of Gaming, Dennis Martin counted eighteen monks who completed an M.A. at the University of Vienna; in 1458, they made up fully half of the Gaming community.[125] Such monasteries could be places of great intellectual vitality. Third, many late medieval houses were located in large towns amid the commercial fabric and wealth of the city. This turn toward the world—a "Copernican change" from the thirteenth century, in the words of one scholar—thrust monks such as Denys the Carthusian into more open engagement with the world through their writings.[126] Fourth, again in contrast to the early history of the order, the fifteenth-century houses were actively involved in the lending and distribution of manuscripts to nonmonastic readers, in some cases even tailoring volumes with special prefaces and abridging texts for those same readers. At Basel, with its sixteen Gerson manuscripts, records survive of some five hundred loans between 1482 to 1528, to printers, priests, students, and schoolmasters.[127] Carthusian libraries became lending libraries for the literate public.

A survey of the most popular titles of Gerson's works in the Charterhouses reveals his legacy taking shape in this particular context as a moral and spiritual authority and guide to the religious life. We should be careful not to oversimplify a complicated picture. Most of these houses possessed a selection of Gerson's works broad enough to reflect the complexity and wide interests of Gerson himself. Nonetheless, beyond a few Constance sermons, readers of the Charterhouse collections would have learned little of Gerson the great Latin orator, and nothing whatsoever of Gerson the vernacular preacher or writer. They would have known from *The Consolation of Theology* that he liked to write poetry, but they would have had great difficulty finding his epic, the

Josephina. Some local opinion pieces like the tract on Joan of Arc never entered the Charterhouse collections. A few readers might have known from the list of Jean the Celestine that Gerson had attacked academic curiosity in lectures at Paris, but they had no access to the work.[128]

The actual transmission to these houses is a shadowy subject that would benefit from more research among the manuscripts. Jean must have had some role in communicating Gerson's last works to the Carthusians. In the year of Gerson's death, 1434, a small collection of works from his last two years reached the Charterhouse of Gaming near Vienna. The manuscript (now in Vienna) includes the *Compilation on the Magnificat* (1427–1428), the *Treatise on the Song of Songs* (1429), and three poems.[129] Gerson had written two of these works in his last two weeks—the *Treatise on the Song of Songs,* which he left incomplete, and a poem, the "Defense of His Songs." The manuscript also includes the epitaph and the second *Annotatio,* the updated list of Gerson's works produced by Jean after his brother's death.[130] All the evidence indicates that Jean was very closely involved in the assembly of this manuscript. The selection suggests an attempt to recover Gerson's final works, to compile others by means of the list, and to commemorate his passing. The list itself survives in at least thirteen copies, eleven of these in the same recension as this manuscript.[131] Another manuscript copied in the early 1450s shows that this exact series of texts had found its way into other Carthusian houses, now in the company of many other texts; it also records the spread of these texts from the Carthusian house at Antwerp to the Canons Regular of Groenendael.[132]

That is an important clue to an enormous development whose contours are now only faintly visible but that would profoundly shape the religious culture of the fifteenth century: the spread of Gerson's works to religious houses of all kinds, perhaps especially to the Benedictines. The foundation for his popularity among members of that order may have been laid in 1418. After his departure from Constance, Gerson may have lingered for a short time (September and October) at the great Benedictine abbey of Melk in Austria, situated on a large outcrop overlooking the Danube and home to one of the greatest libraries in the Latin West. There, a movement for reform or regular observance (that is, strict observance of the Rule) was taking hold that would soon spread to other orders and shake Western monasticism to its foundations.[133] Nicholas of Dinkelsbühl—who reportedly said that he saw no one at Constance more learned than Gerson—played a key role at the outset in a series of visitations from Melk, but Gerson's presence might also have given the movement some of its momentum.[134] In any case, he soon became the single most important spiritual authority for the Melk reform, and therefore one of the most desirable authors for the library

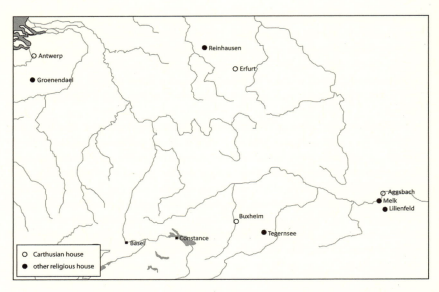

Map 2. The spread of Gerson texts from Carthusian houses to other orders. ©
David Mengel and Daniel Hobbins.

of any observant house.[135] Melk and its satellite houses—the so-called
Congregation of Melk—soon acquired numerous Gerson manuscripts.
The 1483 catalogue at Melk lists forty-three manuscripts containing one
or more Gerson texts.[136] The Charterhouses played a crucial role in this
distribution. We can document the transmission of texts from the Aggsbach Charterhouse to Melk and to the powerful Cistercian house of
Lilienfeld in Lower Austria, from the Erfurt Charterhouse to the
reformed Benedictine house of Reinhausen nearby, and from an
unknown Charterhouse (probably nearby Buxheim) to the reforming
Benedictine abbey of Tegernsee in Bavaria (Map 2).[137]

These manuscripts serve as a reminder of this pattern of transmission
from the Carthusians to other religious orders and hence to new distribution circles, especially to those that shared in the spirit of regular
observance. They also testify not just to the increasing range of Gerson's
audience but to how his works stimulated new patterns of readership
and increased the momentum for reform.

The Celestines deserve more space than I can give them here. From
the surviving evidence, we know that they amassed impressive collections, including works that the Carthusians never obtained, such as the
Treatises on Songs. The best place to find Gerson's works during his lifetime was probably at a Celestine monastery in France.[138] Yet the evidence

for Celestine libraries is meager. Almost no medieval catalogues survive, and therefore all the evidence for Gerson texts in these libraries comes from surviving manuscripts and a few references by Gerson himself.[139] Founded in 1275, the Celestines never caught up to the Carthusians' sophisticated book culture. It is telling that a Carthusian, not a Celestine, asked Gerson the question that inspired *In Praise of Scribes of Healthy Doctrine.*

The circulation among both Carthusians and Celestines may help us to grasp an essential point about medieval distribution circles. Even though religious orders such as these were international, books did not stream effortlessly from one end of Europe to the other. Geography and national boundaries could severely limit the flow of medieval texts. Despite the fact that Gerson lived among the Lyon Celestines and sent his library to the Celestine house at Avignon, his works apparently never crossed the Alps to the numerous and important (and older) Italian Celestine houses. I have not identified a single Gerson text in any Celestine house in Italy.[140] Nor did Gerson texts reach the great English Charterhouses, some of them with rich and important libraries. Monastic distribution circles had an important role for an author like Gerson, but political boundaries were not easily crossed. I shall return to this point below.

The Third Distribution Circle: The Council of Basel

Two years after Gerson's death, as the great distribution began through the Charterhouse network, his works received still greater diffusion through the Council of Basel. Convened to continue the reforms begun at Constance and especially to deal with the Hussites, the council brought together more than 3,200 individuals during the period from 1432 to 1443.[141] Probably no single event was more important than this council for the spread of late medieval texts of all kinds. Churchmen, scholars, lawyers, intellectuals of every variety brought books. They also searched for books in the immediate vicinity of Basel, sometimes acting on instructions.[142] Sensing a magical moment in 1434, the great book collector Humphrey, duke of Gloucester, commissioned Zenone da Castiglione to round up the works of Italian scholars, especially their translations from Greek.[143] The council's impact on the reception of Gerson was deep and lasting. For the first time beyond his immediate circles, his readers could begin to collect his works into single volumes and to gather them into institutional libraries.

The reception of the tract on Joan of Arc demonstrates the importance of the council for the spread of Gerson's works.[144] He had written the work in May 1429. We saw in Chapter 5 that by autumn the tract had reached Paris, where a canon lawyer attacked it in a response piece that he inserted after the closing lines of Gerson's tract. Someone, perhaps an individual in the Anglo-Burgundian camp that had opposed Joan of Arc, then brought this version of the tract to Basel—that is, Gerson's tract (in its short version) followed by the response piece of the canon lawyer from Paris. This copy then became the basis for the majority of our surviving copies of the work. In fact, an entire family of surviving copies—nine in all—descended from a lost manuscript that was copied at the Council of Basel in September 1433. All of these copies have the short version of the text followed by the reply treatise of the canon lawyer. We can even deduce that immediately before the tract on Joan of Arc, the lost original must have contained another work of Gerson, his important and popular letter-treatise on prayer from 1416.

The key to all of this is a scribal mistake. The scribes in four of the surviving manuscripts reproduced in full a colophon from the letter-treatise on prayer just before the title of the tract on Joan; they may have assumed that it was an author's colophon rather than a scribe's. It reads as follows: "Here ends the treatise on prayer at Basel, the year 1433, the month of September."[145] Scribes frequently recopied colophons by mistake, as they did here.[146] Thanks to their error, we can be fairly certain that the entire manuscript family associated with these four manuscripts descended from a copy made at Basel. The existence of another copy dated at Basel in 1435 makes ten surviving manuscripts and at least one lost manuscript (there must have been many more) linked to Basel.[147]

The surviving copies also document the text's spread from Basel. Three of these nine manuscripts cannot be localized within Germany or Austria. But for the most part, the others either were given to or were copied in a cluster of religious houses in Bavaria: the Benedictine abbeys at Augsburg (two copies), Melk, and Wiblingen, the Dominican convent in Nuremberg, and the Cistercian abbey at Fürstenfeld, and one copy belonging to a chaplain in Kaufbeuren (Map 3).[148]

The texts of Gerson copied at the Council of Constance and afterward in Central Europe circulated in all cases with at most one other text of Gerson, usually standing alone. By contrast, the Basel manuscripts reveal a trend toward compilation. In all fifteen manuscripts, the tract on Joan was transmitted in the company of other Gerson texts. We can even deduce that the lost manuscript of September 1433 probably included two other works besides the Joan tract (and the reply treatise, which none of the scribes omitted) and the letter-treatise on prayer from 1416 (with its colophon of 1433): *On Perfecting the Heart* (1423) and *On Mystical Theology*. As in the case of the Lollard compilations studied by Anne Hudson, the gatherers of these compilations were not stitching together

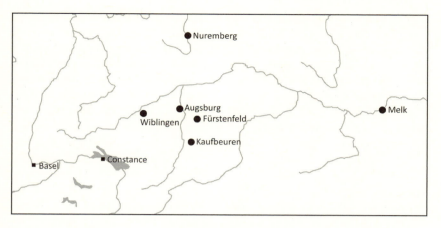

Map 3. The diffusion of Gerson's tract on Joan of Arc. © David Mengel and Daniel Hobbins.

preexisting booklets but copying the texts one after another onto fresh sheets.[149]

Other Gerson manuscripts copied at Basel confirm this impression of a growing collecting impulse. Large clusters of works were being copied there by 1433, including one manuscript with ten works of Gerson.[150] In 1437, Cardinal Juan de Torquemada, a papal apologist and uncle of the notorious Thomas de Torquemada, purchased a manuscript containing *On Ecclesiastical Power* and the sermon on Sigismund's departure, both copied at the council between 1433 and 1436.[151] Between 1436 and 1438, a learned Benedictine monk from Melk named Johannes Schlitpacher, a champion of reform, copied twenty-two works of Gerson, including some of the late works from 1428 that had reached Basel by this time.[152] Other manuscripts with multiple texts of Gerson were copied at Basel in 1437 (two works), 1439 (eight), 1441 (nineteen), and 1444 (at least eleven).[153] By this stage, we are certainly glimpsing just a small fraction of the copying that went on there.[154]

Strategies of Compilation

The trend toward collecting begun at Basel might seem to be an entirely natural development. In fact, it represents something quite new in the history of the medieval book and an important theme in the reception of Gerson's works. Medieval readers might organize a codex according to a theme or topic, or an author in the case of a great authority such as Augustine. But they might not impose any organizing principle at all.

The practice for thirteenth-century schoolmen presents a striking contrast with Gerson. Individual works, especially longer ones such as *Sentences* commentaries, were excerpted rather than gathered whole and entire into an author collection. The large size of such works made collecting them into single volumes much more difficult. Aquinas's *Summa theologiae* was rarely transmitted in its entirety, for example, and even the most popular part, the *Secunda-secundae*, was excerpted 25 percent of the time, a process that began even during the lifetime of Aquinas.[155] The great majority of his works transmitted in the papal collection at Avignon were copied one to a volume.[156] This seems to have been the normal experience of reading thirteenth-century scholarly literature.

Vernacular poets struggled more than Latin writers to achieve authorial status. Sylvia Huot observes that it is "difficult to find manuscripts in which generically diverse works by a single twelfth-, thirteenth-, or early fourteenth-century author are associated."[157] Jean de Meun (d. c. 1305), the continuator of the *Roman de la Rose*, achieved the status of a great authority, and in the prologue to his translation of Boethius's *Consolation of Philosophy* he listed his other poems and translations; yet among hundreds of surviving manuscripts, not a single one transmits his complete works.[158] A. S. G. Edwards likewise finds little evidence of author collections for vernacular English writers before the early fifteenth century. Even the works of Chaucer were normally jumbled with authors in the "Chaucerian tradition," including Hoccleve and especially John Lydgate, and Chaucer's "complete works" were not printed until 1532.[159] By the fifteenth century we do begin to see vernacular authors—rather than readers—taking care to gather their works into collections, as we saw with Hoccleve, who produced "the first 'collected poems' in English" two centuries before Ben Jonson.[160] Another example is Christine de Pizan, who assembled into one volume preexisting copies of her works, possibly in response to a request from Queen Isabeau for her complete works.[161]

That final step, however, does not seem to have come easily or naturally for most writers. Christine may well have compiled her works in part to preserve her legacy. We shall probably never know for sure. Yet it is also telling that the queen had something to do with the compilation, and that after compiling this manuscript (1410–1415), Christine—who died around 1431—apparently never attempted anything like it again. Turning to Gerson, we see him taking much greater care to compile his works and to transmit them to posterity in collections. Chapter 3 traced his efforts to compile his works at Lyon. The five volumes mentioned in 1423 by Jean the Celestine, we saw, were organized by genre and theme.[162] Gerson (or someone close to him) had already organized his sermons. Within his lifetime, then, Gerson had himself begun to organize his works into a coherent body of writings, probably with the help of Jean.

He was not the first schoolman to do so. John Wyclif appears to have revised his own works at the end of his life, Hudson suggests, to support a comparison to his hero Robert Grosseteste or perhaps even Augustine, who late in life had sifted through his own literary remains in his *Retractions*, a work well known to medieval writers.[163] Wyclif's revision involved gathering a heap of unrelated works, sequencing them, and greatly expanding and coordinating their existing cross-references.[164] Wyclif or an editor (or both) likewise put his sermons into liturgical order and supplied cross-references.[165] As Gerson gathered his compilations in his last years at Lyon, so Wyclif assembled his two summas on theology and philosophy from previously written works.[166] Wyclif and Gerson both understood that to reinforce and to project authority, they had to gather for readers the scattered remains of their writings—their academic "detritus" as Hudson has it—and present them as a coherent body of work. We may even view these gatherings as a form of paratext, a "vestibule" for the reader about to enter the text itself, hence a further attempt by authors to control the meaning and reception of their works.[167] The message to a reader confronted by a huge volume of Gerson's works would have been clear: the writer of these works is also an *auctor*, a true authority. Ignore him at your peril.

Within the broader corpus, Gerson identified subgroups of works on common topics. He often grouped his Latin and French works on mystical theology together, the two parts of *On Mystical Theology*, *La montagne de contemplation*, and *La mendicité spirituelle*.[168] At the end of *On the Removability of the Spouse from the Church* (1410), he suggests that the work be joined to his sermon at Tarascon in 1404 and to his *Treatise on the Unity of the Church* from 1409.[169] The prologue to the *Compilation on the Magnificat* recommends that the individual treatises be brought together with the centiloquies.[170] The four works on the heart circulated together from early on, probably by Gerson's design, possibly aided by Jean the Celestine, who describes them in his 1423 list as constituting a single *libellus* in four parts.[171] A note in at least three manuscripts, including two that can be linked to the Council of Basel, indicates that Gerson wanted two works, *On Preparation for Mass* and *On the Need for Lay Communion in Both Kinds*, to circulate and be read with the ninth treatise of the *Compilation on the Magnificat*: "According to the author's intention—that is, master Jean, chancellor of Paris—these last two treatises should be placed after the preceding ninth treatise on the Magnificat, that is, after the verse 'Esurientes,' which is concerned with the sacrament of the altar."[172] Gerson thought of these works as a collection of his teachings on the Eucharist and must have instructed his secretary Jacques de Cerisy—the probable author of this note—to organize them in this way.[173] In compiling his lists of Gerson's works, Jean the Celestine repeatedly noted that certain works could be gathered together. In his first list in 1423, he recommended joining *On Distinguishing True Revelations from False* to *On Testing Spirits*. In his second list (1429–1434), he further recommended joining to these two works *On the Examination of Teachings* and a letter (here called a *cedula*) in praise of Bonaventure (which survives in a single manuscript). The two lectures on mystical theology, he adds, can be brought together to make one book, supplemented by *On the Passions of the Soul*, which "contributes greatly to the understanding of *On Mystical Theology*"; the *Dialogue Apology* can conveniently be joined to *On the Consolation of Theology*.[174]

Gerson himself began the drive toward compilation, and Jean the Celestine gave the trend further momentum through his lists and by actively circulating some of the texts. But perhaps the single most striking feature of Gerson's reception is that so many *readers* took upon themselves the task of compiling his works, in the process making Gerson's authorship the basis of organization for complete codices. Bookmakers and compilers might communicate this principle of organization in various ways. A manuscript with fifteen works of Gerson, once owned by the Augustinian monastery of Herrenchiemsee in Bavaria, has a bookplate mounted on the cover, "Various treatises of the Chancellor of Paris and of others," as well as a running head for the *Opus in Three Parts*, "Cancellarius Parisiensis."[175] A colophon might communicate the same point. A manuscript of French works once owned by an Englishman named Thomas Unton closes: "Here ends the present book composed by master Jean Gerson, doctor."[176] But the usual strategy to signal a Gerson collection was through a contents list. A good example is a huge fifteenth-century folio volume from Seitenstetten Abbey near Melk, containing twenty-eight Gerson texts. The heading on the first folio reads: "The contents of this book are written below, and first (those) of Johannes Gerson." The verso heading, "Here follow the contents of other [authors] besides Gerson," only reinforces Gerson's authorship as the basic organizing principle (Figure 14).[177]

Sometimes the manuscripts reflect a second level of organization beyond the principle of Gerson's authorship, a sign that readers were sorting his works into themes and genres. The Seitenstetten contents list takes care to distinguish sermons from treatises and to list them separately. A much smaller collection, a manuscript of thirty-eight poems (Paris, BnF, Ms. lat. 3624), opens with a rubric that seems to derive from someone who admired Gerson the poet: "Here begins the book of songs [*liber canticorum*] of master Jean Gerson, doctor of theology and chancellor of the University of Paris, which are called songs of the pilgrim."[178]

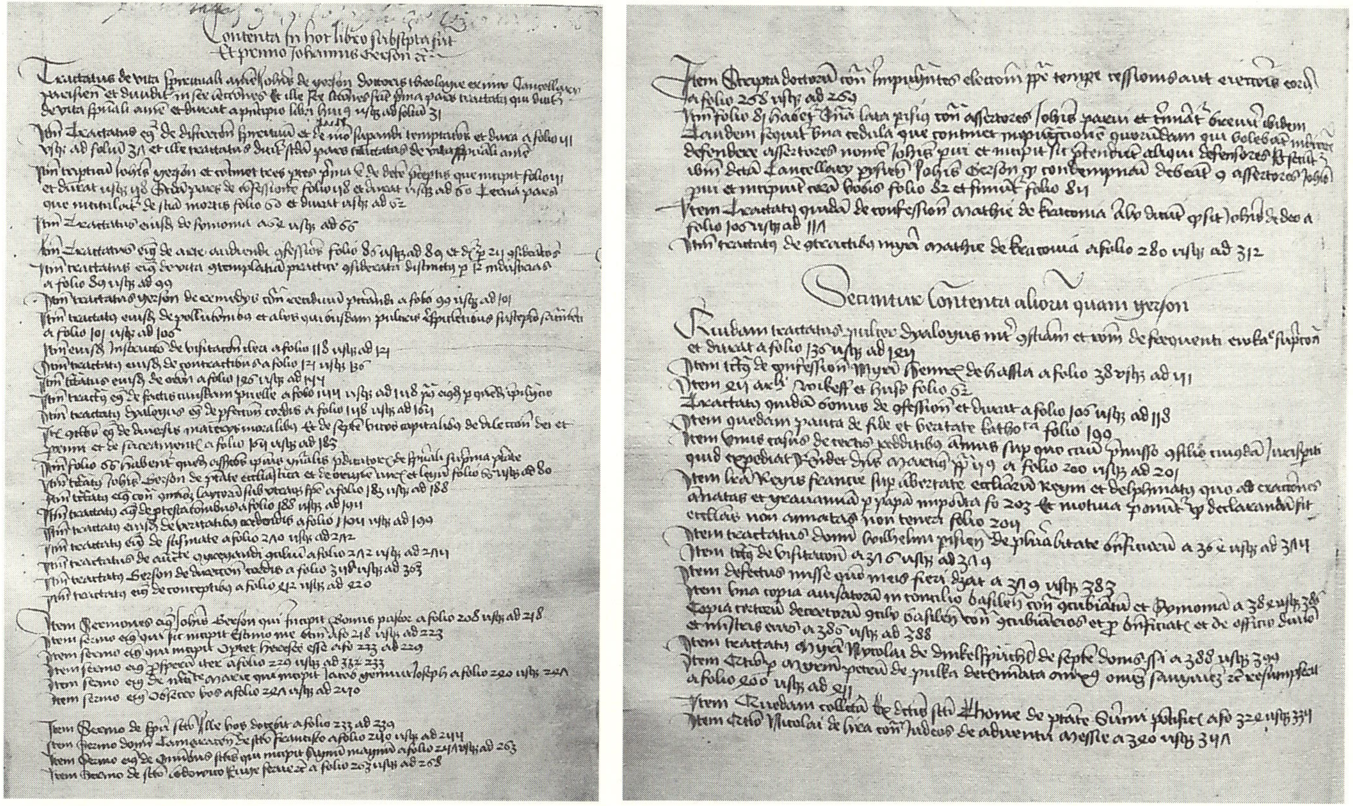

Figure 14. Contents list of a Gerson collection manuscript. Seitenstetten, Stiftsbibliothek, Hs. 49 ff. Ar–v. Used by permission.

The compiler of Brussels, Ms. 9305–6, once owned by Margaret of York, took a similar strategy, presenting *La montagne de contemplation* and *La mendicité spirituelle* as two parts of a "Book of contemplation made by master Jean Gerson, chancellor of the University of Paris."[179] Those two works often traveled together. It was much more difficult to find and bring together works on the same theme but long separated in time, such as the three tracts on discernment of spirits. While most manuscripts copied outside France contain just *On Testing Spirits*, eleven also have *On Distinguishing True Revelations from False* immediately afterward. But I know of only two manuscripts with these two works and *On the Examination of Teachings*.[180] These groupings testify to readers who were not satisfied with a random sequence of works, and who attempted to bring some order to the reading of Gerson, an order that would facilitate comparison and cross-referencing.

This pattern of compilation testifies to the level of respect for Gerson as a theological authority and spiritual guide, to a broad and deep desire to read and to study his works as a unified whole, and to the great advances in manuscript production that made texts more abundant and easier to gather. Such collections allowed for a greater sophistication in the study of authorities. Systematic study of Gerson's complete works could now begin. Subject indexes to his works appeared for the first time following the Council of Basel. In some manuscripts these occupy many folios.[181]

The question remains: Just how representative was Gerson in achieving this kind of recognition as an authority? We can find similar patterns of reception in Wyclif or, closer in time, Nicholas of Dinkelsbühl, whose works survive in over 1,400 manuscripts, as we saw, many of these author collections.[182] But we need only compare Gerson to D'Ailly, a gigantic figure in his own right who also had readers at the Council of Constance, to realize that most writers never achieved this kind of committed readership. Besides those under D'Ailly's immediate control or patronage, we seem to have few manuscripts that indicate a conscious attempt at an "author collection."

As for vernacular writers, Huot has shown that while earlier manuscripts of vernacular poetry rarely collect the works of an author, later manuscripts show a trend toward compilation.[183] Petrarch manuscripts exhibit a similar tendency. A study of more than four hundred copies of *I trionfi*, a major vernacular work, revealed a slow but steady shift. While 53 percent of early fourteenth-century copies contained works of Petrarch alone, that percentage climbed to 63 percent for the late fourteenth century, to 74 percent for the fifteenth century.[184]

The most basic lesson here is the growing importance of the author as an organizing principle in late medieval written culture. In this respect, the printed *opera omnia* that appear on the horizon are only the culmination of a process that had been gaining momentum for several generations.

The Implications of Compilation

We have looked at three distribution circles that gave Gerson's works an unprecedented outreach, and that help to explain at least on a technical level how his works reached so many readers in Central Europe. Several implications follow from this survey. The evidence presented here reveals a shift in the reception of Gerson's works toward collection and compilation, the desire not just to read a specific text of Gerson but to identify his works and to collect them, to have them and to store them. This new pattern, the Gerson collection, would leave a heavy imprint on fifteenth-century libraries. For the first time beyond his immediate circle, Gerson's authorship alone—rather than an event such as the Council of Constance, or a topic such as the Hussites, or a certain moral obligation such as confession—became the guiding principle in compiling his texts. This is no bibliographic footnote; this pattern of reception affected in profound ways how the public received and read his texts. In this interpretation, the collecting begun by Jean Lamasse in the 1430s at St. Victor, which Ouy has so carefully investigated and catalogued, appears as one effort among many to compile Gerson's works—more comprehensive and industrious than the efforts that began at Basel, but also much more dependent on a few individuals and more limited and confined to a single place.[185] Considered in these terms, the editing at St. Victor even begins to take on the appearance of an industry, and as such to foreshadow the printers who would soon be gathering and publishing Gerson's *opera omnia*.

The process of collecting Gerson changed the way his works were read. Opinion pieces lost their local flavor. The reception of each work was absorbed into the reception of other Gerson texts, in many cases texts that were far removed in theme and had nothing in common except Gerson's authorship, in the same way that Lollard compilations bound together texts on unrelated topics.[186] The tract on Joan illustrates this pattern. Strange as it may now appear, we can be confident that the copyists of the fifteen manuscripts recopied the work not because it discussed Joan of Arc but because Gerson had written it.[187] In fact not one of these manuscripts mentions Joan by name, and it even seems likely that some of the copyists—especially those who had transmitted a text with a shortened title, lacking a date and all reference to Orléans, to England, and to France—did not understand the identity of the "puella" at all. Joan was executed in 1431, years before many of these manuscripts were copied. The original context of the work was quite remote from some readers. Not one copyist put Joan's name in the margin. A work originally written in the heat of the moment following a spectacular military victory, which probably circulated originally as a single folded sheet and which drew almost immediate criticism—a true, local opinion piece intended to enlist support for Joan and to tilt history in France's favor—now found itself within a few short years surrounded by texts on Church reform, mystical theology, and prayer. Henceforth, it would be bound into heavy manuscript volumes, sometimes ruled into double columns. Its reappearance at the nullification trial, effectively a distribution circle of its own, put the work into a political context once again, in company with other works on Joan, and gave it a new circulation (thirteen surviving manuscripts) as part of the proceedings.[188] Readers of the proceedings cared less about Gerson than about Joan herself and current political pressures.

This evidence also implies that by the time of Basel, a surge of indiscriminate collecting of Gerson's works had begun. A copyist interested in compiling Gerson texts, when presented with an exemplar of multiple works, would probably recopy every text, no matter the topic. As a result, a text of Gerson that had reached Basel and Constance had an excellent chance of wide circulation, many times what it would have had otherwise. The medieval book trade was uneven and heavily subject to economies of place. The popularity of a text—typically measured by the number of surviving copies—depended on accident and chance as well as choice. The simple fact that Gerson wrote something was insufficient to guarantee its popularity. Earlier, I noted the few surviving copies of *Against the Curiosity of Students* and *On the Two Kinds of Logic*. Can there be any doubt that if these texts had reached Constance or Basel or the Carthusians, readers would have copied them? The copyists of Gerson manuscripts were choosing not from among his complete works in a bookseller's shop but from those at their disposal. The problem can be stated in this way: when we say that one of his texts had greater "success" than another, to some extent what this might mean is merely that one text reached Constance, Basel, or both, and that the other did not. Of course a text's content remained crucial to its success, but its entry into a distribution circle could be just as important. For historians, the challenge is to understand the balance of these two factors, content and availability, in the distribution of any medieval work.

That earliest circulation before the frenzy for compilation took hold interests us most, yet it is the most difficult to uncover. With the tract on Joan, a clue to this early stage appears in the catalogue description of a French manuscript of just four folios that disappeared in the First World War. In this lost manuscript, the work appeared by itself, and the scribe clearly found Joan of Arc much more interesting than Gerson. Here at last she is named in the colophon: "Here ends the treatise of master Jean Gerson, chancellor of Paris, on the Maid of France called Joan. Know that this Maid wore men's clothing, fought wars, and inspired soldiers on the king's behalf against the enemy, saying that she was sent from God to recover the kingdom from the hands of the English."[189] This copyist, a supporter of Charles VII, gives us a glimpse of perhaps the tail end of that swirling, early debate about Joan in which Gerson's tract participated. The text of the tract itself was probably the same as the Basel manuscripts (from the catalogue description we can deduce that this was the short version, without the reply treatise), but the context could not be more different: not Gerson on prayer and mystical theology, but Joan's inspiring story. In this sense, the Council of Basel and the distribution from Lyon through the Charterhouses changed Gerson's readership and flattened it out. Constance had given his works an international audience. Basel and Jean the Celestine with the Carthusians gave readers the chance to collect his works systematically and on a grand scale. As Gerson's name gained weight, so did the volumes of his works.

Why Italians (Mostly) Didn't Read Gerson

I have mostly emphasized the long reach of Gerson's hand, the massive market that allowed him to shape patterns of thought and spirituality in so much of Europe. This discussion would not be complete without giving some thought to the limits of that audience. The textual avalanche into German-speaking regions did not send comparable numbers of his works to Europe's geographical margins. A few did find their way to Italy, and fewer still reached Spain and England.[190] But the number of copies in these countries seems paltry compared to the abundance of copies in the Empire. The reasons for this imbalance, I suspect, have partly to do with cultural forces that marked and distinguished the European landscape in this period, and in turn with the focus of Gerson's works. Here, toward the end of this book, it is worth asking what Gerson's uneven distribution might tell us about the face of Europe itself in the fifteenth century.

The first and simplest explanation for this unevenness is that except for the greatest medieval authors and the most foundational texts (Augustine, Gregory, the Bible), this is simply the nature of the medieval book trade. Imbalance, not evenness, is the rule. To ask why an author did not have readers in a given place is to assume a truly open and fluid market of texts, perfect knowledge of and access to his works. But we are not dealing with a true market at all (despite my chapter title), much less a twenty-first-century mass market. Fifteenth-century readers were choosing not from all existing texts but only from those available nearby. Print did not at once balance the book trade. Even in the sixteenth century, a recent study shows, Spain accounted for only 3.1 percent of recorded printed editions, compared to 32 percent for Germany, 21.4 percent for France, and 18.4 percent for Italy.[191] Thus the solution to the puzzle of Gerson's failure to find readers in Spain must be partly simple geography. All texts circulated slowly, even a literary bombshell like *The Imitation of Christ*, begun around 1420 and circulating by 1424. Of 782 fifteenth-century manuscripts, Uwe Neddermeyer counted sixty from Italy, forty-two from France, thirty-five from England, and fourteen from "elsewhere," compared to 631 from the regions of the Empire, more than 80 percent of the total. The text had almost no readers in Spain.[192]

So we should not expect an even distribution of Gerson's works across Europe. But I have argued that distribution circles like the major councils made possible an international audience even in faraway places. Intellectuals from Spain, England, and Italy did travel to Constance and Basel and did hunt for books. Yet for some reason, many chose not to make copies of Gerson's works available there and to take them back home.

One might also blame different levels of book production, the simple fact that, according to Neddermeyer's best estimate (which quantifies what many experts in this period had assumed), the Empire simply produced many more books at this period, three times the number in France, ten times that in England, and probably an even higher ratio in the case of Spain. So we should not expect to see many Gerson manuscripts in those countries. But this argument does not account for Italy, where Neddermeyer estimates production at 85 percent of that in the Empire.[193] Moreover, it begs more fundamental questions and so brings us right back to where we started: Why was Gerson more popular in some places than in others?

A clue comes from one text that did find an audience in Italy: *On Ecclesiastical Power*, which survives in sixteen copies now in Italian libraries (out of a total of at least eighty surviving copies), far more Italian copies than of any other work of Gerson.[194] Important churchmen owned the work, including Cardinal Domenico Capranica (d. 1458), Cardinal Juan de Torquemada, and Cardinal Bessarion (d. 1472), the famous Greek convert, translator of Xenophon and Aristotle and promoter of a crusade against the Turks.[195] For these princes of the Church, *On Ecclesiastical Power* represented "the quintessential statement of conciliarist thought."[196] It spoke to present concerns. The success of this text in Italy is crucial evidence for us, since it proves that Gerson's texts could and did reach Italy. The deduction is clear: for those texts that did not, one cannot blame simple geography. Why then did Italian readers turn away from Gerson, even as audiences north of the Alps found in his works the answers to all their questions?

Long ago, Paul Kristeller and before him Karl Vossler pointed to the cultural fissures that separated Italy from France, England, Germany, and the Low Countries for most of the Middle Ages. Kristeller thought that until the thirteenth century, Italy lagged far behind the rest of Europe in fields as diverse as architecture, music, religious drama, theology, and even classical studies.[197] Italy, he reasoned, had taken a different cultural trajectory, developing different educational patterns that would soon nurture the humanist movement. More recent scholarship has stressed differences in grammar and rhetorical training in Italy: grammar lifted from the university curriculum and completely divorced from theology, rhetoric limited to "pleading and legal oratory."[198] Social and economic forces in Italy encouraged these developments by providing a market for classical rhetorical skills. Far more easily than elsewhere in Europe, university graduates could make a living in urban settings.[199] Even with the severe mortality of the Black Death, a more civic, urban landscape arose that, with the exception of the Low Countries, looked much different from the rest of Europe.[200] And just below the surface of measurable categories like population, far deeper rifts appear in social structures such as the family and the household—their size (larger in Italy), age differences between husband and wife (greater in Italy), and the position of women (less egalitarian in Italy).[201]

We should add to these factors the growing regionalization of Europe, which the Great Schism accelerated. Every new university reinforced this trend, as fewer students went "abroad" to study. By the fifteenth century, "external migration actually came to a halt."[202] The few local studies we have bear this out: the German nation shrinks at the law faculty of Bologna and at the arts faculty of Paris, foreigners abandon canon law at Paris, students from southern France no longer head south to Italy, the Great Schism stifles mobility everywhere and severs long-established networks of learning, all over Europe students stay closer to home and attend universities nearby.[203]

For these and certainly many other reasons, by the period under consideration here Italy and Germany had two very different reading publics. Book production was surging in both places. But while German demand came from religious and semireligious orders, ecclesiastical careerists, and university graduates, Italy's growth depended on a civic culture fueled by the energy of the city-states, by early humanists, and to some extent by universities. Theology faculties came to Italian universities very late, they were marginal to the university once they did arrive, and they left little evidence of serious and systematic instruction. Usually, they were dominated by mendicants, who had never warmed to Gerson.[204] Italy was home to a reading public that prized classical authors and modern humanists above the theological and spiritual writings so popular in Germany.[205] It also seems that what Gerson accomplished with the tract preachers such as John of Capistrano (d. 1456) and Bernardino of Siena (d. 1444) to some extent accomplished with sermons, some on topics that Gerson never treated independently but that attracted considerable attention in a more urban setting—women's clothing, for example. We are talking here in the broadest generalities, but these differences do help to explain why Gerson failed to reach a wide public in Italy. Ultimately, different tastes prevailed, collecting never began, and Gerson was perhaps best known there for a work he did not write, *The Imitation of Christ.*

Conclusion

The full complexity of Gerson's readership cannot be measured in these few pages. Nonetheless, we can take away from this discussion a much clearer sense of the broad patterns and processes that transformed Gerson from a great and renowned Paris preacher, to the most powerful theologian in France, to the dominant voice at the Council of Constance, to the most popular contemporary author of the fifteenth century in major parts of Europe. Gerson thought first of a specific, local audience. His works soon found a wider readership beyond Paris and a few reached the Low Countries, where he spent some time himself. Constance gave him an unprecedented stage for the distribution of old and new works alike. Retiring from the council, exiled from Paris and wandering through the Empire, confident in the breadth of his audience, he set about writing as never before, and never stopped until three days before his death on 12 July 1429. Then the collecting impulse took over—begun already by Gerson himself, encouraged by Jean the Celestine, carried on with gusto at the Charterhouses, made possible on a grand scale by the Council of Basel, executed most methodically at St. Victor, and slowly spreading from all directions to the great Congregation of Melk. Collecting shaped the reception of Gerson's works through the rest of the century, even leaving a deep imprint on the first complete editions, which often reproduce the order of texts as they appear in surviving manuscripts. For an author who wrote so many works in such a variety of contexts, this was a major shift. The circulation of individual tracts in unbound gatherings came to an end, leaving scarcely a trace in the manuscripts. Gerson's reputation underwent a slow transformation, from preacher and powerful public figure to a mighty moral and spiritual authority. For the first time, deep study and comparison of works long separated in time and place could begin. Decades before print, the author became the central organizing principle of the codex.

Conclusion

In this book we have seen a series of developments and shifts that distinguish Gerson from his thirteenth-century predecessors. The dramatic convergence of these shifts in the period under study here fully justifies the designation of a new historical space. We have seen a new space in the history of reading, a schoolman handling texts more like a humanist, sensitive to their formal literary qualities but evaluating them within strict guidelines set down by thirteenth-century authorities who (in Gerson's view) had stabilized theological language. We have seen a new approach to moral theology, from systematic taxonomy to a focus on individual cases, a momentous and enduring shift in the history of ethics that has as much relevance now as it ever had. We have witnessed a young student brought up in the schools and deeply respectful of the authors in that tradition, yet spellbound by the prospect of literary fame and permanence, and striving desperately in his maturity to fashion a legacy. We have seen him shattering the traditional template of scholarly pursuit, writing poetry, pointing students beyond commentaries and glosses to a more direct encounter with scripture, indulging a taste for logic but championing rhetoric for its capacity to stir the passions, shocked and embarrassed by theologians who talk in jargon. We have seen in Gerson the clearest and best representative of a new type, the medieval public intellectual, concerned far more than his predecessors with the world beyond the schools and more involved in public outreach, especially through the writing of tracts. We have used him to explore a publishing system closer in some ways to print than to the manuscript production of the twelfth century. We have pondered the genesis and stages of authorship through oral and written channels. Finally, we have seen a medieval author harness the communication networks of his day and, perfectly tuned to the desires and needs of fifteenth-century readers, achieve the status of a modern doctor in much of Europe soon after his death.

Certain oppositions stand out here: school learning and humanism, ancients and moderns, logic and rhetoric, systems and cases, orality and writing, internal audience and external public, coterie readership and massive markets. With these in view, we might be tempted to describe

Gerson as a liminal or transitional figure. But such an argument cedes the field to the master narrative; it allows the periodization to interpret our evidence for us. It fails to recognize the nonlinearity of historical development. Above all, it ignores the ways in which some of these cross-currents characterize an entire generation of theologians and even humanists. An entire history vanishes, squeezed out by more familiar and reassuring patterns. In her study of the sixteenth-century "humanist-scholastic" debates, Erika Rummel recognizes both Gerson and Petrarch as figures who resist easy classification and subordination to the demands of later polemicists. The deep links between the two, which form a frequent subtext of this book, extend even to their concern for clear handwriting. For Petrarch, that concern leads off to humanist script in Poggio and Niccolò Niccoli; for Gerson, to the praise of scribes as we find it in Johannes Trithemius (1492). Their connection is more than just a case of simple "influence" of Petrarch upon Gerson. Instead, it reflects a common set of cultural interests, values, and assumptions all linked to problems of expression. Looking ahead to mid-fifteenth-century Germany, we find Gerson's program receiving its warmest reception among early humanists, who profoundly admired and revered him as a doctrinal and spiritual authority, who prized clear expression, and who saw no contradiction between eloquence and piety. Étienne Delaruelle was right. This was the century of Gerson, and we must make room for it in the stories we tell.

But those stories will have complicated plots, wrinkles, and sharp turns. If the picture I have drawn is too clear, then I have probably not explained it well enough. While arguing for Gerson's value as a historical witness, his centrality to the trends of his age, I have also tried to lay bare his utter complexity, the contradictions and the tension in the historical space he occupies. He is so central to his culture that no trend or tradition fully escaped him. All the cultural traffic of the fifteenth century runs through him. But I repeat: he never rationalized the century's traditions into a system. Gerson wrote no summa. Instead, the competing instincts that those traditions encouraged sometimes left him torn and confused, hedging and backtracking. His story is nothing if not full of the unexpected. What good story is not?

Abbreviations

ACC	*Acta concilii Constanciensis.* Ed. Heinrich Finke et al. 4 vols. Münster, 1896–1928.
AHDLMA	*Archives d'Histoire Doctrinale et Littéraire du Moyen Âge*
AHR	*American Historical Review*
BEC	*Bibliothèque de l'École des Chartes*
CALMA	*Compendium auctorum Latinorum Medii Aevi.* Bottai, 2000–.
CPPMA	*Clavis patristica pseudepigraphorum Medii Aevi.* Turnhout, 1990–.
CUP	*Chartularium Universitatis parisiensis.* Ed. Heinrich Denifle and Émile Chatelain. 4 vols. Paris, 1889–1897.
DA	*Deutsches Archiv für Erforschung des Mittelalters*
DLF	*Dictionnaire des lettres françaises: Le Moyen Âge.* Paris, 1994.
DMA	*Dictionary of the Middle Ages.* New York, 1982–1989.
DMT	*Ioannis Carlerii de Gerson De mystica theologia.* Ed. A. Combes. Lugano, 1958.
DNB	*Oxford Dictionary of National Biography.* Oxford, 2004.
DS	*Dictionnaire de spiritualité ascétique et mystique, doctrine et histoire.* Paris, 1932–1995.
GW	*Gesamtkatalog der Wiegendrucke.* Leipzig, 1925–.
LMA	*Lexikon des Mittelalters.* Munich, 1977–1999.
MBKDS	*Mittelalterliche Bibliothekskataloge Deutschlands und der Schweiz.* Vol. 1, *Die Bistümer Konstanz und Chur.* Ed. Paul Lehmann. Vol. 2, *Bistum Mainz, Erfurt.* Ed. Paul Lehmann. Vol. 3, pt. 1, *Bistum Augsburg.* Ed. Paul Ruf. Munich, 1918–.
MBKDSE	*Mittelalterliche Bibliothekskataloge Deutschlands und der Schweiz, Ergänzungsband.* Vol. 1, *Handschriftenerbe des deutschen Mittelalters,* pt. 1, Aachen-Kochel; pt. 2, Köln-Zyfflich. Ed. Sigrid Krämer. Munich, 1989.
MBKO	*Mittelalterliche Bibliothekskataloge Österreichs,* vol. 1, *Niederösterreich.* Ed. T. Gottlieb. Vienna, 1915; rpt. 1974.
OC	*Jean Gerson, Oeuvres complètes.* Ed. P. Glorieux. 11 vols. in 10. Paris, 1960–1973.

OO	*Joannis Gersonii Opera omnia.* Ed. L. E. Du Pin. 4 vols. in 5. Antwerp, 1706.
PL	*Patrologiae latinae*
RBMA	Friedrich Stegmüller, *Repertorium biblicum medii aevi.* Madrid, 1950–1958.
RHE	*Revue d'histoire ecclésiastique*
RHT	*Revue d'histoire des textes*
RSD	*Chronique du religieux de Saint-Denys: Contenant le règne de Charles VI, de 1380 à 1422.* Ed. L. Bellaguet. 6 vols. Paris, 1839–1852.
RSR	*Revue des sciences religieuses*
RTAM/RTPM	*Recherches de théologie ancienne et médievale/Recherches de théologie et philosophie médiévales*
SOP	Thomas Kaeppeli, *Scriptores ordinis praedicatorum medii aevi.* Rome, 1970–1993.
VL	*Die deutsche Literatur des Mittelalters: Verfasserlexikon.* Berlin, 1977–.

Appendix

Gerson Manuscripts in Carthusian and Celestine Monasteries

This list includes manuscripts identified in the course of my research and does not pretend to be exhaustive. The information is drawn from (1) modern catalogues of extant manuscripts; (2) medieval catalogues; (3) scholarly literature; (4) personal examination of manuscripts; and (5) contemporary references (such as a reference by Gerson or by a scribe to a manuscript).

GERSON MANUSCRIPTS AND TEXTS IN CARTHUSIAN AND CELESTINE HOUSES

Carthusian house	MS volumes	Texts unique (total)	Questionable texts
Aggsbach	26	53 (69–71)	15
Antwerp	1–2	2	0
Basel	16	50 (68) [+22]	0
Brno	1	6	0
Buxheim	17	38 (48)	8
Castres	1	4	0
Cologne	18	76 (153)	13
Dijon	1	6	0
Erfurt	21	54 (80)	7
Gaming	1	5	0
Gdańsk	1	1	0
Grande Chartreuse	10 + 4	(?)	(?)
Güterstein	2	3	0
's-Hertogenbosch	1	2	0
Herne	1	1	0
Mainz	13	39 (51)	8
Mont-Dieu	2	9	0
Paris-Vauvert	1–3	20–24	0
Rettel	3	9	0
Roermond	2	3	0
Rostock	1	11	1
Seitz	2	5	0
Trier	9	24 (27)	3
Utrecht	1	1	0
Villeneuve	3–4	15 (16)	0
Wesel	2	44 (54)	0
Würzburg	1	3	0

Celestine house	MS volumes	Texts unique (total)	Questionable texts
Ambert	3	2 (3)	0
Amiens	2	4	0
Avignon	? + 4	(?)	0
Gentilly	2	1 (2)	0
Lyon	? + 6	(?)	0
Marcoussis	4	6 (7)	0
Metz	7	15	0
Offemont	1	2	0
Paris	10	18 (20)	0
Rouen	1	3	0
Sens	1	3	0
Vichy	1	1 (?)	0

Carthusian Monasteries

Aggsbach (26 MSS)
Sources: late fifteenth-century catalogue (*MBKO* 1.530–610)
MSS: Vienna, ONB, Cod. lat. 1158

Antwerp (1–2 MSS)
References: Stuttgart, WLB, Hs. HB I 10, ff. 183v and 304r, refer to original copies at Antwerp

Basel (16 MSS)
References: Gerz von Buren, *Tradition*

Brno (1 MS)
MSS: Vienna, ONB, Cod. lat. 4738

Buxheim (17 MSS)
Sources: catalogue, c. 1450 (*MBKDS* 3.1.91–101)
MSS: London, BL, Add. Ms. 41618; Vienna, ONB, Cod. ser. n. 3896; Cologne, HASK, Hs. W 56 (*MBKDSE* 1.131–43); Philadelphia, UPL, Ms. Codex 96 (Ouy, "Le Célestin," 307 n. 72)

Castres (1 MS)
MSS: Philadelphia, UPL, Ms. Codex 33

Cologne (18 MSS)
Sources: fifteenth-century catalogue
MSS: Berlin, SPK, Hs. lat. fol. 717 and theol. lat. fol. 712; Darmstadt, HLHB, Hss. 2, 707, 798, and 924; London, BL, Add. Ms. 54243; Münster, UB, N.R. 1551; New Haven, Yale Medical Library, Ms. 38; Oxford, Bodleian Library, Ms. lat. th. e. 18; Toledo (Ohio), Toledo Museum of Art, Ms. 1916.48; Vienna, ONB, Cod. lat. 4547. See *MBKDSE* 2.424–34;

Richard Bruce Marks, *The Medieval Manuscript Library of the Charter-house of St. Barbara in Cologne* (Salzburg, 1974).

Dijon (1 MS)
MSS: Dijon, BM, Ms. 214 (*OC* 7.xxxvi–xxxvii)

Erfurt (21 MSS)
Sources: late fifteenth-century catalogue (*MBKDS* 2.239–593; *MBKDSE* 1.215–24; *OC* 1.88)

Gaming (1 MS)
MSS: Vienna, ONB, Cod. lat. 1519 (Ouy, "Le Célestin," 306–8)

Gdańsk (1 MS)
MSS: Strasbourg, BM, Ms. 105 (Hogg, "Kartäuserhandschriften," 458).

Grande Chartreuse (10 + 4 MSS)
Sources: catalogue, c. 1450–1470 (Fournier, *Notice*, 60)
MSS: Grenoble, BM, Mss. 271, 298, 382, 398

Guterstein (2 MS)
Sources: catalogue, 1457 (*MBKDS* 1.153–75)

's-Hertogenbosch (1 MS)
MSS: Paris, BnF, Ms. lat. 10707 (Hogg, "Kartäuserhandschriften," 458)

Herne (1 MS)
MSS: Brussels, BR, Ms. 4935–43 (Kees Schepers, ed., *Ioannis Rusbrochii De ornatu spiritualium nuptiarum* [Turnout, 2004], 105–8)

Mainz (13 MSS)
MSS: Mainz, SB, Hss. I 13, I 30, I 127, I 132, I 134, I 135, I 138, I 161, I 173, I 215a, I 370, II 316 (*MTKDS* 2.532–49)
References: Emery, *Dionysii Cartusiensis Prolegomena*, 1.349 (lost Ms. "F.III.T")

Mont-Dieu (2 MSS)
MSS: Charleville-Mézières, BM, Mss. 52 and 58

Paris-Vauvert (1–3 MSS)
MSS: Paris, BnF, Ms. fr. 1029; possibly Ms. fr. 974 (*OC* 7.xxv, xxiii); possibly the exemplar of Paris, Bibliothèque Mazarine, Ms. 921 (Schepers, *Ioannis Rusbrochii De ornatu spiritualium nuptiarum*, 130–32)

Rettel (3 MSS)
MSS: Metz, BM, Mss. 354, 604 (from Trier), 1439

Roermond (2 MSS)
MSS: Brussels, BR, Ms. 2231–45 (Pons, *L'Honneur*, 161–62)

References: Stuttgart, WLB, Hs. HB I 10, f. 166v, refers to an original copy of *De examinatione doctrinarum* at Roermond

Rostock (1 MS)
MSS: Pelplin, Bibl. Seminarium Duchownego, [Ms.] 170/301 (*MBKDSE* 2.691–92; Seńko and Włodek, "Dzieła Gersona")

Seitz (2 MSS)
MSS: Giessen, UB, Hs. 85; Graz, UB, Hs. 1649

Trier (9 MSS)
MSS: Trier, Stadtbibliothek, Hss. 212/1119 8º, 597, 600, 604, 637, 683, 685, 690, 780

Utrecht (1 MS)
MSS: Utrecht, UB, Hs. 340 (J. P. Gumbert, *Die Utrechter Kartäuser und ihre Bücher im frühen fünfzehnten Jahrhundert* [Leiden, 1974], 335)

Villeneuve-les-Avignon (3–4 MSS)
Sources: early seventeenth-century catalogue (Anneliese Maier, "Ein Handschriftenkatalog der Kartause Vallis Benedictionis bei Avignon," in *Studi offerti a Roberto Ridolfi* [Florence, 1973], 347–67)
MSS: Marseille, BM, Mss. 237, 241
References: The seventeenth-century catalogue (Maier, pp. 356–57) refers to one or two other works of Gerson: *La montagne de contemplation* and possibly the *Monotessaron.*

Wesel (2 MSS)
MSS: Darmstadt, HLHB, Hss. 779, 788 (*MBKDSE* 2.830–31)

Würzburg (Engelgarten) (1 MS)
MSS: Würzburg, UB, Hs. 2 an: I. t. f. CCCXVI

Celestine Monasteries

Ambert (3 MSS)
MSS: Oxford, Bodleian Library, Ms. Rawlinson 156 (Ouy, "Le Célestin," 300); Paris, BnF, Ms. lat. 18572 (Ouy, "Le Célestin," 299–300)
References: *OC* 2.333 refers to a copy of *De distinctione verarum revelationum a falsis* at Ambert

Amiens (2 MSS)
MSS: Armagh, Public Library, Ms. G.IV.6 (Franz Blatt, "Studia Hibernica," *Classica et Mediaevalia* 14 [1953], 226–32); Cambridge, St. John's College, Ms. Y.1 (N. R. Ker, *Medieval Manuscripts in British Libraries* [Oxford, 1969–], 5.7)

Avignon (4+ MSS)
MSS: Avignon, BM, Mss. 329, 331 (?), 342, 615, 1098
References: *OC* 1.28 refers to Gerson's bequest to this house.

Gentilly (2 MSS)
MSS: Avignon, BM, Mss. 329, 1098

Lyon (6+ MSS)
MSS: Vatican City, BAV, Ms. Reg. lat. 335 (Ouy, *Gerson bilingue*, xxi)
References: *OC* 1.25–26 (cf. Ouy, "Le Célestin," 304 and n. 62) and
   10.554–61 refer to manuscripts in the possession of this house.

Marcoussis (4 MSS)
MSS: Oxford, Bodleian Library, Ms. Rawlinson 156 (Ouy, "Manuscrits
   jumeaux"); Paris, BnF, Mss. lat. 10709 and nouv. acq. lat. 3043 (Ouy,
   "Le Célestin," 284–89)
References: A sale catalogue (Jörn Günther Antiquariat [firm], *Fifty
   Manuscripts and Miniatures* [Hamburg, 2006]), describes a manuscript
   from this house, containing *De praeparatione ad missam* and *De arte
   audiendi confessiones.*

Metz (7 MSS)
MSS: Metz, BM, Mss. 266, 530, 600, 603, 611, 614, 617

Offemont (1 MS)
MSS: Paris, Bibl. de l'Arsenal, Ms. 2121

Paris (10 MSS)
MSS: Paris, Bibl. de l'Arsenal, Mss. 2109, 2176; Paris, Bibl. Mazarine,
   Mss. 945, 979; Paris, BnF, Mss. lat. 18572 (Ouy, "Le Célestin," 299–
   300), fr. 1790, fr. 9611; Paris, Bibl. Sainte-Geneviève, Ms. 1363; Vatican
   City, BAV, Mss. Reg. lat. 422 (Ouy, "Le Célestin," 294), 1554 (Roccati,
   "Manuscrits," 108–9)

Rouen (1 MS)
MSS: Avignon, BM, Ms. 331

Sens (1 MS)
MSS: Paris, Bibl. de l'Arsenal, Ms. 2176

Vichy (1 MS)
References: *OC* 2.336 refers to a copy of letter #42 at this house.

Notes

All translations are my own except where indicated.

Introduction

1. The passage is from *Rerum senilium libri* 9.1. Ouy, "L'humanisme du jeune Gerson," 256; Ornato, *Jean Muret*, 273, s.v. "Pétrarque (François)."

2. *OC* 10.7: "Gallia quae viris semper et strenuis bello et omni sapientia eruditis illustrata est, gravium et eloquentium historicorum atque poetarum magnam hactenus passa est inopiam. O si illam attigisset prior illa scriptorum solers industria, quamquam Dei nutu abunde aucta famataque sit, apud omnes tamen, et maxime posteros, clarior et quodammodo immortalior effulsisset. Nam quid Graecorum, Romanorum atque Trojanorum regna, etiam post ruinam, ad semotissimos populos celeberrima reddidit? Interrogati Sallustius atque Naso fatebuntur id elegantem scriptorum eloquentiam effecisse, quae famam illis genuit, muris etiam cadentibus, perire non valentem; adeo longaevior vivaciorque est scriptorum quam urbium duratio."

3. Ouy, "Les recherches," 290. Gerson repeats the idea in a Latin sermon for the feast of St. Louis, preached at the College of Navarre in 1392 (*OC* 5.240–41): "Et utinam ingentibus et maximis regum nostrorum virtutibus pares in eloquentia scriptores accessissent . . . ita in Gallicis fuit factorum quam verborum cura major."

4. *OC* 10.8: "Me frequens horum consideratio impulit ut causam fidei, quam ipsa Universitas Parisiensis nunc et olim prosequitur, quam verissime scriberem."

5. For context, see Marielle Lamy, *L'Immaculée Conception: Étapes et enjeux d'une controverse au Moyen-Âge (XIIe–XVe siècles)* (Paris, 2000), 562–75. See also McLoughlin, "Gerson as Preacher," 276–78. Cf. the résumé in *OC* 10.3–5 and the sources cited in Taber, "Pierre d'Ailly," 167 n. 12.

6. Boureau, "Peut-on parler d'auteurs scolastiques?" 267–79.

7. Ibid., 273–74.

8. Ibid., 271.

9. Cf. Eisenstein, *Printing Press*, 1.121.

10. *De laude scriptorum doctrine salubris* and not merely *De laude scriptorum* is the correct and complete title. See for example Marseille, BM, Ms. 241, f. 144r; Munich, Clm. 17837, f. 287v; Paris, BnF, Ms. lat. 17488, f. 164r and Ms. lat. 18205, f. 54r; Caen, Musée des Beaux Arts, Coll. Mancel Ms. 131, f. 193r–v; Stuttgart, WLB, Hs. HB I 10, f. 166r. The colophon to the Caen manuscript is reproduced in Jehan-Spencer Smith, *Notice bibliographique sur un traité manuscrit du quinzième siècle jusqu-ici inédit . . .* (Caen, 1860), n.p. See also in the text itself,

OC 9.424: "Scriptor idoneus et frequens librorum doctrinae salubris—sic enim semper infra loqui volumus et intelligi."

11. Delaruelle, Labande, and Ourliac, *L'Église au temps du Grand Schisme*, 837.

12. McGuire, *Jean Gerson and the Last Medieval Reformation*. For orientation to Gerson bibliography, see pp. 407–14. See also the essay collection edited by McGuire, *A Companion to Jean Gerson*.

13. The text is *OC* 7.2.519–38.

14. See Nicole Bériou, *L'avènement des maîtres de la Parole: La prédication à Paris au XIIIe siècle*, 2 vols. (Paris, 1998).

15. See esp. his comments at the beginning of *La montagne de contemplation*, *OC* 7.1.16.

16. Thomas Sullivan, *Parisian Licentiates in Theology, A.D. 1373–1500: A Biographical Register*, vol. 1 (Leiden, 2004), 19.

17. The chancellor of St. Geneviève licensed some of the students in the arts faculty. See Bernstein, *Pierre d'Ailly*, 13. On the development of the office before Gerson, see Gabriel, "Conflict," 106–54. On the chancellor's authority over false teaching, see Thijssen, *Censure*, 8–11. My thanks to William Courtenay for clarification on this issue.

18. *OC* 6.299. The year was 1418.

19. Beryl Smalley noted this similarity in "Jean de Hesdin O. Hosp. S. Ioh.," in *Studies in Medieval Thought and Learning from Abelard to Wyclif* (London, 1981 [1961]), 381. The pattern appears more general. Compare, for example, the career of Jean Beaupère, one of the interrogators at the trial of Joan of Arc, who entered the service of the duke of Burgundy. See further C. T. Allmand, "Un conciliariste nivernais du XVe siècle: Jean Beaupère," *Annales de Bourgogne* 35 (1963), 145–54.

20. Vansteenberghe, "Gerson à Bruges," 5–52.

21. For a lively description, see Huizinga, *Autumn*, 270–73.

22. The most recent treatment is Guenée, *Un meurtre, une société*. For a brief summary, see McGuire, *Jean Gerson*, 229–34.

23. For further details, see McGuire, *Jean Gerson*, 245–46.

24. Déniau, *La Commune de Lyon*, 361. Déniau cites the registers from 2 April 1427, but the text quoted in the footnote makes no reference to a journey, and this claim needs independent verification.

25. *OC* 1.146.

26. F. Palacky, *Documenta Mag. Joannis Hus vitam, doctrinam, causam in Constantiensi concilio actam et controversias de religione in Bohemia, annis 1403–1418 motas* (Prague, 1869), 278.

27. *OC* 1.145. The obituary dates from around 1430.

28. Berndt Hamm, "Hieronymus-Begeisterung und Augustinismus vor der Reformation: Beobachtungen zur Beziehung zwischen Humanismus und Frömmigkeitstheologie (am Beispiel Nürnbergs)," in *Augustine, the Harvest, and Theology (1300–1650)*, ed. K. Hagen (Leiden, 1990), 138, 196. For further references to Gerson's popularity, see Mertens, *Iacobus Carthusiensis*, 136; and Martin, *Fifteenth-Century Carthusian Reform*, 38.

29. Hobbins, "The Schoolman as Public Intellectual," 1311–12. The situation in print is no different. See Milway, "Forgotten Best-Sellers," 142.

30. See further Mazour-Matusevich, "Jean Gerson," 963–87.

31. Bejczy, *Erasmus*, 81–82.

32. Monika Ingenhoff-Danhäusr, "Die Kanzel," in *Die Amanduskirche in Bad Urach*, ed. Friedrich Schmid (Sigmaringen, 1990), 101–9.

33. On pulpits with the four Latin doctors, see J. Charles Cox, *Pulpits, Lecterns, and Organs in English Churches* (London, 1915), 70, 74; J. J. G. Alexander, "The Pulpit with the Four Doctors at St James's, Castle Acre, Norfolk," in *England in the Fifteenth Century (Proceedings of the 1992 Harlaxton Symposium)* (Stamford, UK, 1994), 198–206.

34. See for example Kaluza, *Les querelles doctrinales à Paris*, 60–61, 124. For other examples and further discussion, see Hobbins, "Beyond the Schools," 24–33.

35. See among many other important studies, Neddermeyer, *Handschrift*; Ornato, *La face cachée*; Parkes, *Scribes*; Petrucci, *Writers and Readers*; Rouse and Rouse, *Authentic Witnesses* and *Manuscripts*; and Saenger, *Space Between Words*.

36. On cursive scripts, see Saenger, *Space Between Words*, 257–58; Clanchy, *From Memory to Written Record*, 129–30; Parkes, "Literacy," 285.

37. Neddermeyer, *Handschrift*, 1.25, 256–64. On cursive bookhands, see Saenger, *Space Between Words*, 257–58. On the introduction of paper, see Burns, "Paper"; and (for England) Lyall, "Materials."

38. Bozzolo and Ornato, *Pour une histoire*, 31–37. Cf. on prices of earliest printed books Neddermeyer, *Handschrift*, 1.368–77, 2.831–62.

39. Neddermeyer, *Handschrift*, 1.258–62.

40. For bibliography on late medieval literacy, see Marco Mostert (ed.), *New Approaches to Medieval Communication* (Turnhout, 1999), 209, 244–46; Amtower, *Engaging Words*, 32–37; Neddermeyer, *Handschrift*, 1.26–28; Hasenohr, "Religious Reading," 206 n. 3; Watts, "Pressure," 162 n. 18. See also Charles F. Briggs, "Literacy, Reading and Writing in the Medieval West," *Journal of Medieval History* 26 (2000), 397–420. On the growth of grammar schools in the fourteenth century, see Verger, "Schools and Universities," 226.

41. Amtower, *Engaging Words*, 19–31; McGrady, *Controlling Readers*, 3–4, 245–46 nn. 5–8; Hasenohr, "L'essor."

42. The key study is Parkes, "Influence." See also Rouse and Rouse, "*Ordinatio*"; and Rouse and Rouse, "*Statim invenire*," 191–219.

43. Cf. Neddermeyer, *Handschrift*, 1.217–18, on a supposed declining interest in books and libraries, and on contemporary criticism of attitudes toward books.

44. Rouse, "Backgrounds to Print," 450.

45. His methodology involves counting the total number of surviving manuscripts by century in the great European collections and estimating a loss rate derived from the percentage of surviving incunabula in modern libraries. See Neddermeyer, *Handschrift*, 1.47–91 and the diagram on 2.581. The crucial step is the estimate of loss (1.72–85). Neddermeyer bases this estimate on the survival rate of incunabula, where we sometimes know the original print run. He estimates this survival rate as 4.2 percent, but then takes into account factors that would make manuscripts both more and less likely to survive (pp. 79–80). For late medieval manuscripts (up to one hundred years before print), he estimates a survival rate of one out of fifteen or 7 percent, with regional variation. To estimate manuscript production over time, Neddermeyer relied on dated manuscripts but also took into account the higher occurrence of dated manuscripts from the high to the late Middle Ages, from around 5 percent in the twelfth century to around 50 percent in the fifteenth century (1.58).

46. Neddermeyer, *Handschrift*, 1.222, 288–97; 2.657.

47. Clanchy, *From Memory to Written Record*, 50, 58–61; Daniel Lord Smail, *Imaginary Cartographies: Possession and Identity in Late Medieval Marseille* (Ithaca, N.Y., 2000), 21–23. On Italy, see Neddermeyer, *Handschrift*, 1.288–89; Hagen

Keller, "Vom 'heiligen Buch' zur 'Buchführung': Lebensfunktionen der Schrift im Mittelalter," *Frühmittelalterliche Studien* 26 (1992), 1–31.

48. Emily Steiner, *Documentary Culture and the Making of Medieval English Literature* (Cambridge, 2003).

49. Knapp, "Bureaucratic Identity," 366.

50. F. P. van Oostrom, *Court and Culture: Dutch Literature, 1350–1450* (Berkeley, 1992), 9; quoted in Knapp, *Bureaucratic Muse*, 7.

51. See in general Ornato, *Jean Muret*. Cf. Gilli, "L'humanisme français," 55–58.

52. Gabriel, "Conflict," 108.

53. The *CUP* has scattered references to officials of the chancellor. See *CUP* 3.757, s.v. "Cancellarius Parisiensis." See also Bernstein, *Pierre d'Ailly*, 82, 92–93.

54. For orientation to the literature see Watts, "Pressure," 159–80, esp. 162–73. See also Nolan, *Lydgate*, 5–10; and esp. for France and the Continent, Guenée, *L'opinion publique*, 217 n. 3; Guenée, *L'Occident aux XIVe et XVe siècles: Les états*, 6th ed. (Paris, 1998), cvii–cviii.

55. Guenée, "Les campagnes de lettres," 45–65.

56. For France, see Novák, "La source du savoir," 152–58. For England, see esp. Scase, "Imagining Alternatives to the Book"; and Scase, "'Strange and Wonderful Bills.'" See also on Lollard book production Hudson, "A Lollard Quaternion"; and Hudson, "Lollard Book-Production." On the means of diffusion of the Hussite movement, see Marin, *L'archevêque*, 214–29.

57. See the two articles by Scase in the previous note, esp. "'Strange and Wonderful Bills,'" 237–38.

58. Watts, "Pressure," 164.

59. See further Celenza, *Lost Italian Renaissance*, 30, with references to the literature at 170 n. 37.

60. For the vast literature on early French humanism, see Roccati, "Formation"; Ouy, "Les recherches"; and Gilli, "L'humanisme français."

61. Ouy, "Le Collège de Navarre"; Gorochov, *Le Collège de Navarre*, 473–505; Ornato, *Jean Muret*, 272, s.v. "Collège de Navarre."

62. On Petrarch's influence upon the French humanists, see Ouy, "Pétrarque."

63. Ornato, *Jean Muret*, 232.

64. Cecchetti, *L'evoluzione*. Ouy also notes that Clamanges made extensive philological annotations to his copies of Cicero, Virgil, and Macrobius ("'Taedium,'" 10–12).

65. Ouy, "Le Collège de Navarre," 285–86.

66. Ouy, "Gerson, émule de Pétrarque."

67. For the eclogue, ibid. See also *OC* 10.290–95. Nicholas Mann discovered the connection between the sermon *Quaerite Dominum . . . Ces paroles sont escriptes* (*OC* 7.2.969–78) and the *De remediis*, and concluded that for Gerson, Petrarch was "une source non seulement de philosophie mais aussi de style" (Mann, "Fortune," 7–9 [quotation at 9]).

68. Mann, "Petrarch's Role," 7; Mann, "Fortune," 1–4. See also Rummel, *Humanist-Scholastic Debate*, 30–34. Riccardo Fubini sees more ambiguity in the reputation of Petrarch among Italian and French humanists of the succeeding generation, specifically "more radical elements" that were "then turned against his late-fourteenth-century public image." See his *Humanism and Secularization*, 95–100 (quotation at 97).

69. Ouy, "La plus ancienne oeuvre," 440–53.

70. Bejczy, "Erasme explore le moyen âge," 474. Cf. Trithemius on Gerson, described as "sermone scholasticus" (*OC* 1.146).

71. References to the "Sola Gallia monstro caruit" motif (ultimately derived from Jerome, but widely current at the time) include *OC* 2.159; 4.6, 32; 7.2.522–23; 10.10, 19, 87. See further Ouy, "La plus ancienne oeuvre," 449–50, 475; and Ouy, "La preuve," 272–73.

72. Gerson follows D'Ailly in his use of the theme (cf. *CUP* 3.399, no. 1519) in *OC* 7.329. Other references include *OC* 4.31–32 (ll. 33–37); 5.340, 362; and 10.9. See also Lusignan, "L'Université de Paris," 59–72.

73. *OC* 7.2.1116. On Gerson's strong identification with France, see Hobbins, "Joan of Arc," 120. The sermon's date is contested. See most recently Guenée, *Un meurtre, une société,* 217–18.

74. *OC* 7.2.772. Gerson was regularly preaching at court and might have heard such conversations in 1392 when John of Gaunt visited France and spent time with Philip the Good, duke of Burgundy, or perhaps sometime after he became almoner to the duke in April 1393. From what we know of John of Gaunt, this is just the kind of thing he would have said after 1381 when he repented of adultery. Gaunt also withdrew his support for Wyclif from 1382. See on these matters Anthony Goodman, *John of Gaunt: The Exercise of Princely Power in Fourteenth-Century Europe* (New York, 1992), 241–65. Goodman also notes (p. 37) that Gaunt had some training in logic. On Gerson's attachment to the duke of Burgundy, see *OC* 1.109; McGuire, *Jean Gerson,* 59.

75. *OC* 3.334, 340. Cf. on Scotland Michael Van Dussen, "Conveying Heresy: 'A Certayne Student' and the Lollard-Hussite Fellowship," *Viator* 38, no. 2 (2007), 217.

76. *OC* 6.212, 286; 9.449.

77. *OC* 5.238. The sermons on St. Louis are nos. 217, 219, and 223 in *OC* vol. 5.

78. Ornato, *Jean Muret,* 61–62.

79. On Glorieux's edition, see McGuire, *Jean Gerson,* 407; Hobbins, "Beyond the Schools," 4–5 n. 6.

Chapter 1. Gerson as Bookman

1. On the identity of Michael Hartrut, whom Glorieux called Michael Bartine, see Hobbins, "Editing and Circulating Letters," 185–86.

2. *OC* 9.613: "Confitebor autem in insipientia mea quod a triginta annis et amplius familiares habere volui praedictos tractatulos saepe legendo, saepe ruminando, etiam usque ad verba nedum sententias. Et ecce hac aetate, hoc otio, velut ad votum vix perveni usque ad initium gustus eorumdem, qui repetiti mihi semper novi fiunt et placent, juxta illud Flacci de poemate vel imagine compositi eleganter: decies repetita placebit."

3. A brief and elegant introduction to the work is Jordan, *Care of Souls,* esp. 8–20.

4. Letter of 10 December 1513. James B. Atkinson and David Sices (trans. and ed.), *Machiavelli and His Friends: Their Personal Correspondence* (Dekalb, Ill., 1996), 264.

5. Ouy, "Les premiers humanistes," 270.

6. *OC* 2.127, 3.334, 9.188, 3.129, 5.61, 5.96, 6.199 (cf. 8.546). *On the Twelve Fruits of Tribulation* remains unidentified.

7. *OC* 2.126, 56; 3.68, 8.274; 5.234.

8. Grafton, "Humanist as Reader," 181–82.

9. Hamesse, "Scholastic Model," 117–18.

10. See for example Lynn Thorndike (trans.), *University Records and Life in the Middle Ages* (New York, 1971), 194, 244–45.

11. Cf., for southern France, Verger, "Le livre," 407–16.

12. C. H. Talbot, "The Universities and the Mediaeval Library," in *The English Library Before 1700*, ed. F. Wormald and C. E. Wright (London, 1958), 73. On the few large private libraries in the thirteenth century, see Christ, *Handbook*, 297–307.

13. Weiss, "Private Collector," 112–13. I know of no study devoted specifically to private libraries of university masters. On private French libraries in general in this period, see Hasenohr, "L'essor." Rather disappointing in its treatment of private libraries is M. H. Jullien de Pommerol, "Livres d'étudiants, bibliothèques de collèges et d'universités," in *Histoire des bibliothèques françaises*, vol. 1, *Les bibliothèques médiévales du VIe siècle à 1530*, ed. A. Vernet (Paris, 1989), 93–111.

14. On the reading of French laity, see Hasenohr, "Religious Reading."

15. On its possible destruction in 1413, see Ouy, "Les premiers humanistes," 270; *OC* 10.512.

16. Ouy, "Le Célestin," 284–85; the manuscript is Paris, BnF, Ms. lat. 2768.

17. Talbot, "Universities," 73; Verger, "Le livre," 409.

18. Autrand, "Les librairies," 1225.

19. Ibid., 1226; Ouy, "Les premiers humanistes," 269–70. In general on Courtecuisse, see *DLF*, 765. There is disagreement over the size of Pierre d'Ailly's library. See Boudet, "Un prélat," 128.

20. Adam Ludwik Szafrański, *Materiały do historii teologii średniowiecznej w Polsce* (Warsaw, 1974), 1.58–64; Hoenen, *Marsilius of Inghen*, 10, 20.

21. *OC* 5.385: "Vidi nuper sanctum Thomam et Bonaventuram; hic reliquorum libros non habeo."

22. Ouy's suggestion, that he may have lost some or most of it during the civil uprising at Paris in 1413, is plausible but remains a supposition. "Les premiers humanistes," 270. See also Hobbins, "Editing and Circulating Letters," 182–83. Ouy suggests ("Les premiers humanistes," 277) that the library of Jean de Montreuil was destroyed at the time of the massacre at Paris in 1418, when he was killed. Gerson's library might have been destroyed at this time.

23. *OC* 1.27–28, 2.334. His precise references to Bernard's sermons on the Song of Songs throughout his career suggest that he probably owned this text as well. See *OC* 2.54 (1402), 2.127 (probably 1409), 2.298–99 (c. 1427–1428).

24. Ong, *Orality*, 119–20.

25. Carruthers, *Book of Memory*.

26. Trapp, "Augustinian Theology," 146–52.

27. *OC* 2.314–19. Other lengthy quotations include: from a *Sentences* commentary of Henry of Oyta (3.242), from a sermon of Bernard on the Song of Songs (2.54), from an anonymous sermon to the Carthusians (2.99–100), from Bede's commentary on the Gospel of Mark (3.27), from Quintilian's *Institutio oratoria* (5.162), from Seneca's tragedies (5.375), from Boethius's *De consolatione* (5.400, 523), from Hugh of St. Victor's *De arrha animae* (8.557), from Aquinas's *De regimine principum* (10.192–94), and from Nicole Oresme's translation of Aristotle's *Politics* (10.196–98). The work containing the last two quotations, from Aquinas and Oresme, also includes a long schedule of passages on tyrannicide from many different authors (10.199–206).

28. On Denys, see Emery, "Denys the Carthusian and the Invention of

Preaching Materials," 381. On reference consultation more generally, see Saenger, "Silent Reading," 376, 385.

29. The manuscript is briefly described in *BEC* 96 (1935), 218. On the evolution of author portraits, see Saenger, *Space Between Words*, 251, with references. Cf. Lesley Smith, "*Scriba, Femina*: Medieval Depictions of Women Writing," in *Women and the Book: Assessing the Visual Evidence*, ed. Lesley Smith and Jane H. M. Taylor (London, 1996), 21–44.

30. In 1409 or 1413 Gerson did not have a copy of his lecture *Super victu et pompa praelatorum* (*OC* 2.127). See on this instance Lieberman, "Chronologie gersonienne" (1960), 90–91. In 1427, he did not have a work that he had written on confessing diurnal pollution (2.298–99). But Gerson may well have said this (*sed apud me non habeo*) with the knowledge that the Celestines of Lyon, a short walk's distance, did have a copy.

31. Hobbins, "Editing and Circulating Letters," 179.

32. Besides the letter, see *OC* 2.101, 246, 307–8; 7.133; 8.154–55, 172, 292, 553; 9.10, 193, 538, 551.

33. On Clamanges, see Ouy, "Les premiers humanistes," 275.

34. See Gerson's letter of May 1423 to Jean the Celestine (*OC* 2.246), where Gerson refers to *De theologia mystica* as being "now in your possession." See also the letter of Jean the Celestine to a correspondent at the Grande Chartreuse (*OC* 10.561), in which he refers to the "excellent works" Gerson had "recently" shared with him.

35. On the Sorbonne, see Rouse, "Early Library." On the College of Navarre, see E. Châtelain, "Les manuscrits du collège de Navarre en 1741," *Revue des bibliothèques* 11 (1901), 362–411. On the different kinds of libraries available in the fifteenth century, see other essays in Rouse and Rouse, *Authentic Witnesses*, and Martin, *The History and Power of Writing*, 186–88. See further references in Autrand, "Les librairies," 1222 nn. 15–16.

36. Rouse, "Early Library."

37. Gilli, "L'humanisme français," 47–48, mentions the bequest of a copy of Cicero's *Verrine Orations* possibly in 1395 or 1396.

38. Mary A. and Richard H. Rouse (eds.), *Registrum Anglie de libris doctorum et auctorum veterum* (London, 1991). Other union catalogues are mentioned in Talbot, "Universities," 78, and Christ, *Handbook*, 43–44, 244. See also Neddermeyer, *Handschrift*, 1.285.

39. Rouse and Rouse, "Bibliography," 480–86.

40. Neddermeyer, *Handschrift*, 1.286.

41. Bozzolo and Ornato, *Pour une histoire*, 93.

42. Ibid., 93, 95, 116–18.

43. *OC* 6.149. Gerson refers to him as the "Cardinal de Chalanco," probably Antoine de Challant, who attended the Council of Constance. See *LMA* 2.1656–57. Cf. *CUP* 4.201.

44. *OC* 9.465.

45. The manuscript is Paris, BnF, Ms. lat. 3348A. Bourgain, "L'édition," 53. Jacques Lefèvre d'Etaples also knew of these copies. See A. Renaudet, *Préreforme et humanisme à Paris pendant les premières guerres d'Italie (1494–1517)*, 2nd ed. (Paris, 1953), 483 n. 1.

46. *OC* 2.316. Otto Pächt, "Jean Fouquet: A Study of His Style," *Journal of the Warburg and Courtauld Institutes* 4, nos. 1–2 (Oct. 1940–Jan. 1941), 100–101.

47. *OC* 7.133.

48. *OC* 2.333: "Vel in Aurelianis reperietur vel in Amberto." The Celestine

house of St. Mary of the Assumption in Ambert (dioc. Orléans) was founded in 1304. It is not clear what religious house Gerson had in mind by referring Bassand to Orléans. Cf. the list of Celestine houses in Borchardt, *Cölestiner*, 355–70.

49. *OC* 2.336. Gerson also said that he shared his *Dialogus de perfectione cordis* with the Celestines, presumably at Lyons (2.295).

50. Ouy, *Gerson bilingue*, xvii–xxi.

51. *OC* 2.112. See also on this point Ouy, *Gerson bilingue*, xv–xvi.

52. Ornato, *Jean Muret*, 159–60, 76, 154–55. For more on the French humanists and their pursuit of the classics, see Ornato, "Les humanistes français."

53. *OC* 2.126. Cf. 8.174, 581. On this letter, see the studies of Lieberman listed on *OC* 2.xviii.

54. Lieberman, "Chronologie gersonienne" (1959), 289–336, esp. 303ff.

55. Rudolf Goy, *Die Überlieferung der Werke Hugos von St. Viktor* (Stuttgart, 1976), 329–40.

56. Bozzolo, "La production manuscrite," 221, and, more generally on this point, 219–30.

57. Autrand, "Les librairies," 1236. See also Verger, "Le livre," 409–11.

58. Reiter, "Masters, Students, and Their Books," 389–401.

59. Minnis, *Medieval Theory of Authorship*, 5.

60. In *Medieval Theory of Authorship*, Minnis traces the influence on Middle English writers. For the influence on Dante, Boccaccio, and Petrarch, see A. J. Minnis and A. B. Scott (eds.), *Medieval Literary Theory and Criticism c. 1100–c. 1375: The Commentary Tradition* (Oxford, 1987). The classic study on academic prologues as a genre is Edwin A. Quain, "The Mediaeval Accessus ad Auctores," *Traditio* 3 (1945), 215–64. This article was reprinted with "slight modifications" as an independent volume (New York, 1986).

61. *OC* 2.94; 5.196; 6.204; 8.113, 380; 10.142, 215.

62. Constable, "Forgery," 9.

63. Examples of works not by Gerson include *La danse macabre* (*OC* 7.286–301) and the *Regulae de modis titulandi et apificandi* (9.700–703).

64. See the many essays on this general topic in *Fälschungen im Mittelalter: Internationaler Kongress der Monumenta Germaniae Historica München, 16–19 September 1986*, 6 vols. (Hannover, 1988).

65. Minnis, *Medieval Theory of Authorship*, 10–12 (quotation at 11).

66. Blanche B. Boyer and Richard McKeon (eds.), *Sic et non: A Critical Edition* (Chicago, 1975), 91–92; Minnis, *Medieval Theory of Authorship*, 59.

67. *OC* 10.142.

68. *OC* 2.320. Cf. 3.293, 5.486. Gerson refers to the work by incipit even after he discovered the author: "Viae Sion lugent." It has been known by other titles, including *De triplici via* and *De mystica theologia*. On the problem of the work's authorship, see Dennis D. Martin, *Carthusian Spirituality: The Writings of Hugh of Balma and Guigo de Ponte* (New York, 1997), 9–14; on the more than one hundred manuscripts, with reference to some that attribute the work to Hugh of Balma, pp. 12 and 258 n. 38.

69. See for example the note on *De remediis contra pusillanimitatem* in Salzburg, SBSP, Hs. b.V.13, f. 242v: "Visum est aliquibus quod non Gerson sed alter auctor sit huius tractatus propter stili discrepanciam sed potuit ita fieri quod Gerson fecerit in vulgari gallice et alter transtulit in latinum quod et ego opinor. Quidquid tamen sit materie utiles sunt et bene fundate que amplectantur prius nomine auctoris." Cf. Gerson's own use of stylistic criteria in *OC* 9.64: "Item tractatus quem ascribunt aliqui sancto Thomae, sed magis apparet ex stylo et

materia quod sit Bonaventurae, qui incipit: Quoniam fundamentum et janua, etc. et est utilis multum." The work in question is the *De confessione vel de munditia cordis*, which appears in one of the manuscripts of the library at St. Victor (Paris, BnF, Ms. lat. 14920 ff. 69r–101r; Calvot and Ouy, *L'oeuvre de Gerson*, 71). On Guigo, see Constable, "Forgery," 18.

70. *OC* 9.470: "Remittamus ad illam quam libenter hic et alibi commemoramus Summam; quoniam ex optimis undecunque collecta est: cujus auctor contemporaneus satis fuit Guillelmo Parisiensi, et sancto Thomae de Aquino, vir sine gradu, de conventu Praedicatorum Lugdunensium." On Peraldus, see Antoine Dondaine, "Guillaume Peyraut, vie et oeuvres," *Archivum Fratrum Praedicatorum* 18 (1948), 162–236; on the *Summa*, 184–97; on the interpretation of this passage, with reference to Combes, 174–75. The Bibliothèque nationale de France in Paris has forty MSS from the thirteenth century alone.

71. Two early sermons, in 1392 and 1397, attribute the work to Augustine: *OC* 5.231, 585. All other references drop the attribution: *OC* 2.275; 3.203, 215; 8.174, 179, 294–95, 312, 571. See also 10.555, where Jean the Celestine has Gerson refer to "the author" of both the *Summa on Vices and Virtues* and *On the Spirit and the Soul*. On the widespread attribution of *On the Spirit and the Soul* (*De spiritu et anima*) to Augustine, see *CPPMA*, 2A, 76–78; Wilson, "Contents," 88.

72. Chenu, *Toward Understanding Saint Thomas*, 132 n. 7. The work is edited in *PL* 40.779–832.

73. *OC* 10.104: "Auctor libri De vetula . . . et false adscripserit Ovidio."

74. See the two modern editions of the *De vetula*: Dorothy M. Robathan, *The Pseudo-Ovidian De vetula* (Amsterdam, 1968), 9; and Paul Klopsch, *Pseudo-Ovidius De vetula: Untersuchungen und Text* (Leiden, 1967), 84. Robathan notes that D'Ailly had some contact with Arnoldus Geilhovenus, a Dutch humanist who first suggested the attribution to Richard de Fournival (d. before 1261).

75. Thomas Netter, *Doctrinale antiquitatum fidei catholicae ecclesiae* (Venice, 1757–59; rpt., Farnborough, U.K., 1967), 2.293–94. See Catto, "Wyclif," 260 and n. 274, who says that the author was Rupert of Deutz. For further discussion, see Catto, "Scholars," 771–73.

76. Eisenstein, *Printing Press*, 1.183–90.

77. Grafton, "Importance," 281–82.

78. Borchardt, *Cölestiner*, 97 (quotation), 135.

79. On Ubertino, see G. L. Potestà, "Ubertino de Casale," *DS* 16 (1992), 3–15.

80. *OC* 2.274: "Scripsit fatemur, immo libere confitemur; et utinam stetisset in illis stylus suus; utinam conformasset se doctrinis illorum quos allegat quandoque. Saepe vero magnas partes excerpit et rapit in propria forma tacitis auctorum nominibus; nescimus si par esse voluerit Aesopi corniculae, plumis aliarum volucrum se ornantis. Creber fuit apud istum Bonaventura cum suo Breviloquio, sed vix nominatus ex illo. Multi praeterea sunt sermones sub contextu suae locutionis quos in forma legimus apud libros alios non modicae vetustatis."

81. See here Constable, "Forgery," 1–41.

82. *OC* 2.322; 9.64, 410, 475, 612.

83. Boureau, "Peut-on parler d'auteurs scolastiques?" 270.

84. *OC* 10.455–56; *CUP* 4, no. 1761. On the period at Bruges, still indispensable is Vansteenberghe, "Gerson à Bruges."

85. *OC* 2.30–35. On the dating of this letter, see Vansteenberghe, "Quelques écrits de Jean Gerson," *RSR* 13 (1933), 411–24. On the letter itself, see Kaluza, *Les querelles doctrinales à Paris*, 13–15.

86. *OC* 2.32. Cf. the letter of Jean the Celestine in 1423 (*OC* 10.555): "Quorum [i.e., doctorum] equidem in elucidatione divinae legis tantus fuit labor ut incredibili studio pene plures ediderint libros quam exiguitas ingenii sequentium vel legere vel apprehendere potuerit."

87. *OC* 2.33: "Quosdam in transitu raptim videamus quasi eos non penitus ignorasse satis sit, et eis fiat vale perpetuum. Aliis per vices utamur prout se dederit necessitas delectationisve congruitas. At vero quosdam familiares advocemus nobis assiduos et tamquam domesticos fidelissimos eos intra mentis nostrae cubilia, inter secreta quotidianaque colloquia jugiter collocemus."

88. *OC* 2.33.

89. A crucial passage on the importance of terminology appears in *De modis significandi*, *OC* 9.629–30.

90. See Hasenohr, "La littérature religieuse," 287; *CPPMA*, 2B, 700–703.

91. *OC* 2.212, in the list of reading for the dauphin, sent to his tutor. The Meditations of Pseudo-Augustine and Pseudo-Anselm survive in more than 150 manuscripts, those of Pseudo-Bernard in two hundred. Neddermeyer, "*Radix Studii*," 459.

92. *OC* 2.33–34. On *De contemplatione et eius speciebus*, see István Bejczy, "*De contemplatione et eius speciebus*: A Work Falsely Attributed to Hugh of Saint Victor," *Studi Medievali* 45 (2004), 433–43.

93. Hamesse, "Scholastic Model," 107–10. This entire article addresses this theme.

94. Hamesse, *Auctoritates*, 24–35, 48–50.

95. Hamesse, "Scholastic Model," 111.

96. Ibid., 105.

97. René Gandilhon, *Sigillographie des universités de France* (Paris, 1952), nos. 8, 26, 35, 103, 173. Cf. Verger, "Le livre," 405–7. For further context, see Saenger, *Space Between Words*, 258–61.

98. The phrase of Marcel Jousse, quoted in Hamesse, "Scholastic Model," 104. On the monastic model of reading, see the classic study of Jean Leclercq, *The Love of Learning and the Desire for God: A Study of Monastic Culture*, 3d ed. (New York, 1982).

99. On the concept of the canon and its distinction from other kinds of lists, I have found helpful Jonathan Z. Smith, *Imagining Religion: From Babylon to Jonestown* (Chicago, 1982), 44–48.

100. John Guillory, *Cultural Capital: The Problem of Literary Canon Formation* (Chicago, 1993), 29.

101. *OC* 2.126; 3.68–69; 5.55–56, 100, 486; 8.32, 294–95; 9.612–13. On bibliographies in general, see Neddermeyer, *Handschrift*, 1.285–87.

102. This is the *Annotatio doctorum aliquorum qui de contemplatione locuti sunt*, *OC* 3.293. Lieberman ("Chronologie gersonienne" [1958], 339–75) challenged its authenticity and preferred an attribution to Jean the Celestine. I accept its authenticity, as does Ouy, but the issue needs revisiting. Cf. Ouy, "Le Célestin," 293–94. A fourth, previously unknown version exists in Giessen, UB, Hs. 763 f. 222r–v. The version of the text in this manuscript contains a portion of a letter of Gerson to Oswald of Bavaria. This inclusion of another text of Gerson at the end of the list is important evidence. By far the most thorough critical edition is Combes, *Essai*, 1.652–64, 822–24, 868–69.

103. I have compiled these figures from the sources in the previous two notes, as well as from the lists to the hermit addressed in letter 21 (*OC* 2.83), to the new bishop in letter 24 (2.112), and to the dauphin's tutor in letter 42 (*OC* 2.212–13).

104. *OC* 2.32, 33; 9.630; 10.556.

105. *OC* 3.256.

106. *OC* 10.256.

107. *OC* 5.250. Gerson might have mistaken Guillelmus Durandus, who did attend but is not considered a major theologian (at least not by Gerson), for Durandus of St. Pourçain. On the meeting at Vincennes, see William J. Courtenay, "The Parisian Faculty of Theology in the Late Thirteenth and Early Fourteenth Centuries," in *After the Condemnation of 1277: Philosophy and Theology at the University of Paris in the Last Quarter of the Thirteenth Century: Studies and Texts*, ed. Jan A. Aaertsen, Kent Emery Jr., and Andreas Speer (Berlin, 2001), 244.

108. Hoenen, "Via Antiqua," 19.

109. See the English translation in Van Engen, *Devotio Moderna*, 70–71. On later adaptations, see Kock, *Buchkultur*, 122–53.

110. Maureen Quilligan, "The Allegory of Female Authority: Christine de Pizan and Canon Formation," in *Displacements: Women, Tradition, Literatures in French*, ed. Joan DeJean and Nancy K. Miller (Baltimore, 1991), 126–27; Knapp, *Bureaucratic Muse*, 9–12, 51, 107–27 (quotation at 116); Lerer, *Chaucer and His Readers*.

111. A good survey of scholarship on Capreolus can be found in Guy Bedouelle, Romanus Cessario, and Kevin White (eds.), *Jean Capreolus en son temps (1380–1444)* (Paris, 1997).

112. *Doctoris ecstatici D. Dionysii Cartusiani Opera omnia* (Monstrolii, 1896–1913), 38.542, 41.625–26; Kock, *Buchkultur*, 130.

113. Karl A. E. Enenkel and Jan Papy (eds.), *Petrach and His Readers in the Renaissance* (Leiden, 2006); Grendler, *Universities*, 203–4.

114. Hoenen, "Tradition," 462–63, and 473 nn. 2 and 5 for further literature. On the *via antiqua* and the *via moderna*, see Hoenen, "Via Antiqua," 13–22; and Courtenay, "Antiqui," 3–10. The two *viae* represented two methods of explaining Aristotle, but the stakes were much higher than just this, and though the debate arose out of the arts faculty, it came to include theologians involved with accusations of heresy. Hoenen notes ("Via Antiqua," 19) that Scotus marked the chronological dividing line between the two camps. The first use of the terms *antiqui* and *moderni* in this sense occurred in 1425. Hoenen, *Marsilius of Inghen*, 13–14.

115. Guillory, *Cultural Capital*, 26–27.

116. See Lusignan, *"Vérité garde le Roy."* References to the "Sola Gallia monstro caruit" motif (ultimately derived from Jerome, but widely current at the time) include *OC* 2.159; 4.6, 32; 7.2.522–23; 10.10, 19, 87. See further Ouy, "La plus ancienne oeuvre," 449–50, 475; and Ouy, "La preuve," 272–73.

117. *OC* 5.384–85: "Huic veritati fundatae supra petram Sacrae Scripturae quisquis a proposito detrahit cadit in haeresim jam damnatam quam nullus unquam theologus, maxime Parisiensis, et sanctus asseruit."

118. *OC* 2.32. On the long history of the expression *tritum iter*, and with special reference to Gerson, see Andrea Robiglio and Zénon Kaluza, "Appunti sulla 'strada battuta,'" *Bulletin Du Cange* 63 (2005), 251–67.

119. Cf. Pierre Ceffons, who characterized the opponents of Jean de Mirecourt as "shriveled old women" (*vetulae rugosae*) who cannot read or write a *quaestio*. See D. Trapp, "Peter Ceffons of Clairvaux," *RTAM* 24 (1957), 138, 148, 152. My thanks to William Courtenay for this reference.

120. *OC* 8.303: "Cognovimus, proh dolor, aliquos quibus omnis doctrina miscens cum speculativa pietatem fidei ad effectum, reddebatur gravis, molesta,

nauseans et onerosa ita ut doctores deriderent devotos ut idiotas et vetulas, quales sunt apud tales Gregorius, Bernardus, immo, damnata arrogantia et amentia, Augustinus et dominus Bonaventura cum similibus. Est, inquiunt, doctrina eorum ad praedicationem et devotionem, quasi stare nequeant pariter devotio et eruditio. . . . Devotio nihil habens de philosophia vel theologia scholastica speculativa, sufficit ad salutem; . . . Philosophia vero et theologia sine devotione dispergunt superbos mente cordis sui, deprimunt et avertunt ut se misceant quaestionibus infinitis." Cf. Kaluza, *Les querelles doctrinales à Paris*, 60–61.

121. *OC* 8.366: "Collaudandus est ad extremum doctor theologus cujus doctrina sic erudit ad intellectus distinctionem quod non minus allicit, trahit et inducit ad affectus unionem."

122. For an overview of Gerson's views on Bonaventure, see Glorieux, "Gerson et saint Bonaventure."

123. *OC* 10.256. On Gerson's critique of Albert, see Kaluza, "Gerson critique." Kaluza is modifying Combes, who saw Albert solely as the means of introducing Gerson to Pseudo-Dionysius. The *De intellectu et intelligibili* is edited in *B. Alberti Magni . . . Opera omnia*, ed. A. Borgnet, vol. 9 (Paris, 1890), 477–521. For context, see Benedict M. Ashley, "St. Albert and the Nature of Natural Science," in *Albertus Magnus and the Sciences: Commemmorative Essays 1980*, ed. J. A. Weisheipl (Toronto, 1980), 73–102.

124. *OC* 8.601. This passage provides the key to another, in the *Tractatus de canticis* (*OC* 9.565), where Gerson speaks of "two outstanding theologians," one of whom followed the philosophy of Aristotle rather than Augustine in his terminology of the passions.

125. Pierre d'Ailly, *Tractatus ex parte universitatis*, quoted in Hoenen, "Via Antiqua," 24 n. 62.

126. The two manuscripts with this different version are Paris, BnF, Ms. lat. 14902, f. 163v; and Giessen, UB, Hs. 763, f. 180r. (I did not consult Vienna, ONB, Cod. Ser. n. 3887, ff. 156r–160r.) Because of the importance of this passage, I provide here the reading in full from the Giessen manuscript (cf. *OC* 2.33–34; *OO* 1.108): "Ad primum iuvant, exempli gratia, questiones doctorum super sententias et presertim illorum qui purius et solidius conscripserunt. Inter quales, meo iudicio, dominus Antisiodorensis, Bonaventura et Durandus utique resolutissimus numerandi videntur. Excellit quidem in suis quolibet Henricus de Gandavo, excellit sanctus Thomas [Paris 14902 and *OO* 1.108 add: "praesertim"] Secunda-secundae, excellunt multi recensiores." Glorieux knew of only two manuscripts of this letter.

127. The manuscript with the first version, Paris, Bibl. de l'Arsenal, Ms. 523, is clearly an early and important manuscript (Glorieux dated it to 1408: *OC* 1.101; cf. Combes, *Essai*, 1.99), and seems to be closely connected to Jean the Celestine. The table of contents of this manuscript indicates that the works have been listed "non eo quidem ordine quo compilata sunt sed quo presenti volumine reponuntur" (f. 5r). Cf. the letter of Jean the Celestine to Anselm in 1423, describing the accompanying list of Gerson's works: "Non autem eo tempore vel ordine quo peracta sunt ordinavi omnia, sed prout occurrerunt memoriae" (*OC* 10.561). The Arsenal manuscript requires further, careful study. My thanks to Gilbert Ouy for his insight on this point.

128. *OC* 2.112. On the dating, see Ouy, *Gerson bilingue*, xl n. 4. The intended audience of the work is clear from the reference to the work as "de casibus reservatis ad episcopos" in *OC* 8.52. See also the praise of the *Secunda-secundae* in the prologue to the *Monotessaron* possibly written by Jean the Celestine, *OC* 9.246–47.

129. Boyle, "Setting," 16.

130. See further Krieger, " 'Theologica perscrutatio.' "

131. *OC* 2.277–78. Thomas Netter likewise saw Berengar of Tours as an outstanding heretic. See M. Hurley, "A Pre-Tridentine Theology of Tradition: Thomas Netter of Walden (†1430)," *Heythrop Journal* 4 (1963), 352.

132. *OC* 9.475: "Sed dum studet illuminationi intellectus, totum refert ad pietatem et religiositatem affectus."

133. *OC* 9.475.

134. Hamm, "Hieronymus-Begeisterung," 139. On Gerson and *Frömmigkeitstheologie*, see Grosse, *Heilsungewissheit*; more generally but still with frequent reference to Gerson, see Hamm, *Frömmigkeitstheologie*.

135. Catto, "Theology After Wycliffism," 265; Hoenen, "Tradition," 462 and 473 n. 4.

136. Schreiner, "Laienfrömmigkeit," 42.

137. For another interpretation of the common school, see Combes, *Essai*, 2.422–35.

138. This listing could easily be lengthened. Catto, "Theology After Wycliffism," 264–65; Braakhuis and Hoenen, "Marsilius," 9–10; Post, *Modern Devotion*, 80–82 (on Salvarvilla). See also Courtenay, *Teaching Careers*, 32.

139. Smoller, *History, Prophecy, and the Stars*, 95–101.

140. Hoenen shows that Gerson saw in Plato two tendencies, one positive and one negative. Positively, Gerson identified Plato's Ideas with God, and therefore placed him within the tradition of belief in God. Negatively, Gerson rejected Plato's equation of human and divine thought as independent and eternal, since this challenged the Christian notion of creation, in which only God is eternal. See Hoenen, " 'Modus loquendi platonicorum,' " 329.

141. *OC* 2.97. See also 9.629.

142. Kaluza, *Les querelles doctrinales à Paris*, 14–15, 43, 60–63.

143. Asztalos, "Faculty," 434, 437. As chancellor, Gerson presumably would have had immediate access to an archive, though its exact nature is unclear. But see Gabriel, "Conflict," 108.

144. See esp. the comments in *OC* 5.245.

145. *OC* 2.98. Cf. the prologue to the *Monotessaron*, perhaps written by Jean the Celestine, *OC* 9.246, which states that Christians need to find order in theology, to reduce variety to a few terms: "Sibi resolutionem et ordinem ad pauca, quoniam habet omnis varietas ad unum vel pauca reduci."

146. *OC* 2.277: "Secutus est doctor iste [Bonaventure], se testante, doctrinam communem et solidam quae Parisius vigebat maxime tempore suo."

147. *CUP* 2.588.

148. Gerson refers variously to a *communis veritas* (*OC* 3.239, 8.274), a *communis scola* (2.62, 273–74; 3.182; 5.181; 9.630; *DMT*, 227 [*OC* 8.157]), a *communis Minerva* (*OC* 2.32). See further below. On *infertilis varietas* and *singularitas doctorum et doctrinarum*, see Kaluza, *Les querelles doctrinales à Paris*, 16 and 28 n. 11.

149. Courtenay, "Inquiry"; Thijssen, *Censure*.

150. Courtenay, "Inquiry," 173–77; Thijssen, *Censure*, 111, 113–16.

151. Courtenay, "Preservation," 1663.

152. Courtenay, "Inquiry," 178–81 (quotation at 181).

153. *OC* 2.279: "Egregie dudum mihi tunc adolescentulo dixit unus in theologia doctor et famatissimus: dum quaesiverit, inquit aliquis si praescindatur essentia divina ab intellectu divino, quid est illa essentia, dic quod est Deus et quod non est Deus. Est itaque Deus quia nihil est in Deo quod non sit Deus; et

tamen non est Deus quia Deus est suus intellectus nec esse potest sine ipso. Hoc est sententialiter argumentum beati Bernardi contra Gilbertum." Cf. 2.27.

154. *OC* 2.28. Gerson's suggestion is important evidence for an early attempt to publicize condemned articles. On the lack of any institutional mechanism for gathering together lists of condemned articles in this period, see Courtenay, "Preservation," 1659–67, esp. 1663–64.

155. *OC* 2.273–74, 3.182, 5.181, 8.157, 9.630.

156. *OC* 3.245.

157. *OC* 3.244.

158. For Gerson's references to the translations of Eriugena, see *OC* 8.553, 9.638. For his awareness of different translations of Aristotle, see *OC* 5.231. Kaluza notes that late in his career, Gerson was still using Eriugena's translation of the *De mystica theologia* of Pseudo-Dionysius. Kaluza, "Gerson critique," 192–93 n. 42. But since Gerson knew of Grosseteste's translations, the problem was likely one of access.

159. *OC* 3.245.

160. "Nobis ad certam regulam loqui fas est" (from *The City of God*, bk. 10, ch. 23; *PL* 41.300). Cf. *CUP* 3.492, 501. I have slightly modified the translation by J. W. C. Wand (London, 1963). See *OC* 2.26, 61, 97, 278; 3.244, 336; 5.228, 476, 477. The passage in Augustine continues: "For fear that a looseness of language might give rise to a blasphemous opinion about the realities to which the words refer."

161. *CUP* 3.492, 501. Wolfgang Hübener first connected Gerson's use of this passage in Augustine to the Monzon affair: "Konservativismus," 171–72. Cf. Combes, *Essai*, 1.387, 629 note b.

162. Hübener, "Konservativismus," 172.

163. Rummel, *Humanist-Scholastic Debate*, 83, 155, 177–81.

164. Cf. Courtenay, "Inquiry," 172–74, 178–79.

165. A good introduction is James A. Wiseman, *John Ruusbroec, The Spiritual Espousals and Other Works* (New York, 1985), 7–22.

166. Jan de Grauwe corrects the spelling found in Glorieux (Clantier), and provides further details about his family, in *Historia Cartusiana Belgica*, Analecta Cartusiana 51 (Salzburg, 1985), 13. On the exchange more generally, see Combes, *Essai*.

167. *OC* 2.56.

168. *OC* 2.57–59.

169. *OC* 2.60–61.

170. *OC* 3.293.

171. *OC* 2.62. This idea of nonimitation of the fathers is an important theme in Gerson. See esp. *De remediis contra tentationes*, *OC* 9.521–23. On the history behind Climacus's terminology, see *DS* 1.727–46. Cf. Combes, *Essai*, 1.634 note *a*.

172. Coville, *Jean Petit*, 142–59; Willard, "Manuscripts," 271–80, esp. 274–76.

173. Coville, *Jean Petit*, 138–39, 403–501.

174. *OC* 2.162–66. Cf. Matthew Spinka, *John Hus: A Biography* (Princeton, 1968), 241. Some manuscripts transmit just the articles. See *OC* 2.xx. The articles also appear in Vienna, ONB, Cod. lat. 4933, ff. 56v–58r.

175. Matthew Spinka, *John Hus at the Council of Constance* (New York, 1965), 228–31.

176. On this point, see the crucial passage in the sermon of 21 July 1415 with the application of this passage to Hus (*OC* 5.476–77, and cf. the same point

made a year or two earlier in *De sensu litterali sacrae scripturae*, 3.334–35). Gerson repeated much of the language of the sermon less than a year later in a work related to the condemnation of Jean Petit's articles in defense of tyrannicide (10.259–60).

177. Gerson refers to this decision in *Contra curiositatem studentium*, *OC* 3.245. Cf. *CUP* 4, no. 1749.

178. *OC* 2.102. Other important passages on Lull include *OC* 9.465, and of course the entire tract, *OC* 10.121–28.

179. *OC* 10.256.

180. Courtenay, "Inquiry," 181.

181. Thijssen, *Censure*, 117.

182. Anne Hudson, "Netter, Thomas (*c.*1370–1430)," *DNB* 40.444–47. On the spread of Wyclif's teachings, see *OC* 3.334, 340.

183. *BRUO* 1.386–87.

184. Norman Tanner (ed.), *Heresy Trials in the Diocese of Norwich* (London, 1977); *Correspondence of Bekynton*, iii (Rolls Series, 1872), 275–76.

185. Catto, "Wyclif," 260.

186. Cf. Ullmann, *Humanism*, 101.

187. Quoted in Graff, "Literacy Patterns," 78.

188. Graff, "Literacy Patterns," 79. See further Harvey J. Graff, *The Labyrinths of Literacy: Reflections on Literacy Past and Present* (Pittsburgh, 1995); Graff, *The Legacies of Literacy: Continuities and Contradictions in Western Culture and Society* (Bloomington, Ind., 1987).

Chapter 2. Justifying Authorship

1. *OC* 10.556.

2. *OC* 2.232, 286; 3.57, 250–51; 8.47. See further Hobbins, "Beyond the Schools," 147–48.

3. For what follows, see Minnis, *Medieval Theory of Authorship*, 192–210.

4. *Troilus and Criseyde*, bk. 2, st. 2, lines 4–7; st. 3, lines 1–4 (ed. Skeat), quotation at st. 3, l. 4. See further examples in Minnis, *Medieval Theory of Authorship*, 192–93, 197–98, 203–4.

5. *OC* 8.565. Cf. on the circumstances of the writing of this work, 2.313.

6. Cf. *OC* 8.79, though here Gerson claims to hesitate (*sub dubio fluctuare*) because of the difficulty of the task: "Denique tanta reperitur difficultas, tanta pro diversitate hominum varietas in practicando doctrinam verae sanctaeque meditationis, quod an silere vel aliquid scribere consultius sit, videor egomet mihi quandoque sub dubio fluctuare."

7. *OC* 2.42: "Neque enim famam meam in ore hominum . . . neque opuscula mea ita velut proprios filios diligere." Cf. Lieberman, "Chronologie gersonienne" (1958), 366.

8. *OC* 2.42.

9. Harold Bloom, *The Anxiety of Influence: A Theory of Poetry*, 2nd ed. (New York, 1997); Elizabeth Cheresh Allen, *A Fallen Idol Is Still a God: Lermontov and the Quandaries of Cultural Transition* (Stanford, 2007), 14–15, 19.

10. *OC* 9.420.

11. "Metrum contra curiositatem scribendi plures libros" (*OC* 4.160). Glorieux's edition has been superseded by that of Ouy, " 'Taedium,' " 25–26.

12. *OC* 10.8.

13. Mourin, *Jean Gerson*. No similar study of the Latin sermons exists.

14. My definition recalls the tract as understood in early modern English usage: "a short pamphlet on some religious, political, or other topic, suitable for distribution or for purposes of propaganda" (*Oxford English Dictionary*, 2nd ed., s.v. "tract," I.3.a). Cf. the discussion of "Schreitschriftenliteratur" during the Schism in Miethke, "Die Konzilien als Forum," 741–42.

15. *OC* 2.159. Cf. *OC* 5.223–24. Although Gerson normally appears to have used the term *novissimi* to refer to his own time, he does apply it to Aquinas and Bonaventure as well. See also *OC* 10.256, where he refers to thirteenth-century theologians as ancient doctors.

16. *OC* 2.33–34. Cf. *OC* 2.277, 8.364, and 9.465. See further Kaluza, *Les querelles doctrinales à Paris*, 44–45 and 72 n. 34. On the term *recentiores*, see Hobbins, "Beyond the Schools," 141 n. 5.

17. Kaluza, *Les querelles doctrinales à Paris*, 40–45, 60–63, 124.

18. On Maisonneuve, Kaluza, *Les querelles doctrinales à Paris*, 92–106, 124; and on Denys, Emery, "Denys the Carthusian," 334.

19. On Henry of Oyta, see *OC* 3.241–42. Among many references to D'Ailly, see in particular 2.64; 5.362, 524; 6.303.

20. Edith Sylla, "Autonomous and Handmaiden Science: St. Thomas Aquinas and William of Ockham on the Physics of the Eucharist," in *The Cultural Context of Medieval Learning* (Dordrecht, 1975), 352; Murdoch, "From Social into Intellectual Factors," 278; Bert Hansen, *Nicole Oresme and the Marvels of Nature: A Study of His De causis mirabilium with Critical Edition, Translation, and Commentary* (Toronto, 1985), 111 n. 46.

21. Murdoch, "From Social into Intellectual Factors," 276.

22. The image is from *Africa*, IX, 553; quoted in Peter Burke, *The Renaissance* (London, 1964), 2.

23. Eugene F. Rice Jr., "The Humanist Idea of Christian Antiquity: Lefèvre d'Etaples and His Circle," in *French Humanism 1470–1600*, ed. W. L. Gundersheimer (London, 1969), 174.

24. Key passages in Gerson here include *OC* 2.33–34, 98. See also the prologue to the *Monotessaron*, probably written by Jean the Celestine, *OC* 9.246. For Gerson, this view of the thirteenth century took shape as part of his reaction against the perceived abuses of more recent authors. Besides the passages above, see *OC* 2.277, 8.364, 9.465; and Kaluza, *Les querelles doctrinales à Paris*, 44–45, 72 n. 34, 124.

25. *OC* 2.98.

26. Brian Stock, *The Implications of Literacy: Written Language and Models of Interpretation in the Eleventh and Twelfth Centuries* (Princeton, 1983), 517–21.

27. Thijssen, *Censure*, 94–95.

28. Ibid., 111–12, summarizing 99–107.

29. See the excellent study of Douglass Taber Jr., "Pierre d'Ailly."

30. *OC* 9.462.

31. *OC* 3.201. Gratian attributed to theologians a "gift of knowledge" but insisted that bishops and pope have the authority to supervise the community of believers. See further Thijssen, *Censure*, 95–96. And especially on the "determination" for D'Ailly, Taber, "Pierre d'Ailly," 172.

32. Gerson refers to the quotation from Peter of Spain as a "maxim of the logicians": "Cuilibet experto in arte sua magis credendum est" (*OC* 2.62, 98, 211, 228; 6.230; 7.2.545, 600; 9.420; 10.86, 117; cf. *OC* 2.244; 9.218). This adage appears in Peter of Spain's *Summulae logicales* (ed. de Rijk), 76. He received the adage of Horace (epist. 2,1,15) through an epistle of Jerome (epist. 53.6; *PL* 22,

544): "Quod medicorum est promittunt medici, tractant fabrilia fabri" (*OC* 2.26; 5.130; 9.471, 491; 10.86).

33. *OC* 7.2.1076.

34. On this and subsequent development of the doctrine, see Marielle Lamy, *L'Immaculée Conception: Étapes et enjeux d'une controverse au Moyen-Âge (XIIe–XVe siècles)* (Paris, 2000).

35. Gerson mentions the stubbornness of the Dominicans and attempts to solve the passage they use to reject the Immaculate Conception in one of the late letters to Oswald, *OC* 2.326.

36. *OC* 7.2.1077.

37. *OC* 7.2.1076. See Gregory's homilies on Ezekiel (bk. 2, hom. 4; *PL* 76.980). Similar notions were current from at least the twelfth century onward. See Constable, "Forgery," 36–38.

38. The statement appears in the context of four considerations on why holy doctors such as Jerome, Augustine, and Bernard seem to speak against the Immaculate Conception. *OC* 7.2.1076.

39. *OC* 5.353; 7.1.15, 72. On the cult of St. Joseph, see Hobbins, "Beyond the Schools," 283–85.

40. *OC* 2.329–30.

41. On D'Ailly, cf. Taber, "Pierre d'Ailly," esp. 170–74.

42. For Gerson's attitude toward canon lawyers, see Posthumus Meyjes, "Exponents," 308–11; Posthumus Meyjes, *Jean Gerson,* 220–30. Krynen, "Les légistes," 193–98, provides valuable historical context for Gerson's hostility toward jurists, with special reference to Nicole Oresme. On Gerson's influence on Nicholas of Kempf in this area, see Martin, *Fifteenth-Century Carthusian Reform,* 73 n. 7, 74.

43. *OC* 6.154.

44. Gerson praised *De consideratione* as early as his sermon for the feast of St. Louis in 1393 (*OC* 5.152).

45. Valois, "Un nouveau témoignage," 175–79.

46. Guillaume de Mota is named in some manuscripts. See, for example, Erlangen-Nürnberg, UB, Hs. 541, f. 226v (*Katalog der Handschriften der Universitätsbibliothek Erlangen* [Erlangen, 1928–], 2.167).

47. Gerson's attack on the canon lawyer appears in *De contractibus* (*OC* 9.409–21). The author is identified as Catalonian in certain manuscripts of the work, but not in the edition. The treatise (which Gerson identifies with the incipit "Contractus quidam") has not been identified, but Gerson's summary of the work suggests it was written by a canon lawyer. Cf. Glorieux, "Gerson et les Chartreux," 133–34 and n. 51. Various manuscripts add the *consilium* of Johannes of Imola after the close of Gerson's *De contractibus,* prefacing it with the following (Seitenstetten, SB, Hs. 49 [f. 135v]): "After the above there was also a conference at the studium of Bologna for the purpose of quieting consciences. There, a very distinguished and famous doctor of both laws took up the preceding matter, and he—that is the reverend H. Imola—likewise examined the Chancellor's treatise. At length, agreeing with the said Catalonian, he concluded that the aforesaid contracts were illicit, although not usurious" ("Post predictam etiam habitum est consilium de studio Bononiensis propter securiorem conscientiarum tranquilitatem, ubi precipue egregius utriusque juris et famosus doctor materiam precedentem discutiendam suscipiens, et ipse tractatum Cancellarii similiter perspiciens, videlicet dominus H. Ymola, pro et contra, ut moris est, arguit; et tandem cum predicto Cathalano idem sentiens, predictos contractus

concludit illicitos etsi non usurarios"). The date 1429 appears at the end of the *consilium*. "H. Imola" is certainly a mistake for "J. Imola." In 1429, Johannes of Imola is known to have been at the University of Bologna. See D. Staffa, "De Iohannis ab Imola vita et operibus," *Apollinaris* 10 (1937), 90. Frankfurt, SUB, Hs. Barth. 141, f. 283v has "Jo. de ymo. bononie." Gerhardt Powitz and Herbert Buck, *Die Handschriften des Bartholomaeusstifts und des Karmeliterklosters in Frankfurt am Main* (Frankfurt, 1974), 327.

48. Grévy-Pons, *Célibat*, *OC* 9.476; Pascoe, "Nobility," 315–18.

49. *OC* 3.167. This passage is taken from the fourth lecture of the *De vita spirituali animae*, which deals with the abuse of positive law. Another important reference appears in Gerson's address in 1408 to the licentiates in canon law, *OC* 5.439.

50. For further orientation on this debate between canonists and theologians, see Van Engen, "Practical Theology," 873–96 (quotation at 895). See also Takashi Shogimen, "The Relationship between Theology and Canon Law: Another Context of Political Thought in the Early Fourteenth Century," *Journal of the History of Ideas* 60 (1999), 417–32.

51. *OC* 5.220–21.

52. *OC* 5.226–27.

53. *OC* 5.225.

54. *OC* 5.226. Cf. 9.471–72; 5.173–76.

55. See the overview in *OC* 10.52–54. The Hussite position is edited in Hermann von der Hardt, *Magnum oecumenicum Constantiense Concilium* (Frankfurt, 1700), 3.761–66. Gerson alludes to the "general warning" (*monitio generalis*) in the first line: "Oblaturus iuxta seniorum huius sacri Concilii Constanciensis monitionem generalem" (*OC* 10.55).

56. *OC* 10.58–59. See also *OC* 5.430–31: "Cuius Facultatis auctoritas major est in hac parte quam unius glossatoris, quia Decreta sunt dicta doctorum sanctorum theologorum quae melius intelligi possunt a theologis quam a solis juristis, sicut architectonica judicat de ceteris."

57. *OC* 6.154.

58. The summary occupies *OC* 9.410–15, the ten observations 9.415–20.

59. *OC* 9.420: "Doctores autem viventes non minorem habent auctoritatem doctrinaliter exponendi Sacram Scripturam vel interpretandi jura, quam mortui, et qui non scripserunt quam qui scripserunt. Et ideo frustra fit aliquando tot allegationum multiplicatio, confestim ut unus aliquid scripsit, et contemnitur viventium consilium, qui saepius attendere magis possunt circumstantias particulares secundum quas variari judicium saepe necesse est, quemadmodum dicunt experientissimi medicorum in hominibus sanandis quod regulae generales traditae sub arte, vix inveniuntur practicabiles absque exceptione; multo magis in moralibus hoc evenit, quanto plures sunt mutationes animorum quam corporum. . . . Patet exinde quorumdam nimia humilitas vel vanitas, qui requisiti dicere quid sentiant de aliquo casu morali, confugiunt statim ad allegationes super allegationes, et ad glossas super glossas, dimissis etiam quandoque textibus aut principiis universalibus ad quae debet resolutio fieri, dicentes: iste sic sentit, alter sic sentit, alter approbat eum, alter sentit cum isto; quibus recte dici potest: dic non quod alii scripserunt, sed qui tu ipse dicis vel sentis." A record of the actual case survives and was printed in *ACC* 4.709–10. (Another copy appears to be in Paris, Bibliothèque Mazarine, Ms. 1330, ff. 310–312.) According to this record, D'Ailly argued that the contracts in question were permissible as long as the intention of those who purchased the contracts (pensions, in this case, purchased by members of a religious house) was not usurious.

60. *Quodl. IV*, art. 18, cited in Chenu, *Toward Understanding Saint Thomas*, 87–88 n. 15 (Chenu's translation, slightly modified).

61. *OC* 9.409: "Expertus sum, inquit, dum in allegationibus iurium mihi veritas impugnari videbatur, si dismissis glossis super glossa recursus mihi fiebat ad nudam textus litteram, mox apertior patebat intellectus, fatentibus hoc idem et mirantibus allegantibus in adversum." See also *OC* 6.211 and 8.343.

62. Cf. Lk 5:31–32: "Et respondens Iesus dixit ad illos non egent qui sani sunt medico sed qui male habent. Non veni vocare iustos sed peccatores in paenitentiam." See further Tentler, *Sin and Confession*, 157–58.

63. J. Alberigo et al. (eds.), *Conciliorum oecumenicorum decreta* (Bologna, 1973), 245: "Sacerdos autem sit discretus et cautus, ut more periti medici superinfundat vinum et oleum vulneribus sauciati, diligenter inquirens et peccatoris circumstantias et peccati, per quas prudenter intelligat, quale illi consilium debeat exhibere et cuiusmodi remedium adhibere, diversis experimentis utendo ad sanandum aegrotum."

64. The teaching of civil law had been prohibited at Paris in the university's early history. But Hilde de Ridder-Symeons notes that "foreigners regarded the law university of Orléans as the faculty of civil law of the University of Paris." "Mobility," 291.

65. For example, Gerson once consulted medical masters on the causes of pollution, in preparation for his *De cognitione castitatis* (*OC* 9.51). He also addressed the faculty of medicine on at least one occasion (5.44–51). Joseph Ziegler notes that the themes in that address correspond to themes in an earlier sermon of Humbert of Romans to students in medicine. Ziegler, *Medicine and Religion c. 1300* (Oxford, 1998), 2.

66. *OC* 9.425.

67. Siraisi, "Surgery," 105.

68. Jacquart, "Medical Scholasticism," 224–26, quotation at 226.

69. Pesenti, "Generi e pubblico," 523–24.

70. Cohn, "Black Death," 709; and at greater length in *The Black Death Transformed*, 67–68, 233–38.

71. *OC* 8.107. Gerson included a large section of *De directione cordis* (nearly seven pages in the edition), including the section summarized, in a letter to his brother, Jean the Celestine (*OC* 2.175–91). Glorieux dated the letter to 1416–1417. Glorieux gives a date of 23 July 1417 to the treatise but, as usual, fails to explain where he found the date or to justify it. The corresponding texts are *OC* 2.183–91 ("Descendamus consequenter . . . de moribus judicat") and *OC* 8.101–7 ("Descendamus consequenter . . . judicat alienis").

72. *OC* 9.425.

73. See Hamesse, *Auctoritates*, 235: "Virtus est habitus electus in mente consistens quo ad nos declarata ratione ut utique sapiens determinabit."

74. *OC* 8.129.

75. *OC* 2.43 (on the variety of spiritual tastes), 2.236 (that the Carthusian order is successful in part because it allows for individual differences), 2.328 (that laws must take into account the variety of persons), 8.79 (on whether to write because of human diversity), 9.18 (that wine affects people differently because it changes the "accidental disposition" of blood and the humors and spirits), 9.497 (that according to the distribution of tasks in the body [Rom. 12:14], a particular church such as the church of Lyon can be distinguished by a "hierarchical and beautiful variety").

76. Van Engen, "Practical Theology," 882–90. On the older tradition, see Baldwin, *Masters*, 1.53–57.

77. Boyle, "Quodlibets," 245.

78. Cf. Van Engen, "Practical Theology," 894: "Theologians had come to follow the canonists or practical theologians in thinking of simony as essentially not a problem of heresy or of heretical sacraments but of endless moral *casus* involving transactions at all levels between the spiritual and the material."

79. On the traditional province of the canonists, see Van Engen, "Practical Theology," 882–83.

80. Cf. Van Engen, "Practical Theology," 880–83, 894.

81. Most of the emphasis is on the early modern period. I found the following essay collections helpful: Braun and Vallance, *Contexts of Conscience;* James F. Keenan and Thomas A. Shannon (eds.), *The Context of Casuistry* (Washington, D.C., 1995); Edmund Leites (ed.), *Conscience and Casuistry in Early Modern Europe* (Cambridge, 1988).

82. For Gerson's use of *epikeia,* see Posthumus Meyjes, *Jean Gerson,* 242–46. Cf. Bernstein, *Pierre d'Ailly,* 55–56. Still useful is Riley, *Epikeia,* 52–54. See also D'Agostino, "Un contributo."

83. Riley, *Epikeia,* 28–32.

84. *OC* 9.126.

85. *OC* 9.72.

86. *OC* 5.452.

87. *OC* 3.166.

88. See the following examples: on confessions in the sermon *Si non lavero te,* 1399 (*OC* 5.509); again in *Quaestiones 4 circa poenitentiam, et de detractione,* 1400–1415 (*OC* 9.72); and again in *Regulae morales,* 1400–1415 (*OC* 9.126); on revelations in *De distinctione verarum revelationum a falsis,* 1401 (*OC* 3.37; Gerson refers to this passage more than twenty-five years later in the *Collectorium super Magnificat, OC* 8.351); on restitution when a prelate has spent the *bona ecclesiastica* lavishly, in *Super victu et pompa praelatorum,* 1402 (*OC* 3.102); on moral cases generally, besides *De vita spirituali animae,* in *Multum valet deprecatio,* 1416–1417 (*OC* 2.183) and in *De directione cordis,* 1417 (*OC* 8.101); and again (contrasting moral probabilities with mathematical certainties) in the *Collectorium super Magnificat,* 1426 (*OC* 8.364–65); on the danger of simony in the performance of spiritual offices and in pluralism, in the sermon *Poenitemini et credite,* 1404 (*OC* 5.452); on visions in *De probatione spirituum,* 1415 (9.178–79); on the uncertainty of astrological judgments, in the sermon *Jacob autem genuit Joseph,* 1416 (*OC* 5.347; see also *De respectu coelestium siderum,* 1419, *OC* 10.112); on prayer in *De directione cordis,* 1417 (*OC* 8.105); on the celebration of Mass in *De contractibus,* 1421 (*OC* 9.402); on the danger of simony in the granting of temporalities in return for spiritual services, in *Tractatus de sollicitudine ecclesiasticorum,* before 1423 (*OC* 9.439, and see further on 440). Cf. *OC* 3.86; 6.113; 9.99, 363; 10.133.

89. Astrology: *OC* 5.347, and see also 10.112; revelations: 3.37 (cf. the later reference to this passage, 8.351); public vices: 9.99, 409–10. Yet when it came to heresy, Gerson occasionally saw himself as crafting the general rules that could then be applied to stamp out the heresy. See, for example, *OC* 10.59. Cf. in the *Contra superstitionem sculpturae leonis, OC* 10.133.

90. On scrupulosity, see Tentler, *Sin and Confession,* 156–62.

91. *OC* 8.364–65.

92. Stone, "Probabilism," 114–57 (here at 116–17). On probabilism, with some reference to Gerson, see also James Franklin, *The Science of Conjecture: Evidence and Probability Before Pascal* (Baltimore, 2001), 69–76.

93. *OC* 9.402: "Sed haec et similia dimittimus exercitio logicorum, dicentes

quod probabilis certitudo sufficit in moralibus ut non exponat se quis periculo, sicut dicunt doctores de celebrante missam et similibus ubi requiritur status gratiae, quod sufficit ad hoc probabilis conjectura; quia certitudo alia sine revelatione non habetur, prout in moralibus dicit Aristoteles sumendam esse certitudinem grosse et figuraliter."

94. See further Hobbins, "Joan of Arc," 109–10 and n. 47.

95. *OC* 9.402: "Propterea consilium est quod in materia morali non ita leviter asseratur aliquid esse peccatum mortale dum aliquis doctor dat consilium super aliquo actu quod non fiat; maxime dum plures alii posse bene fieri dicunt, aut quod cadit sub dubio, prout in casu nostro notatum est. Ubi patet quale labyrinthum conscientiarum timoratarum incurritur si quaelibet opinio vel consilium doctoris sufficit ad incertitudinem faciendam, cum frequenter opiniones nedum variae sed adversae sint inter doctores, nunc propter passiones animorum, nunc propter varios aspectus circumstantiarum, modo illarum solum, modo aliarum, modo omnium, unde ortum est illud comicum: quot capita, tot sententiae."

96. *OC* 2.292. See 9.50–51 for another reference to experience gleaned from confessions.

97. Ouy, "Gerson and the Celestines," 113–40. Ouy dates the work to "ca. 1400."

98. E. F. Jacob, *The Fifteenth Century 1399–1485* (Oxford, 1976), 311.

99. The manuscript figures are my own. For the incunabula figures, see *GW*, vol. 9, nos. 10830, 10808–15, 10733–40, 10831.

100. Mormando, "'To Persuade Is a Victory,'" 58–59.

101. Quotation from the *Oxford English Dictionary*, s.v. "casuistry."

102. Braun and Vallance, *Contexts of Conscience*, x.

103. Braun and Vallance, *Contexts of Conscience*, x and 180 n. 6. A thoughtful plea for casuistry in resolving modern ethical problems is Richard B. Miller, *Casuistry and Modern Ethics: A Poetics of Practical Reasoning* (Chicago, 1996).

104. Ouy, "De Gerson à Geiler von Kaysersberg," 136 and n. 28; Grosse, *Heilsungewissheit*, 3.

105. Ouy, citing B. Möller, in "De Gerson à Geiler von Kaysersberg," 656. See also 661 for reasons given for Gerson's popularity with Geiler's circle. And Hamm, *Frömmigkeitstheologie*, 136, discussing the separation of Gerson as a nominalist from his status as a spiritual authority: "Seine mächtige Wirkung, die er als Lehrer geistlicher Lebensführung, als 'doctor consolatorius,' ausübte und die ihn in Deutschland geradezu zum Kirchenvater des 15. Jahrhunderts machte, war gegenüber seinem Nominalismus weitgehend abgeschirmt." See also Grosse, *Heilsungewissheit*, 3 n. 18. For the placement of Gerson in the nominalist tradition, see Oberman, *Harvest*; for criticism, see Steven Ozment, "Mysticism, Nominalism and Dissent," in *The Pursuit of Holiness in Late Medieval and Renaissance Religion*, ed. C. Trinkaus (Leiden, 1974), 67–92.

106. In his *Protestatio ad superiorem suum* (c. 1440–1441). Emery, "Denys the Carthusian," 329.

107. From his *De vita et miraculis Joannis Gerson*: "Neque enim inhaerebat curiosis speculationum ambagibus nec circa vanam subtilitatum ostentationem sollicitus nec in novitatibus adinveniendis turgidus fuit. Versabatur autem in his studiis, quae ad dei laudem, ad fidei robur, ad plantandam ecclesiam, ad conscientiae pacem, ad consolandos pusillanimes, ad morum aedificationem, ad animarum salutem utilia et necessaria esse videbantur." Petrus Schott (1460–1490) describes Gerson as one "non haerentem in curiosis ambagibus, non in vana

subtilium ostentatione sollicitum neque affectatione exquisitae novitatis turgen-tem." Cited in Hamm, *Frömmigkeitstheologie*, 137 and 138 n. 36.

Chapter 3. A Tour of Medieval Authorship

1. *OC* 9.425. At the beginning of the work, Gerson glosses *dictator* as a syn-onym for *scriba*, distinguished from the *scriptores*, who are the "mechanical" scribes. The *dictatores* were equivalent to the scribes among the Jews, learned in the law, or doctors of theology among the Christians. Gerson's usage should be distinguished from the *dictatores* who were the teachers of the *ars dictaminis*, the skill of letter writing, manuals on which first appeared in the late eleventh cen-tury. Cf. Witt, "Medieval *Ars Dictaminis*." Jean the Celestine seems to have read this passage and incorporated it into his own defense of Gerson's writings in his letter to Ambrose. Cf. *OC* 10.557–59.

2. *OC* 2.43.

3. Combes, *Théologie mystique*, 2.374–76; Roccati, "Gerson e il problema del-l'espressione poetica," 285.

4. Summarizing here *OC* 10.559–61.

5. Cf. in *De consolatione theologiae*, *OC* 9.187: "Evolavit sicut passer erepta de laqueo venantium; undique nimirum sibi parabantur insidiarum tendiculae; enatavit ut potuit a naufragio reipublicae, praestolans si forte postmodum sit spes." See also Combes, *Théologie mystique*, 2.301–4.

6. Cf. in *De consolatione theologiae*, *OC* 9.186: "Miserabilem denique civitatis celeberrimae desolationem, tamquam Jeremias ruinas Jerusalem, lamentatur."

7. Cf. Combes, *Théologie mystique*, 2.374, on the works written at Lyon: "Aucune obscurité ne pèse sur les oeuvres alors composées. On en connaît le nombre et la nature."

8. The monastery, formerly owned by the Knights Templar, was granted to the Celestines in 1407 and refounded in 1421. Borchardt, *Cölestiner*, 90–91, 362. McGuire notes (*Jean Gerson*, 327–28) that the oft-repeated claim that Gerson taught children at Saint-Paul is unsubstantiated. Nonetheless, Gerson was con-nected to the church of Saint-Paul in some way. In a letter to Gérard Machet written on 10 July 1424, Gerson refers to a chapel of St. Margaret that he uses "as a cell and a place of solitude" (*tamquam loco cellae et solitudinis*, *OC* 2.259). A chapel dedicated to St. Margaret was founded in the cloister of the church of Saint-Paul sometime before 1415. See Martin, *Histoire*, 1.176. According to Mar-tin (*Histoire*, 1.181), whose source I have not discovered, the chapter of the adja-cent church of Saint-Laurent provided a domicile for Gerson "and those who accompanied him," and on 21 October 1428 established an anniversary for him on 14 December (his birthday) of each year.

9. Gerhart Ladner, "Homo Viator: Mediaeval Ideas on Alienation and Order," *Speculum* 42 (1967), 233–59.

10. Thomson, *Latin Writings*, 79–80.

11. Combes clarifies the problem of the date of Gerson's departure in *Théo-logie mystique*, 2.268–70. Glorieux, tacitly repeating the date in earlier sources, had suggested "le 6 ou plutôt le 15 mai" (*OC* 1.133). McGuire (*Jean Gerson*, 282, 362) gives 17 May.

12. Combes, *Théologie mystique*, 2.269, with references to the sources in n. 166. Glorieux is hopelessly confused on this point. See on the general situation in Paris, Jean Favier, *Nouvelle histoire de Paris: Paris au XVe siècle, 1380–1500*, 2nd ed. (Paris, 1997), 169; *RSD* 6.229–69. Gerson's own works provide important evi-

dence for the impact of the devastation in Paris. See especially the *Deploratio super civitatem aut regionem quae gladium evaginavit super se* (*OC* 10.407–14); and the poems "Deploratio studii parisiensis" (*OC* 4.5–7), "Carmen de miseriis Franciae" (*OC* 4.100–101), "Carmen de causa canendi" (*OC* 4.18–19), "Carmen de multiplici martyrio" (*OC* 4.134), and "Carmen in laudem ducis Austriae" (*OC* 4.169–70). For context on some of this literature, see Pons, "Intellectual Patterns." On the *Deploratio super civitatem*, see further Ouy, "'Deploratio.'" On the possible death of Laurent de Premierfait, see Ouy, "'Taedium,'" 10.

13. M. G. A. Vale, *Charles VII* (Berkeley, 1974), 25.

14. Gerson spent some time at Rattenberg in Bavaria (July), at Neuberg am Inn (perhaps a more likely route than Neuberg an der Donau) (August 10), presumably at the abbey of Melk in Austria (September–October?), and at Vienna. Cf. Combes, *Théologie mystique*, 2.302–3 n. 278 (on the letter from Neuberg), 306–11 (on Melk, p. 308 nn. 9–10; but on Melk 2, cf. *OC* 8.xxiii–xxv, esp. p. xxv, which notes that this manuscript reproduces Aggsbach I. 4. I), 366–69; Roccati (ed.), *Josephina*, 19, 40–41; *OC* 1.133–34; Calvot and Ouy, *L'oeuvre de Gerson*, 117–18, 133 (two colophons placing the *De consolatione theologiae* in Rattenberg); McGuire, *Jean Gerson*, 286–88. The case for Gerson at Melk was made by Ignaz Franz Keiblinger, *Geschichte des Benedictiner-Stiftes Melk in Niederösterreich: Seiner Besitzungen und Umgebungen* (Vienna, 1851–1869), 1122. For Gerson in Vienna, see the "Carmen in laudem ducis Austriae" (*OC* 4.169–70) and in *OC* 8.351. The dates of his stay there are uncertain; Glorieux dated the "Carmen" without explanation to September 1419 (*OC* 4.xxv), probably to give Gerson enough time to reach Lyon by November. Gerson also seems to have visited Nuremberg at some point (*OC* 5.492). On Gerson's personal losses, see the letter of Jean the Celestine, *OC* 10.559: "Veritatis tuendae causa domo, patria, civitate, cognatis, amicis, dignitatibus rebusque propriis privatus est et ex illis propulsus ac innumeris insidiis expetitus." Mazour-Matusevich, "Jean Gerson," 980–81, suggests that Gerson's exile in Germany may have been invented by his German editors, but the documentary evidence shows otherwise. Nonetheless, the entire topic of Gerson's exile before arriving at Lyon needs revisiting.

15. *OC* 10.553. I take it that the date of 25 January 1419 should be read new style. For Gerson's support for the French Crown, see further Hobbins, "Joan of Arc," 120.

16. Claassen, *Displaced Persons*. See also the recent collection, Laura Napran and Elisabeth Van Houts (eds.), *Exile in the Middle Ages: Selected Proceedings from the International Medieval Congress, University of Leeds, 8–11 July 2002* (Turnhout, 2004).

17. References to the *Tusculan Disputations* include *OC* 5.412, 9.11. On Ovid, see 7.2.839: "Notez des odes de Ovide qui en fut en ezil." On Seneca, see, among other passages, 5.61, 93–94, 103, 233–34, 366, 497. A careful study of Gerson's sources would require a true critical edition.

18. Including the "Pastorium carmen," *De remediis utriusque fortunae, De vita solitaria* (*OC* 7.2.784), and *De viris illustribus* (5.237). On the "Pastorium carmen," see Ouy, "Gerson, émule de Pétrarque," 175–231 (see 181 on Petrarch's self-designation as *peregrinus ubique*). On *De remediis*, see Mann, "Fortune," 9–10.

19. *OC* 2.199: "Quatenus ego peregrinus et advena,—sic enim Gerson interpretatum significat." See also *OC* 4.104, and Roccati (ed.), *Josephina* l. 2840 (p. 152) = *OC* 4.98. For Petrarch's usage, see Ouy, "Gerson, émule de Pétrarque," 181. Petrarch uses *Monicus* in *Bucolicum carmen*, ecl. 1, *Volucer* in ecl. 12.

20. "Nostra autem conversatio in caelis est." The letter is *OC* 2.199.

21. Glorieux (*OC* 1.134) and McGuire (*Jean Gerson*, 288, 362) give November 1419 as the date of Gerson's arrival in Lyon, while Combes gives June or July 1419 (*Théologie mystique*, 2.369–73).

22. See the colophons in *OC* 8.534, 565.

23. D'Ailly referred to Gerson as "peregrinus" (*OC* 2.221). Amadeus of Talaru spoke of Gerson's "long exile for truth" (*OC* 1.144). See also the epitaph of Jean the Celestine (*OC* 1.145). On the early editions, see Walter L. Strauss (ed.), *Albrecht Dürer Woodcuts and Wood Blocks* (New York, 1980), 592. With the 1488 edition, this image at once became standard. For the 1489 and 1502 editions, see pp. 28–29, 102–3.

24. Derolez, *Palaeography*, 17–20; for further literature, see 18 n. 52.

25. Gerson completed the work at Rattenberg in July 1418 (see the colophons in Calvot and Ouy, *L'oeuvre de Gerson*, 117–18, 133). Combes challenged the dating (*Théologie mystique*, 2.306–11) as found in Glorieux (*OC* 1.133), which he wished to push back to September or October at Melk to make a better chronology with Gerson's letter of 10 August 1418 to his brothers Nicolas and Jean the Celestine. Combes's argument is unconvincing, and in any case flatly contradicts the evidence from the colophons.

26. On this text see Burrows, *Jean Gerson*; and Combes, *Théologie mystique*, 2.304–66.

27. Roccati (ed.), *Josephina*, 60; Combes, *Théologie mystique*, 2.314 n. 24.

28. *OC* 9.240: "Conquereris, o homo, quod aetate tua multi depereunt; quid quaeso novum accidit? Habet aetas omnis mortuos suos."

29. Cf. in the second *Annotatio*, compiled by Jean the Celestine (*OC* 1.32): "Item egregius liber de consolatione theologie per dialogum duorum fratrum, unius theologi et alterius monachi celestini, more Boetii de consolatione philosophie." Note, however, that Gerson did address two poems to his brother Jean the Benedictine in 1420 (*OC* 2.224–26), in each case addressing him as *Monicus*. Another poem, "Carmen de causa canendi" (*OC* 4.18–19), uses the same address, which could refer to either Jean the Celestine or Jean the Benedictine. It is not clear why the first two are edited with the letters and the third with the poetry.

30. Ouy, "Gerson, émule de Pétrarque," 181; Mann, *Petrarch*, 5.

31. Combes, *Theologie mystique*, 2.316–19. For a careful reading of the entire text, see Burrows, *Jean Gerson*.

32. Glorieux (*OC* 9.xiii) lists 42 (Vienna, ONB, Hs. 5086, ff. 257–61 contains *De probatione spirituum*, not *De consolatione theologiae*), and I have located close to forty more.

33. *OC* 6.296–304. Glorieux dates the work speculatively to September 1418 at Melk (*OC* 1.133). The work does refer (6.304) to *De consolatione theologiae*. But to my knowledge, there is no solid evidence for its exact date or place of composition.

34. *OC* 1.24: "Item dialogus apologeticus; ejus collocutores sunt Volucer et Monicus prout in praecedenti servatum est, et convenienter adjungi potest praedicto libro ut sit unus."

35. See here Claassen, *Displaced Persons*, 155–81.

36. The work has mostly been overlooked. But see Posthumus Meyjes, *Jean Gerson*, 202–3; and McGuire, *Jean Gerson*, 282–83.

37. The entire subject of medieval Gospel harmonies is very poorly studied, and the question of Gerson's originality cannot be fully determined until more

critical editions and studies are published. The date of 1420 for the *Monotessaron* comes from two manuscripts: Tours, BM, Ms. 379, f. 78v; and Paris, BnF, Ms. lat. 17488, f. 173v. The date appears in the heading of the "Prohemium" (*OC* 9.248: "Prohemium super Unum ex quatuor compilatum anno 1420") and is supported by a letter that appears as a prologue in some of the manuscripts (*OO* 4.87–90), where Gerson refers to the current political situation in terms that suggest he was writing after the calamities of 1418: "Sed heu nostra hec aetate misera! Quis leget haec? Quis studebit? Quis transcribet? Cernis et sentis, frater Christianissime, quantus modo bellorum plusquam civilium horror circumtonat, quanta succrescit haereseum infelix pullulatio." Cf. Vial, "Funktion," 41–42 n. 4. Because of similarities in one of the prologues to works written in 1400–1402, Vial argues that Gerson had produced a draft of the work by 1402, "vielleicht noch nicht fertiggestellt, aber doch wenigstens im Geiste konzipiert" (67). However, Gerson did not write the prologue that bears most of the resemblance (*OC* 9.245–48). Jean the Celestine is the most likely author. See Lieberman, "Chronologie gersonienne" (1958), 370–71. The author was probably the same individual who prepared a prologue to the *Collectorium super Magnificat* (*OC* 8.163–64). Whoever it was, he does appear at 9.247 to be summarizing Gerson's letters to the College of Navarre. This is exactly what we would expect of Jean the Celestine, who did the same thing in his letter to Ambrose in 1423 (see Chapter 2). Another piece of evidence to consider for the date is Gerson's reference to the work in the *Collectorium super Magnificat* as "recently composed" (*nuper edita*; *OC* 8.481), a description that accords better with a date of 1420 than with a date of 1402.

38. Vial points out ("Funktion," 49) that the harmony of Ammonius, which may never even have existed in the form of a Gospel harmony, was sometimes confused with Tatian's *Diatessaron*, which stood at the fountainhead of medieval Gospel harmonies. On the canon tables of Eusebius, see Grafton and Williams, *Christianity*, 195–200.

39. *OO* 4.87–90. In the Dupin edition, the letter appears as a prologue, but closes "Vale Frater"—indicating that it was originally a letter, or perhaps "lettre d'envoi," to one of Gerson's brothers. Some manuscripts of the *Monotessaron* contain this letter, such as Vienna, ONB, Cod. lat. 3710, ff. 199v–200r, whose rubric also describes the text as a letter. See also *RBMA* vol. 3, no. 4486. Augustine used the Vetus Latina rather than Jerome's Vulgate, though it is unclear if Gerson knew this.

40. Vial, "Funktion," 47–48, and see the two appendices, pp. 69–72.

41. *OC* 9.247. A proximate source for this complaint might well have been the criticism of Aquinas in the introduction to the *Summa theologiae*, of the "useless questions, articles, and arguments." See *Sancti Thomae Aquinatis doctoris angelici Opera omnia*, vol. 4 (Rome, 1888), 5.

42. Glorieux omitted these abbreviations along with other apparatus from his edition. See instead the edition of Dupin, *OO* 4.83–202. Zacharias of Besançon (twelfth century) had also used abbreviations in his commentary on the second-century *Diatessaron* of Tatian. On speculation about whether Gerson knew of Zacharias, see Vial, "Funktion," 51–52 and n. 28. A twelfth-century English Austin friar named Clement of Llanthony (d. after 1169) appears to have been the first to tackle the problem of producing a Latin Gospel harmony without reference to the second-century *Diatessaron* of Tatian, and he apparently used the same abbreviation system as Zacharias. On Gerson's *Monotessaron* in the context of other Gospel harmonies, see also Hörner, *Evangelienharmonie*, 141–56. Hörner

does not mention Clement of Llanthony's *Unum ex quattuor*. On Clement, see G. R. Evans, "Llanthony, Clement of (*d.* after 1169)," *DNB* 34.91. The text of Clement is unedited.

43. See further Lang, "Harmony."

44. C. S. Lewis, *English Literature in the Sixteenth Century Excluding Drama* (Oxford, 1954), 179.

45. Vial, "Funktion," 42–44.

46. The first three rubrics give the basic idea (*OC* 9.249–51): 1. On the eternal generation of Christ, J. 1; 2. On the annunciation and conception of John the Baptist, L. 1; 3. On the annunciation of Christ to Mary by Gabriel, L. 1.

47. *OC* 9.246. Glorieux distinguished this prologue with italics; it appears in 9.245–48. See also Lang, "Harmony."

48. *OC* 9.357.

49. *OC* 9.248.

50. Glorieux knew of ten copies. On the translation, see Axel Mante (ed.), *Monotessaron: Eine mittelniederdeutsche erweiterte Fassung vom Jahre 1513 (Diözesanarchiv, Trier, Nr. 75)* (Lund, 1952). A commentary on the third section, probably by a Carthusian monk, survives in at least two manuscripts: Innsbruck, UB, Cod. 9, ff. 74r–91v; and Partridge Green, St. Hugh's Charterhouse, Parkminster, Ms. bb.8 (C.100), ff. 2–28. Another commentary with numerous illuminations exists in two manuscripts. See Albert Derolez, "L'Editio Mercatelliana du Monotessaron de Gerson," in *Hommages à Andre Boutemy*, ed. Guy Cambier (Brussels, 1976), 42–54.

51. *The Complete Works of St. Thomas More*, vol. 13, ed. Garry E. Haupt (New Haven, 1976), 50.

52. *OC* 6.303: "Ita enim fas erit tibi vel alteri cui placuerint illa, sub collectorio uno seu pluribus scriptis dare."

53. Glorieux thought that this last work, the *Carmen super Magnificat*, work was "un recueil factice, dû peut-être à Jean le Célestin" (*OC* 4.xviii; "Note sur le 'Carmen super Magnificat,'" 148–49). Glorieux knew of no manuscripts. I have located two: Paderborn, EAB, Hs. Hux 15a, ff. 75v–85v; and Melk, SB, Hs. 1583, ff. 217v–218v. In the Paderborn manuscript, it is called "Carmen super Magnificat" (f. 75v). Gerson refers to the work twice, in *OC* 8.569 and 633. See also the reference to the work in the letter of Jacques de Cerisy, *OC* 1.27. The question of editorial responsibility needs to be revisited with the manuscript evidence in hand.

54. See now Fabre, *Doctrine*. On this edition, see the important review by Roccati, "La production."

55. See further on this point Roccati, "La production," 358 and n. 13.

56. Fabre, *Doctrine*, 34–35. Note the discrepancy in Roccati, "La production," 357, which dates *On the Original Reason for Songs* to before August 1426.

57. *OC* 9.525; Fabre, *Doctrine*, 311.

58. Fabre, *Doctrine*, 46.

59. Roccati ("La production," 357) suggests that the centiloquy was probably not the definitive form of the work but "juste un canevas, destiné à être développé." Yet Gerson published a whole series of centiloquies that take this same form. The question of whether or not Gerson himself or Jean the Celestine published the work is unresolved.

60. Fabre, *Doctrine*, 29, 51–73; Roccati, "La production," 359–60.

61. For an overview of the contents, see Fabre, *Doctrine*, 19–27.

62. On these matters, see Fabre, *Doctrine*, 148–57.

63. Fabre, *Doctrine*, 111–34.

64. Fabre, *Doctrine*, 274.

65. Roccati, "La production," 356–57 n. 5.

66. *OC* 9.708–10; Fabre, *Doctrine*, 549. See further Ouy, "Manuscrits jumeaux," 128.

67. On the translations, see *DLF*, 728–31. Cf. H. J. R. Murray, *A History of Chess* (Oxford, 1913), 537–46. Christine de Pizan was "inspired by" the *Liber* in the translation of Jean de Vignay, in her *Livre de la mutacion de Fortune* (*DLF*, 285). See further on all these matters Jenny Adams, *Power Play: The Literature and Politics of Chess in the Later Middle Ages* (Philadelphia, 2006).

68. In the *Liber*, the king and knight stand for those ranks, the queen for both queen and women in general, the pawns for various trades and professions, such as farmer, carpenter, and scribe.

69. Fabre, *Doctrine*, 60. See further on this text pp. 60–63. On the manuscripts, see *OC* 9.xx.

70. *OC* 2.249–50.

71. Carruthers, *Book of Memory*, 328.

72. For context on the modes of signifying, see Louis G. Kelly (ed.), *Pseudo-Albertus Magnus, Quaestiones Alberti De modis significandi* (Amsterdam, 1977). On the *Centilogium de conceptibus* and the *De modis significandi*, see the entries by R. Schönberger in Franco Volpi and Julian Nida-Rümelin (eds.), *Lexikon der philosophischen Werke* (Stuttgart, 1988), 63, 96, 127.

73. Dallas G. Denery, *Seeing and Being Seen in the Later Medieval World* (Cambridge, 2005).

74. Lehmann, "Mittlelalterliche Büchertitel," 47; Smoller, *History, Prophecy, and the Stars*, 48. Gerson might also have known of the *Centiloquium* of Pseudo-Ockham. But the form of that work bears little resemblance to Gerson's centilo-quies. The modern edition is *Opera dubia et spuria Venerabili Inceptori Guillelmo de Ockham adscripta* (Opera philosophica 7), *Centiloquium*, ed. P. Böhner (St. Bonaventure, N.Y., 1988), 373–505. Cf. Smalley, *English Friars*, 51–52 on the various works of John of Wales with names ending in "-loquium."

75. We know this from a letter to Oswald of Bavaria in 1428, *OC* 2.314: "Mitto Collectorium septem sportarum cujus principium est De verbo et hymno gloriae, ad intelligentiam theologiae mysticae Dyonisii, et pro complemento hujus versiculi Gloria Patri."

76. The *Collectorium septem sportarum* is mentioned in a letter to Oswald of Bavaria (*OC* 2.314), in the beginning of his *Collectorium super Magnificat* (8.163–64), in the *Tractatus super Cantica Canticorum* (8.579), in the list of Jacques de Cerisy (1.27), and in an unedited recension of the second *Annotatio* (found in various manuscripts: see for example Vienna, ONB, Cod. lat. 1519, f. 32r). See also *OC* 4.xxxvii, 8.viii. Combes, *Théologie mystique*, 2.614–19. Cf. Glorieux's comments in *OC* 8.vii–viii. Cf. the use of *collectorium* in *OC* 2.212, 6.303.

77. *OC* 8.149–54.

78. This reconstruction is based on a note probably provided by Jean the Celestine in Marseille, BM, Ms. 241, f. 126v, as reproduced in *OC* 8.viii. This is a list of the works included in the *Collectorium septem sportarum*; the *Centilogium de oculo* is described as follows: "Centilogium de oculo triplici et una pretiosa margarita, sub duplici partitione, et additione xii. propositionum de concordia theologie cum scholastica; sed numerus amplior et complexior intellectus, habetur ex ana-gogico de verbo et hymno glorie." The two works in question are *OC* 8.154–61, 2.252–59. Gerson completed the *Tractatus de oculo* sometime shortly before 1

June 1424, he completed the *De concordia theologiae mysticae cum scholastica* on 1 June 1424, and he wrote the *De una pretiosa margarita* on 10 July 1424. On the date for the first two works, see Combes, *Théologie mystique*, 2.396 n. 107. Combes suggested that Gerson wrote the entire *De concordia* on 1 June 1424.

79. On the organization of the *Anagogicum de verbo et hymno gloriae*, see the colophon to the work on 8.565. Glorieux prints "190," but at least one manuscript has 195, the actual number of "notulae." See Colledge and Marler, "Tractatus," 357 and n. 13 (but note that the Colledge and Marler misread Glorieux's apparatus: the final "u" is the manuscript *U*, not the Roman numeral *v*).

80. Glorieux lists eleven manuscripts for both the *Anagogicum de verbo et hymno Gloriae in excelsis* and the *Centilogium de conceptibus*. He gives anywhere from two to eight manuscripts for the others.

81. *OC* 8.134–49.

82. For Thomas of Erfurt, see the edition of G. L. Bursill-Hall, *Grammatica speculativa* (London, 1972).

83. See the description in Thomson, *Latin Writings*, 79–80.

84. The best treatment remains Combes, *Théologie mystique*, 2.572–613. See also Combes, *Essai*, 1.329–45. The work has two prologues, but the first (8.163–64), which Combes cites extensively, appears not to be by Gerson and is probably by Jean the Celestine.

85. *OC* 8.164–65.

86. Combes, *Théologie mystique*, 2.576.

87. Combes, *Essai*, 1.329–30.

88. *OC* 8.204–9.

89. The structure is as follows: dialogue (8.239–45), twelve considerations (245–48), dialogue (248–52), and treatise on the holy name of God (253–65). For the reference to this treatise, see 8.317.

90. *OC* 8.289–90.

91. The structure is as follows: dialogue (8.265–85), eighteen considerations (285–88), unfinished selection (288–89).

92. Before he had finished the compilation, in September 1426, Gerson also referred to treatises 7 and 9 as separate, independent works. *OC* 2.270. See also 2.291. At the end of 1428, he referred to treatise 8 as a *specialis tractatus* (2.332–33).

93. The first prologue is *OC* 8.163–64. The references in the text itself are 8.168, 170, 185, 194, 250, 301–2, 332, 346–47, 358, 376.

94. Theology and philosophy, 8.201; music, 8.168–71, 227; studying pagan authors, 8.274; devotion and learning, 8.293, 301–4; lay spirituality, 8.314–17; the vices of the schoolmen, 8.341–42, 366; incendiary preachers, 8.343; heresy and Bible reading, 8.350–51; misguided speculation, 8.356.

95. The insertion is *OC* 8.168–71 of 9.714–17. For the references to other works (not counting the references in the first prologue), see 8.168, 170, 172, 185, 194, 239, 250, 269, 275, 292, 301–2, 317, 332, 346–47, 351, 354, 358, 376, 380, 416, 424, 432, 440, 481, 487, 495, 513, 528. In some cases, the work in question is unclear.

96. Perhaps the only discussion is Combes, *Théologie mystique*, 572–613.

97. *OC* 8.413–26.

98. *OC* 8.528.

99. *GW*, vol. 9, nos. 10765–66.

100. On this work, see Glorieux, "Gerson et les Chartreux," 150–51; Combes, *Théologie mystique*, 2.650–60 (on the work's incompleteness, 658–60); McGuire, "Jean Gerson, the Shulammite, and the Maid," 183–92.

101. *OC* 8.566–76.

102. *OC* 8.576–77, 566.

103. *OC* 8.577.

104. *OC* 8.577–78.

105. *OC* 8.578.

106. *OC* 8.576.

107. Glorieux's edition has been superseded by that of Ouy, " 'Taedium,' " 25–26. For the work's date, see p. 23.

108. *OC* 8.293.

109. Ouy, "Gerson, émule de Pétrarque."

110. See the first item in the first *Annotatio*, *OC* 1.23; also 1.109. On the fifteenth century as an *aetas Boethiana*, cf. Lerer, *Chaucer and His Readers*, 13–14.

111. Roccati (ed.), *Josephina*, 40, 60.

112. E. R. Curtius, *European Literature and the Latin Middle Ages*, trans. Willard R. Trask (Princeton, 1953), 224.

113. For this paragraph, I have drawn on Minnis, *Medieval Theory of Authorship*, 138–45, 211–17. For the older view, see Curtius, *European Literature*, 214–27.

114. Minnis, *Medieval Theory of Authorship*, 138–39. On these ancient charges, see Curtius, *European Literature*, 204; Witt, "Coluccio Salutati," 539.

115. "Poetica scientia est de his quae proper defectum veritatis non possunt a ratione capi; unde oportet quod quasi quibusdam similitudinibus ratio seducatur." The quotation comes from Aquinas's commentary on the *Sentences*, the prologue to bk. 1 art. 5 ad. 3, quoted in Witt, "Coluccio Salutati," 540 n. 7.

116. Minnis, *Medieval Theory of Authorship*, 139.

117. Bernard G. Dod, "Medieval Philosophical Literature," in *The Cambridge History of Later Medieval Philosophy*, ed. Anthony Kenny, Norman Kretzmann, and Jan Pinborg (Cambridge, 1982), 63; Minnis, *Medieval Theory of Authorship*, 140–42, 216. See also Witt, "Coluccio Salutati," 538. Witt stresses their notion of the "sacral character of ancient poetry, which in their own eyes gave it nobility, without having to resort to medieval arguments for a direct divine influence acting on the poet or for a secret tradition of divine truth initially derived from God's Revelation."

118. Ouy, " 'Taedium,' " 22.

119. Ullmann, *Humanism*, 63–69, here 64–65.

120. Ibid., 66–68.

121. Ornato, *Jean Muret*, 138–39, 149 n. 223.

122. *OC* 5.321. See also in *Contra curiositatem studentium*, 3.240: "Idem de rethoricis et poeticis et mathematicis scientiis judico, quarum notitia nonnihil ancillatur theologiae, nonnihil quoque sibi praestat ornamenti."

123. *PL* 192.648. *Iohannis Dominici Lucula noctis*, ed. Edmund Hunt (Notre Dame, Ind., 1940), xiv, 2. Cf. *OC* 8.274: "Veritas a quocumque dicatur, est communis omnibus et singulis."

124. Ornato, *Jean Muret*, 149.

125. *OC* 7.2.1059–60.

126. See especially Roccati, "Gerson e il problema dell'espressione poetica." See also Roccati, "Humanisme," 107–22, esp. 116; and Roccati, "Gersonian Text."

127. See the new edition and translation in Roccati, "Gersonian Text," 372–76, 380–85. See also Roccati, "Gerson e il problema dell'espressione poetica," 282.

128. Roccati, "Gerson e il problema dell'espressione poetica," 282; *OC* 4.137.

129. Roccati, "Gersonian Text," 372–73 n. 25.

130. Translation, very slightly modified, from Roccati, "Gersonian Text," 372–73, 381, ll. 15–18. On the use of mnemonic verses, see Carruthers, *Book of Memory*, 99.

131. Roccati, "Gerson e il problema dell'espressione poetica," 280; *OC* 4.18, 176.

132. Roccati (ed.), *Josephina*, ll. 1–10: "Fontem sueverunt veteres celebrare poete | Sacratum musis Parnasi, monte subortum | Quem pes fodit equi. Sed habet sapientia montem | Nostra alium, fontem et musas quibus altera vox est. | Fons vite, verbum Domini sublimibus exit | A celis jugi puro salubrique meatu, | Cristallo similis, manans a sede superni | Montibus eternis; musas nec curat agrestes | Que mortale sonant, que noxia carmina texunt, | Que solas vanis demulcent corporis aures."

133. I quote from the translation in Rummel, *Humanist-Scholastic Debate*, 32.

134. Allen, *Ethical Poetic.*

135. See *OC* 4, poems 113, 130, 140, 165, 175, 206.

136. McGuire summarizes the first three distinctions in *Jean Gerson*, 295–99. For the *Josephina* in earlier scholarship, see Lieberman, "Chronologie gersonienne" (1955), 290 and n. 3. The studies of Roccati are fundamental. See "La 'Josephina'" and "Humanisme." See also Antonius Placanica, "'Verbis texta sacris': Fonti bibliche ed esegesi nella 'Iosephina' di Giovanni Gerson," in *Gli umanesimi medievali: Atti del II Congresso dell' "Internationales Mittellateinerkomitee," Firenze, Certosa del Galluzzo, 11–15 settembre 1993*, ed. C. Leonardi (Florence, 1998), 515–38; and Placanica, "In prologum ad Ioannis Gersonii 'Iosephinam' animadversiones," *Filologia mediolatina* 2 (1995), 293–306.

137. Roccati, "Humanisme," 109 n. 17.

138. See also Roccati (ed.), *Josephina*, 7 and nn. 13–15. On Ludolf of Saxony, see the article by Walter Baier and K. Ruh in *VL* 5.967–77. On the *Meditationes vitae Christi*, see the article by K. Ruh in *VL* 6.282–90. On Carthusian authors, see Dennis D. Martin, "Behind the Scene: The Carthusian Presence in Late Medieval Spirituality," in *Nicholas of Cusa and His Age: Intellect and Spirituality*, ed. T. M. Izbicki and C. M. Bellitto (Leiden, 2002), 39–52.

139. See Roccati, "La 'Josephina.'"

140. Roccati, "Humanisme," 108, 117 and n. 63.

141. Lines 60–77 in both editions. For further discussion, see Roccati, "Humanisme," 111–12. Throughout the *exordium*, Gerson refers to himself as "theosophus" or "peregrinus." On the pilgrim motif, found throughout Gerson's writings, see p. 112; Lieberman, "Chronologie gersonienne" (1955), 291–92.

142. For a more detailed overview, see Roccati (ed.), *Josephina*, 24–26.

143. Ibid., ll. 407–753 (pp. 95–102); *OC* 4.40–48.

144. Cf. *OC* 6.184–85, the sixth level of truth that does not require belief but nourishes piety.

145. Roccati (ed.), *Josephina*, ll. 1950–54, 874–84. *OC* 4.76–77, 51–52.

146. Roccati (ed.), *Josephina*, ll. 925–33, 940–56 (pp. 106–7); ll. 1796–1802 (p. 127). *OC* 4.53, 73.

147. Roccati (ed.), *Josephina*, ll. 1955–2023 (pp. 130–31); *OC* 4.77–48.

148. Thomas H. Bestul, *Texts of the Passion: Latin Devotional Literature and Medieval Society* (Philadelphia, 1996), 26–68. For a general overview of the shift, see Rachel Fulton, *From Judgment to Passion: Devotion to Christ and the Virgin Mary, 800–1200* (New York, 2002).

149. *OC* 7.2.449–519.

150. Roccati (ed.), *Josephina*, ll. 2068–74, 2094–95, 2103–4. *OC* 4.79–80.

151. See *OC* 8.55–61.

152. Roccati (*Josephina*, 187) refers here to M. Lieberman, "St. Joseph, Jean Gerson et Pierre d'Ailly dans un manuscrit de 1464," *Cahiers de Joséphologie* 20 (1972), 64–65, 80–81.

153. On Virgil, see Roccati, "La 'Josephina,'" 3–19; on Petrarch, see Roccati (ed.), *Josephina*, 9 (see esp. nn. 25–26), 12–15.

154. Roccati, "Humanisme," 109 n. 17.

155. I have recently identified a reference to the *Imitation* in a later revision of the *Annotatio doctorum aliquorum qui de contemplatione locuti sunt.* Gerson there refers to a passage from the beginning of book 1: "Eleganter quidam: Opto inquit magis sentire compunctionem, quam scire eius diffinitionem." Giessen, UB, Hs. 763, f. 222r–v. This is one of the earliest references to the work. A study of the text is in progress.

156. On the authorship debate, see Nikolaus Staubach, "Eine unendliche Geschichte? Der Streit um die Autorschaft der 'Imitatio Christi,'" in *Aus dem Winkel in die Welt: Die Bücher des Thomas von Kempen und ihre Schicksale*, ed. Ulrike Bodemann and Nikolaus Staubach (Frankfurt am Main, 2006), 9–35.

157. A lengthy gloss appears in Innsbruck, UB, Cod. 97, ff. 2r–17v; Melk, SB, Hs. 799, ff. 4r–41r (dated 15 October 1449); and Tübingen, Wilhelmsstift, Hs. Gi 211. What appears to be a shorter version is in Vienna, ONB, Cod. lat. 4428, ff. 140r–160v.

Chapter 4. Literary Expression

1. *OC* 2.98: "Tolerent igitur patienter homines inferioris gradus et scientiae si dicta eorum quaerantur ad proprium usum coarctari, non in perniciem doctrinae catholicae dilatari. Hac consideratione permotos existimo doctores novissimos Thomam, Bonaventuram et similes, dum omisso omni verborum ornatu tradiderunt theologiam per quaestiones ut sub certis regulis et sub praecisa verborum forma tutissimam haberemus theologiam tam practicam quam speculativam, reducendo doctorers omnes priores ad unam securamque locutionis proprietatem."

2. Erwin Panofsky, *Gothic Architecture and Scholasticism* (New York, 1951), 35.

3. *OC* 10.12.

4. Nauert, "Humanism as Method," 432–33. Partly responding to Nauert is Bose, "The Issue of Theological Style."

5. Rummel, *Humanist-Scholastic Debate*, 30–40.

6. Ibid., 30.

7. Ibid., 32–33.

8. Ibid., 32, 34.

9. Ibid., 39.

10. *OC* 5.321. See here Vasoli, "Débuts," 274.

11. Smalley, *English Friars.*

12. Ouy, "Le Collège de Navarre."

13. Catto, "Scholars," 770–78.

14. Minnis, "Theorizing the Rose," 17–18, 35, 35–36 n. 97. For Gerson's involvement in literary discussions in Paris in 1398, see Ornato, *Jean Muret*, 80, 142 n. 198.

15. Chenu, *Toward Understanding Saint Thomas*, 85.

16. Anthony Goodman, *John of Gaunt: The Exercise of Princely Power in Fourteenth-Century Europe* (New York, 1992), 37.

17. *OC* 9.475.

18. *OC* 10.125. Cf. Peter of Spain, *Summulae logicales*, ed. L. M. de Rijk (Assen, 1972), 1.

19. *OC* 9.641.

20. *OC* 5.293–96.

21. *Paradise Lost*, bk. 5, ll. 772–895.

22. *OC* 2.98: "De summa theologia quae mystica nominatur et quam scholastico more Albertus magnus et quidam alii claram proprioque sermone exposuerunt."

23. *OC* 6.265: "Libellus articulorum theologicorum et scholastice compositorum."

24. *Disputatio de schismate tollendo* (*OC* 6.99–105); *An liceat in causis fidei a Papa appellare* (*OC* 6.283–90); *De sententia Pastoris semper tenenda* (*OC* 6.291–94).

25. *OC* 3.241.

26. Maurice Accarie, *Theatre sacré de la fin du Moyen Âge: Étude sur le sens moral de la Passion de Jean Michel* (Geneva, 1979), 79. The great French orator Olivier Maillard (c. 1430–1502) likewise employed numerous dialogues in his sermons (Ibid., 78).

27. Bossuat, "Gerson et le théâtre," 295–98. Cf. Fabre, *Doctrine*, 41 n. 43; Pierre Yves Badel, "Le débat," in *La littérature française aux XIVe et XVe siècles*, ed. Daniel Poirion (Heidelberg, 1988), 102 n. 19.

28. *OC* 5.500–501.

29. Cf. Oberman, *Contra vanam curiositatem*, 29–30, on the understanding of *studiositas* according to Aquinas, as a positive contrast to reprehensible *curiositas*.

30. *OC* 5.273. See also *OC* 5.73, 5.82.

31. *OC* 5.546–62 (1397), 498–511 (1399), 70–73 and 81–90 (1404), 435–47 (1408), 398–405 (1415), 376–98 (1417) (amplified in 6.190–210), and 538–46 (1418). The eighth sermon, from 1408 or 1411, was discovered in 1976 by Alexandre Olivar ("Sermon," 273). On the dating, see further Hobbins, "Beyond the Schools," 134 n. 162. Cf. *Studiositas religiosa* in *OC* 5.353. *Curiosité* apparently has the same function in the French sermons as *Studiositas* in the Latin sermons. See *OC* 7.2.642–43, 695–96, 785–88, 954–57, and 1041–42. Cf. "Desir de savoir," described as "Ung bon estudiant, soutil et ingenieux," in 7.2.1031. Sometimes the questions (occasionally expressed merely as doubts) come without the character of *Curiosité*. *OC* 7.2.804–9, 814–15, 817–21, 864, 886, 900. On questions in the French sermons, see also Brown, *Pastor and Laity*, 31–32, 161–62. Cf. *OC* 8.373 and 421, where *studiositas* is contrasted with *curiositas*. On the use of questions in the sermons of other fifteenth-century French preachers, see pp. 22–23. On dialogues in general in the French sermons, see Mourin, *Jean Gerson*, 467–74.

32. *OC* 5.557, 70, 444.

33. For clarification on these points, my thanks to William Courtenay.

34. *OC* 2.332. Occasionally, Gerson also used "distinctions," which "greatly illumine the understanding and, with no heavy exertion, allure the affections" (*OC* 2.276). See also in the *Josephina*.

35. *OC* 2.97.

36. *OC* 3.251 (*DMT* 5–6).

37. Cf. Pierre d'Ailly in Guenée, *Between Church and State*, 138–39, 195, 199, and 216–17. Gerson mentions the device of Bonaventure in the letter *Si quis vult* (*OC* 2.332).

38. *OC* 3.39. For references in patristic literature to the metaphor of the moneychanger, see Elliott, "Seeing Double," 41–42 n. 69.

39. *OC* 10.55, 91; 6.127; 9.524 (= Fabre, *Doctrine*, 310).

40. The classic study is Parkes, "Influence." See also the works of the Rouses listed in the Bibliography.

41. *OC* 10.58.

42. See on this text Posthumus Meyjes, *Jean Gerson*, 247–86. At the time of the treatise, the leadership of the Church was in a state of chaos. Pope John XXIII had already been deposed, the deposition of Benedict XIII would soon follow, and Gerson felt compelled to justify these actions of the council.

43. *OC* 6.211: "Haec me consideratio movit ut de potestate ecclesiastica sub pauculis considerationibus dissererem, quatenus materia quae quodammodo videtur infinita sicut tractari solet ab aliquibus per auctoritates, et allegationes, resolveretur ad paucos certos et claros terminos per descriptiones et divisiones resolutive procedendo, allegationum confusione dimissa, quales apud doctores invenire non est difficile."

44. *OC* 7.2.599: "Je prendray selon les termes de nostre theume aucunes consideracions, plus par maniere de dottrine et de lecon que de curieuse oracion, et sans me charger d'allegacions non necessaires, mais entendray a venir au point et au vif de la matiere comme il me samble." See also *OC* 7.2.644, 648, 1059, 1126; 8.343; 9.420; 10.58.

45. *OC* 5.384: "Quae verba quomodo sint accipienda tractatulus quidam nuper editus pandit quid prodiet in publicum magis ad examinationem quam determinationem, magisque ad elucidationem veritatis quam ostentationem vanitatis." See also *OC* 6.24: "In inquisitione veritatis tangentis proximum schisma et statum ejus." 6.136: "Non quidem ad determinandum, absit haec temeritas, sed ad examinandum et dandum sapientibus occasionem et offerendum in tabernaculo Dei cum hominibus id quod ex talento qualisque scientiae commissum est." 6.250: "Finit tractatulus . . . magis ad inquisitionem veritatis quam ad determinationem editus et pronuntiatus Constantiae." 6.290: "Haec autem dicta sint vel argumentata magis ad veritatis inquisitionem quam ad alicujus, praesertim sanctissimi domini nostri papae Martini reprehensionem." Cf. 10.51: "Haec interim notata . . . magis ad rememorandum quam docendum."

46. Weijers, *Terminologies*, 348–55. See also Mariken Teeuwen, *The Vocabulary of Intellectual Life in the Middle Ages* (Turnhout, 2003). For Aquinas's position, see Wei, "Self-Image," 409.

47. *The Mirror of Simple Souls*, trans. Edmund Colledge, J. C. Marler, and Judith Grant (Notre Dame, Ind., 1999), 9.

48. Van Engen, *Devotio Moderna*, 68.

49. *OC* 7.2.1077: "Les sains docteurs touchant la foy et la religion crestienne ont toudis procédé meurement sans tost determiner veritez doubteuses; si ont parlé en ceste matiere plus en enquerent que en determinant; par quoy aucunes foys ilz semblent dire choses contraires et non font. Et si puet on tenir en tel cas contre leur oppinion sans errer perilleusement."

50. *OC* 9.475: "Permittendum est idcirco religiosis aliquibus inquirere de doctrinis scholasticorum, quae tractari solent circa libros Sententiarum."

51. Ward, "Rhetoric," 159–231, here at 172, 178, 182, 204, 207, 216.

52. Bose, "The Issue of Theological Style," 6.

53. *OC* 2.98, 262; 5.344, 400; 8.577. Cf. the frequent references to the appropriate parameters of scholastic exercise (5.92, 559) and to matters relating "more to school than to preaching" (7.2.624, 676, 942).

54. *OC* 3.57: "Non tam ex mea quam aliorum sententia, neque tam magistrali locutione quam collocutione familiari, non demum polito curiosoque sermone sed quotidiano loquendi more et extra lectiones ordinarias"; 5.500: "Adde quod materia haec de poenitentia non accuratum stylum vel elaboratum sed quotidianum exigit, quod locutionis genus quasi sordidum jam apud modernos dissolutum, flaccidum et nauseans contemnitur, praesertim in sermocinationibus extra scholam." Cf. *OC* 5.400.

55. Gerson refers to Cicero's works as the old and new rhetoric (see, e.g., *OC* 3.59, 8.636). In his 1393 sermon for the feast of St. Louis, he quotes from Quintilian's description of the ideal teacher in book 2 (5.162–63; cf. M. Winterbottom [ed.], *M. Fabi Quintiliani Institutionis oratoriae libri duodecim* [Oxford, 1970], 76–77). On the rediscovery of the complete text of Quintilian, see my Chapter 7.

56. *OC* 8.293: "Deinde fastidium tollitur dum eadem sententia varie describitur. Unde fundatur color rhetoricus expolitio nominatus." On *expolitio*, see Lausberg, *Handbook*, 372.

57. On the place of rhetoric as part of the trivium in the university curriculum, see Copeland, *Rhetoric*, 158–60.

58. Quintilian (*Inst.* 2.17.37; also *bene dicendi scientia, Inst.* 2.14.5) defined rhetoric broadly as the "art of speaking well" (*ars bene dicendi*). Cf. the definition of grammar as the *scientia recte loquendi, Inst.* 1.4.2. See here Lausberg, *Handbook*, 17. For fuller discussion, see Witt, "Medieval Italian Culture," 31–32.

59. The dating of this work is circumstantial. See Glorieux, "L'enseignement universitaire," 88–113.

60. *OC* 3.58–59. On the importance of this distinction between rhetoric and logic in the debates at Constance with Hus, see Shank, *Logic*, 180–83.

61. *OC* 3.61–62. Cf. Kaluza, *Les querelles doctrinales à Paris*, 39, where Kaluza argues that *phantasticus* for Gerson is loosely equivalent to "Scotist." This link to English logic is certainly in the background of this passage, but Gerson's usage suggests that the term is being applied broadly (unfortunately in his view) to all theologians *by the members of other faculties*, and as a near synonym of the words *sophistae* and *verbosi*. Cf. in the *Contra curiositatem studentium, OC* 2.249: "For this reason we theologians are known as *phantastici*" ("Ob hanc quippe rationem notamur nos theologici esse phantastici"). Gerson expresses the same fear in his letter to D'Ailly on the reform of teaching, *OC* 2.26–27. And cf. usages of *phantasticus* in other contexts, *OC* 3.56, 76, 271, 284; 5.575; 8.83, 636; 9.635.

62. Copeland, *Rhetoric*, 160.

63. Korolec, "Jean Buridan," 622–27; and Shank, *Logic*, 182, citing Georg Wieland, "The Reception and Interpretation of Aristotle's *Ethics*," in *The Cambridge History of Later Medieval Philosophy*, ed. Norman Kretzmann, Anthony Kenny, and Jan Pinborg (Cambridge, 1982), 668. On the relation between rhetoric and ethics, see also Ward, "Rhetoric," 217–18.

64. Copeland, *Rhetoric*, 64.

65. Courtenay, "Force of Words."

66. Ibid., 118–21.

67. Here summarizing Courtenay, "Reception," 49, 52–53; Courtenay, "Force of Words," 122–24, and 124–25 for the later examples of Richard Brinkley and Angelus Dobelin.

68. Now summarizing Copeland, *Rhetoric*, 59.

69. Bose, "The Issue of Theological Style," 7–8.

70. Rummel, *Humanistic-Scholastic Debate*, 31.

71. *Praise of Folly*, trans. Betty Radice (New York, 1971), 152.

72. Rummel, *Humanistic-Scholastic Debate*, 180–81.

73. No good study of the work exists. For orientation, see Courtenay, "Antiqui." Not without problems is Kelly, "*Modus significandi rhetoricus.*" For context, see Louis G. Kelly (ed.), *Pseudo–Albertus Magnus, Quaestiones Alberti De modis significandi* (Amsterdam, 1977), introduction. See also Rummel, *Humanist-Scholastic Debate*, 35–36.

74. For all of this, see the usual clear treatment in Courtenay, "Antiqui," 3–10. On nominalism, still essential is Courtenay, "Nominalism and Late Medieval Religion."

75. Kelly, "*Modus significandi rhetoricus,*" 44.

76. Hamesse, *Auctoritates*, 305 (from the authorities of the *Peri hermeneias*): "Significare est intellectum constituere"; E. J. Ashworth, "Signification and Modes of Signifying in Thirteenth-Century Logic: A Preface to Aquinas on Analogy," *Medieval Philosophy and Theology* 1 (1991), 44.

77. *OC* 9.625–26; cf. 8.194.

78. *OC* 9.627. The definition appears in various places in Cicero, among them *De oratore*, 69.

79. *OC* 9.627, 629–30.

80. *OC* 9.639.

81. *OC* 9.636: "Vae igitur illis qui gaudent in confusione linguarum per contemptum terminorum quos posuerunt patres nostri, qui in impositione terminorum fuerunt magni metaphysici."

82. *OC* 2.70: "Animadvertes, crede mihi, non esse factam injuriam tyrannicam eloquentiae si eam theologiae sociaverimus."

83. Rummel, *Humanist-Scholastic Debate*, 168–72.

84. *OC* 3.58: "Ceterum vulgari usitataeque locutioni plurimum condescendit quaerens ut sua quadam tum familiaritate tum speciositate auditorum affectus impellat quo vult, et vel in iram vel indignationem, odium vel amorem concitet audientes. Dicta est idcirco logica haec esse necessaria ad scientias morales quia ad effectus concitandos generandosque si boni sunt, aut ad sedandos aut compescendos seu tollendos si mali reperiantur, logica praecedens non sufficit. Illa enim inquirit tantummodo veritatem in rebus prout veritas est adaequatio rei intellectae ad intellectum speculativum; ista autem prout est adaequatio quaedam ad affectum seu practicum intellectum."

85. On this topic, see Bernard McGinn, "Love, Knowledge, and Unio Mystica in the Western Christian Tradition," in *Mystical Union in Judaism, Christianity, and Islam: An Ecumenical Dialogue*, ed. Moshe Idel and Bernard McGinn (New York, 1996), 59–86.

86. Gerson explains these operations in *On mystical theology*, *OC* 3.256–63. For orientation, see Ozment, *Homo Spiritualis*, 59–71.

87. Henry of Suso, *Horologium Sapientiae* (Freiburg, 1977), 388; quoted in Krieger, "Theologica perscrutatio," 619 n. 56.

88. *The Mirror of Simple Souls*, 9.

89. Van Engen, *Devotio Moderna*, 31, 33.

90. Magnus Ditsche, "Zur Herkunft und Bedeutung des Begriffes der Devotio Moderna," *Historisches Jahrbuch* 79 (1960), 139; quoted in Schreiner, "Laienfrömmigkeit," 43 (for more on this theme, see pp. 43–46).

91. See Martin, "Via Moderna," 190–92.

92. For context, see McGinn, *Harvest*, 449–51; and Kent Emery Jr., "Mysticism and the Coincidence of Opposites in Sixteenth- and Seventeenth-Century

France," in *Monastic, Scholastic and Mystical Theologies from the Later Middle Ages* (Brookfield, Vt., 1996), XI.3–4.

93. *Itinerarium*, Prologus 5 (*Doctoris seraphici S. Bonaventurae . . . Opera omnia* [Quaracchi, 1896], 5.296): "Rogo igitur, quod magis pensetur intentio scribentis quam opus, magis dictorum sensus quam sermo incultus, magis veritas quam venustas, magis exercitatio affectus quam eruditio intellectus." For more on Bonaventure and *affectus*, see Elizabeth Dreyer, "Bonaventure the Franciscan: An Affective Spirituality," in *Spiritualities of the Heart: Approaches to Personal Wholeness in Christian Tradition*, ed. Annice Callahan (New York, 1990), 33–44.

94. For context on this theme as it relates to Gerson's philosophical position, see Krieger, "Theologica perscrutatio," 605–19.

95. *OC* 9.579. Cf. 3.127, 217; 8.1.

96. *OC* 3.127; 2.275.

97. *OC* 2.61: "Vult ergo aliquis esse et dici vere sapiens? Habeat utramque contemplationis speciem, illam videlicet affectus quae saporem dat, et illam intellectus quae scientiae luminositatem praestat ut constituatur sapientia id est sapida scientia. Quod si altera carendum esset, eligibilius judicarem communicare in prima quam in secunda, sicut optabilius est habere pium affectum humilem et devotum ad Deum quam intellectum frigidum solo studio illuminatum. Scientia quippe inflat, intellige si sola est, caritas aedificat. Nihilominus ubi de veritate fidei quaeritur tradita in sacris scripturis, magis interrogandi consulendique sunt theologi vigentes in contemplatione secunda quam idiotae pollentes in prima, secluso in eis patenti revelationis miraculo, et nisi forte manifesta esset in hujusmodi theologis depravatio voluntatis et intolerabilis morum perversitas."

98. *OC* 9.641: "Theologica perscrutatio sistere non debet in sola intelligentia vel illuminatione intellectus sed labi debet et liquefieri ad inflammationem affectus."

99. *OC* 8.366: "Collaudandus est ad extremum doctor theologus cuius doctrina sic erudit ad intellectus distinctionem quod non minus allicit, trahit et inducit ad affectus unionem."

100. *OC* 8.107, 2.191: "Attendatur denique . . . quod doctores sancti priores utentes rhetoricis persuasionibus in aggravationem vitiorum et laudem virtutum, non ita tradiderunt resolutionem moralium materiarum, immo nec speculabilium sicut doctores recentiores qui per quaestiones et argumenta processerunt ad utramque partem et per decisiones. Propterea magis insistendum est illis doctrinis quantum ad eruditionem intellectus licet quantum ad inflammationem affectus efficaciores aliae judicentur."

101. Jordan, *Care of Souls*, 2–7, 16–20, 41–46 and passim.

102. Quinto, *Scholastica*, 89–90.

103. Ibid., 58–61.

104. Ibid., 64–84, quotation at 82: "Disciplina autem duplex est: *scholastica* et *monastica* sive morum; et non sufficit ad habendam sapientiam *scholastica* sine *monastica*; quia non audiendo solum, sed observando fit homo sapiens."

105. Cf. Wisdom 11:21: "Sed omnia mensura et numero et pondere disposuisti."

106. *OC* 2.32: "Scribimus, sed absque pondere sententiarum, absque numero et mensura verborum; est enim illud omne quod scribimus flaccidum, illiberale, fluidum. Scribimus non nova sed antiqua noviterque versando et transmutando, dum nostra conamur efficere, prava reddimus et inepta quasi videlicet juxta vulgare proverbium antiquorum fossatarum quae solida sunt non tam reparatores

quam demolitores; hiis praeterea similes quos notat Terentius qui ex bonis com-oediis graecis latinas fecerunt non bonas. Sic quidem excerpentes, aut magis proprie lacerantes, ex libris optimis et probatis particulis [Paris, Bibliothèque de l'Arsenal, Ms. 523, f. 2v: 'particulas'], ingentia tendunt volumina obnubilantes et per incuriam scribendi legendique reddentes originalia velut superflua et mortua a corde. Vides in Sententiarum lecturis dum pudet quemlibet etiam majores sequi, quam infertilis varietas in immensam crescit" (cf. Arsenal 523, f. 2v: "Quam facilis lecturarum varietas in immensum successerit"). Giessen, UB, Hs. 763, f. 178v has the same readings as the Arsenal manuscript.

107. *OC* 2.32: "Porro quanto consultius erat uti bene inventis quam dum quaeruntur invenienda, nec illa afferre quin etiam subvertere bene jam inventa." On *inventio*, see Lausberg, *Handbook*, 119: "The discovery of ideas . . . a process of exhaustive productivity."

108. Verger and Vulliez, "Crise et mutations," 126–33.

109. Quinto, *Scholastica*, 118–19.

110. Rummel, *Humanist-Scholastic Debate*, 153–92, esp. 155–56.

111. Rouse and Rouse, "Development," 249–51.

112. Quillen, *Rereading the Renaissance*, 76; Fubini, *Humanism and Secularization*, 98.

113. Gilli, "L'humanisme français," 49.

114. Baptista Guarino continued to describe reading as the making of excerpts. See the discussion in Eckhard Kessler, "Renaissance Humanism: The Rhetorical Turn," in *Interpretations of Renaissance Humanism*, ed. Angelo Mazzocco (Leiden, 2006), 186–88. Guarino's *De modo et ordine docendi et discendi* is translated in Craig W. Kallendorf (ed. and trans.), *Humanist Educational Treatises* (Cambridge, Mass., 2002).

115. *OC* 3.230: "Curiositas est vitium quo dimissis utilioribus homo convertit studium suum ad minus utilia vel inattingibilia sibi vel noxia." The fullest discussion of *curiositas* appears in this set of lectures. Cf. the definition of William of Auvergne, "libido sciendi non necessaria." *De legibus* (*Guilielmi Alverni Opera omnia* [1674; rpt. Frankfurt, 1963]), 70. Steven Ozment provided historical and bibliographical notes to his translation of the *Contra curiositatem studentium: Selections from "A deo exivit,"* 82–84. Gerson restates many of the earlier attacks on *curiositas* in *De modis significandi*, *OC* 9.625–42. On the connection between curiosity and images, see Jeffrey F. Hamburger, "Idol Curiosity," in *Curiositas: Welterfahrung und ästhetische Neugierde in Mittelalter und früher Neuzeit*, ed. Klaus Krüger (Göttingen, 2002), 19–58.

116. André Cabassut, "Curiosité," *DS* 2.2, 2654–61, here 2655; Courtenay, "Spirituality," 116; Peters, "Transgressing the Limits," 339–40. For further references to the literature on *curiositas*, see Martin, *Fifteenth-Century Carthusian Reform*, 76 n. 16.

117. Kaluza, *Les querelles doctrinales à Paris*, 43–45; Courtenay, "Reception," 43–64. On the study of logic and theology in fourteenth-century England, see Courtenay, *Schools and Scholars*. Also relevant is Murdoch, "'Subtilitates Anglicanae.'"

118. *CUP* 2.588. On this letter, see Courtenay, "Reception," 54.

119. Roccati, "Formation," 68 n. 82.

120. Witt, *Hercules at the Crossroads*, 220 and n. 21.

121. The image of a blind man who disputes about colors is common in Gerson. See, e.g., *OC* 3.36, 276, 255, 339; 5.556; 7.29; 9.211, 505–6. On the doctor who disputes on his deathbed, see 3.247 and 8.374. Cf. 5.501.

122. *OC* 3.240: "Signum curiositatis et singularitatis poenitentiam atque credulitatem impedientis apud scholasticos est gaudere potius in impugnatione doctorum aut in defensione unius pertinaci quam ad eorum dicta concordanda operam dare."

123. Heb. 13:9. In fact, Gerson gives this meaning not to curiosity but to "singularity" (*singularitas*), which he figures as the sister of curiosity. But he distinguished between the two inconsistently, and this division of labor is in my view a rhetorical rather than an analytical device. See *OC* 3.230: "Superbia scholasticos a poenitentia et fide viva praepediens, duas in eis filias infelices, nisi providerint, gignere solita est, curiositatem et singularitatem. . . . Singularitas est vitium quo dimissis utilioribus homo convertit studium suum ad doctrinas peregrinas et insolitas."

124. *OC* 3.238: "Hanc esse magnam aut praecipuam causam existimo cur opiniones toties revertuntur et mutantur. Mavult enim curiositas quaerere invenienda quam inventa cum veneratione studiosa intelligere."

125. Connolly, *John Gerson*, 82–83; Oberman, *Contra vanam curiositatem*, 33–38; Rummel, *Humanist-Scholastic Debate*, 38–39. For a succinct explanation of the distinction between *potentia ordinata* and *absoluta*, see Francis Oakley, *The Western Church in the Later Middle Ages* (Ithaca, N.Y., 1979), 98. For this distinction within the context of nominalism, see Courtenay, "Nominalism and Late Medieval Religion," 37ff.

126. *OC* 3.247: "Contemnere claras et solidas doctrinas, quia leves videntur, et ad obscuriores se transferre, signum est curiositatis et originalis corruptelae poenitentiae et credulitati adversae. Nulla est in omni doctrina major virtus quam claritas, neque evidentius aliud habetur excellentis ingenii et clari argumentum, quam ex claritate dictorum vel scriptorum. Obscurum siquidem ingenium et confusum impossibile est ut perspicue et resolute quidquam edoceat: verumtamen apud multorum curiositatem tanta est judicii corruptio, qualem in me alias fuisse non nego, quod latinitas aliqua vel stylus eo judicetur pulchrior quo difficilior, et quo turgidior et ex consequenti vitiosior eo elegantior appareat, cum longe aliter sit. Omnis enim oratio quanto clarior, tanto est speciosior, atque laudabilior; nisi forte abjecta omni elegantia et accuratione tota sordeat, langueat et effluat."

127. *OC* 10.13: "Habet subtilis hic theologus noster quod optabat: obscuris verborum ambagibus, neque aliis intelligibilibus neque sibi, aures astantium replevit in admirationemque convertit." See also Ouy, "L'humanisme du jeune Gerson," 264. See esp. on this point Cecchetti, *L'evoluzione*, 14 and 32 n. 8.

128. For numerous examples of the theme of darkness in a variety of disciplines, see Mehtonen, *Obscure Language*.

129. De Vooght, *Sources*, 416–17.

130. Hoenen, "'Modus loquendi platonicorum,'" 336–37.

131. Dag Nikolaus Hasse, "Plato arabico-latinus: Philosophy—Wisdom Literature—Occult Sciences," in *The Platonic Tradition in the Middle Ages: A Doxographic Approach*, ed. Stephen Gersh and Maarten J. F. M. Hoenen (Berlin, 2002), 36–39, 52–64.

132. Hoenen, "'Modus loquendi platonicorum,'" 337 and n. 42.

133. Morris Bishop, *Petrarch and His World* (Bloomington, Ind., 1963), 243; Mehtonen, *Obscure Language*, 86–90.

134. D. Cecchetti, "Temi umanistici nell'opera di Jean de Montreuil," *Le Moyen Français* 8–9 (1981), 49–50. On *vis* in Cicero, see Courtenay, "Force of Words," 111; on the shift from *vis* to *virtus* in scholastic authors, 113–14.

135. Gerson: "Omnis enim oratio quanto clarior, tanto est speciosior, atque laudabilior." And Giovanni Moccia (c. 1345–?) in a letter to Laurent de Premierfait: "Quanto clara quidem magis est oracio, tanto | Pulchrior esse solet." Ornato, "L'umanista Jean Muret," 287 n. 133, and, more generally, 286–87. On humanism at Avignon, see Ornato, *Jean Muret*, 256, references s.v. "Humanisme. *Avignonnais*."

136. Witt, "Medieval Italian Culture," 47–48, 67–68 n. 89; and Witt, "Medieval *Ars Dictaminis*," 15 n. 34, 16, 16 n. 36; Mehtonen, *Obscure Language*, 106–8.

137. Mehtonen, *Obscure Language*, 117–18.

138. Hamm, *Frömmigkeitstheologie*, 176–77. The style of Denys the Carthusian has been characterized in a similar way. See Emery, *Dionysii Cartusiensis Prolegomena*, 1.29.

139. Martin, *Fifteenth-Century Carthusian Reform*, 38.

140. A recent treatment of Gerson's reception in Germany is Mazour-Matusevich, "Jean Gerson."

141. Rummel, *Humanist-Scholastic Debate*, 75–76, 79–80.

142. Pettegree and Hall, "The Reformation and the Book," 801–2.

143. Rummel, *Humanist-Scholastic Debate*, 72.

Chapter 5. The Schoolman as Public Intellectual

1. *OC* 2.28. See also 5.132. On the notion of the "simple people," cf. Susan J. Dudash, "Christine de Pizan and the 'menu peuple'," *Speculum* 78 (2003), 788–831.

2. H. Emile Rébouis, *Étude historique et critique sur la peste* (Paris, 1888), 72.

3. D. W. Singer, "Some Plague Tractates (Fourteenth and Fifteenth Centuries)," *Proceedings of the Royal Society of Medicine* 9, no. 2 (1915–1916), 179. On the French translations, see Sylvie Bazin-Tacchella, "Rupture et continuité du discours médical à travers les écrits sur la peste de 1348: Le *Compendium de epidemia* (1348) et ses adaptations françaises," in *Air, miasmes et contagion: Les épidémies dans l'Antiquité et au Moyen Âge*, ed. Sylvie Bazin-Tacchella and Evelyne Samama (Langres, 2001), 109. On the influence, see A. Coville, "Écrits contemporains sur la peste de 1348 à 1350," *Histoire littéraire de la France* 37 (1937), 357.

4. *OC* 2.73; 5.451–52. Cf., on the correction of the calendar, 2.315.

5. The key study is Schreiner, "Laienfrömmigkeit." See also Watts, "Pressure," 167; Catto, "Theology After Wycliffism," 265–66; and Hobbins, "Gerson on Lay Devotion," 49–55.

6. On the move away from the interpretation of books, see Marenbon, *Later Medieval Philosophy*, 33.

7. Recent studies on this theme include Shank, *Logic*; Hoenen, "Academics"; Hoenen, "Denys the Carthusian"; and Lusignan, "Intellectuels." More generally, see Verger, "Les professeurs."

8. For modern context of discussions about the public intellectual, see the introduction by Helen Small in Small (ed.), *Public Intellectual*, 1–18.

9. Le Goff, *Intellectuals in the Middle Ages*. For further orientation, see Rita Copeland, "Pre-Modern Intellectual Biography," in Small (ed.), *Public Intellectual*, 40–61.

10. Swanson, *Universities*, 16 n. 25; Kouamé, *Dormans-Beauvais*, 68 and n. 391.

11. Grundmann, "Sacerdotium."

12. Lusignan, "*Vérité garde le Roy*"; Wei, "Self-Image."

13. Habermas, *Structural Transformation*. James Van Horn Melton, *The Rise of*

the Public in Enlightenment Europe (Cambridge, 2001), 3–15, is extremely helpful for orientation.

14. Guglielmo Cavallo, "Between Volumen and Codex: Reading in the Roman World," in *A History of Reading in the West*, ed. Guglielmo Cavallo and Roger Chartier (Amherst, Mass., 1999), 65–71.

15. Michael Camille, *The Gothic Idol: Ideology and Image-Making in Medieval Art* (Cambridge, 1989), 219. For more on various forms of publicity in a medieval urban landscape, see the stimulating treatment in Carol Symes, *A Common Stage: Theater and Public Life in Medieval Arras* (Ithaca, N.Y., 2007), chapter 3: "Access to the Media: Publicity, Participation, and the Public Sphere."

16. Huizinga, *Autumn*, xix.

17. Scase, "'Strange and Wonderful Bills,'" 226–27, 247. See also Symes, *Common Stage*, 127–30.

18. Habermas, *Structural Transformation*, 7–9 (quotation at 9).

19. On the medieval public, see most recently Watts, "Pressure"; Nolan, *Lydgate*, 5–6; and Hruza, "Propaganda."

20. *Sancti Thomae Aquinatis doctoris angelici Opera omnia*, vol. 4 (Rome, 1888), 5: "Quia catholicae veritatis doctor non solum provectos debet instruere, sed ad eum pertinet etiam incipientes erudire, secundum illud Apostoli I ad Corinth. III: *tanquam parvulis in Christo, lac vobis potum dedi, non escam*; propositum nostrae intentionis in hoc opere est, ea quae ad Christianam religionem pertinent, eo modo tradere, secundum quod congruit ad eruditionem incipientium." Cf. Chenu, *Toward Understanding Saint Thomas*, 298: "The *Disputed Questions* were the book suited to masters, the *Summa* is the book of the pupil."

21. This evolution from the spoken to the written word is best described by Jürgen Miethke, "Die mittelalterlichen Universitäten und das gesprochene Wort," 1–44 (here 13–32). General surveys of these forms include Weijers, *Le maniement du savoir*; Courtenay, "Programs of Study"; Asztalos, "Faculty"; Catto, "Theology and Theologians"; Kenny and Pinborg, "Medieval Philosophical Literature"; and Glorieux, "L'enseignement au Moyen Âge." See also Schönberger, *Was ist Scholastik?* 52–102.

22. A brief description of the manuscript (in Swedish) appears in *Gyllene böcker: Illuminerade medeltida handskrifter I dansk och svensk ägo* (Stockholm, 1952), 38 (no. 43). On Eustratius, see H. P. F. Mercken, "The Greek Commentators on Aristotle's *Ethics*," in *Aristotle Transformed: The Ancient Commentators and Their Influence*, ed. Richard Sorabji (London, 1990), 410–19.

23. Murdoch, "From Social into Intellectual Factors," 275–78; Bert Hansen, *Nicole Oresme and the Marvels of Nature* (Toronto, 1985), 109–13; Konstanty Michalski, "Les sources du criticisme et du scepticisme dans la philosophie du XIVe siècle," in *La philosophie au XIVe siècle: Six études* (Frankfurt, 1969), 37. On the *Sentences* commentary, see G. R. Evans (ed.), *Mediaeval Commentaries on the Sentences of Peter Lombard*, vol. 1, *Current Research* (Leiden, 2002).

24. R. W. Southern, *Scholastic Humanism and the Unification of Europe*, vol. 1, *Foundations* (Oxford, 1995), 45–51. For scholastic teaching on "avoidance of offspring" and abortion, see Peter Biller, *The Measure of Multitude: Population in Medieval Thought* (Oxford, 2000), esp. 57–59 and 166–77 on *Sentences* commentaries, where the subject is treated at book 4 dist. 31. In the same vein is Odd Langholm, *Economics in the Medieval Schools* (Leiden, 1992).

25. Courtenay, "Bible," 181–82, 187.

26. Wippel, "Quodlibetal Questions," 158 and n. 3, also 221–22. On Henry of Ghent's and Godfrey of Fontaines' quodlibets dealing with economic ques-

tions, see Joel Kaye, *Economy and Nature in the Fourteenth Century: Money, Market Exchange, and the Emergence of Scientific Thought* (Cambridge, 1998), 101–15.

27. Boyle, "Quodlibets," 249, 252. On the quodlibet in general, see Glorieux, *La littérature quodlibétique de 1260 à 1320*, 2 vols. (Le Saulchoir, 1925–1935); Christopher Schabel (ed.), *Theological Quodlibeta in the Middle Ages*, 2 vols. (Leiden, 2006); Amédée Teetaert, "La littérature quodlibétique," *Ephemerides Theologicae Lovanienses* 14 (1937), 75–105; Wippel, "Quodlibetal Questions," with a valuable annotated bibliography (153–56); and Wippel, "Quodlibetal Quaestio." See also Wei, "Masters of Theology."

28. B. C. Bazán, "Les questions disputées," in *Les questions disputées et les questions quodlibétiques dans les facultés de théologie, de droit et de médecine* (Turnhout, 1985), 43, 46–48, 146–47. Cf. Catto, "Wyclif," 178–80; and Courtenay, "Parisian Theology," 5–7.

29. Glorieux, *La littérature quodlibétique*, 1.57. Also Courtenay, *Schools and Scholars*, 251–52; Courtenay, "Postscript," esp. 699. Like other genres, the quodlibet enjoyed renewed popularity in the younger foundations of Central Europe after 1350. On quodlibets in the arts faculty at Prague, see Frantisek Smahel, "Die Verschriftlichung der Quodlibet-Disputationen an der Prager Artistenfakultät bis 1420," in *Schriften im Umkreish mitteleuropäischer Universitäten um 1400: Lateinische und volkssprachige Texte aus Prag, Wien und Heidelberg: Unterschiede, Gemeinsamkeiten, Wechselbeziehungen*, ed. Jürgen Miethke et al. (Leiden, 2004), 63–91.

30. Bazán, "Les questions disputées," 48 n. 74.

31. See Miethke, "Die mittelalterlichen Universitäten," 1–44, esp. 30–36.

32. Weijers, *Disputatio*, 31–32.

33. For the implications of this problem, see Hobbins, "The Schoolman as Public Intellectual," 1314 n. 35.

34. Weijers, *Le maniement du savoir*, 66. Cf. Courtenay, "Programs," 338.

35. Ong, *Orality*, 157.

36. Saenger, *Space Between Words*, 264.

37. Courtenay, "Bible," 183. Cf. Glorieux, "L'oeuvre littéraire de Pierre d'Ailly," 67–68.

38. Courtenay, "Bible," 187; Hamm, *Frömmigkeitstheologie*, 179; see also p. 135 n. 21.

39. Glorieux, "'Lectiones duae,'" 347; and Glorieux, "L'enseignement universitaire." Cf. Burger, *Aedificatio*, 35–40. See further Hobbins, "The Schoolman as Public Intellectual," 1315.

40. For what follows see P. Glorieux, "*Sentences*," *Dictionnaire de Théologie Catholique* 14 (1941), 1871–77, esp. 1874–76. See also Courtenay, *Schools and Scholars*, 252–55, 327–74; Courtenay, "Programs," 332–33, 340–42; John Marenbon, *Later Medieval Philosophy (1150–1350): An Introduction* (London, 1987), 31–33; and Catto, "Wyclif," 178–80, 255–56.

41. *OC* 2.27–28.

42. The suggestion of Katherine Tachau, cited in Courtenay, "Programs," 340–42.

43. Glorieux, "L'année universitaire," 461–62.

44. Ibid., 463–64.

45. Ibid., 443.

46. He began book 1 on October 11, book 2 on December 30, book 3 on March 27, and book 4 on May 20 ("L'année universitaire," 465–66).

47. Questions and commentaries appear nearly indistinguishable by 1400 (Catto, "Wyclif," 178). For developments in the arts faculty with commentaries on Aristotle, see Hobbins, "The Schoolman as Public Intellectual," 1316 n. 50.

48. A practice termed *lectura secundum alium* ("lecture according to another") by modern scholars. See most recently Bakker and Schabel, "*Sentences* Commentaries." For more literature, see Hobbins, "The Schoolman as Public Intellectual," 1316 n. 51.

49. While the genre survived elsewhere, it was not being used for what we would call serious "research." Bakker and Schabel state ("*Sentences* Commentaries," 462) that early fifteenth-century *Sentences* commentaries at Vienna are often virtually identical.

50. *CUP* 3.14–15 (nos. 1206–8), 17–18 (no. 1212). For earlier practice, 2.691–95 (no. 1188), and William J. Courtenay, *Adam Wodeham: an Introduction to his Life and Writings* (Leiden, 1978), 49–51, cited by Tachau, "French Theology," 56. Cf. Glorieux, "*Sentences*," 1876. On bachelor lectures on the Bible during a summer vacation at Oxford, see Courtenay, "Bible," 181 and n. 15.

51. On low survival rates for scholastic works written in England, see Courtenay, *Schools and Scholars*, 360. After 1360, although bachelors still lectured on Lombard's *Sentences*, the commentary as a circulated text virtually disappeared. Catto ("Wyclif," 178–79) sees Thomas Claxton's *Sentences* commentary of 1409 as perhaps a conscious attempt at a revival of the form.

52. See the sources and discussion in Hobbins, "The Schoolman as Public Intellectual," 1317 n. 55. And see Courtenay, "Course of Studies," 89–90 and n. 72.

53. *OC* 3.ix. See further Hobbins, "The Schoolman as Public Intellectual," 1317 n. 56.

54. See Hobbins, "The Schoolman as Public Intellectual," 1317–18 n. 57.

55. Glorieux, "L'enseignement au Moyen Âge," 95, 115; *CUP* 4.419–20, 436, etc. (nos. 2217–18, 2244–45). At Paris, each bachelor was required to lecture on two books of the Bible before lecturing on the *Sentences*. These lectures were called the first and second *cursus*. On the *cursus*, see Courtenay, "Course of Studies," 72–74. Here too the trend was toward easing the restrictions. The statutes of 1387 allow a bachelor to substitute an ordinary lecture or a disputation at the Sorbonne during the summer (sometimes called a "Sorbonic lecture") for a *cursus* (*CUP* 3.441–42 [no. 1534]). On the Sorbonic lecture, see Glorieux, "L'enseignement au Moyen Âge," 134–36; Hastings Rashdall, *The Universities of Europe in the Middle Ages* (Oxford, 1936), 1.479–80.

56. *CUP* 4.499 (nos. 2349–50). See further Hobbins, "The Schoolman as Public Intellectual," 1318 n. 59.

57. Important fifteenth-century *Sentences* commentaries include those of Jean Capreolus, Denys the Carthusian, and Gabriel Biel. See further on the late fifteenth and early sixteenth centuries Elie, "Quelques maîtres"; and Farge, *Orthodoxy and Reform*.

58. On the pecia system, see Rouse and Rouse, "Book Trade." On the pecia system's abrupt halt in the middle of the fourteenth century, Rouse and Rouse, *Manuscripts*, 96–97; Fink-Errera, "Institution," 231–32. On the lack of an offical system at Oxford, M. B. Parkes, "Book Provision and Libraries at the Medieval University of Oxford," reprinted in Parkes, *Scribes*, 304–7. The Rouses (in *Manuscripts*) link the demise of the pecia system to the Hundred Years' War and the Black Death, Fink-Errera ("Institution") to a shift in teaching methods and the growing abundance of paper. See also Hillgarth, *Who Read Thomas Aquinas?* 6.

59. On the readership of one very important scholastic author, see Hillgarth, *Who Read Thomas Aquinas?*

60. François Bérier, "La traduction en français," in *La Littérature française aux*

XIVe et XVe siècles (Heidelberg, 1988), 225; Hillgarth, *Who Read Thomas Aquinas?* 30–31. On translations into German, see the important comments of Georg Steer, "Die Rezeption des theologischen Bonaventura-Schrifttums im deutschen Spätmittelalter," in *Bonaventura: Studien zu seiner Wirkungsgeschichte*, ed. Ildefons Vanderheyden (Werl, Germany, 1976), 153–54. German readers had access to Bonaventure's ascetic and mystical works, but not to his formal theological works.

61. For the phrase *in transcursu*, see *OC* 6.105, 165; 9.471; 10.51. Cf. *haec . . . in transito* (2.166), *sub hiis paucis raptim annotatis* (2.231), *haec . . . dicta, licet satis cursorie, sufficient* (9.613), *haec sub brevitate* (10.43), *cursim* (9.185, 473), and (on reading) *in transitu raptim* (2.33).

62. On Gerson and French recovery, see Hobbins, "Joan of Arc," 120.

63. On John of Příbram, see William R. Cook, "John Wyclif and Hussite Theology 1415–1436," *Church History* 42 (1973), 335–49. Manuscripts of the treatise of John of Příbram (inc. "Quamvis pridem magnifici" or "Quamvis quidam magnifici") include Bernkastel-Kues, BSNH, Hs. 95, ff. 212r–221v; Prague, KMK, Cod. D.51, ff. 167v–176v; Cod. D.109.2, ff. 131v–150r. To my knowledge, the work is unedited. For the description of the tract as having been written *celeriter*, see the description of Cod. D.51 and D.109.2 in Antonín Podlaha, *Soupis rukopisu knihovny metropolitní kapitoly pražské* (Prague, 1922), 354, 356, 403.

64. Paul Schrodt and Ingeborg Berlin Vogelstein, *The Reformation Era Pamphlet in the Ambrose Swasey Library* (Lanham, Md., 1997), xiv. See also Joad Raymond, *Pamphlets and Pamphleteering in Early Modern Britain* (Cambridge, 2003), 4–26; and Miriam Usher Chrisman, *Conflicting Visions of Reform: German Lay Propaganda Pamphlets, 1519–1530* (Atlantic Highlands, N.J., 1996), 3.

65. Schrodt and Vogelstein, *Pamphlet*, xvi.

66. Ibid.

67. Cf. Oliver, "The First Political Pamphlet?" 266–68.

68. Madre, *Nikolaus von Dinkelsbühl*, 256 n. 13.

69. *OC* 5.451–52.

70. Justice, *Writing and Rebellion*, 28–29, 77–80 (quotation on 77).

71. Ibid., 78.

72. Hudson, "Lollard Book-Production," 134, 141 n. 39.

73. Marin, *L'archevêque*, 219–20.

74. Sue Powell, "The Transmission and Circulation of *The Lay Folks' Catechism*," in *Late-Medieval Religious Texts and Their Transmission*, ed. A. J. Minnis (Cambridge, 1994), 75–76; A. S. G. Edwards, "The Transmission and Audience of Osbern Bokenham's *Legendys of Hooly Wummen*," in Minnis (ed.), *Late-Medieval Religious Texts*, 162; Julia Boffey and John J. Thompson, "Anthologies and Miscellanies: Production and Choice of Texts," in *Book Production and Publishing in Britain, 1375–1475*, ed. Jeremy Griffiths and Derek Pearsall (Cambridge, 1989), 288–91.

75. *OC* 5.248, 347.

76. Karl Sudhoff, "Pestschriften aus den ersten 150 Jahren nach der Epidemie des 'schwarzen Todes' 1348," *Archiv für Geschichte der Medizin* 5 (1912), 58–69 (the work is called a *cedula* on pp. 63 and 67). On the work's circulation, see Lister M. Matheson, "*Médecin sans Frontières?* The European Dissemination of John of Burgundy's Plague Treatise," *ANQ* 18, no. 3 (2005), 17–28.

77. Hudson, "Aspects," 183; Hudson, "A Lollard Quaternion"; Hudson, "Lollard Book-Production," 134.

78. Besides the works of Hudson and Scase, see Taylor, "Authors," 359; Robinson, "The 'Booklet.'"

79. Catto, "Wyclif," 210; Zénon Kaluza, "Note sur Guillaume de Salvarvilla, auteur de deux poèmes sur le Grande Schisme," *Mediaevalia Philosophica Polonorum* 19 (1974), 168–71; Swanson, *Universities*, 22–44.

80. *OC* 10.11.

81. See for D'Ailly, *OC* 2.44, 63–64, 127, 315, 316; 5.474; and for Langenstein, 6.114, 124; 9.181. See further Hobbins, "The Schoolman as Public Intellectual," 1326.

82. *SOP* 1.80–82, 87–89. See further Thomas M. Izbicki, "The Origins of the *De ornatu mulierum* of Antoninus of Florence," *Modern Language Notes* 119 Supplement (2004), S142–61.

83. Bozzolo and Ornato, *Pour une histoire*, 95.

84. Ibid., 113 and n. 172. By comparison, the Merton College Library had fifteen copies of the *Sentences* in 1360. R. M. Ball, "Thomas Cyrcetur, a Fifteenth-Century Theologian and Preacher," *Journal of Ecclesiastical History* 37 (1986), 220.

85. Wilson, "Contents," 87 and 107 n. 16

86. France produced 226 copies in the twelfth and thirteenth centuries, and just 37 in the fourteenth and fifteenth centuries, whereas Germany produced 72 and 183, respectively. Agneta Sylwan (ed.), *Petri Comestoris Scolastica historia: Liber Genesis* (Turnhout, 2005), xxxiii. See also Stanislaw Wielgus, "Die mittelalterlichen polnischen Bibelkommentare," *Probleme der Bearbeitung mittelalterlicher Handschriften*, ed. Helmar Härtel et al. (Wiesbaden, 1986), 277–99.

87. Bozzolo and Ornato, *Pour une histoire*, 96. Cf. the situation in print, Milway, "Forgotten Best-Sellers," 118.

88. Kenny and Pinborg, "Medieval Philosophical Literature," 33; M. de Wulf, *Scholasticism Old and New*, trans. P. Coffey (London, 1910), 25. For Aquinas's *De ente et essentia*, see *Sancti Thomae de Aquino Opera omnia iussu Leonis XIII P. M. edita*, vol. 43 (Rome, 1976), 370–81; Chenu, *Toward Understanding Saint Thomas*, 330–32.

89. *OC* 9.385–421.

90. Cf. D. P. Lockwood, *Ugo Benzi: Medieval Philosopher and Physician, 1376–1439* (Chicago, 1951), 79: "The consilium . . . becomes an embryonic treatise when the individual patient is eliminated. . . . By expansion, this may then become a monograph on a disease, treating its causes, nature, symptoms, and therapy."

91. Miethke, *De potestate papae*, and Miethke, "Practical Intentions of Scholasticism," 211–28, esp. 213–14.

92. Likewise, in their treatments of Carthusian diet, Pierre d'Ailly and Gerson both referred to the treatise *On the Eating of Meat* by Arnau de Vilanova. See Joseph Ziegler, *Medicine and Religion c. 1300: The Case of Arnau de Vilanova* (Oxford, 1998), 161–62; *OC* 3.80.

93. *Contre le Roman de la Rose* is fifteen pages long in the modern edition, and *De parvulis ad Christum trahendis* is seventeen.

94. Such as: *avisamentum, defensio, determinatio, disputatio, exhortatio, invectiva, opusculum, propositio, quaestio, regulae, responsio*, and *scriptum*.

95. *Super facto puellae et credulitate sibi praestanda*. On this title, see Hobbins, "Joan of Arc," 140–44.

96. When discussing the circumstances of Joan's life as evidence for her authenticity, Gerson passes them by with the remark that "nothing is included about them here" ["De quibus hic nil inseritur"] (*OC* 9.664). Also *OC* 9.665: "De quibus non est hic dicendum per singula."

97. For a more detailed summary, see Hobbins, "Joan of Arc," 113–19.

98. For the law faculties, see Philippe Godding, *La jurisprudence* (Turnhout, 1973), 28; G. Fransen, "Les questions disputées dans les facultés de droit," in *Les questions disputées et les questions quodlibétiques dans les faculté de théologie, de droit et de médecine* (Turnhout, 1985), 239–40; Paul Ourliac and Henri Gilles, *La période post-classique (1378–1500)* (Paris, 1971), 147–49; Ingrid Baumgärtner, ed., *Consilia im späten Mittelalter* (Sigmaringen, 1995). For the medical faculty, see Lockwood, *Ugo Benzi*, 47; Jole Agrimi and Chiara Crisciani, *Les consilia médicaux* (Turnhout, 1994), 18 (39–61 on the trend toward the *consilia*); Pesenti, "Generi e pubblico," 533–38.

99. Agrimi and Crisciani, *Les consilia médicaux*, 19–21; Lockwood, *Ugo Benzi*, 79–80; and Ourliac and Gilles, *La période post-classique*, 111–14.

100. Cf. Ourliac and Gilles, *La période post-classique*, 132.

101. Pesenti, "Generi e pubblico," 534–35.

102. Swanson, *Universities*; Serge Lusignan and Gilbert Ouy, "Le bilinguisme latin-français à la fin du Moyen Âge," in *Acta Conventus Neo-Latini Torontonensis (Proceedings of the Seventh International Congress of Neo-Latin Studies)*, ed. Alexander Dalzell, Charles Fantazzi, and Richard J. Schoeck (Binghamton, N.Y., 1991), 157 n. 6; Cohn, *The Black Death Transformed*, 67–68.

103. Luis García-Ballester, "Changes in the *Regimina sanitatis*: The Role of the Jewish Physicians," in *Health, Disease and Healing in Medieval Culture*, ed. Sheila Campbell, Bert Hall, and David Klausner (New York, 1992), 122.

104. Cohn, *The Black Death Transformed*, 66.

105. J. N. Biraban, *Les hommes et la peste en France et dans les pays européens et méditerranéens* (Paris, 1975), 1.56 n. 64.

106. Indeed, the trend toward shorter occasional pieces extends well beyond these fields. For example, Christopher Given-Wilson notes the trend toward tracts and pamphlets on political themes: "Adam Usk, the Monk of Evesham and the Parliament of 1397–8," *Historical Research* 66 (1993), 333. On newsletters, see Antonia Gransden, *Historical Writing in England*, vol. 2, *c. 1307 to the Early Sixteenth Century* (London, 1982), 238–39; Novák, "La source du savoir," 152–55. Cf. Oliver, "The First Political Pamphlet?" 251–68, esp. 266–68.

107. Baldwin, *Masters*, 1.xi.

108. See further Baldwin, *Masters*, 1.58. Such works could still circulate widely. Peter seems to have attempted to reach a wider public with his ethical manual, the *Verbum abbreviatum*, which survives in various versions in eighty-five manuscripts. Baldwin, *Masters*, 1.15–16, 2.246–65.

109. Lerner, "Writing and Resistance," 189–90. A similar example comes from England, where Archbishop Pecham prepared a Latin catechism but left the translation into English to others. Taylor, "Authors," 360.

110. Among many studies on Arnau, I have found helpful Ziegler, *Medicine and Religion*; and many of the essays in Daniel Le Blèvec (ed.), *L'Université de Médecine de Montpellier et son rayonnement (XIIIe–XVe siècles)* (Turnhout, 2004). For overviews, see *CALMA* 1.442–59; *DLF* 92–93.

111. Donatella Nebbiai, "L'école de Montpellier et les bibliothèques médicales: Arnaud de Villeneuve, son milieu, ses livres (XIIIe–XIVe siècles)," in Le Blèvec (ed.), *L'Université de Médecine de Montpellier*, 257–58.

112. Lluís Cifuentes, "Université et vernacularisation au bas Moyen Âge: Montpellier et les traductions catalanes médiévales de traités de médecine," in Le Blèvec (ed.), *L'Université de Médecine de Montpellier*, 277–81.

113. Ziegler, *Medicine and Religion*, 21–26 (quotation at 23); Clifford R. Backman, "The Reception of Arnau de Vilanova's Religious Ideas," in *Christendom*

and Its Discontents: Exclusion, Persecution, and Rebellion, 1000–1500, ed. Scott L. Waugh and Peter D. Diehl (Cambridge, 1996), 118–19.

114. Wei, "Masters of Theology," 41–43.

115. See D. L. d'Avray, *Medieval Marriage Sermons: Mass Communication in a Culture Without Print* (Oxford, 2001); D'Avray, *Medieval Marriage: Symbolism and Society* (Oxford, 2005); and D'Avray, "Printing, Mass Communication, and Religious Reformation: the Middle Ages and After," in *The Uses of Script and Print, 1300–1700,* ed. Julia Crick and Alexandra Walsham (Cambridge, 2004), 50–70. D'Avray argues that thirteenth-century mendicant sermons, by virtue of being mass produced, standardized, and repeatedly preached, constitute a kind of "mass communication" that approaches the "printing revolution" in its impact. Despite the solid textual scholarship on which these studies are based, the argument in my view relies too much on an unprovable hypothesis—and indeed in the case of *pecia* manuscripts on a *lack* of surviving manuscripts—that is, on an argument from silence. His assumptions about the uniqueness of sermon manuscripts and mendicant libraries are open to debate, and the comparison to print seems overstated, in part because print was the climax of a tremendous growth in manuscript production during the fourteenth and fifteenth centuries, a growth that D'Avray does not address. To be convincingly applied to a medieval context, the phrases "mass production" and "mass communication" require clear definition and differentiation from their modern manifestations. Cf. the review of *Medieval Marriage Sermons* by Robert Lerner in *Speculum* 79 (2004), 163–65; and the brief response in Stallybrass, "Broadsides," 319–20 n. 16.

116. See further Peter Francis Howard, *Beyond the Written Word: Preaching and Theology in the Florence of Archbishop Antoninus, 1427–1459* (Florence, 1995); Cynthia L. Polecritti, *Preaching Peace in Renaissance Italy: Bernardino of Siena and His Audience* (Washington, D.C., 2000).

117. Courtenay, "Spirituality," 112–13; Courtenay, *Teaching Careers,* 31–32; Francis Rapp, "Rapport introductif," in *Le clerc séculier au Moyen Âge* (Paris, 1993), 13. This trend at Paris continued into the sixteenth century. See Farge, *Orthodoxy and Reform,* 55–56.

118. Addresses survive to the faculties of arts (5.339–44), canon law (5.168–79, 218–29, 435–47), and medicine (5.144–51). The treatise *De erroribus circa artem magicam* (*OC* 10.77–90) began as an address to the medical faculty.

119. On Gerson preaching, *OC* 1.108; on the French sermons, see Mourin, *Jean Gerson.* On Gerson's connections to nobility, see for example his letter to the duke of Berry (*OC* 2.155–57), and his poem to Albert V, archduke of Austria (*OC* 4.169–70). On Gerson's relations with the duke of Burgundy, see Vansteenberghe, "Gerson à Bruges." On taxation, *OC* 7.2.650, 1158; 10.360. On Gerson's personal background, *OC* 2.3; Ouy, *Gerson bilingue,* xi–xiv; Hobbins, "Gerson and Lay Devotion," 52.

120. On the increase of basic literacy in the fifteenth century, see Derville, "L'alphabétisation du peuple."

121. On Gerson's positive attitudes toward the "simple people," specifically their aptitude for mystical theology, see Schreiner, "Laienfrömmigkeit," 50–51. For another view, Elliott, "Seeing Double," 35. On the churches where Gerson preached, Mourin, *Jean Gerson,* 62 (the royal church of Saint-Paul), 103 (Saint-Antoine des Champs), 121 (Saint-Jean-en-Grève), 123 (Saint-Germain-l'Auxerrois), 148 (Saint-Antoine), and 163 (Saint-Severin).

122. See Ouy, *Gerson bilingue,* xv–li. Ouy has newly edited both the Latin and the French versions of the work (pp. 2–93). For further manuscripts see Brunelli, "Traité"; and Hasenohr, "Aperçu," 72–73 nn. 58–60.

123. *OC* 2.75.

124. Vansteenberghe, "Doctrinal"; and Ouy, *Gerson bilingue,* xvii–xviii.

125. Rieckenberg, "Katechismus-Tafel," 555–81, esp. 569–70; Donald Sullivan, "Cusanus and Pastoral Renewal: The Reform of Popular Religion in the Germanies," in *Nicolas of Cusa on Christ and the Church,* ed. Gerald Christianson and Thomas M. Izbicki (Leiden, 1996), 171–72.

126. For precedents, cf. Ouy, *Gerson bilingue,* xv; and André Vauchez, "Un réformateur religieux dans la France de Charles VI: Jean de Varennes," in *Académie des Inscriptions et Belles-Lettres (Comptes rendus des séances de l'année 1998 novembre-decembre)* (Paris, 1998), 1112 n. 6. Gabriel Biel also translated Gerson's *Opus tripartitum* into German: Kraume, *Gerson-Übersetzungen,* 49–55.

127. On the early editions, *GW* vol. 9, nos. 10774–96. On its impact, Bast, *Honor Your Fathers,* 13–28.

128. Hasenohr, "Aperçu," 57–90; Hasenohr, "Religious Reading," 205–21.

129. The *Ad Deum vadit* is in *OC* 7.2.449–519. The manuscript figures here come from Hasenohr, "Aperçu," 90. The owners come from the manuscript catalogues. My thanks to Maureen Boulton for her help with these manuscripts. These figures do not include many manuscripts with unknown provenance. For Jeanne de Velle, Hasenohr, "L'essor," 242.

130. This includes the *Montagne de contemplation,* the *A.B.C. des simples gens,* the three works constituting the French *Opus tripartitum,* and the *Mendicité spirituelle. OC* 7.1.16–55, 154–57, 193–206, 393–400, 404–7, 220–80.

131. For the *Roman de la Rose,* see Sylvia Huot, *The Romance of the Rose and Its Medieval Readers: Interpretation, Reception, Manuscript Transmission* (Cambridge, 1993), 84.

132. See Celenza, *Lost Italian Renaissance,* 1–15.

133. Pettegree and Hall, "The Reformation and the Book," 792, 796–97.

134. See further Neddermeyer, *Handschrift,* 1.88, 104–5.

135. Cornelius O'Boyle, *The Art of Medicine: Medical Teaching at the University of Paris, 1250–1400* (Leiden, 1998), 45–46. An excellent illustration of this kind of clerical audience appears at the Council of Constance. See here Miethke, "Die Konzilien als Forum," 746–48.

136. Verger, "Les universités françaises," 248.

137. Martin, *History,* 196.

138. Autrand, "Librairies," 1236.

139. For sources and further details on what follows, see Hobbins, "Joan of Arc," 99–155.

140. G. W. Coopland, *Nicole Oresme and the Astrologers* (Liverpool, 1952), 1–2.

Chapter 6. Publishing Before Print (1)

1. *OC* 5.384: "Quae verba quomodo sint accipienda tractatulus quidam nuper editus pandit quid prodiet in publicum."

2. Munich, BS, Clm 7505, f. 197r; Clm 17837, f. 229r. The colophon in Clm 17837 reads: "Hec interim habui que de ecclesiastica potestate et de origine juris summatim desorcon [!] sic complete, fecit deus per me quod volui, si nimis feci quod potui, suppleat imperfectum meum prudens lector, etc. Scriptum Constantie tempore generalis Concilii, anno domini M° cccc° xvi die septima Octobris, etc." At present, it is not clear whether Gerson changed the text of the work for the February publication. This text awaits a critical edition.

3. *OC* 6.250: "Finit tractatulus de potestate ecclesiastica et de origine juris et

legum; magis ad inquisitionem veritatis quam ad determinationem editus et pro-nuntiatus Constantiae tempore concilii generalis pro parte cancellarii Parisien-sis; anno a Nativitate Domini 1417, die vi Februarii."

4. The *pronuntiatio* is very poorly understood. See in the first place Hamesse, "Approche." See also Miethke, "Die Konzilien als Forum," 753–55; Fink-Errera, "Institution," 232–35; Christ, *Handbook*, 247.

5. The technique may have been in use as early as the thirteenth century, though probably in much more limited form. See Clanchy, *From Memory to Written Record*, 270.

6. Cf. *OC* 10.280: "Responsiones Gersonistarum ad predictum questionis dubium . . . Pronunciata in ecclesia beati Stephani per Jacobum Sauer clericum omnibus scribere volentibus."

7. For Petit, see Willard, "Manuscripts," 276, 278–79; Coville, *Jean Petit*, 134–37; *OC* 5.195. For Hus, see Marin, *L'archevêque*, 216 and n. 4.

8. Miethke, "Die Konzilien als Forum," 754–55 n. 61.

9. This is my figure, supplementing the total of thirty-seven in *OC* 6.xv. For more on the manuscripts, see below, Chapter 7. A good recent discussion of the text is Posthumus Meyjes, *Jean Gerson*, 247–86.

10. On risk, see Stallybrass, "Broadsides," 320–22.

11. Eisenstein, *Printing Press*, 1.11. For an early criticism, see Grafton, "Importance," 280–81.

12. Nichols, "Introduction," 6.

13. Bourgain, "L'édition," 49–75, esp. 51 and references in notes 14 and 23. Cf. Fink-Errera, "Institution," 240 n. 16.

14. *OC* 2.74, 333; 5.132, 384; 10.77. An example from Christine de Pizan comes at the close of her *Trois Vertus*, where she expresses the remarkable desire that her work will be "ventillee, espandue et publiee en tout païs." *Le livre des trois vertus*, ed. Charity Cannon Willard and Eric Hicks (Paris, 1989), 225. My thanks to Lori Walters for this reference.

15. *OC* 2.291, 333.

16. In general on scribal publication after print, see Love, *Scribal Publication*; and Richardson, "From Scribal Publication to Print Publication." Other studies include George Justice and Nathan Tinker (eds.), *Women's Writing and the Circulation of Ideas: Manuscript Publication in England, 1550–1800* (New York, 2002); and Peter Beal, *In Praise of Scribes: Manuscripts and Their Makers in Seventeenth-Century England* (New York, 1998).

17. On this topic, see first of all Bourgain, "L'édition." This important article has been overlooked in more recent discussions. Other studies include Doyle, "Publication"; and Riddy, " 'Publication' before Print." A study of ancient publication that is well worth consulting is Gamble, *Books and Readers*. On Carolingian publication, see Meyvaert, "Medieval Notions of Publication."

18. Bourgain, "L'édition," 54; Doyle, "Publication," 110. Instructive comparisons can be drawn to publication in the early Church, on which see Gamble, *Books and Readers*, 82–143, esp. 138–39 on Augustine and Jerome, and 139 on Rufinus of Aquileia (and see also the references to publication in antiquity, pp. 279–80 n. 6).

19. Chartier, *Order of Books*, 28.

20. On the advantages that Pietro Bembo saw in printing his verse, see Richardson, "From Scribal Publication to Print Publication," 684–95, esp. 691–93.

21. This seems to be the case with many of the items relating to the Jean Petit affair.

22. Neddermeyer, *Handschrift*, 23; Saenger, *Space Between Words*, 273; McGrady, *Controlling Readers*, 39–44.

23. On this point, see Doyle, "Publication," 110.

24. Love, *Scribal Publication*, 35–46, esp. 36; Richardson, "From Scribal Publication to Print Publication," 686.

25. For Petrarch and Boccaccio, see Root, "Publication," 420–22.

26. Gamble, *Books and Readers*, 135–36.

27. Doyle, "Publication," 111.

28. *OC* 2.95. On the work's five manuscripts (two in the original French—one of these the actual copy sent to Gerson—and three in a Latin translation), see Claude Arnaud-Gillet, *Entre Dieu et Satan: Les visions d'Ermine de Reims (†1396) recueillies et transcrites par Jean Le Graveur* (Florence, 1997), 35–43.

29. See Root, "Publication," 420–23.

30. McGrady, *Controlling Readers*, 9–10.

31. Poor, *Mechthild of Magdeburg*, 3, 168.

32. *OC* 1.29: "De hiis incertum est si et ubi supersint."

33. Martin, *Mise en page*, 85–91; Marina Belozerskaya, *Rethinking the Renaissance: Burgundian Arts Across Europe* (Cambridge, 2002).

34. Richard Vaughan, *Philip the Bold: The Formation of the Burgundian State* (Cambridge, Mass., 1962), 201.

35. *OC* 5.154–55.

36. *OC* 10.463. Glorieux gives the date of this letter as "1397/1403."

37. McGuire, *Jean Gerson*, 81; Mourin, *Jean Gerson*, 169–75; *RSD* 3.346; *DLF* 1250–51.

38. The manuscript is Paris, BnF, Ms. fr. 926. See on this manuscript besides the catalogue description *Paris, 1400: Les arts sous Charles VI* (Paris, 2004), 328.

39. *OC* 2.72.

40. The sermon *Redde quod debes* from 8 October 1421, delivered at a synod before his patron the archbishop of Lyon, Amadeus of Talaru (*OC* 5.487–93).

41. I am using Glorieux's totals here (*OC*, vol. 6). The exception is the *De modo se habendi tempore schismatis*, written in 1398, which survives in at least nineteen MSS. The next work to survive in more than five MSS (again using Glorieux's figures) is the *De auctoritate Concilii universalem Ecclesiam repraesentantis*, from 1408–1409, which survives in at least seven MSS.

42. On the early letter, see Ouy, "Pétrarque," 419 n. 10.

43. *OC* 2.43. See further Calvot and Ouy, *L'oeuvre de Gerson*, 22 and n. 44.

44. *OC* 2.151–52.

45. *OC* 2.157–61. Cf. Kaminsky, *Simon de Cramaud*, 301.

46. This fact is not always appreciated in conversations about the orality of late medieval culture. Cf. Suzanne Fleischman, "Philology, Linguistics, and the Discourse of the Medieval Text," *Speculum* 65 (1990), 20: "It is now commonly accepted that the European Middle Ages were 'oral,' insofar as writing was dictated and reading was carried out viva voce."

47. Gamble, *Books and Readers*, 139.

48. Monique-Cécile Garand, "Auteurs latins et autographes des XIe et XIIe siècles," *Scrittura e civiltà* 5 (1981), 77–104.

49. On Aquinas and Albert, see Hamesse, "Les autographes," 191, 195–96. On late medieval French authors, among many studies by Gilbert Ouy on this subject, see "Manuscrits autographes." See further on the subject the essays in this same volume, and Saenger, "Silent Reading," 388. Saenger (*Space Between Words*, 249–51) links autograph composition to a more private or interior writ-

ing process. Petrucci (*Writers and Readers*, 145–68) uses it as a window to the production of medieval texts.

50. Combes cites a passage from the *Tractatus super Cantica Canticorum* to show that Gerson may have dictated at least part of that work. The passage in question, however, remains open to interpretation. Combes, *Théologie mystique*, 2.654–55 n. 374.

51. *OC* 1.144.

52. Ouy has discovered two autograph copies of individual works: an early draft of the treatise against Juan de Monzon, and the first part of the *Opus tripartitum*, copied by Gerson in March 1405 as a fair copy for further duplication. Ouy, "La plus ancienne oeuvre"; Calvot and Ouy, *L'oeuvre de Gerson*, 60–62; Ouy, *Gerson bilingue*, xxii–xxxiv.

53. References to autograph composition include *OC* 2.26, 161, 163, 216–17, 292; 10.253. Further references appear in Ouy, "Enquête," 280–81. Ouy's most recent discussion of this topic appears in his "Le Célestin," 281–83.

54. See on these stages Beadle, "English Autograph Writings," 249–68, here at 260–64. Cf. Lucas, *From Author to Audience*, 69–89.

55. Ouy, *Gerson bilingue*, xxii–xxxiv.

56. Calvot and Ouy, *L'oeuvre de Gerson*, 20–22.

57. Ouy, "Le Célestin."

58. The chancellorship had official notaries, but we have no evidence at all that they copied theological texts. A shadowy figure named André de Curia had served as Gerson's chaplain and assistant for at least ten years until his death in 1418 (McGuire, *Jean Gerson*, 220, 287). For the Lyon period at least, one of Gerson's copyists may have been Jacques de Cerisy, who returned with Gerson to Lyon from Constance and probably outlived him (*OC* 1.27–28, 2.217).

59. In chronological order, by Glorieux numbers: nos. 234, 281, 529, 248, 282 and 447, 284, 286, 42, 497, 498. For other memoirs, poems, and letters, see *OC* 10.593. Glorieux dated to the summer the four treatises on the heart (nos. 409–12), the last of these (no. 412) to July 28. Combes rejected the dating based on his own understanding of Gerson's doctrinal development over time. His arguments invite criticism. See Combes, *Théologie mystique*, 2.249–61. The dating of these works is unresolved.

60. Anne Hudson, *The Premature Reformation: Wycliffite Texts and Lollard History* (Oxford, 1988), 241 n. 72, citing Thomson, *Latin Writings*.

61. On the date of completion, see Chapter 3.

62. *OC* 8.481; 9.248: "Visus est protinus labor vix explebilis, maxime propter ordinis rerum gestarum incertitudinem."

63. *OC* 2.313; 8.639; Combes, *Théologie mystique*, 2.650–56.

64. Guenée, *Between Church and State*, 138.

65. Hobbins, "Joan of Arc," 133–34 and n. 131; *OC* 10.163, 2.274, 7.xvii–xviii, 2.203. On the dialogue on clerical celibacy, see further Grévy-Pons, *Célibat*, 109–10.

66. An edition of the work is in preparation. The manuscript is Stuttgart, WL, Hs. HB I 10, ff. 275v–276r.

67. McGrady, "Authorship and Audience," 26–27. See the essays on Lebègue by Anne D. Hedeman and Gilbert Ouy in *Patrons, Authors and Workshops: Books and Book Production in Paris around 1400*, ed. Godfried Croenen and Peter Ainsworth (Louvain, 2006).

68. Cf. Doyle, "Publication," 119.

69. Laidlaw, "Christine and the Manuscript Tradition," 231–32.

70. Gerson addressed his "Carmen in laudem ducis Austriae" to Archduke Albert of Austria in September 1419 (*OC* 4.169–70). Gerson also dedicated the *De nobilitate* to the archbishop of Lyon, Amadeus of Talaru, his "most generous benefactor" in Lyon. Gerson states in the letter of introduction that the archbishop had treated Gerson "like an archbishop," even as Ambrose had treated Augustine "like a bishop." *OC* 2.248.

71. Of course there are other kinds of "publishing conditions" that are beyond my scope here. For example, authors of visionary literature wrote "under constraint": see the discussion in Kathryn Kerby-Fulton, *Books Under Suspicion: Censorship and Tolerance of Revelatory Writing in Late Medieval England* (Notre Dame, Ind., 2006), 15–20.

72. On diagrams and spatial elements, see Chapter 3. Cf. Ouy, "Maquette," which argues that Gerson gave instructions on the illustration of a manuscript of Honoré Bouvet's *Somnium prioris de Sallono super materia Scismatis*.

73. Carruthers, *Book of Memory*, 324–37.

74. For an excellent study of the scientific diagrams in manuscripts of Pierre d'Ailly, see Boudet, "Un prélat."

75. Eisenstein, *Printing Press*, 1.53, 67, 81; 2.467–68, etc.

76. McGrady, *Controlling Readers*, 11, 14–15.

77. Gamble, *Books and Readers*, 104–5, 118 (and see further 122–27); Johannes Pedersen, *The Arabic Book* (Princeton, N.J., 1984), 48–49; Beit-Arié, *Unveiled Faces*, 57; C. H. Talbot, "The Universities and the Mediaeval Library," in *The English Library Before 1700*, ed. F. Wormald and C. E. Wright (London, 1958), 75; Henry Suso, *The Exemplar, with Two German Sermons*, trans. Frank Tobin (New York, 1989), 304.

78. Petrucci, *Writers and Readers*, 158–68.

79. Petrucci, quoted in Chartier, *Order of Books*, 55. See also Petrucci, *Writers and Readers*, 145–68.

80. Steinberg, *Accounting for Dante*, 9.

81. Mooney, "Chaucer's Scribe," 122.

82. Bowers, "Holographs," 45. Bowers makes the case for considering the two Huntington manuscripts as originally a single codex of Hoccleve's complete poems.

83. *OC* 2.43, 3.320.

84. *OC* 9.424; Petrucci, *Writers and Readers*, 193. Cf. Carruthers, *Book of Memory*, 280–81.

85. See here Ouy, "Manuscrits autographes," 270–71; Petrucci, *Writers and Readers*, 193–94. Petrarch wrote about scribes in the *De remediis utriusque fortunae*, in the chapter "De librorum copia," which is edited in *Mostra di codici petrarcheschi* (Florence, 1974), 74–86.

86. *OC* 9.425.

87. *OC* 9.423: "Verum quomodo scrutabuntur scripturae si non habeantur? Qualiter habebuntur si non scribantur? Qua ratione scribentur sine scriptoribus? Sunt igitur necessarii scriptores; et hoc est quod hic et nunc intendimus suadere, compellente nos ad hoc multiplici circa scriptores librorum utilium defectu quem patitur aetas nostra."

88. *OC* 9.424.

89. *OC* 9.428: "Videat autem scriptor ne suum sal infatuet . . . si corruptum per ineptias scribendi reddiderit. Quales vere protulit aetas nostra plurimos quorum mendosa fuerunt adeo volumina ut consultius fuisset nulla quam talia ministrari cum litteris inconditis, sine lege, sine sensu vel ordine, adeo quidem ut

auctori proprio seu dictatori non intelligibilia redderentur quantumlibet intro-specta."

90. *OC* 9.428. Gerson's source must have been Eusebius's *Historia ecclesiastica*. See Gamble, *Books and Readers*, 124. For the efforts of Eusebius to manage scribal production, see Grafton and Williams, *Christianity*, 178–232.

91. Chartier, *Order of Books*, 28.

92. For *tituli*, see Hudson, "Lollard Book-Production," 139 n. 17, citing Richard H. and Mary A. Rouse, *Preachers, Florilegia and Sermons* (Toronto, 1979), 29. Cf. Sharpe, *Titulus*, 29–31.

93. Grafton and Williams, *Christianity*, 102–6, 137–43, 173, 194–200.

94. Beadle, "English Autograph Writings," 261–62.

95. On paratext, see Genette, *Paratexts*, 1: "The paratext is what enables a text to become a book and to be offered as such to its readers and, more generally, to the public."

96. Parkes, "Influence."

97. Rouse and Rouse, "*Ordinatio*," 124, 127.

98. *OC* 9.430.

99. Rouse and Rouse, "Development," and "*Statim invenire*."

100. Keiser, "Serving the Needs of Readers," 212.

101. Siraisi, "Surgery," 93.

102. Beit-Arié, *Unveiled Faces*, 53–59.

103. Emery, *Dionysii Cartusiensis Prolegomena*, 1.48–49.

104. Gillespie, "Vernacular Books of Religion," 328.

105. Bowers, "Holographs," 39 and 48 n. 17.

106. Keiser, "*Ordinatio*," 140–44. For broader context, see the studies cited in Lerer, *Chaucer and His Readers*, 226–27 n. 17.

107. Mooney, "Chaucer's Scribe," 97–138, here at 105.

108. Hudson, "Accessus ad auctorem," 323–44; on Hus, 328.

109. For example, Melk, SB, Hs. 889; Vienna, ONB, Cod. lat. 4738 (begun 4 July 1446, finished 14 August 1446); Paris, BnF, Ms. lat. 17488; Tours, BM, Ms. 379.

110. *OC* 2.332. Gerson calls the *Monotessaron* here the "Unum ex quatuor."

111. *OC* 8.487.

112. For manuscripts, see *RBMA* vol. 2, nos. 1175–82. Such mnemonic devices were commonplace by Gerson's day. Cf. Mary Carruthers and Jan M. Ziolkowski (eds.), *The Medieval Craft of Memory: An Anthology of Texts and Pictures* (Philadelphia, 2002), 255–93, for an anonymous *Method for Recollecting the Gospels* that relies on images rather than verse. The abbot of Melk, Peter of Rosenheim, also included metrical summaries in his *Roseum memoriale* (c. 1430). See Carruthers and Ziolkowski, *Medieval Craft of Memory*, 255.

113. A random sampling of manuscripts with the table includes Giessen, UB, Hs. 762; Hs. 763a, ff. 84–85v (completed 1467); Cologne, HASK, GB fol. 188; Melk, SB, Hs. 799, ff. 4r–5v (dated 15 October 1449); Hs. 1915, ff. 78r–80r; Salzburg, SBSP, b.XII.26, ff. 8v–9r; Vorau, SB, Hs. 308 (CXCII), ff. 223r–224r; Vienna, ONB, Cod. lat. 4374, ff. 2r–3r; Cod. lat. 4428; Vienna, Schottenkloster 321 (4254) [Glorieux's L²], ff. 1r–2v.

114. *OC* 9.175–77.

115. *OC* 8.577–78.

116. Kerby-Fulton, "Langland," 79.

117. Destrez and Fink-Errera, "Des manuscrits apparemment datés," 67–70. Cf. Neddermeyer, *Handschrift*, 1.20.

118. On Ockham, see Léon Baudry, *Guillaume d'Occam, sa vie, ses oeuvres, ses idées sociales et politiques* (Paris, 1949); on Wyclif, Thomson, *Latin Writings*; and on Chaucer, Derek Pearsall, *The Life of Geoffrey Chaucer: A Critical Biography* (Oxford, 1992).

119. On secretaries and monarchs, see Knapp, *Bureaucratic Muse*, 34; and Knapp, "Bureaucratic Identity," 369. One way to get some sense of the chronology of author signatures is through catalogues of dated manuscripts, when these specify manuscripts incorrectly dated in modern catalogues by authors who based their dates on authorial rather than scribal colophons. See, for example, *Katalog der datierten Handschriften in lateinischer Schrift in Österreich*, 8 vols. in 16 (Vienna, 1969–1988). See also Destrez and Fink-Errera, "Des manuscrits apparemment datés"; and Giovanni Murano, *Manoscritti prodotti per exemplar e pecia conservati nelle biblioteche austriache* (Vienna, 2003).

120. In fact, early modern books took this over from late antique codices. Neddermeyer, *Handschrift*, 1.24–25. Cf. Eisenstein, *Printing Press*, 1.52 and n. 35. On the development of title pages, see Anneliese Schmitt, "Zur Entwicklung von Titelblatt und Titel in der Inkunabelzeit," *Beiträge zur Inkunabelkunde*, 3rd ser., 8 (1983), 11–29; M. M. Smith, *The Title-Page: Its Earliest Development, 1460–1510* (London, 2000); Sharpe, *Titulus*, 26–27.

121. Kerby-Fulton, "Langland," 70.

122. Three of seven manuscripts add "Gerson," but this was probably a scribal addition.

123. Hobbins, "Joan of Arc," 141: "Lugduni 1429 die 14 Maii in vigilia Penthecostis post signum habitum Aurelianis in depulsione obsidionis Anglicane. Actum autem est a famosissimo et solemnissimo sacre theologie professore magistro Johanne [Gerson] cancellario Parisiensis super facto puelle et credulitate sibi prestanda."

124. Ibid., 143: "Quoddam compilatum super facto puelle de credulitate sibi prestanda a Johanne cancellario Parisiensi Lugduni anno Domini m° cccc° xxix die quartadecima Maii in vigilia Penthecostes post signum habitum Aurelianis in depulsione obsidionis Anglicane."

125. In some of the following cases, the form of the name appears in the first lines of the letter. See letters 8, 14, 16, 20, 21, 22 (with Pierre d'Ailly), 27, 28, 32, 34, 36, 40, 41, 43, 50, 51, 54, 56, 57, 59, and 85. The other texts are 299, 326, 413 (see Combes, *Essai*, 1.314), 415, 416, 418, 421, 448, 453, 456, 465, 468, 475, 510.

126. *OC* 8.565: "Explicit anagogicum de verbo et hymno gloriae, a Joanne Cancellario Parisiensi, Lugduni anno 1428. Et continet quatuor partitiones principales in quarum qualibet sunt decem verba seu considerationes et in quolibet versu multae notulae seu verbula per litteras alphabeti usque ad numerum 190; praesulatum tunc agente Reverendissimo Patre Domino A. Archipraesule et comite Lugdunensi primate Galliarum nostrae peregrinationis benevolissimo suceptore."

127. *OC* 8.534.

128. *OC* 6.181, 8.47. For *In Praise of Scribes of Healthy Doctrine*, see Paris, BnF, Ms. lat. 17488, f. 164r, and below, Chapter 7.

129. A corrupt form of *cancellarius*.

130. Hobbins, "Joan of Arc," 141–42.

131. Ibid., 142–43.

132. I have set aside the two manuscripts copied from the first edition in this accounting.

133. Eisenstein, *Printing Press*, 1.107.

134. *OC* 6.250: "Magis ad inquisitionem veritatis quam ad determinationem editus et pronuntiatius." Cf. 5.384: "Qui prodiet in publicum magis ad examinationem quam determinationem, magisque ad elucidationem veritatis quam ostentationem vanitatis."

135. *OC* 10.51.

136. *OC* 8.47.

137. Manuscripts include Cologne, HASK, GB fol. 94, f. 74v: "Superscripta visitandi formula correcta fuit Constan[tia] provincie maguntium 28 Augusti dum generale concilium illic esset." Also Salzburg, UB, Hs. M II 99.

138. Nicholson, "Poet and Scribe"; Roger Lovatt, "The *Imitation of Christ* in Late Medieval England," *Transactions of the Royal Historical Society*, 5th ser., 18 (1968), 101; Laidlaw, "Christine and the Manuscript Tradition," 232–40 (quotation on 235); and see further Laidlaw, "Christine de Pizan: An Author's Progress," *Modern Language Review* 78 (1983), 532–50.

139. Pearsall, *Life of Geoffrey Chaucer*, 189. See also Nichols, "Philology," 6–7.

140. Studies on the editing and rewriting of scholastic works include Constantine Michalski, "Die vielfachen Redaktionen einiger Kommentare zu Petrus Lombardus," *Miscellanea Francesco Ehrle*, vol. 1, *Per la storia della teologia e della filosofia* (Rome, 1924), 219–64; and Damasus Trapp, "Dreistufiger Editionsprozess und dreiartige Zitationsweise bei den Augustinertheologen des 14. Jahrhunderts?" *Augustiniana*, 25 (1975), 283–92. Early Christian writers also had a clear sense of edition. See the example of Tertullian in Gamble, *Books and Readers*, 118–19.

141. Petrucci, *Writers and Readers*, 149–50.

142. Hobbins, "Joan of Arc," 129–34. The final section (see below), however, was later added to two of the twelve manuscripts. I am not counting here two manuscripts copied from the 1488 edition.

143. Gerson probably added this section within a few days, because the entire work, including this additional section, found its way to Rome by early June. Hobbins, "Joan of Arc," 131.

144. Ibid., 129–30.

145. For a list of works that Gerson revised, which is not comprehensive, see ibid., 131 n. 121.

146. Petrucci, *Writers and Readers*, 150.

147. See the description of Paris, BnF, lat. 3126 in *OC* 5.xx.

148. On what follows, see Hobbins, "Editing and Circulating Letters."

149. Ibid., 171, 177–78.

150. Ibid., 176–77. Original version: "Ut denique peculiares oraciones in cella que sub precepto sunt presertim ecclesie, proferri non committantur nisi forte de maioris consilio." Amplified version: "Ut denique orationes in cella quae sub praecepto praesertim Ecclesiae cadunt, ore offerri et proferri non omittantur nisi forte id fieret de consilio et licentia superioris."

151. Glorieux, " 'Contre l'observation superstitieuse des jours.' "

Chapter 7. Publishing Before Print (2)

1. Boudet, "Jean Gerson et la Dame à la licorne"; Connolly, *Mourning into Joy*, chapter 5: "The Song of the Heart: Raphael's Commissioners and Jean Gerson," 111–50.

2. See the discussion by Richard S. Field of the colored woodcut of the Holy

Family, c. 1430, in Peter Parshall and Rainer Schoch (eds.), *Origins of European Printmaking: Fifteenth-Century Woodcuts and Their Public* (Washington, D.C., 2005), 133–35 and 136 n. 8.

3. For Gerson's reception, see Mazour-Matusevich, "Jean Gerson"; and Mazour-Matusevich, "Gerson's Legacy." The author's focus in these articles is on the many individuals who embraced Gerson's teachings and legacy. My focus is instead on the creation of authorial identity and on networks and patterns of manuscript transmission.

4. Hillgarth, *Who Read Thomas Aquinas?* 1–5.

5. The judgment of H. V. Shooner, quoted in Hillgarth, *Who Read Thomas Aquinas?* 6.

6. Ibid.

7. Ibid., 30.

8. The most thorough discussion is Neddermeyer, *Handschrift*, 1.254–88.

9. Verger, "Schools and Universities," 225–27.

10. Neddermeyer, *Handschrift*, 1.231–32.

11. Kock, *Buchkultur.*

12. Ouy, "Gerson and the Celestines."

13. Glorieux, "L'activité littéraire," 238–43.

14. Miethke, "Kirchenreform," 29.

15. Neddermeyer, *Handschrift*, 1.282–88; Derek Pearsall, "The Whole Book: Late Medieval English Manuscript Miscellanies and Their Modern Interpreters," in *Imagining the Book*, ed. Stephen Kelly and John J. Thompson (Turnhout, 2005), 17–29.

16. One of the Paris manuscripts was originally copied in Germany. Madre, *Nikolaus von Dinkelsbühl*, 342–401.

17. See the discussion in Neddermeyer, *Handschrift*, 1.428–29. Cf. the graphs in Bozzolo, "La production manuscrite," 225–28.

18. *OC* 9.459: "Concilii Constantiensis, cui forte par in duratione nullum fuit; duravit enim annos tres et menses sex."

19. See on this point the articles in the section "Expansion et tentations urbaines," in *La naissance des Chartreuses (Actes du VI Colloque International d'Histoire et de Spiritualité Cartusiennes)*, ed. Bernard Bligny and Gérald Chaix (Grenoble, 1986), 195–368, esp. the articles of F. Stoelker (215–35) and F. Rapp (237–58).

20. Neddermeyer, *Handschrift*, 1.229–31. Carthusian houses were among the intended market for the Gutenberg Bible. See Christopher de Hamel, *The Book: A History of the Bible* (London, 2001), 196, 212–14.

21. Gerz von Buren, *Tradition*, 119. The prior was Heinrich Arnold (priorate 1449–1480).

22. Kerby-Fulton, "Langland," 113. See also Kerby-Fulton and Justice, "Langlandian Reading Circles." And see now on coterie readership of French poetic anthologies, Jane H. M. Taylor, *The Making of Poetry: Late-Medieval French Poetic Anthologies* (Turnhout, 2007).

23. Kerby-Fulton, "Langland," 113, 118.

24. Among many studies, see McGrady, "Authorship and Audience."

25. Root, "Publication," 418–19.

26. Raymond J. Starr, "The Circulation of Literary Texts in the Roman World," *Classical Quarterly* 37 (1987), 213–23; Grafton and Williams, *Christianity*, 54–55.

27. Cf. Madre, *Nikolaus von Dinkelsbühl*, 338–40.

28. For an overview of the debate, see *OC* 10.25–26.

29. On Agnes of Auxerre, see Hobbins, "Gerson on Lay Devotion," 64 and n. 49.

30. Mourin, *Jean Gerson*, 170, 173 nn. 4–5.

31. For the immediate context of these works see the chronological survey of the Schism in *OC* 6.xxxix–lx. A fine study is Posthumus Meyjes, *Jean Gerson*.

32. See the overview in *OC* 10.73–75.

33. P. Glorieux, "Gerson et les Chartreux."

34. See the historical overview in *OC* 10.52–54.

35. M. Lieberman, "Lettre de Gerson au duc de Berry (23 novembre 1413)," *Cahiers de Joséphologie* 9 (1961), 199–265.

36. Cf. Mertens's comment (*Iacobus Carthusiensis*, 23) on the earliest readers of Jacobus de Paradiso: "Daher bleibt in der Mehrzahl der Fälle nur die Tatsache, daß sich die Kopie eines Traktates zu einem gewissen Zeitpunkt in der Hand eines bestimmten Besitzers befunden hat, Ausgangpunkt der rezeptionsgeschichtlichen Interpretation."

37. *OC* 2.218–21 (Pierre d'Ailly's response to Gerson), 10.90–91.

38. *OC* 2.72–73; Vansteenberghe, "Doctrinal"; and Ouy, *Gerson bilingue*, xvii–xviii.

39. Gerson's letter that accompanied the sermon is in *OC* 2.71–72. For the sermon, see 5.64–90.

40. Kerby-Fulton, "Langland," 119.

41. Davies, "Humanism," 53.

42. The groundbreaking study is Jean Destrez, *La pecia dans les manuscrits universitaires du XIIIe et du XIVe siècle* (Paris, 1935). See now G. Murano, *Opere diffuse per "exemplar" e pecia* (Turnhout, 2005); and Murano, *Manoscritti prodotti per exemplar e pecia conservati nelle biblioteche austriache* (Vienna, 2003).

43. Rouse and Rouse, *Manuscripts*.

44. Nolan, *Lydgate*, 5. On imagined audiences and their connection to an "imaginary public" of the nation, cf. Watts, "Pressure," 165–66.

45. See *OC* 10.105–6. On Gerson's frustration with court astrologers and physicians, see references in Mourin, *Jean Gerson*, 59, 75–76, 87, 100 n. 1, 111–13, 127–33, 170–71, 274–76.

46. On this text, see E. Vansteenberghe, "Le traité contre Nicolas Colne," *RSR* 15 (1935), 532–39.

47. For general context, see Michael D. Bailey, "The Disenchantment of Magic: Spells, Charms, and Superstition in Early European Witchcraft Literature," *AHR* 111 (2006), 383–404. The manuscript figures are mine, supplementing Glorieux.

48. *OO* 2.3: "Ad tollendam quorumdam in praesenti schismate pertinaciam, improbitatemque nimiam, specialiter in Patria Flandrensi."Of the five manuscripts I consulted, four include the reference to Flanders. These four are Seitenstetten, SB, Hs. 49, f. 270r; Vienna, ONB, Cod. lat. 4576, f. 120r; Darmstadt, HLHB, Hs. 779, f. 119v; and Paris, BnF, Ms. lat. 14904, f. 114r (in margin). The manuscript lacking the phrase is Würzburg, UB, Hs. M. ch. F. 244, f. 174v. Apparently, the manuscript Glorieux used, Paris, BnF, Ms. lat. 3126, also lacks the phrase. See *OC* 6.29.

49. *OC* 2.xxv. The manuscript is Charleville-Mézières, BM, Ms. 58.

50. Paris, BnF, lat. 17488, f. 164r: "Tractatulus de laude scriptorum doctrine salubris ad cartusienses et celestinos ymo totam ecclesiam generaliter ordinatus; lugduni 1423 in aprili." The text in Dupin (*OO* 2.694) is clearly corrupt, linking

the place of composition, Lyon, with the substantive *ecclesia*: "Imo totam Ecclesiam Lugdunensem."

51. My totals, supplementing Glorieux. For manuscripts of the letter to Guillaume Minaud, see Hobbins, "Editing and Circulating Letters," 173–75, with additional manuscripts in the subsequent volume 47 (2005), 162. If we accept Neddermeyer's estimate for loss rates, then there were once nearly one thousand copies of each one.

52. I am borrowing this term (*Verbreitungskreis*) from Jürgen Miethke, who applied this concept to humanists, religious orders, and universities. Miethke, however, did not distinguish between a small coterie and a larger distribution circle; this distinction is crucial to my argument. Miethke, "Kirchenreform," 30–31; Miethke, "Die Konzilien als Forum," 763.

53. Gloss on Apoc. 1, "Septem ecclesiis": "Deus dedit Christo, Christus Johanni, Johannes autem ecclesiis; vel per septem universe ecclesie, quia septem universitatem significant, vel qui septiformi spiritu illustrantur." *Biblia Latina cum glossa ordinaria*, vol. 4 (Strasbourg, 1480–1481; facsimile: Turnhout, 1992).

54. Gamble, *Books and Readers*, 105–6; William Mitchell Ramsay, *The Letters to the Seven Churches of Asia and Their Place in the Plan of the Apocalypse* (London, 1904), 171–96 (quotation at 191).

55. Emery, *Dionysii Cartusiensis Prolegomena*, 1.36.

56. Joachim Stieber, *Pope Eugenius IV, the Council of Basel, and the Secular and Ecclesiastical Authorities in the Empire: The Conflict over Supreme Authority and Power in the Church* (Leiden, 1978), 78–80.

57. Mertens, *Iacobus Carthusiensis*, 80.

58. Stieber, *Pope Eugenius IV*, 92–112, esp. 102–3.

59. Ibid., 78–81.

60. Cf. Miethke, "Kirchenreform," 32–33.

61. *OC* 3.x, xii; 9.xvi. One additional copy of *Contra curiositatem studentium* was made from the 1502 Strasbourg edition: Munich, BSB, Clm 28301, ff. 167r–169v.

62. *OC* 1.100–101. On this manuscript, see above, Chapter 1.

63. See the description in *OC* 4.xxxvi–xxxvii.

64. *GW*, vol. 9, no. 10833. The other items in this volume are *OC* vol. 3, nos. 97, 92, 89, 96.

65. Roccati, "Geiler von Kaysersberg," 284.

66. Miethke, "Die Konzilien als Forum," 747 n. 34; Guenée, *Between Church and State*, 238; Joseph Gill, *Constance et Bâle-Florence* (Paris, 1965), 41–42.

67. Derolez, *Palaeography*, 167.

68. Priscilla S. Boskoff, "Quintilian in the Late Middle Ages," *Speculum* 27 (1952), 71–78 (76 on Poggio); Gilli, "L'humanisme français," 48; Ornato, "Redécouverte," 87–88 and 97 n. 17.

69. On the Councils of Constance and Basel as "bookmarkets," see Neddermeyer, *Handschrift*, 1.280–82; Miethke, "Die Konzilien als Forum"; and Helmrath, "Kommunikation." On greater demand for "theological, canonistic, and spiritual" works than for ancient classics, see Helmrath, pp. 163–64. On Guillaume Fillastre's manuscripts at the Council of Constance, see Ornato, "Les humanistes français," 20–23.

70. Miethke, "Die Konzilien als Forum," 762–63; Helmrath, "Kommunikation," 163.

71. *OC* 2.291.

72. For the *De theologia mystica*, see Combes, *Essai*, 1.805 and note *b*; and Lieberman, "Chronologie gersonienne" (1959), 330–31 n. 1. The *De parvulis ad*

Christum trahendis was copied in Zwolle in 1412 by a self-styled disciple of Henry of Langenstein: Cologne, HASK, GB oct. 76.

73. Neddermeyer, *Handschrift*, 1.294–99. On illuminators leaving Paris, see Martin, *Mise en page*, 86, with reference to François Avril and Nicole Reynaud, *Manuscrits à peinture en France, 1440–1520* (Paris, 1993).

74. Neddermeyer, *Handschrift*, 1.91–92, 2.657.

75. Originally, Gerson probably wished to circulate his epic poem, the *Josephina*, at the council, but apparently he failed to do so (Roccati [ed.], *Josephina*, 20). See also Ouy, "Le Célestin," 297–300.

76. For D'Ailly's manuscripts, see Aldo Pasquero, "L'Inedito 'Tractatus supra Boetium' di Pierre d'Ailly: Edizione critica" (Ph.D. dissertation, University of Turin, 1982), 96–98; Izbicki, "Ecclesiological Texts" (1988), 199; Izbicki, "Ecclesiological Texts" (1989), 207; and Miethke, "Die Konzilien als Forum," 754–55 n. 61.

77. For example, the *Avisamentum* of Job Vener from 1417, which survives in just two manuscripts. Miethke, "Kirchenreform," 29.

78. Dietrich von Niem, *Dialog über Union und Reform der Kirche 1410*, ed. Hermann Heimpel (Leipzig, 1933), xviii–xix.

79. *OC* 5.132.

80. See the full discussion of the manuscript, London, BL, Add. Ms. 29279, in Ouy, *Gerson bilingue*, xxxix–xli. Gerson may also have attempted something similar for the Council of Pisa in 1409. Although he did not attend, he apparently sent along his *Tractatus de unitate Ecclesiae*. See the opening lines of the treatise, *OC* 6.136.

81. Jürgen Miethke and Lorenz Weinrich, *Quellen zur Kirchenreform im Zeitalter der grossen Konzilien des 15. Jahrhunderts* (Darmstadt, 1995), 1.188, 220–22.

82. *OC* 2.49.

83. McGuire, *Jean Gerson*, 249–50; *OC* 10.528–29.

84. *OC* 2.102, 333; 8.94, 351; 9.474.

85. These are my totals, supplementing Glorieux, who lists eleven MSS for the *De distinctione*, fifty-one for the *De probatione*, and six for the *De examinatione*. I have not included five small fragments of *De examinatione*, and one of *De probatione*. The German translation is in Munich, BSB, Cgm 830.

86. Carl-Gustaf Undhagen (ed.), *Sancta Birgitta Revelaciones* (Stockholm, 1977), 1.ix–xi. On discussions about St. Birgitta at Basel, see Anna Fredriksson Adman, *Heymericus de Campo: Dyalogus super Reuelacionibus beate Birgitte* (Uppsala, 2003), esp. 15–32.

87. Adam Ludwik Szafrański, *Materiały do historii teologii średniowiecznej w Polsce* [Materials for the History of Medieval Theology in Poland] (Warsaw, 1974), 1.58–64.

88. The sermons are nos. 241 (fifty-nine MSS), 232 (forty-four), and 235 (thirty-four). The sermon preached at the provincial synod at Reims in 1408 also survives, in fifteen manuscripts. The figures for the Constance sermons come from Nighman and Stump, *Biographical Register*, 260; supplemented by my own findings. For nos. 241, 232, and 235, Seitenstetten, Stiftsbibliothek, Hs. 49, ff. 229r–233r, 239v–246v, and 246v–249v. For nos. 232 and 235, Berlin, SBPKB, lat. fol. 717. For no. 241, Kraków, BJ, Cod. 4962, ff. 147r–150r; Vatican City, BAV, Vat. lat. 4905, ff. 225r–227r; and Vat. lat. 5598, ff. 186r–191r. For no. 232, Darmstadt, HLHB, Hs. 2; Melk, SB, Hs. 1100, pp. 545–56; Toledo (Ohio), Toledo Museum of Art, Ms. 1916.48; Wrocław, BU, Cod. I.F.619, ff. 1r–7r. For no. 235, Berlin, SBPKB, Hs. lat. 534; Melk, SB, Hs. 620, ff. 106r–109v. The works relating

to Church reform are nos. 282 (thirty-seven MSS), 280 (thirty), and 276 (twenty-four). These manuscript figures come from Glorieux and could easily be doubled.

89. Basel, UB, Hs. A.X.73. On Gerson's awareness of the *De theologia mystica*, see Hobbins, "Editing and Circulating Letters," 179–80.

90. Uppsala, UB, Mss. C.77 and C.618 (Mornet, "Gerson en Scandinavie," 94–95); Munich, UB, quart. Cod. Ms. 125.

91. *OC* 3.299–300. See further Posthumus Meyjes, *Jean Gerson*, 166–71. On the pronunciation, see Miethke, "Die Konzilien als Forum," 755 n. 61a. Cf. the explicit in Munich, BSB, Clm. 7505, f. 180v: "Explicit tractatus de aufferibilitate pape ab ecclesia editus a magistro Johanne Gerson Canc. Parisiensis in concilio Constantie anno domini 1415."

92. Barcelona, ACC, Cod. 11, f. 182r: "Editus Constancie per cancellarium Parisiensi. Editus, id est publicatus, nam ex eius tenore constant quod fuit factus tempore concilii pisani." This appears at the beginning of the work.

93. Munich, BSB, Clm. 7505, f. 119v: "Explicit tractatus magistri Johannis de Gersona eximii doctoris et cancellarii Paris[iensis] de decem preceptis et confessione et scientia mortis editus sub Concilio Constanciensi."

94. The complete copy is in Uppsala, UB, Ms. C.26 (Mornet, "Gerson en Scandinavie," 94). The copy of part 2 is in Cologne, HASK, GB fol. 94.

95. Cologne, HASK, GB fol. 94, f. 74v. Another copy of the version corrected at Constance is Salzburg, UB, Hs. M II 99, unfoliated. Munich, BSB, Clm. 14120, which has the same two texts as the Cologne manuscript, was copied shortly after 1415, possibly at Constance as well.

96. Vienna, ONB, Cod. lat. 4659; Vienna, Schottenkloster, Cod. 133; Herzogenburg, SB, Hs. 23; Cologne, HASK, GB oct. 84; Uppsala, UB, Ms. C.220, owned by a Swedish student at Leipzig, who brought the text back to Sweden (Mornet, "Gerson en Scandinavie," 95).

97. Bast, *Honor Your Fathers*, 14–15 and n. 50.

98. Augsburg, UB, Cod. II.1.2°.173; Basel, UB, Hs. A II 36.

99. Cologne, HASK, GB quart. 100; GB quart. 108.

100. Munich, UB, fol. 84; Basel, UB, Inc. 51.

101. The sermon, *Prosperum iter faciat*, was copied in 1418 in southern Germany (Augsburg, UB, Cod. II. 1.2°.86). *On Ecclesiastical Power* was copied in the diocese of either Salzburg or Passau around 1423 to 1425 (Ljubljana, EA, Ms. 11 –Kos. 99). The letter-treatise on prayer was copied at Constance possibly in 1416 (Uppsala, UB, Ms. C.77).

102. Mornet, "Gerson en Scandinavie," 93, 97.

103. Glorieux, "Gerson et les Chartreux," 115–17.

104. Jean Aurelien, *La vie admirable de notre père Saint Pierre Celestin, Pape: suivie du texte de la règle* (Bar-le-Duc, 1873), 320. The source for this claim is unclear.

105. Ouy, "Le Célestin," 284–85.

106. On the context of these works, see Glorieux, "Gerson et les Chartreux," 121–31. See also McGuire, "Loving the Holy Order."

107. A manuscript probably dating from early 1409 survives from the Charterhouse at Herne with Gerson's first letter to Barthélémy Thonis. On this manuscript, see Kees Schepers, *Ioannis Rusbrochii De ornatu spiritualium nuptiarum* (Turnout, 2004), 105–8.

108. *OC* 1.25–26, items 46, 47, 51, 52, 56. Item 66, which is called a "libellus," could also refer to a manuscript volume. It too contained short works, "multa brevia et utilia."

109. *OC* 1.23. Cf. 10.561. See also 2.295, where Gerson says that he had sent his *De perfectione cordis* to the Celestines.

110. In his correspondence with the Grande Chartreuse, Gerson refers to various works of his, which I assume the monks there possessed. See *OC* 2.251 ("certain works"), 289 (the *Collectorium super Magnificat*), 303 and 309 (*De valore orationis, De sollicitudine ecclesiasticorum*), 307–8 (*De non esu carnium, De theologia mystica*), 314 ("Collectorium septem sportarum"), 320 (*De elucidatione scholastica mysticae theologiae*). For other works owned by the Grande Chartreuse, see the following note. On the transmission of *De theologia mystica* to the Grande Chartreuse, see Hobbins, "Editing and Circulating Letters," esp. 179–84. In his letter to the Celestines of Avignon, Jacques de Cerisy tells them that it is Gerson's wish that they allow the Grande Chartreuse to make copies of the works (*OC* 1.28).

111. Fournier, *Notice*, 60. The list of volumes specifies the following works: "De consolatione theologie," "Dyalogus . . . de perfectione cordis," "Super Cantica," "Unum ex quator," "Super Magnificat," "Josephina," and another "Tractatus . . . super Cantica." See p. 64 for other possible works: "De monte contemplationis," and "De consolatione theologie, in papiro."

112. Fournier, *Notice*, 27.

113. *OC* 1.28, 2.334.

114. Ouy, "Le Célestin," 281–308 and plates 71–79.

115. Ouy, "Le Célestin," 281.

116. For example, he may have supplied the colophon to the second revision of *On Mystical Theology* in 1422, which says that Gerson (described as *olim cancellarii ecclesiae parisiensis*) completed the work in 1407 and later corrected it and sent a copy from Lyon to the Carthusians. See further Hobbins, "Editing and Circulating Letters," 181.

117. An interesting piece of evidence survives to support this theory in the case of the *Monotessaron*. Some manuscripts of the work include a letter of Gerson which follows the preface and which the editor Glorieux left out of the modern edition for no apparent reason. (The work's authenticity is not in doubt. Glorieux overlooked this letter for his edition, even though Dupin had included it in his. See *OO* 4.87–90, and above, Chapter 3.) There, Gerson situates the *Monotessaron* within earlier efforts to harmonize the Gospels, deplores the wicked age, and takes consolation from promises in scripture. The letter's closing reads "Vale frater," which I take to refer to Jean the Celestine. If I am correct, this letter supplies a link between Jean the Celestine and the anonymous preface. Apparently, before he circulated the work Jean the Celestine added this letter and then supplied his own preface in which he justifies the work, just as he would justify Gerson's entire literary corpus in his letter to Anselm in 1423.

118. *OC* 10.561.

119. Jean might have lived with Gerson for a time in Paris before 1408, but that is conjecture. Cf. McGuire, *Jean Gerson*, 169, who relies on Glorieux's biographical essay, *OC* 1.111. Glorieux based this opinion on a letter of Gerson's mother to Nicholas and Jean the Celestine (*OC* 2.6–8), which Glorieux dates to 1396. The authorship of this letter remains open to question. The early connections between Jean the Celestine and Gerson need fresh critical examination.

120. See further Calvot and Ouy, *L'oeuvre de Gerson*, 9, 27; and below.

121. Rouse and Rouse, *Manuscripts*, 88–89.

122. On Basel, see Gerz von Buren, *Tradition*. The author argued that the Charterhouse of Basel had a much larger Gerson collection than other Charterhouses, but her comparison was far too limited to justify this claim.

123. For the sources used in compiling the map, see the Appendix.

124. Gerz von Buren, *Tradition*, 42–75.

125. Martin, *Fifteenth-Century Carthusian Reform*, 22, 332–33.

126. The phrase is that of Hubert Jedin, quoted in Martin, *Reform*, 230 and n. 164. On the urbanization of the order, see pp. 230–31; and Emery, "Denys the Carthusian and the Invention of Preaching Materials," 378–79.

127. Martin, *Reform*, 231–33. For the English Carthusians, see Taylor, "Authors," 355. On this paragraph in general, see also Nedermeyer, *Handschrift*, 1.229–30.

128. *Contra curiositatem studentium* is item 17 in the second *Annotatio* (*OC* 1.30).

129. *OC* 4.176, 144–46, 176–77. The last poem is dated 1 July 1429. The manuscript is Vienna, ONB, Cod. lat. 1519.

130. Ouy, "Le Célestin," 306–7.

131. Gotha, FB, Chart. A 19, ff. 330v–331v; Marseille, BM, Ms. 241, ff. 57r–60r; Melk, SB, Hs. 889, ff. 326r–327v; Munich, BSB, Clm. 3414, ff. 302r–303v; Paris, BnF, lat. 14904, ff. 53v–57r; Philadelphia, UPL, Ms. 96, ff. 2v–3v; St. Pölten, DB, Hs. 25, ff. 260r–261v; Hs. 71, ff. 107r–108r; Vienna, ONB, Cod. lat. 1519, ff. 32r–33v; Cod. lat. 3710, ff. 144r–145r; Cod. lat. 4318, ff. 392r–393v; Cod. lat. 4487, ff. 341r–342v; Cod. lat. 4913, ff. 274r–276r.

132. The manuscript is Stuttgart, WLB, Hs. HB I 10.

133. See now James Mixson, *Poverty's Proprietors: Ownership and Mortal Sin at the Origins of the Observant Movement* (Leiden, 2009).

134. *OC* 1.146. Schreiner, "Benediktinische Klosterreform," 105–95 (on Gerson, esp. 152–53); Madre, *Nikolaus von Dinkelsbühl*, 29–35; Martin, *Reform*, 62–63.

135. Eisermann, *"Stimulus amoris,"* 308.

136. *MBKO*, 156–261.

137. Two manuscripts appear to derive from a manuscript listed in the Aggsbach catalogue: Melk, SB, Hs. 619, copied at Basel around 1436–1438 by Johannes Schlitpacher, and Lilienfeld, SB, Hs. 75 (*OC* 8.xxiii). The Lilienfeld manuscript appears to derive from Melk 619. The Erfurt librarian Jacobus Volradi gave Weimar, Landesbibliothek, Cod. Fol. 25 to Reinhausen (*MBKDS* 2.225–26). Munich, BSB, Clm. 18651, from the reforming abbey of Tegernsee, refers to a copy of *Super Cantica Canticorum* that was obtained from a Charterhouse. The indication comes at the end of Jean the Celestine's notice of Gerson's death on f. 15v: "Velut olor morte parata, modulatus est [cf. *OC* 10.565]. Illud scriptum habemus a domo Cartusie, etc."

138. See above, Chapter 1.

139. For a very brief overview of Celestine libraries, see Françoise Bérard, "Bibliothèques des Célestins," in *Histoire des bibliothèques françaises*, vol. 1, *Les bibliothèques médiévales du VIe siècle à 1530*, ed. A. Vernet (Paris, 1989), 272–74. See also *Bibliothèques de manuscrits medievaux en France*, ed. A.-M. Genevois et al. (Paris, 1987), 346.

140. For a map of Celestine houses, see Borchardt, *Cölestiner*, n.p.

141. Miethke, "Die Konzilien als Forum," 749.

142. See the interesting example of a book search in E. F. Jacob, "The Bohemians at the Council of Basel in 1433," in *Prague Essays*, ed. R. W. Seton-Watson (Oxford, 1949), 91–92.

143. Weiss, "Private Collector," 117.

144. On what follows, see Hobbins, "Joan of Arc," 119–39.

145. "Explicit tractatus de oratione Basilee anno 1433 mensis Septembris." Hobbins, "Joan of Arc," 138.

146. See further Jordan, "Problems in Interpreting Dated Manuscripts."

147. Hobbins, "Joan of Arc," 138.

148. Ibid., 123–26.

149. Hudson, "Lollard Book-Production," 135.

150. Vienna, Schottenkloster, Cod. 408. *OC* 9.xxxii. Glorieux omitted the year for the *De potestate ecclesiastica*, on f. 244v, which the catalogue includes, 1433.

151. Vatican City, BAV, Vat. lat. 4117. Roccati, "Manuscrits," 104–5.

152. *OC* 8.xxiii–xxv. On Schlitpacher, see F. J. Worstbrock, "Schlitpacher, Johannes," *VL* 8.727–48; on this manuscript and on Schlitpacher's interest in Gerson, see Schreiner, "Klosterreform," 150–51.

153. Basel, UB, Hs. A.II.34; and New York, Pierpont Morgan Library, Bühler Collection Ms. 23 were both copied at Basel (the New York manuscript in 1437), and both contain two works by Gerson, the *Tractatus de parvulis ad Christum trahendis* and the *Tractatus de duplici statu in Dei ecclesia*. Vienna, ONB, Cod. lat. 4748 was copied in 1439 (f. 73v). Basel, UB, Hs. A.VII.37, was copied at Basel in 1441, and Hs. E.II.3 was copied at Basel in 1444. For the texts in Hs. A.VII.37, see *OC* 10.xx–xxii; for those in Hs. E.II.3, see *OC* 10.618. Another manuscript, Vienna, ONB, Cod. lat. 4482, was copied at Basel in 1436. It contains only the *De necessaria communione laicorum sub utraque specie*, but this manuscript, which has the label "No. IV" at the head of the title, appears once to have been part of a larger manuscript.

154. Another manuscript, Munich, BSB, Clm. 18651, twice refers to its exemplar, which was copied at the Council of Basel in 1435 and 1436. The two works in question are *De necessaria communione laicorum sub utraque specie* (f. 98v) and *Pro coelibatu ecclesiasticorum* (f. 117r).

155. Hillgarth, *Who Read Thomas Aquinas?* 3–4.

156. See the 1369 catalogue and the 1375 catalogue in Franz Ehrle, *Historia bibliothecae romanorum pontificum tum Bonifatianae tum Avenionensis* (Rome, 1890), 1.284–432, 454–532.

157. Huot, *From Song to Book*, 233.

158. Ibid.

159. Edwards, "Author Collections," 102–3, 109.

160. Bowers, "Holographs," 27–51, esp. 28, 39, 43.

161. Sandra Hindman, "The Composition of the Manuscript of Christine de Pizan's Collected Works in the British Library: A Reassessment," *British Library Journal* 9 (1983), 111–12.

162. The evidence for this appears in the first *Annotatio* of Jean the Celestine, compiled in May 1423. See items 46–47, 51–52, and 66 (*OC* 1.25–26).

163. Allan D. Fitzgerald, "*Retractiones*," in *Augustine Through the Ages*, ed. Allan D. Fitzgerald (Grand Rapids, Mich., 1999), 723–24.

164. Hudson, "Development," 69.

165. Hudson, "Aspects," 126–29.

166. Hudson also notes the traces of a third summa, "heavily biassed towards commentary on Aristotle." Hudson, "Development," 69–70.

167. For the term vestibule, see Genette, *Paratexts*, 2.

168. *OC* 8.79, 553, 610; 9.193.

169. *OC* 3.313.

170. *OC* 8.163–64. Note the similarity to the way Gerson compiled the "Centiloquy on the eye": see above, Chapter 3.

171. *OC* 1.24. The works in question are the *De meditatione cordis*, the *De simplificatione cordis*, the *De directione cordis*, and the *De perfectione cordis*, all in *OC* vol. 8. In the second list, Jean the Celestine describes them as "four opuscules on the heart" (*OC* 1.31).

172. Vienna, ONB, Cod. lat. 4210, f. 212r: "Isti duo ultimi tractatus secundum intentionem auctoris, scilicet magistri Johannis Cancellarii parisien[sis] debent poni post tractatum nonum precedentem de magnificat, scilicet post versum esurientes in quo agitur de sacramento altaris. Deo gratias." This manuscript was copied at the Council of Basel in 1433. See the description in Michael Denis, *Codices manuscripti theologici Bibliothecae Palatinae Vindobonensis Latini aliarumque Occidentis linguarum* (Vienna, 1795), vol. 1, pt. 2, pp. 2184–87. This note also appears in Eichstätt, UB, Cod. st 682, f. 190r; and in Munich, BSB, Clm. 18651, f. 98v. The Munich manuscript follows the note with a colophon copied from an exemplar that was copied at the Council of Basel: "Scripta sunt haec Basilee tempore generalis Concilii ibi celebrati per quemdam fratres professum Monasterii Mellic[ensis] etc. 1436." We know from several references that the ninth treatise of the *Collectorium super Magnificat* was originally independent: see *OC* 2.270, 291.

173. In his 1429 list of Gerson's works, Jacques de Cerisy calls for the ninth treatise of the *Collectorium super Magnificat* to be joined with the same two works mentioned here, and perhaps with a third, *De simonia*. See *OC* 1.27. This direct parallel in the 1429 list to the note in the three manuscripts provides strong evidence that Jacques wrote the note.

174. See items 5–6 in the first *Annotatio*, and items 4–6, 14–16, and 58 in the second *Annotatio*, *OC* 1.23, 29–32.

175. Munich, BSB, Clm. 5338. See also Basel, UB, A.VII.32, which has a label on the front cover: "Tractatuli XX Gerson et aliorum doctorum" (Gerz von Buren, *Tradition*, 53). These two examples could be multiplied indefinitely.

176. "Cy fine le present livre composé par maistre Jehan Jarson doct(eur)." London, BL, Royal Ms. 19.B.V. Yet the manuscript also includes after three works of Gerson a work by Jean de Varennes, *Medicine de l'âme en l'article de la mort*, and a translation of the Credo into French by "Jean Sarrazin, docteur en theologie." For an example of such an explicit in an English manuscript, see Edwards, "Author Collections," 107.

177. Other manuscripts with contents lists that emphasize Gerson as the unifying ingredient include (among many others) Paris, BnF, Ms. lat. 3125, f. Iv; Ms. lat. 3126, f. 1r; Ms. lat. 14905, before f. 1; Ms. lat. 15899, f. 4r.

178. *OC* 4.xxxii. See also on this manuscript G. Matteo Roccati, "A propos de la tradition manuscrite," 279, 290–303.

179. The rubric is visible in Figure 13 above. For a manuscript description, see J. Van den Gheyn et al. (eds.), *Catalogue des manuscrits de la Bibliothèque Royale de Belgique* (Brussels, 1901–1909), 3.88–89.

180. The eleven manuscripts are as follows: Bamberg, SB, th. 48, ff. 140r–152v; Bautzen, SB, Hs. 40. 4° 8; Berlin, SBPKB, Hs. Magdeb. 15, ff. 53r and 55r; Hs. theol. lat. fol. 658, f. 99v and f. 103v; Düsseldorf, private collection of Dr. K.-J. Miesen, ff. 87v–101r; Giessen, UB, Hs. 762, ff. 118vb–121rb, 249vb–252rb (both copies of *De probatione spirituum*), 303ra–310va; Leipzig, UB, Hs. 581, f. 59v and f. 62v; Leipzig, UB, Hs. 582, f. 72v and f. 75r; Prague, NKCR, Ms. 996, ff. 137v–143r and ff. 143r–158v; Ms. 1693, f. 32r and f. 35r; and Würzburg, UB, Hs. M. ch. f. 244, ff. 85r–97v. The Giessen and Würzburg manuscripts also have *De examinatione doctrinarum*: Giessen, ff. 295vb–301va; Würzburg, ff. 97v–104v.

Prague, KMK, N.9, has *De probatione spirituum* (ff. 200r–202v), followed by the short *Tractatus de unione ecclesiae* (ff. 202v–203v), and then *De examinatione doctrinarum* (ff. 203v–207v).

181. See for example Seitenstetten, SB, Hs. 49, ff. 2r–13r; and Vienna, ONB, Cod. lat. 4576, ff. 3r–20v. Some individual works also acquired tables, such as the *Regulae morales*: Paris, BnF, lat. 3125 ff. 106r–108r, probably copied around 1479–1480.

182. Madre, *Nikolaus von Dinkelsbühl*, 342–401. For Wyclif, see the manuscript index in Thomson, *Latin Writings*, 311–17.

183. Huot, *From Song to Book*, 233–34 n. 27.

184. Chartier, *Order of Books*, 57, with reference to a study by Gemma Guerrini.

185. Calvot and Ouy, *L'oeuvre de Gerson*. St. Victor was a house of canons regular that served as a college in the university and that opened its library to university members. See Hillgarth, *Who Read Thomas Aquinas?* 15.

186. Hudson, "Lollard Book-Production," 135.

187. The possible exception is Melk, SB, Hs. 751/2, where the text appears with just one other Gerson text, *De non esu carnium*, and with other writings of a more political nature. See Vinzenz Staufer, *Catalogus codicum manu scriptorum qui in Bibliotheca Monasterii Mellicensi O.S.B. servantur* (handwritten catalogue, Vienna, 1889), 1092–93.

188. Hobbins, "Joan of Arc," 121.

189. Ibid., 127 n. 109.

190. I use "Italy" as many scholars do, as shorthand for the area of the modern nation-state. An example of an English manuscript is London, BL, Ms. Royal 19.B.V, with English glosses.

191. Pettegree and Hall, "The Reformation and the Book," 791–92.

192. Neddermeyer, "*Radix Studii*," 460–61.

193. Neddermeyer, *Handschrift*, 1.91–92.

194. For manuscripts besides Glorieux, see Roccati, "Manuscrits," 103–11; Izbicki, "Ecclesiological Texts" (1988), 197–201; and Miethke, "Kirchenreform," 29 n. 60. Add to these lists Rome, Biblioteca Angelica, Ms. 90, ff. 1r–14v; and Subiaco, Biblioteca del Monumento Nazionale Santa Scolastica, Ms. 209 CCV, ff. 61ra–79vb.

195. Miethke, "Kirchenreform," 29 n. 60.

196. Izbicki, "Ecclesiological Texts" (1989), 205. See also Izbicki, "Ecclesiological Texts" (1988), 197.

197. Kristeller, *Renaissance Thought*, 86.

198. Black, *Humanism*, 29–30, 72–74; Eckhard Kessler, "Renaissance Humanism: The Rhetorical Turn," in *Interpretations of Renaissance Humanism*, ed. Angelo Mazzocco (Leiden, 2006), 183; Ward, "Rhetoric," 210 (quotation).

199. Moraw, "Careers," 255.

200. For a recent synthetic study on the different levels of urbanization in European states and regions for this period, see Robert C. Allen, "Economic Structure and Agricultural Productivity in Europe, 1300–1800," *European Review of Economic History* 4 (2000), 1–25, esp. 8–9. Donald Weinstein and Rudolph M. Bell, *Saints and Society: The Two Worlds of Western Christendom, 1000–1700* (Chicago, 1982), 176–77, argue that patterns of sainthood in the Italian communes reflect a much closer connection between "popular piety and civic patriotism" in Italy than in the north.

201. See Myriam Carlier and Tim Soens (eds.), *The Household in Late Medieval*

Cities: Italy and Northwestern Europe Compared (Proceedings of the International Conference Ghent, 21st–22nd January 2000) (Louvain, 2001). And see especially Carlier's introduction, pp. 1–3.

202. Ridder-Symoens, "Mobility," 287.

203. Ibid., 285–91, 298–99. See also Grendler, *Universities*, 355. For more on mobility, see the essays in section 3 in Rainer C. Schwinges, Christian Hesse, and Peter Moraw (eds.), *Europa im späten Mittelalter: Politik—Gesellschaft—Kultur* (Munich, 2006).

204. Grendler, *Universities*, 353–60; Denley, "Medieval and Renaissance Italian Universities," 169–70 (Denley minimizes Grendler's contribution to the subject); Kristeller, *Renaissance Thought*, 100. On Gerson's relationship with the Mendicants, see Hobbins, "Beyond the Schools," 214–16; McLoughlin, "Gerson as Preacher," 274–91.

205. Neddermeyer, *Handschrift*, 1.304.

Selected Bibliography

The bibliography includes works pertaining to Jean Gerson and to late medieval written culture that are essential to the book's argument, not all of the works (primary and secondary) cited in the notes. For bibliographical orientation to Gerson, see McGuire, *Jean Gerson and the Last Medieval Reformation*, 407–14, and the bibliography in McGuire, ed., *A Companion to Jean Gerson*.

Selected Editions of Gerson's Works

Combes, André, ed. *Ioannis Carlerii de Gerson De mystica theologia*. Lugano, 1958.
Du Pin, L. E., ed. *Joannis Gersonii Opera omnia*. 4 vols. in 5. Antwerp, 1706.
Fabre, Isabelle. *La doctrine du chant du coeur de Jean Gerson*. Paris, 2005.
Glorieux, P., ed. *Jean Gerson, Oeuvres complètes*. 11 vols. in 10. Paris, 1960–1973.
Hobbins, Daniel. "Editing and Circulating Letters in the Fifteenth Century: Jean Gerson, *Uberius quam necesse*, 10 November 1422." *Bulletin de philosophie médiévale* 46 (2004): 169–90; 47 (2005): 162.
———. "Jean Gerson's Authentic Tract on Joan of Arc: *Super facto puellae et credulitate sibi praestanda* (14 May 1429)." *Mediaeval Studies* 67 (2005): 99–155.
Olivar, Alexandre. "Le sermon pour la Toussaint sur 'Beati qui persecutionem patiuntur' de Jean Gerson." *Bulletin de la litterature ecclesiastique* 77 (1976): 265–85.
Ouy, Gilbert. "Gerson and the Celestines: How Jean Gerson and His Friend Pierre Poquet Replied to Various Questions of Discipline and Points of Conscience (ca. 1400)." In *Reform and Renewal in the Middle Ages and the Renaissance*. Ed. Thomas M. Izbicki and Christopher M. Bellitto. Leiden, 2000. 113–40.
———. *Gerson bilingue: Les deux rédactions, latine et française, de quelques oeuvres du chancelier parisien*. Paris, 1998.
Roccati, G. M., ed. *Jean Gerson Josephina*. CD-ROM. Paris, 2001.

Secondary Sources

Allen, Judson Boyce. *The Ethical Poetic of the Later Middle Ages: A Decorum of Convenient Distinction*. Toronto, 1982.
Amtower, Laurel. *Engaging Words: The Culture of Reading in the Later Middle Ages*. New York, 2000.
Asztalos, Monika. "The Faculty of Theology." In Ridder-Symoens (1992). 409–41.

Autrand, Françoise. "Les librairies des gens du Parlement au temps de Charles VI." *Annales* 28 (1973): 1219–44.

Bakker, Paul J. J. M., and Chris Schabel. "*Sentences* Commentaries of the Later Fourteenth Century." In *Mediaeval Commentaries on the Sentences of Peter Lombard*. Vol. 1, *Current Research*. Ed. G. R. Evans. Leiden, 2002. 425–64.

Baldwin, John W. *Masters, Princes, and Merchants: The Social Views of Peter the Chanter and His Circle*. 2 vols. Princeton, 1970.

Bast, Robert James. *Honor Your Fathers: Catechisms and the Emergence of a Patriarchal Ideology in Germany, 1400–1600*. Leiden, 1997.

Beadle, Richard. "English Autograph Writings of the Later Middle Ages: Some Preliminaries." In *Gli autografi medievali: Problemi paleografici e filologici (Atti del convegno di studio della Fondazione Ezio Franceschini, Erice, 25 settembre–2 ottobre 1990)*. Ed. Paolo Chiesa and Lucia Pinelli. Spoleto, 1994. 249–68.

Beit-Arié, Malachi. *Unveiled Faces of Medieval Hebrew Books: The Evolution of Manuscript Production—Progression or Regression?* Jerusalem, 2003.

Bejczy, István. "Erasme explore le moyen âge: Sa lecture de Bernard de Clairvaux et de Jean Gerson." *RHE* 93 (1998): 460–76.

———. *Erasmus and the Middle Ages: The Historical Consciousness of a Christian Humanist*. Leiden, 2001.

Bernstein, Alan. E. *Pierre d'Ailly and the Blanchard Affair: University and Chancellor of Paris at the Beginning of the Great Schism*. Leiden, 1978.

Black, Robert. *Humanism and Education in Medieval and Renaissance Italy: Tradition and Innovation in Latin Schools from the Twelfth to the Fifteenth Century*. Cambridge, 2001.

Borchardt, Karl. *Die Cölestiner: Eine Mönchsgemeinschaft des späteren Mittelalters*. Husum, 2006.

Bose, Mishtooni. "The Issue of Theological Style in Late Medieval Disputations." In *Medieval Forms of Argument: Disputation and Debate*. Ed. Georgiana Donavin, Carol Poster, and Richard Utz. Eugene, Ore., 2002. 1–21.

Bossuat, R. "Gerson et le théâtre." *BEC* 109 (1952): 295–98.

Boudet, Jean-Patrice. "Les condemnations de la magie à Paris en 1398." *Revue Mabillon* 12 (2001): 121–57.

———. "Jean Gerson et la Dame à la licorne." In *Religion et société urbaine au Moyen Âge: Études offertes à Jean-Louis Biget*. Ed. Patrick Boucheron and Jacques Chiffoleau. Paris, 2000. 551–63.

———. "Un prélat et son équipe de travail à la fin du Moyen Âge: Remarques sur l'oeuvre scientifique de Pierre d'Ailly." In *Humanisme et culture géographique à l'époque du Concile de Constance autour de Guillaume Fillastre (Actes du Colloque de l'Université de Reims, 18–19 novembre 1999)*. Ed. Didier Marcotte. Turnhout, 2002. 127–50.

Boureau, Alain. "Peut-on parler d'auteurs scolastiques?" In *Auctor et auctoritas: Invention et conformisme dans l'écriture médiévale*. Ed. M. Zimmermann. Paris, 2001. 267–79.

Bourgain, Pascale. "L'édition des manuscrits." In *Histoire de l'édition française*, vol. 1, *Le livre conquérant: Du Moyen Âge au milieu du XVIIe siècle*. Ed. Henri-Jean Martin and Roger Chartier. Paris, 1982. 49–75.

Bowers, John M. "Hoccleve's Huntington Holographs: The First 'Collected Poems' in English." *Fifteenth-Century Studies* 15 (1989): 27–51.

Boyle, Leonard E. "The Quodlibets of St. Thomas and Pastoral Care." *The Thomist* 38 (1974): 232–56.

———. "The Setting of the *Summa Theologiae*." In *Aquinas's Summa Theologiae: Critical Essays*. Ed. Brian Davies. Lanham, Md., 2006 [Toronto, 1992]. 1–25.

Bozzolo, Carla. "La production manuscrite dans les pays rhénans au XVe siècle (à partir des manuscrits datés)." *Scrittura e Civiltà* 18 (1994): 183–242.

Bozzolo, Carla, and Ezio Ornato. *Pour une histoire du livre manuscrit au Moyen Âge.* Paris, 1983.

Braakhuis, H. A. G., and M. J. F. M. Hoenen. "Marsilius: A Dutch Philosopher and Theologian." In *Marsilius of Inghen (Acts of the International Marsilius of Inghen Symposium, Nijmegen, 18–20 December 1986).* Ed. H. A. G. Braakhuis and M. J. F. M. Hoenen. Nijmegen, 1992. 1–11.

Braun, Harald E., and Edward Vallance, eds. *Contexts of Conscience in Early Modern Europe, 1500–1700.* New York, 1994.

Brown, D. Catherine. *Pastor and Laity in the Theology of Jean Gerson.* Cambridge, 1987.

Brunelli, G. A. "Le traité La science de bien mourir ou médecine de l'âme de Jean Gerson." *Le Moyen Âge* 70 (1964): 265–84.

Burger, Christoph. *Aedificatio, Fructus, Utilitas: Johannes Gerson als Professor der Theologie und Kanzler der Universität Paris.* Tübingen, 1986.

Burns, R. I. "Paper Comes to the West, 800–1400." In *Europäische Technik im Mittelalter 800 bis 1200: Tradition und Innovation.* Ed. Uta Lindgren. Berlin, 1996. 413–22.

Burrows, Mark S. *Jean Gerson and* De consolatione theologiae *(1418): The Consolation of a Biblical and Reforming Theology for a Disordered Age.* Tübingen, 1991.

Calvot, Danièle, and Gilbert Ouy. *L'oeuvre de Gerson à Saint-Victor de Paris.* Paris, 1990.

Carruthers, Mary. *The Book of Memory: A Study of Memory in Medieval Culture.* 2nd ed. Cambridge, 2008.

Catto, J. I. "Scholars and Studies in Renaissance Oxford." In *The History of the University of Oxford.* Vol. 2, *Late Medieval Oxford.* Ed. J. I. Catto and Ralph Evans. Oxford, 1992. 769–83.

———. "Theology After Wycliffism." In *The History of the University of Oxford.* Vol. 2, *Late Medieval Oxford.* Ed. J. I. Catto and Ralph Evans. Oxford, 1992. 263–80.

———. "Theology and Theologians, 1220–1320." In *The History of the University of Oxford.* Vol. 1, *The Early Oxford Schools.* Ed. J. I. Catto. Oxford, 1992. 471–517.

———. "Wyclif and Wycliffism at Oxford, 1356–1430." In *The History of the University of Oxford.* Vol. 2, *Late Medieval Oxford.* Ed. J. I. Catto and Ralph Evans. Oxford, 1992. 175–261.

Cazelles, Raymond. *Nouvelle histoire de Paris: De la fin du règne de Philippe Auguste à la mort de Charles V, 1223–1380.* Paris, 1994.

Cecchetti, Dario. *L'evoluzione del latino umanistico in Francia.* Paris, 1986.

Celenza, Christopher S. *The Lost Italian Renaissance: Humanists, Historians, and Latin's Legacy.* Baltimore, 2006.

Chartier, Roger. *The Order of Books: Readers, Authors, and Libraries in Europe Between the Fourteenth and Eighteenth Centuries.* Trans. Lydia G. Cochrane. Stanford, 1994 [1992].

Chenu, M.-D. *Toward Understanding Saint Thomas.* Trans. A.-M. Landry and D. Hughes. Chicago, 1964.

Christ, Karl. *The Handbook of Medieval Library History.* Trans. Theophil M. Otto. Metuchen, N.J., 1984 [1950–1965].

Claassen, Jo-Marie. *Displaced Persons: The Literature of Exile from Cicero to Boethius.* Madison, Wisc., 1999.

Clanchy, M. T. *From Memory to Written Record: England, 1066–1307.* 2nd ed. Oxford, 1993.

Cohn, Samuel K., Jr. "The Black Death: End of a Paradigm." *AHR* 107 (2002): 703–38.
———. *The Black Death Transformed: Disease and Culture in Early Renaissance Europe.* London, 2002.
Coleman, Joyce. *Public Reading and the Reading Public in Late Medieval England and France.* Cambridge, 1996.
Colledge, Edmund, and J. C. Marler. "Tractatus Magistri Johannis Gerson De mistica theologia: St. Pölten, Diözesanarchiv MS. 25." *Mediaeval Studies* 41 (1979): 354–86.
Combes, André. *La théologie mystique de Gerson: Profil de son évolution.* 2 vols. Rome, 1963–1964.
———. *Essai sur la critique de Ruysbroeck par Gerson.* 3 vols. Paris, 1945.
Connolly, James L. *John Gerson, Reformer and Mystic.* Louvain, 1928.
Connolly, Thomas. *Mourning into Joy: Music, Raphael, and Saint Cecilia.* New Haven, Conn., 1994.
Constable, Giles. "Forgery and Plagiarism in the Middle Ages." *Archiv für Diplomatik* 29 (1983): 1–41.
Copeland, Rita. *Rhetoric, Hermeneutics, and Translation in the Middle Ages: Academic Traditions and Vernacular Texts.* Cambridge, 1991.
Courtenay, William J. "Antiqui and Moderni in Late Medieval Thought." *Journal of the History of Ideas* 48 (1987): 3–10.
———. "The Bible in the Fourteenth Century: Some Observations." *Church History* 54 (1985): 176–87.
———. "The Course of Studies in the Faculty of Theology at Paris in the Fourteenth Century." In *"Ad ingenii acuitionem": Studies in Honour of Alfonso Maierù.* Ed. Stefano Caroti et al. Louvain-la-Neuve, 2006. 67–92.
———. "Force of Words and Figures of Speech: The Crisis over *Virtus sermonis* in the Fourteenth Century." *Franciscan Studies* 44 (1984): 107–28.
———. "Inquiry and Inquisition: Academic Freedom in Medieval Universities." *Church History* 58 (1989): 168–81.
———. "Late Medieval Nominalism Revisited: 1972–1982." *Journal of the History of Ideas* 44 (1983): 159–64.
———. "Nominalism and Late Medieval Religion." In *The Pursuit of Holiness in Late Medieval and Renaissance Religion.* Ed. Charles Trinkaus and Heiko A. Oberman. Leiden, 1974. 26–59.
———. "Parisian Theology, 1362–1377." In *Philosophie und Theologie des Ausgehenden Mittelalters: Marsilius von Inghen und das Denken seiner Zeit.* Ed. Maarten J. F. M. Hoenen and Paul J. J. M. Bakker. Leiden, 2000. 3–19.
———. "Postscript: The Demise of Quodlibetal Literature." In *Theological Quodlibeta in the Middle Ages.* 2 vols. Ed. Christopher Schabel. Turnhout, 2006. 2.693–99.
———. "The Preservation and Dissemination of Academic Condemnations at the University of Paris in the Middle Ages." In *Les philosophies morales et politiques au Moyen Âge (Actes du IXe Congrès international de Philosophie Médiévale, Ottawa, du 17 au 22 août 1992).* Ed. B. Carlos Bazán, Eduardo Andújar, and Léonard G. Sbrocchi. New York, 1995. 3.1659–67.
———. "Programs of Study and Genres of Scholastic Theological Production in the Fourteenth Century." In *Manuels, programmes de cours et techniques d'enseignement dans les universités médiévales (Actes du Colloque international de Louvain-la-Neuve, 9–11 septembre 1993).* Ed. Jacqueline Hamesse. Louvain-la-Neuve, 1994. 325–50.

————. "The Reception of Ockham's Thought at the University of Paris." In *Preuve et raisons à l'Université de Paris, logique, ontologie et théologie au XIVe siècle.* Ed. Z. Kaluza and P. Vignaux. Paris, 1984. 43–64.

————. *Schools and Scholars in Fourteenth-Century England.* Princeton, N.J., 1987.

————. "Spirituality and Late Scholasticism." In *Christian Spirituality: High Middle Ages and Reformation.* Ed. Bernard McGinn, Jill Raitt, and John Meyendorff. London, 1987. 109–20.

————. *Teaching Careers at the University of Paris in the Thirteenth and Fourteenth Centuries.* Notre Dame, Ind., 1988.

Coville, A. *Jean Petit: La question du tyrannicide au commencement du XVe siècle.* Paris, 1932.

D'Agostino, F. "Un contributo alla storia dell'idea di equita: Jehan de Gerson e la lotta per il concilio." *Angelicum* 48 (1971): 448–89.

Davies, Martin. "Humanism in Script and Print in the Fifteenth Century." In *The Cambridge Companion to Renaissance Humanism.* Ed. Jill Kraye. Cambridge, 1996. 47–62.

De Vooght, Paul. *Les sources de la doctrine chrétienne d'après les théologiens du XIVe siècle et du début du XVe siècle.* Paris, 1954.

Delaruelle, Étienne, E.-R. Labande, and Paul Orliac. *L'Église au temps du Grand Schisme et de la crise conciliaire.* 2 vols. Paris, 1962–1964.

Déniau, J. *La Commune de Lyon et la Guerre Bourguignonne, 1417–1435.* Lyon, 1934.

Denley, Peter. "Medieval and Renaissance Italian Universities and the Role of Foreign Scholarship." *History of Universities* 19, no. 1 (2004): 159–81.

Derolez, Albert. *The Palaeography of Gothic Manuscript Books.* Cambridge, 2003.

Derville, A. "L'alphabétisation du peuple à la fin du Moyen Âge." *Revue du Nord* 66 (1984): 761–76.

Destrez, Jean, and G. Fink-Errera. "Des manuscrits apparemment datés." *Scriptorium* 7 (1958): 56–93.

Doyle, A. I. "Publication by Members of the Religious Orders." In *Book Production and Publishing in Britain, 1375–1475.* Ed. Jeremy Griffiths and Derek Pearsall. Cambridge, 1989. 109–23.

Edwards, A. S. G. "Fifteenth-Century Middle English Verse Author Collections." In *The English Medieval Book: Studies in Memory of Jeremy Griffiths.* Ed. A. S. G. Edwards, Vincent Gillespie, and Ralph Hanna. London, 2000. 101–12.

Eisenstein, Elizabeth L. *The Printing Press as an Agent of Change: Communications and Cultural Transformations in Early-Modern Europe.* 2 vols. Cambridge, 1979.

Eisermann, Falk. *"Stimulus amoris": Inhalt, lateinische Überlieferung, deutsche Übersetzungen, Rezeption.* Tübingen, 2001.

Elie, H. "Quelques maîtres de l'Université de Paris vers l'an 1500." *AHDLMA* 25–26 (1950): 193–243.

Elliott, Dyan. "Seeing Double: John Gerson, the Discernment of Spirits, and Joan of Arc." *AHR* 107 (2002): 26–54.

Emery, Kent, Jr. "Denys the Carthusian and the Doxography of Scholastic Theology." In *Ad litteram: Authoritative Texts and Their Medieval Readers.* Ed. Mark D. Jordan and Kent Emery Jr. Notre Dame, Ind., 1992. 327–59.

————. "Denys the Carthusian and the Invention of Preaching Materials." *Viator* 25 (1994): 377–409.

————. *Dionysii Cartusiensis Prolegomena: Bibliotheca manuscripta.* 2 vols. Turnhout, 1991.

Fabre, Isabelle. *La doctrine du chant du coeur de Jean Gerson.* Paris, 2005.

Farge, James K. *Orthodoxy and Reform in Early Reformation France: The Faculty of Theology of Paris, 1500–1543.* Leiden, 1985.

Fink-Errera, G. "Une institution du monde médiéval, la pecia." *Revue philoso-phique de Louvain* 60 (1962): 184–243.

Fournier, Paul. *Notice sur la bibliothèque de la Grande-Chartreuse au Moyen-Âge suivie d'un catalogue de cette bibliothèque au XVme siècle.* Grenoble, 1887.

Fubini, Riccardo. *Humanism and Secularization from Petrarch to Valla.* Durham, N.C., 2003.

Gabriel, Astrik L. "The Conflict Between the Chancellor and the University of Masters and Students at Paris During the Middle Ages." *Miscellanea mediae-valia* 10 (1976): 106–54.

Gamble, Harry Y. *Books and Readers in the Early Church: A History of Early Christian Texts.* New Haven, Conn., 1995.

Genette, Gérard. *Paratexts: Thresholds of Interpretation.* Trans. Jane E. Lewin. Cambridge, 1997.

Gerz-von Buren, Veronika. *La tradition de l'oeuvre de Jean Gerson chez les chartreux: La chartreuse de Bâle.* Paris, 1973.

Gillespie, Vincent. "Vernacular Books of Religion." In *Book Production and Pub-lishing in Britain, 1375–1475.* Ed. Jeremy Griffiths and Derek Pearsall. Cambridge, 1989. 317–44.

Gilli, Patrick. "L'humanisme français au temps du Concile de Constance." In *Humanisme et culture géographique à l'époque du Concile de Constance: Autour de Guillaume Fillastre (Actes du Colloque de l'Université de Reims, 18–19 novembre 1999).* Ed. Didier Marcotte. Turnhout, 2002. 41–62.

Glorieux, P. "L'activité littéraire de Gerson à Lyon: Correspondance inédite avec la Grande Chartreuse." *RTAM* 18 (1951): 238–307.

———. "Les années d'études de Pierre d'Ailly." *RTAM* 44 (1977): 127–49.

———. "L'année universitaire 1392–1393 à la Sorbonne à travers les notes d'un étudiant." *RSR* 19 (1939): 429–82.

———. "Les 'Considerations sur saint Joseph' de Jean Gerson." *Cahiers de Josépho-logie* 28 (1975): 5–22.

———. " 'Contre l'observation superstitieuse des jours': Le traité de Gerson et ses divers états." *RTAM* 35 (1968): 177–82.

———. "L'enseignement au Moyen Âge: Techniques et méthodes en usage à la Faculté de théologie de Paris au XIIIe siècle." *AHDLMA* 35 (1968): 65–186.

———. "L'enseignement universitaire de Gerson." *RTAM* 23 (1956): 88–113.

———. "Gerson et les Chartreux." *RTAM* 28 (1961): 115–53.

———. "Gerson et saint Bonaventure." In *S. Bonaventura, 1274–1974.* 5 vols. Rome, 1974. 4.773–92.

———. "Les 'Lectiones duae super Marcum' de Gerson." *RTAM* 27 (1960): 344–56.

———. "Note sur le Carmen super Magnificat de Gerson." *RTAM* 25 (1958): 144–50.

———. "L'oeuvre littéraire de Pierre d'Ailly: Remarques et précisions." *Mélanges de science religieuse* 22 (1965): 61–78.

———. "La vie et les oeuvres de Gerson: Essai chronologique." *AHDLMA* 25–26 (1950–1951): 149–92.

Gorochov, Nathalie. *Le Collège de Navarre de sa fondation (1305) au début du XVe siècle (1418): Histoire de l'institution, de sa vie intellectuelle et de son recrutement.* Paris, 1997.

Graff, Harvey. "Literacy Patterns in Historical Perspective." In *Reading Across the Life Span.* Ed. Steven R. Yussen and M. Cecil Smith. New York, 1993. 73–91.

Grafton, Anthony. "The Humanist as Reader." In *A History of Reading in the West.* Ed. Guglielmo Cavallo and Roger Chartier. Amherst, Mass., 1999. 179–212.

————. "The Importance of Being Printed." *Journal of Interdisciplinary History* 11 (1980): 265–86.

Grafton, Anthony, and Megan Hale Williams. *Christianity and the Transformation of the Book: Origen, Eusebius, and the Library of Caesarea.* Cambridge, Mass., 2006.

Grendler, Paul F. *The Universities of the Italian Renaissance.* Baltimore, 2002.

Grévy-Pons, Nicole. *Célibat et nature, une controverse médiévale: À propos d'un traité du début du XVe siècle.* Paris, 1975.

Grosse, Sven. *Heilsungewissheit und Scrupulositas im späten Mittelalter: Studien zu Johannes Gerson und Gattungen der Frömmigkeitstheologie seiner Zeit.* Tubingen, 1994.

Grundmann, Herbert. "Sacerdotium—Regnum—Studium: Zur Wertung der Wissenschaft im 13. Jahrhundert." *Archiv für Kulturgeschichte* 34 (1952): 5–21.

Guenée, Bernard. *Between Church and State: The Lives of Four French Prelates in the Late Middle Ages.* Chicago, 1991.

————. "Les campagnes de lettres qui ont suivi le meurtre de Jean sans Peur, duc de Bourgogne (septembre 1419–février 1420)." *Annuaire-Bulletin de la Société de l'Histoire de France* (1993): 45–65.

————. *L'opinion publique à la fin du Moyen Âge.* Paris, 2002.

————. *Un meurtre, une société: L'assassinat du duc d'Orléans, 23 novembre 1407.* N.p., 1992.

Habermas, Jürgen. *The Structural Transformation of the Public Sphere: An Inquiry into a Category of Bourgeois Society.* Trans. Thomas Burger. Cambridge, Mass., 1989.

Hamesse, Jacqueline. "Approche de la terminologie spécifique des scribes dans les colophons: À propos de la transmission des textes universitaires." In *Scribi e colofoni: Le sottoscrizioni di copisti dalle origini all'avvento della stampa.* Ed. E. Condello and G. De Gregorio. Spoleto, 1995. 145–65.

————. *Les Auctoritates Aristotelis, un florilège médiéval: Étude historique et édition critique.* Louvain, 1974.

————. "Les autographes à l'époque scolastique." In *Gli autografi medievali: Problemi paleografici e filologici (Atti del convegno di studio della Fondazione Ezio Franceschini, Erice, 25 settembre–2 ottobre 1990).* Ed. P. Chiesa and L. Pinelli. Spoleto, 1994. 179–205.

————. "The Scholastic Model of Reading." In *A History of Reading in the West.* Ed. G. Cavallo and R. Chartier. Amherst, Mass., 1999. 103–19.

Hamm, Berndt. *Frömmigkeitstheologie am Anfang des 16. Jahrhundert.* Tübingen, 1982.

————. "Hieronymus-Begeisterung und Augustinismus vor der Reformation: Beobachtungen zur Beziehung zwischen Humanismus und Frömmigkeitstheologie (am Beispiel Nürnbergs)." In *Augustine, the Harvest, and Theology (1300–1650).* Ed. Kenneth Hagen. Leiden, 1990. 127–233.

Hasenohr, Geneviève. "Aperçu sur la diffusion et la réception de la littérature de spiritualité en langue française au dernier siècle du Moyen Âge." In *Wissensorganisierende und wissensvermittelnde Literatur im Mittelalter.* Ed. N. R. Wolf. Wiesbaden, 1987. 57–90.

————. "L'essor des bibliothèques privées aux XIVe et XVe siècles." In *Histoire des bibliothèques françaises.* Ed. André Vernet. Paris, 1989. 215–63.

————. "La litterature religieuse." In *La litterature française aux XIVe et XVe siècles.* Heidelberg, 1988. 266–305.

————. "Religious Reading Amongst the Laity in France in the Fifteenth Century." In *Heresy and Literacy, 1000–1530.* Ed. Peter Biller and Anne Hudson. Cambridge, 1994. 205–21.

Helmrath, J. "Kommunikation auf den spätmittelalterlichen Konzilien." In *Die Bedeutung der Kommunikation für Wirtschaft und Gesellschaft*. Ed. Hans Pohl. Stuttgart, 1989. 116–72.

Hillgarth, J. N. *Who Read Thomas Aquinas?* Toronto, 1992.

Hobbins, Daniel. "Beyond the Schools: New Writings and the Social Imagination of Jean Gerson." Ph.D. dissertation, University of Notre Dame, 2002.

———. "Editing and Circulating Letters in the Fifteenth Century: Jean Gerson, *Uberius quam necesse*, 10 November 1422." *Bulletin de philosophie médiévale* 46 (2004): 169–90; 47 (2005): 162.

———. "Gerson on Lay Devotion." In *A Companion to Jean Gerson*. Ed. Brian Patrick McGuire. Leiden, 2006. 41–78.

———. "Jean Gerson's Authentic Tract on Joan of Arc: *Super facto puellae et credulitate sibi praestanda* (14 May 1429)." *Mediaeval Studies* 67 (2005): 99–155.

———. "The Schoolman as Public Intellectual: Jean Gerson and the Late Medieval Tract." *AHR* 108 (2003): 1308–37.

Hoenen, Maarten. J. F. M. "Academics and Intellectual Life in the Low Countries: The University Career of Heymeric de Campo (†1460)." *RTAM* 61 (1994): 173–209.

———. "Denys the Carthusian and Heymeric de Campo on the Pilgrimages of Children to Mont-Saint-Michel (1458)." *AHDLMA* 61 (1994): 387–418.

———. *Marsilius of Inghen: Divine Knowledge in Late Medieval Thought*. Leiden, 1993.

———. "'Modus loquendi platonicorum': Johannes Gerson und sein Kritik an Platon und den Platonisten." In *The Platonic Tradition in the Middle Ages: A Doxographic Approach*. Ed. Stephen Gersh and Maarten J. F. M. Hoenen. Berlin, 2002. 325–43.

———. "Tradition and Renewal: The Philosophical Setting of Fifteenth-Century Christology. Heymericus de Campo, Nicolaus Cusanus, and the Cologne Quaestiones vacantiales (1465)." In *Christ Among the Medieval Dominicans: Representations of Christ in the Texts and Images of the Order of Preachers*. Ed. Kent Emery, Jr., and Joseph P. Wawrykow. Notre Dame, Ind., 1998. 462–92.

———. "Via Antiqua and Via Moderna in the Fifteenth Century: Doctrinal, Institutional, and Church Political Factors in the Wegestreit." In *The Medieval Heritage in Early Modern Metaphysics and Modal Theory, 1400–1700*. Ed. Russell L. Friedman and Lauge O. Nielsen. Boston, 2003. 9–36.

Hogg, James. "Kartäuserhandschriften in öffentlichen Bibliotheken Frankreichs." In *Bücher, Bibliotheken und Schriftkultur der Kartäuser*. Ed. Sönke Lorenz. Stuttgart, 2002. 423–74.

Hörner, Petra. *Zweisträngige Tradition der Evangelienharmonie: Harmonisierung durch den Tatian und Entharmonisierung durch Georg Kreckwitz u. a.* Hildesheim, 2000.

Hruza, Karel. "Propaganda, Kommunikation und Öffentlichkeit im Mittelalter." In *Propaganda, Kommunikation und Öffentlichkeit (11.–16. Jahrhundert)*. Ed. Karel Hruza. Vienna, 2002. 9–25.

Hübener, Wolfgang. "Der theologisch-philosophische Konservativismus des Jean Gerson." *Miscellanea mediaevalia* 9 (1974): 171–200.

Hudson, Anne. "Accessus ad auctorem: The Case of John Wyclif." *Viator* 30 (1999): 323–44.

———. "Aspects of the 'Publication' of Wyclif's Latin Sermons." In *Late-Medieval Religious Texts and Their Transmission*. Ed. A. J. Minnis. Cambridge, 1994. 121–29.

———. "The Development of Wyclif's Summa theologie." In *John Wyclif: logica, politica, teologia (Atti del Convegno internazionale, Milano, 12–13 febbraio 1999).* Ed. Mariateresa Fumagalli, Beonio Brocchieri, and Stefano Simonetta. Florence, 2003. 57–70.

———. "Lollard Book-Production." In *Book Production and Publishing in Britain, 1375–1475.* Ed. Jeremy Griffiths and Derek Pearsall. Cambridge, 1989. 125–42.

———. "A Lollard Quaternion." In *Lollards and Their Books.* London, 1985. 193–200.

Huizinga, Johan. *The Autumn of the Middle Ages.* Trans. Rodney J. Payton and Ulrich Mammitzsch. Chicago, 1996.

Huot, Sylvia. *From Song to Book: The Poetics of Writing in Old French Lyric and Lyrical Narrative Poetry.* Ithaca, N.Y., 1987.

Ingenhoff-Danhäusr, Monika. "Die Kanzel." In *Die Amanduskirche in Bad Urach.* Ed. Friedrich Schmid. Sigmaringen, 1990. 101–9.

Izbicki, Thomas M. "Ecclesiological Texts of Jean Gerson and Pierre d'Ailly Among the Codices Vaticani Latini." *Manuscripta* 32 (1988): 197–201.

———. "Ecclesiological Texts of Jean Gerson and Pierre d'Ailly in Vatican Manuscript Collections Other Than the Codices Vaticani Latini." *Manuscripta* 33 (1989): 205–9.

Jacquart, D. "Medical Scholasticism." In *Western Medical Thought from Antiquity to the Middle Ages.* Ed. Mirko D. Grmek. Cambridge, Mass., 1998. 197–240.

Jordan, Louis. "Problems in Interpreting Dated Manuscripts Based on Examples from the Biblioteca Ambrosiana." In *Scribi e colofoni: Le sottoscrizioni di copisti dalle origini all'avvento della stampa.* Ed. Emma Condello and Giuseppe De Gregorio. Spoleto, 1995. 367–84.

Jordan, Mark. *The Care of Souls and the Rhetoric of Moral Teaching in Bonaventure and Thomas.* St. Bonaventure, N.Y., 1993.

Justice, Steven. *Writing and Rebellion: England in 1381.* Berkeley, 1994.

Kaluza, Zénon. "Gerson critique d'Albert le Grand." *Freiburger Zeitschrift für Philosophie und Theologie* 45 (1998): 169–205.

———. *Les querelles doctrinales à Paris: Nominalistes et realistes aux confins du XIVe et du XVe siècles.* Bergamo, 1988.

Kaminsky, Howard. "From Lateness to Waning to Crisis: The Burden of the Later Middle Ages." *Journal of Early Modern History* 4 (2000): 85–125.

———. *Simon de Cramaud and the Great Schism.* New Brunswick, N.J., 1983.

Keiser, George R. "*Ordinatio* in the Manuscripts of John Lydgate's Lyf of Our Lady: Its Value for the Reader, Its Challenge for the Modern Editor." In *Medieval Literature: Texts and Interpretation.* Ed. T. W. Machan. Binghamton, N.Y., 1991. 139–57.

———. "Serving the Needs of Readers: Textual Division in Some Late-Medieval English Texts." In *New Science Out of Old Books: Studies in Manuscripts and Early Printed Books in Honour of A. I. Doyle.* Ed. Richard Beadle and A. J. Piper. Aldershot, 1995. 205–26.

Kelly, Louis G. "*Modus significandi rhetoricus*: Jean Gerson Against Dialectic." *Studies in Medieval and Renaissance Teaching* 7 (1999): 43–59.

Kenny, Anthony, and Jan Pinborg. "Medieval Philosophical Literature." In *The Cambridge History of Later Medieval Philosophy.* Ed. Anthony Kenny, Norman Kretzmann, and Jan Pinborg. Cambridge, 1982. 11–34.

Kerby-Fulton, Kathryn. "Langland and the Bibliographic Ego." In *Written Work: Langland, Labor, and Authorship.* Ed. Steven Justice and Kathryn Kerby-Fulton. Philadelphia, 1997. 67–143.

Kerby-Fulton, Kathryn, and Steven Justice. "Langlandian Reading Circles and the Civil Service in London and Dublin, 1380–1427." *New Medieval Literatures* 1 (1997): 59–83.

Knapp, Ethan. "Bureaucratic Identity and the Construction of the Self in Hoccleve's *Formulary* and *La male regle.*" *Speculum* 74 (1999): 357–76.

———. *The Bureaucratic Muse: Thomas Hoccleve and the Literature of Late Medieval England.* University Park, Penn., 2001.

Kock, Thomas. *Die Buchkultur der Devotio moderna: Handschriftenproduktion, Literaturversorgung und Bibliotheksaufbau im Zeitalter des Medienwechsels.* Frankfurt, 1999.

Korolec, Jerzy B. "Jean Buridan et Jean de Jandun et la relation entre la Rhétorique et la Dialectique." In *Sprache und Erkenntnis im Mittelalter.* Ed. Wolfgang Kluxen et al. Berlin, 1981. 622–27.

Kouamé, Thierry. *Le collège de Dormans-Beauvais à la fin du Moyen Âge: Stratégies politiques et parcours individuels à l'Université de Paris (1370–1458).* Leiden, 2005.

Kraume, Herbert. *Die Gerson-Übersetzungen Geilers von Kaysersberg: Studien zur deutschsprachigen Gerson-Rezeption.* Munich, 1980.

Krieger, Gerhard. "'Theologica perscrutatio labi debet ad inflammationem affectus': Der Zusammenhang von mystischer Theologie und Philosophie bei Johannes Gerson." In *Scientia und ars im Hoch- und Spätmittelalter.* 2 vols. Ed. Ingrid Craemer-Ruegenberg and Andreas Speer. Berlin, 1994. 2.605–19.

Kristeller, Paul Oskar. *Renaissance Thought and Its Sources.* Ed. M. Mooney. New York, 1979.

Krynen, J. "Les légistes 'idiots politiques': Sur l'hostilité des théologiens à l'égard des juristes, en France, au temps de Charles V." In *Théologie et droit dans la science politique de l'État moderne (Actes de la Table ronde E.F.R., C.N.R.S., Rome, 1987).* Rome, 1991. 171–98.

Laidlaw, James. "Christine and the Manuscript Tradition." In *Christine de Pizan: A Casebook.* Ed. Barbara K. Altmann and Deborah L. McGrady. New York, 2003. 231–49.

Lang, Marijke H. de. "Jean Gerson's Harmony of the Gospels (1420)." *Dutch Review of Church History* 71 (1991): 37–49.

Lausberg, Heinrich. *Handbook of Literary Rhetoric.* Trans. Matthew T. Bliss, Annemiek Jansen, and David E. Orton. Ed. David E. Orton and R. Dean Anderson. Leiden, 1998 [1973].

Le Goff, Jacques. *Intellectuals in the Middle Ages.* Trans. Teresa Lavender Fagan. Cambridge, Mass., 1993.

Lehmann, Paul. "Konstanz und Basel als Buchermarkte während der grossen Kirchenbersammlungen." In *Erforschung des Mittelalters.* 5 vols. Leipzig, 1941 [1921]. Vol. 1, 253–80.

———. "Mittelalterliche Büchertitel." In *Erforschung des Mittelalters.* 5 vols. Stuttgart, 1962. Vol. 5, 1–93.

Lerer, Seth. *Chaucer and His Readers: Imagining the Author in Late-Medieval England.* Princeton, N.J., 1993.

Lerner, Robert E. "Writing and Resistance Among Beguins of Languedoc and Catalonia." In *Heresy and Literacy, 1000–1530.* Ed. Peter Biller and Anne Hudson. Cambridge, 1994. 186–221.

Lieberman, M. "Autour de l'iconographie gersonienne." *Romania* 84 (1963): 307–53; 85 (1964): 49–100, 230–68; 91 (1970): 341–77, 467–90.

———. "Chronologie gersonienne." *Romania* 70 (1948): 51–67; 73 (1952): 480–96; 74 (1953): 289–337; 76 (1955): 289–333; 78 (1957): 433–62; 79

(1958): 339–75; 80 (1959): 289–336; 81 (1960): 44–98, 338–79; 83 (1962): 52–89.

Love, Harold. *Scribal Publication in Seventeenth-Century England.* Oxford, 1993.

Lucas, Peter J. *From Author to Audience: John Capgrave and Medieval Publication.* Dublin, 1997.

Lusignan, Serge. "Intellectuels et vie politique en France à la fin du Moyen Âge." In *Les philosophies morales et politiques au Moyen Âge.* Ottawa, 1995. 267–81.

———. "L'Université de Paris comme composante de l'identité du royaume de France: Étude sur le thème de la translatio studii." In *Identité régionale et conscience nationale en France et en Allemagne du Moyen Âge à l'époque moderne (Actes du colloque organisé par l'Université Paris XII).* Ed. R. Babel and Jean-Marie Moeglin. Paris, 1997. 59–72.

———. *"Vérité garde le Roy": La construction d'une identité universitaire en France (XIIIe–XVe siècle).* Paris, 1999.

Lyall, R. J. "Materials: The Paper Revolution." In *Book Production and Publishing in Britain, 1375–1475.* Ed. Jeremy Griffiths and Derek Pearsall. Cambridge, 1989. 11–29.

Madre, Alois. *Nikolaus von Dinkelsbühl: Leben und Schriften.* Münster, 1965.

Mann, Nicholas. "La fortune de Pétrarque en France: Recherches sur le 'De remediis.'" *Studi Francesi* 37 (1969): 1–15.

———. *Petrarch.* Oxford, 1984.

———. "Petrarch's Role as Moralist in Fifteenth-Century France." In *Humanism in France at the End of the Middle Ages and in the Early Renaissance.* Ed. A. H. T. Levi. Manchester, 1970. 6–28.

Marenbon, John. *Later Medieval Philosophy (1150–1350): An Introduction.* London, 1987.

Marin, Olivier. *L'archevêque, le maître et le dévot: Genèses du mouvement réformateur pragois années 1360–1419.* Paris, 2005.

Martin, Dennis D. *Fifteenth-Century Carthusian Reform: The World of Nicholas Kempf.* Leiden, 1992.

———. "The Via Moderna, Humanism, and the Hermeneutics of Late Medieval Monastic Life." *Journal of the History of Ideas* 51 (1990): 179–97.

Martin, Henri-Jean. *The History and Power of Writing.* Trans. Lydia G. Cochrane. Chicago, 1994.

———. *Mise en page et mise en texte du livre français: La naissance du livre moderne (XIVe–XVIIe siècles).* Ed. Isabelle Diu. Paris, 2000.

Martin, J.-B. *Histoire des églises et chapelles de Lyon.* 2 vols. Lyon, 1908.

Mazour-Matusevich, Yelena. "Gerson's Legacy." In *A Companion to Jean Gerson.* Ed. Brian Patrick McGuire. Leiden, 2006. 357–99.

———. "Jean Gerson (1363–1429) and the Formation of German National Identity." *RHE* 101 (2006): 963–87.

McConica, James K. *The Waning of the Middle Ages: An Essay in Historiography.* Toronto, 1995.

McGinn, Bernard. *The Harvest of Mysticism in Medieval Germany, 1300–1500.* New York, 2005.

McGrady, Deborah. "Authorship and Audience in the Prologues to Christine de Pizan's Commissioned Poetry." In *Au champ des escriptures (IIIe Colloque international sur Christine de Pizan).* Ed. Eric Hicks. Paris, 2000. 25–40.

———. *Controlling Readers: Guillaume de Machaut and His Late Medieval Audience.* Toronto, 2006.

McGuire, Brian Patrick. *Jean Gerson and the Last Medieval Reformation.* University Park, Penn., 2005.

————. *Jean Gerson: Early Works.* New York, 1998.

————. "Jean Gerson, the Shulammite, and the Maid." In *Joan of Arc and Spirituality.* Ed. Ann W. Astell and Bonnie Wheeler. New York, 2003. 183–92.

————. "Loving the Holy Order: Jean Gerson and the Carthusians." *Analecta Cartusiana* 62 (1993): 100–139.

————, ed. *A Companion to Jean Gerson.* Leiden, 2006.

McLoughlin, Nancy. "Gerson as a Preacher in the Conflict Between Mendicants and Secular Priests." In *A Companion to Jean Gerson.* Ed. Brian Patrick McGuire. Leiden, 2006. 249–91.

Mehtonen, Päivi. *Obscure Language, Unclear Literature: Theory and Practice from Quintilian to the Enlightenment.* Trans. Robert MacGilleon. Helsinki, 2003.

Mertens, Dieter. *Iacobus Carthusiensis: Untersuchungen zur Rezeption der Werke des Kartäusers Jakob von Paradies (1381–1465).* Göttingen, 1976.

Meyvaert, Paul. "Medieval Notions of Publication: The 'Unpublished' *Opus Caroli regis contra synodum* and the Council of Frankfort (794)." *Journal of Medieval Latin* 12 (2002): 78–89.

Miethke, Jürgen. *De potestate papae: Die päpstliche Amtskompetenz im Widerstreit der politischen Theorie von Thomas von Aquin bis Wilhelm von Ockham.* Tübingen, 2000.

————. "Die Konzilien als Forum der öffentliche Meinung." *DA* 37 (1981): 736–73.

————. "Kirchenreform auf den Konzilien des 15. Jahrhunderts: Motive— Methoden—Wirkungen." In *Studien zum 15. Jahrhundert (Festschrift für Erich Meuthen).* 2 vols. Ed. Johannes Helmrath and Heribert Müller. Munich, 1994. 1.13–42.

————. "Die mittelalterlichen Universitäten und das gesprochene Wort." *Historische Zeitschrift* 251 (1990): 1–44.

————. "Practical Intentions of Scholasticism: The Example of Political Theory." In *Universities and Schooling in Medieval Society.* Ed. William J. Courtenay and Jürgen Miethke. Leiden, 2000. 211–28.

Milway, Michael. "Forgotten Best-Sellers from the Dawn of the Reformation." In *Continuity and Change: The Harvest of Late Medieval and Reformation History.* Ed. Robert J. Bast and Andrew C. Gow. Leiden, 2000. 113–42.

Minnis, Alastair J. *Medieval Theory of Authorship: Scholastic Literary Attitudes in the Later Middle Ages.* 2nd ed. Aldershot, 1988.

————. "Theorizing the Rose: Commentary Tradition in the Querelle de la Rose." In *Poetics: Theory and Practice in Medieval English Literature.* Ed. Piero Boitani and Anna Torti. Cambridge, 1991. 13–36.

Mooney, Linne R. "Chaucer's Scribe." *Speculum* 81 (2006): 97–138.

Moraw, Peter. "Careers of Graduates." In Ridder-Symoens (1992). 244–79.

Mormando, Franco. "'To Persuade Is a Victory': Rhetoric and Moral Reasoning in the Sermons of Bernardino of Siena." In *The Context of Casuistry.* Ed. J. F. Keenan and T. A. Shannon. Washington, D.C., 1995. 55–84.

Mornet, E. "Gerson en Scandinavie." In *Pratiques de la culture écrite en France au XVe siècle (Actes du Colloque international du CNRS Paris, 16–18 mai 1992).* Ed. Monique Ornato and Nicole Pons. Louvain-la-Neuve, 1995. 93–108.

Mourin, Louis. *Jean Gerson, prédicateur français.* Bruges, 1952.

Murdoch, John E. "From Social into Intellectual Factors: An Aspect of the Unitary Character of Late Medieval Learning." In *The Cultural Context of Medieval Learning.* Ed. John Murdoch and Edith Sylla. Dordrecht, 1975. 271–339.

———. "'Subtilitates Anglicanae' in Fourteenth-Century Paris: John of Mirecourt and Peter Ceffons." In *Machaut's World: Science and Art in the Fourteenth Century*. Ed. Madeleine Pelner Cosman and Bruce Chandler. New York, 1978. 51–86.

Nauert, Charles G. "Humanism as Method: Roots of Conflict with the Scholastics." *Sixteenth Century Journal* 29 (1998): 427–38.

Neddermeyer, Uwe. "*Radix Studii et Speculum Vitae*: Verbreitung und Rezeption der 'Imitatio Christi' in Handschriften und Drucken bis zur Reformation." In *Studien zum 15. Jahrhundert (Festschrift für Erich Meuthen)*. 2 vols. Ed. J. Helmrath and H. Müller. Munich, 1994. 1.457–81.

———. *Von der Handschrift zum gedruckten Buch: Schriftlichkeit und Leseinteresse im Mittelalter und in der frühen Neuzeit, quantitative und qualitative Aspekte*. 2 vols. Wiesbaden, 1998.

Nichols, Stephen G. "Introduction: Philology in a Manuscript Culture." *Speculum* 65 (1990): 1–10.

Nicholson, Peter. "Poet and Scribe in the Manuscripts of Gower's Confessio amantis." In *Manuscripts and Texts: Editorial Problems in Later Middle English Literature*. Ed. Derek Pearsall. Cambridge, 1987. 130–42.

Nighman, Chris, and Phillip Stump. *A Biographical Register of the Sermons and Other Orations Delivered at the Council of Constance (1414–1418)*. The Bibliographical Society of America, 2007. http://www.bibsocamer.org/BibSite/bibsite.htm.

Nolan, Maura. *John Lydgate and the Making of Public Culture*. Cambridge, 2005.

Novák, Veronika. "La source du savoir: Publication officielle et communication informelle à Paris au début du XVe siècle." In *Information et société en Occident à la fin du Moyen Âge (Actes du colloque international tenu à l'Université du Québec à Montréal et à l'Université d'Ottawa, 9–11 mai 2002)*. Paris, 2004. 151–63.

Oberman, Heiko A. *Contra vanam curiositatem*. Zurich, 1974.

———. *The Harvest of Medieval Theology: Gabriel Biel and Late Medieval Nominalism*. 3rd ed. Durham, N.C., 1983.

Olivar, Alexandre. "Le sermon pour la Toussaint sur 'Beati qui persecutionem patiuntur' de Jean Gerson." *Bulletin de littérature ecclésiastique* 77 (1976): 265–85.

Oliver, Clementine. "The First Political Pamphlet? The Unsolved Case of the Anonymous Account of the Good Parliament of 1376." *Viator* 38 (2007): 251–68.

Ong, Walter J. *Orality and Literacy: The Technologizing of the Word*. London, 1982.

Ornato, Ezio. *La face cachée du livre médiéval: L'histoire du livre vue par Ezio Ornato, ses amis et ses collègues*. Rome, 1997.

———. "Les humanistes français et la redécouverte des classiques." In *Préludes à la Renaissance: Aspects de la vie intellectuelle en France au XVe siècle*. Ed. C. Bozzolo and E. Ornato. Paris, 1992. 1–46.

———. *Jean Muret et ses amis Nicolas Clamanges et Jean de Montreuil*. Geneva, 1969.

———. "La redécouverte des classiques, révélateur de ruptures et de continuités dans le mouvement humaniste en France au XVe siècle." In *L'aube de la Renaissance*. Ed. D. Cecchetti, L. Sozzi, and L. Terreaux. Geneva, 1991. 83–101.

———. "L'umanista Jean Muret ed il suo dialogo 'De contemptu mortis.'" In *Miscellanea di Studi e Ricerche sul Quattrocento francese*. Ed. Franco Simone. Torino, 1967. 243–353.

Ouy, Gilbert. "Le Célestin Jean Gerson: Copiste et éditeur de son frère." In *La collaboration dans la production de l'écrit médiéval (Actes du XIIIe Colloque interna-*

tional de paléographie latine, Weingarten, 22–25 septembre 2000). Ed. Herrad Spilling. Paris, 2003. 281–308 and plates 71–79.

———. "Le Collège de Navarre, berceau de l'humanisme français." In *Enseignement et vie intellectuelle, IXe–XVIe siècle (Actes du 95e congrès national des sociétés savantes, Reims, 1970)*. Paris, 1975. 276–99.

———. "De Gerson à Geiler von Kaysersberg: À propos d'un ouvrage récent." *Francia* 12 (1984): 654–65.

———. "La 'Deploratio super civitatem aut regionem que gladium evaginavit super se.'" *Divinitas* 11 (1967): 747–84.

———. "Enquête sur les manuscrits autographes du chancelier Gerson et sur les copies faites par son frère le célestin Jean Gerson." *Scriptorium* 16 (1962): 275–301.

———. *Gerson bilingue: Les deux rédactions, latine et française, de quelques oeuvres du chancelier parisien*. Paris, 1998.

———. "Gerson, émule de Pétrarque: Le 'Pastorium Carmen,' poème de jeunesse de Gerson, et la renaissance de l'églogue en France à la fin du XIVe siècle." *Romania* 88 (1967): 175–231.

———. "Humanism and Nationalism in France at the Turn of the Fifteenth Century." In *The Birth of Identities: Denmark and Europe in the Middle Ages*. Ed. Brian Patrick McGuire. Copenhagen, 1996. 107–26.

———. "L'humanisme du jeune Gerson." In *Genèse et débuts du Grand Schisme d'Occident (Colloque International, Avignon, 25–28 septembre 1978)*. Paris, 1980. 253–68.

———. "Manuscrits autographes d'humanistes en Latin et en Français." In *Gli autografi medievali: Problemi paleografici e filologici (Atti del convegno di studio della Fondazione Ezio Franceschini, Erice, 25 settembre–2 ottobre 1990)*. Ed. Paolo Chiesa and Lucia Pinelli. Spoleto, 1994. 269–305.

———. "Manuscrits jumeaux et copies en fac-similé: Deux couples de manuscrits gersoniens." *Codices manuscripti* 11 (1985): 124–36.

———. "Une maquette de manuscrit à peintures." In *Mélanges Frantz Calot*. Paris, 1960. 43–51.

———. "Pétrarque et les premiers humanistes français." In *Petrarca, Verona e l'Europa*. Padua, 1997. 415–34.

———. "La plus ancienne oeuvre retrouvée de Jean Gerson: Le brouillon inachevé d'un traité contre Juan de Monzón." *Romania* 83 (1962): 433–92.

———. "Les premiers humanistes et leurs livres." In *Histoire des bibliothèques françaises*. Ed. André Vernet. Paris, 1989. 267–83.

———. "La preuve par les textes de l'authenticité gersonienne du traité contre Juan de Monzon." *Romania* 88 (1967): 270–73.

———. "Les recherches sur l'humanisme français des XIVe et XVe siècles." In *La filologia medievale e umanistica greca nel secolo XX (Atti del Congresso Internazionale, Roma, Consiglio Nazionale delle Ricerche, Università La Sapienza, (11–15 dicembre 1989)*. 2 vols. Rome, 1993. 1.275–327.

———. "Le thème du 'Taedium scriptorum gentilium' chez les humanistes, particulièrement en France au début du XVe siècle." *Cahiers de l'Association Internationale des Études Françaises* 23 (1971): 9–26.

Ozment, Steven E. *Homo Spiritualis: A Comparative Study of the Anthropology of Johannes Tauler, Jean Gerson and Martin Luther (1509–16) in the Context of Their Theological Thought*. Leiden, 1969.

———. *Selections from "A deo exivit," "Contra curiositatem studentium" and "De mystica theologia speculativa."* Leiden, 1969.

Parkes, M. B. "The Influence of the Concepts of *Ordinatio* and *Compilatio* on the Development of the Book." In *Medieval Learning and Literature: Essays Presented to R. W. Hunt.* Ed. J. J. G. Alexander and M. T. Gibson. Oxford, 1976. 115–40. Reprinted in Parkes, *Scribes, Scripts, and Readers*, 35–70.

———. "The Literacy of the Laity." In *The Mediaeval World.* Ed. David Daiches and Anthony Thorlby. London, 1973. 555–77. Reprinted in Parkes, *Scribes, Scripts, and Readers*, 275–97.

———. *Scribes, Scripts, and Readers: Studies in the Communication, Presentation, and Dissemination of Medieval Texts.* London, 1991.

Pascoe, Louis. "Nobility and the Ecclesiastical Office in Fifteenth-Century Lyons." *Mediaeval Studies* 38 (1976): 313–31.

Peters, Edward. "Transgressing the Limits Set by the Fathers: Authority and Impious Exegesis in Medieval Thought." In *Christendom and Its Discontents: Exclusion, Persecution, and Rebellion, 1000–1500.* Ed. Scott L. Waugh and Peter D. Diehl. Cambridge, 1996. 338–62.

Petrucci, Armando. *Writers and Readers in Medieval Italy: Studies in the History of Written Culture.* Trans. Charles M. Radding. New Haven, Conn., 1995.

Pettegree, Andrew, and Matthew Hall. "The Reformation and the Book: A Reconsideration." *The Historical Journal* 47 (2004): 785–808.

Pons, Nicole. "Intellectual Patterns and Affective Reactions in Defence of the Dauphin Charles, 1419–1422." In *War, Government and Power in Late Medieval France.* Ed. Christopher Allmand. Liverpool, 2000. 54–69.

Poor, Sara S. *Mechthild of Magdeburg and Her Book: Gender and the Making of Textual Authority.* Philadelphia, 2004.

Post, R. R. *The Modern Devotion: Confrontation with Reformation and Humanism.* Leiden, 1968.

Posthumus Meyjes, G. H. M. "Exponents of Sovereignty: Canonists as Seen by Theologians in the Late Middle Ages." In *The Church and Sovereignty, c. 590–1915: Essays in Honour of Michael Wilks.* Ed. Diana Wood. Oxford, 1991. 299–328.

———. *Jean Gerson Apostle of Unity: His Church Politics and Ecclesiology.* Trans. J. C. Grayson. Leiden, 1999.

Pesenti, Tiziana. "Generi e pubblico della letteratura medica padovana nel Tre e Quattrocento." In *Università e società nei secoli XII–XVI (Pistoia, 20–25 settembre 1979).* Pistoia, 1982. 523–45.

Quillen, Carol Everhart. *Rereading the Renaissance: Petrarch, Augustine, and the Language of Humanism.* Ann Arbor, 1998.

Quinto, Riccardo. *Scholastica: Storia di un concetto.* Padua, 2001.

Reiter, Eric H. "Masters, Students, and Their Books in the Late Medieval German Universities." *Paedagogica Historica* 34 (1998): 389–401.

Richardson, Brian. "From Scribal Publication to Print Publication: Pietro Bembo's *Rime*, 1529–1535." *The Modern Language Review* 95, no. 3 (2000): 684–95.

Ridder-Symoens, Hilde de, ed. *A History of the University in Europe.* 3 vols. Vol. 1, *Universities in the Middle Ages.* Cambridge, 1992.

———. "Mobility." In Ridder-Symoens (1992). 280–304.

Riddy, Felicity. "'Publication' Before Print: The Case of Julian of Norwich." In *The Uses of Script and Print, 1300–1700.* Ed. Julia Crick and Alexandra Walsham. Cambridge, 2004. 29–49.

Rieckenberg, Hans-Jürgen. "Die Katechismus-Tafel des Nikolaus von Kues in der Lamberti-Kirche zu Hildesheim." *DA* 39 (1983): 555–81.

Riley, Lawrence Joseph. *The History, Nature, and Use of Epikeia in Moral Theology.* Washington, D.C., 1948.

Robinson, P. R. "The 'Booklet': A Self-Contained Unit in Composite Manuscripts." In *Codicologica 3: Essais typologiques*. Ed. A. Gruys. Leiden, 1980. 46–69.

Roccati, G. Matteo. "À propos de la tradition manuscrite de l'oeuvre poétique latine de Gerson: Les manuscrits Paris, Bibl. nat., lat. 3624 et 3628." *RHT* 10 (1980): 277–304.

———. "La formation des humanistes dans le dernier quart du XIVe siècle." In *Pratiques de la culture écrite en France au XVe siècle (Actes du Colloque international du CNRS Paris, 16–18 mai 1992)*. Ed. Monique Ornato and Nicole Pons. Louvain-la-Neuve, 1995. 55–73.

———. "Geiler von Kaysersberg et la tradition imprimée des oeuvres de Gerson." *Revue française d'histoire du livre*, n.s., 47 (1985): 271–93.

———. "Gerson e il problema dell'espressione poetica: Note su alcuni temi e immagini ricorrenti nelle poesie latine." *Studi Francesi* 77 (1982): 278–85.

———. "A Gersonian Text in Defense of Poetry: De laudibus elegie spiritualis (ca. 1422–1425)." *Traditio* 60 (2005): 369–85.

———. "Humanisme et préoccupations religieuses au début du XVe siècle: Le prologue de la 'Josephina' de Jean Gerson." In *Préludes à la Renaissance: Aspects de la vie intellectuelle en France au XVe siècle*. Ed. C. Bozzolo and E. Ornato. Paris, 1992. 107–22.

———. "La 'Josephina' di Jean Gerson (1418): Un poema virgiliano di contenuto biblico." *Studi Francesi* 121 (1997): 3–19.

———. "Manuscrits de la Bibliothèque Vaticane contenant des oeuvres de Gerson: Compléments à l'édition Glorieux." *Scriptorium* 36 (1982): 103–11.

———. "La production *de canticis* de Jean Gerson: Les circonstances de composition et de diffusion. À propos d'un ouvrage récent." *Le Moyen âge* 112 (2006): 355–61.

Root, R. K. "Publication Before Printing." *Publications of the Modern Language Association* 28 (1913): 417–31.

Rouse, Mary A., and Richard H. Rouse. *Authentic Witnesses: Approaches to Medieval Texts and Manuscripts*. Notre Dame, Ind., 1991.

———. "Bibliography Before Print: The Medieval *De viris illustribus*." In *Authentic Witnesses*. 469–94.

———. "The Book Trade at the University of Paris, ca. 1250–ca. 1350." In *Authentic Witnesses*. 259–338.

———. "The Development of Research Tools in the Thirteenth Century." In *Authentic Witnesses*. 221–55.

———. *Manuscripts and Their Makers: Commercial Book Producers in Medieval Paris, 1200–1500*. 2 vols. Turnhout, 2000.

———. "*Ordinatio* and *Compilatio* Revisited." In *Ad litteram: Authoritative Texts and Their Medieval Readers*. Ed. Mark D. Jordan and Kent Emery, Jr. Notre Dame, Ind., 1992. 113–34.

———. "*Statim invenire*: Schools, Preachers, and New Attitudes to the Page." In *Authentic Witnesses*. 191–219.

Rouse, Richard H. "Backgrounds to Print: Aspects of the Manuscript Book in Northern Europe of the Fifteenth Century." In Rouse and Rouse, *Authentic Witnesses*. 449–66.

———. "The Early Library of the Sorbonne." In Rouse and Rouse, *Authentic Witnesses*. Notre Dame, Ind., 1991. 341–408.

Rummel, Erika. *The Humanist-Scholastic Debate in the Renaissance and Reformation*. Cambridge, Mass., 1995.

Saenger, Paul. "Silent Reading: Its Impact on Late Medieval Script and Society." *Viator* 13 (1982): 367–414.

———. *Space Between Words: The Origins of Silent Reading.* Stanford, 1997.

Scase, Wendy. "Imagining Alternatives to the Book: The Transmission of Political Poetry in Late Medieval England." In *Imagining the Book.* Ed. Stephen Kelly and John J. Thompson. Turnhoult, 2005. 237–50.

———. "'Strange and Wonderful Bills': Bill-Casting and Political Discourse in Late Medieval England." *New Medieval Literatures* 2 (1998): 225–47.

Schönberger, Rolf. *Was ist Scholastik?* Hildesheim, 1991.

Schreiner, Klaus. "Benediktinische Klosterreform als zeitgebundene Auslegung der Regel." *Blätter für württembergische Kirchengeschichte* 86 (1986): 105–95.

———. "Laienfrömmigkeit—Frömmigkeit von Eliten oder Frömmigkeit des Volkes?" In *Laienfrömmigkeit im späten Mittelalter.* Ed. Klaus Schreiner. Munich, 1992. 1–78.

Schwab, J. B. *Johannes Gerson, Professor der Theologie und Kanzler der Universität Paris.* Wurzburg, 1858; rpt., New York, 1960.

Seńko, Władysław, and Zofia Włodek. "Dzieła Gersona zachowane w bibliotekach polskich." (Works of Gerson Preserved in Polish Libraries.) *Materiały i studia. Seria A: Materiały do historii folozofii średniowiecznej w Polsce* 7 (1967): 101–17.

Shank, Michael H. *"Unless You Believe, You Shall Not Understand": Logic, University, and Society in Late Medieval Vienna.* Princeton, N.J., 1988.

Sharpe, Richard. *Titulus: Identifying Medieval Latin Texts, An Evidence-Based Approach.* Turnhout, 2003.

Siraisi, Nancy G. "How to Write a Latin Book on Surgery: Organizing Principles and Authorial Devices in Guglielmo da Saliceto and Dino del Garbo." In *Practical Medicine from Salerno to the Black Death.* Ed. Roger French, Luis Garcîa-Ballester, Jon Arrizabalaga, and Andrew Cunningham. Cambridge, 1994. 88–109.

Small, Helen, ed. *The Public Intellectual.* Oxford, 2002.

Smalley, Beryl. *English Friars and Antiquity in the Early Fourteenth Century.* Oxford, 1960.

Smoller, Laura Ackerman. *History, Prophecy, and the Stars: The Christian Astrology of Pierre d'Ailly, 1350–1420.* Princeton, N.J., 1994.

Stallybrass, Peter. "Broadsides and the Printing Revolution." In *Agent of Change: Print Culture Studies After Elizabeth L. Eisenstein.* Ed. Sabrina Alcorn Baron, Eric N. Lindquist, and Eleanor F. Shevlin. Amherst, Mass., 2007. 315–41.

Steinberg, Justin. *Accounting for Dante: Urban Readers and Writers in Late Medieval Italy.* Notre Dame, Ind., 2007.

Stone, M. W. F. "The Origins of Probabilism in Late Scholastic Moral Thought: A Prolegomenon to Further Study." *RTPM* 67 (2000): 114–57.

Swanson, R. N. *Universities, Academics, and the Great Schism.* Cambridge, 1979.

Taber, Douglass, Jr. "Pierre d'Ailly and the Teaching Authority of the Theologian." *Church History* 59 (1990): 163–74.

Tachau, Katherine. "French Theology in the mid-Fourteenth Century." *AHDLMA* 51 (1984): 41–80.

Taylor, Andrew. "Authors, Scribes, Patrons and Books." In *The Idea of the Vernacular: An Anthology of Middle English Literary Theory, 1280–1520.* Ed. Jocelyn Wogan-Browne, Nicholas Watson, Andrew Taylor, and Ruth Evans. University Park, Penn., 1999. 353–65.

Tentler, Thomas. *Sin and Confession on the Eve of the Reformation.* Princeton, N.J., 1977.

Thijssen, J. M. M. H. *Censure and Heresy at the University of Paris, 1200–1400.* Philadelphia, 1998.

Thomson, W. R. *The Latin Writings of John Wyclyf.* Toronto, 1983.

Trapp, D. "Augustinian Theology of the Fourteenth Century." *Augustiniana* 6 (1956): 146–274.

Ullmann, Berthold L. *The Humanism of Coluccio Salutati.* Padua, 1963.

Valois, Noël. "Un nouveau témoignage sur Jeanne d'Arc: Réponse d'un clerc parisien à l'apologie de la Pucelle par Gerson." In *Annuaire-Bulletin de la Société de l'Histoire de France, 1906.* Paris, 1907.

Van Engen, John. *Devotio Moderna Basic Writings.* New York, 1988.

———. "From Practical Theology to Divine Law: The Work and Mind of Medieval Canonists." In *Proceedings of the Ninth International Congress of Medieval Canon Law, Munich, 13–18 July 1992.* Ed. Peter Landau and Joers Mueller. Vatican City, 1997. 873–96.

Vansteenberghe, E. "Le Doctrinal de Gerson à la cathédrale de Thérouanne." *Bulletin de la Société des Antiquaires de la Morinie* 15 (1924): 467–74.

———. "Gerson à Bruges." *RHE* 31 (1935): 5–52.

Vasoli, C. "Les débuts de l'humanisme à l'Université de Paris." In *Preuve et raisons à l'Université de Paris: logique, ontologie et théologie au XIVe siècle.* Ed. Zénon Kaluza and Paul Vignaux. Paris, 1984. 269–86.

Verger, Jacques. "Le livre dans les universités du Midi de la France à la fin du Moyen Âge." In *Pratiques de la culture écrite en France au XVe siècle.* Ed. Monique Ornato and Nicole Pons. Louvain, 1995. 403–20.

———. "Les professeurs des universités françaises à la fin du Moyen Âge." In *Les universités françaises au moyen âge.* Leiden, 1995. 174–98.

———. "Schools and Universities." In *The New Cambridge Medieval History.* 7 vols. Vol. 7, *c. 1415–c. 1500.* Ed. Christopher Allmand. Cambridge, 2005. 220–42.

———. "Les universités françaises au XVe siècle: Crise et tentatives de réforme." In *Les universités françaises au moyen âge.* Leiden, 1995. 228–55.

Verger, Jacques, and C. Vulliez. "Crise et mutations des Universités françaises à la fin du Moyen Âge." In *Histoire des Universités en France.* Ed. J. Verger. Toulouse, 1986. 109–37.

Vial, Marc. "Zur Funktion des Monotessaron des Johannes Gerson." In *Evangelienharmonien des Mittelalters.* Ed. August den Hollander, Christoph Burger, and Ulrich Schmid. Assen, 2004. 40–72.

Ward, J. O. "Rhetoric in the Faculty of Arts at the Universities of Paris and Oxford in the Middle Ages: A Summary of the Evidence." *Archivum Latinitatis Medii Aevi* 54 (1996): 159–231.

Watts, John. "The Pressure of the Public on Later Medieval Politics." In *Political Culture in Late Medieval Britain.* Ed. Linda Clark and Christine Carpenter. Woodbridge, UK, 2004. 159–80.

Wei, Ian P. "The Masters of Theology at the University of Paris in the Late Thirteenth and Early Fourteenth Centuries: An Authority Beyond the Schools." *Bulletin of the John Rylands University Library Manchester* 75 (1993): 37–63.

———. "The Self-Image of the Masters of Theology at the University of Paris in the Late Thirteenth and Early Fourteenth Centuries." *Journal of Ecclesiastical History* 46 (1995): 398–431.

Weijers, Olga. *La disputatio à la faculté des Arts de Paris (1200–1350 environ): Esquisse d'une typologie.* Turnhout, 1995.

———. *Le maniement du savoir: Pratiques intellectuelles à l'époque des premières universités (XIIIe–XIVe siècles).* Turnhout, 1996.

―――. *Terminologies des universités au XIIIe siècle.* Rome, 1987.

Weiss, Roberto. "The Private Collector and the Revival of Greek Learning." In *The English Library Before 1700.* Ed. Francis Wormald and C. E. Wright. London, 1958. 112–35.

Willard, Charity Cannon. "The Manuscripts of Jean Petit's Justification: Some Burgundian Propaganda Methods of the Early Fifteenth Century." *Studi Francesi* 38 (1969): 271–80.

Wilson, R. M. "The Contents of the Mediaeval Library." In *The English Library Before 1700.* Ed. Francis Wormald and C. E. Wright. London, 1958. 87–111.

Wippel, J. F. "The Quodlibetal Quaestio as a Distinctive Literary Genre." In *Les genres littéraires dans les sources théologiques et philosophiques médiévales: Définition, critique et exploitation (Actes du Colloque international de Louvain-la-Neuve, 25–27 mai 1981).* Louvain-la-Neuve, 1982. 67–87.

―――. "Quodlibetal Questions, Chiefly in Theology Faculties." In *Les questions disputées et les questions quodlibétiques dans les facultés de théologie, de droit et de médecine.* Ed. B. C. Bazán, G. Fransen, D. Jacquart, and J. Wippel. Turnhout, 1985. 153–222.

Witt, Ronald G. "Coluccio Salutati and the Conception of the Poeta Theologus in the Fourteenth Century." *Renaissance Quarterly* 30 (1977): 538–63.

―――. *Hercules at the Crossroads: The Life, Works, and Thought of Coluccio Salutati.* Durham, N.C., 1983.

―――. "Medieval *Ars Dictaminis* and the Beginning of Humanism: A New Construction of the Problem." *Renaissance Quarterly* 35 (1982): 1–35.

―――. "Medieval Italian Culture and the Origins of Humanism as a Stylistic Ideal." In *Renaissance Humanism: Foundations, Forms, and Legacy.* Ed. A. Rabil, Jr. Philadelphia, 1988. 29–70.

Index of Manuscripts

Index of Works by Gerson

Works are indexed according to their number in the modern edition of P. Glorieux (ed.), *Jean Gerson, Oeuvres complètes* (Paris, 1960–73). Works not numbered in the modern edition appear at the end. The translated or informal titles used in this book appear in parentheses following the original titles (as given by Glorieux, with occasional modification). I have omitted merely passing references to a text in the notes.

General Index

Acknowledgments

This book concerns authorship and the material conditions within which it occurs. Many individuals and institutions have generously supported my own authorship, and it is a pleasure to be able to thank them for helping to make this book possible. Among the many research librarians who have assisted me, I should mention especially David Lincove at Ohio State University and Marina Smyth at the University of Notre Dame. Christine Glassner generously shared with me her inventory of Gerson manuscripts in Lower Austria. Brother Florian Ehebruster kindly sent me images of a manuscript from Seitenstetten Abbey. The staff at the Hill Monastic Manuscript Library in Collegeville, Minnesota, welcomed me as a Heckman Research Fellow; for the study of Gerson, their collection is priceless. I also wish to thank the many librarians in Europe who helped me canvass the manuscript evidence that underlies important parts of this book: at the British Library in London; at the Institut de Recherche et d'Histoire des Textes, the Bibliothèque nationale de France, and the Bibliothèque de l'Arsenal in Paris; and at the Bayerische Staatsbibliothek in Munich.

A year of study in Paris was made possible through support from a fellowship provided by the Newberry Library and the École des Chartes. During that year, Gilbert Ouy welcomed me warmly to his *équipe* at Villejuif, now in its third incarnation as the Laboratoire de médiévistique occidentale de Paris; he also read my work many times with great care. My few disagreements with him pale next to my respect and admiration for his accomplishments. Without his pioneering research, this book would not have been possible in its current form. Ezio and Monique Ornato, Carla Bozzolo, and Nicole Pons answered many questions and offered me a comfortable place to work in their magnificent library.

I wrote three chapters in Toronto while on a Mellon Postdoctoral Fellowship at the Pontifical Institute of Mediaeval Studies under the direction of Father James McConica. Father James Farge and Joseph Goering both read early versions of Chapters 6 and 7 and gave helpful advice and criticism. I also learned much from the participants in the Interdisciplinary Seminar. I must also thank the University of Texas at Arlington for generously allowing me to defer my position for a year to take the fellowship at Toronto, and especially my department chair, Don Kyle, and my dean, Beth Wright, for their support in making that happen.

Since arriving at Ohio State in 2006, I've enjoyed working in a wonderful community of scholars. The College of Humanities and the Department of History provided a generous subvention to help with the cost of publication. I enjoyed a stimulating discussion of Chapter 7 with David Cressy, Geoffrey Parker, Dale Van Kley, and the other participants (including a very sharp group of graduate students) in the Early Modern Seminar. I also wish to thank the History of the Book Group, under the organization of Cynthia Brokaw, for their helpful discussion of Chapter 6.

Many other scholarly and personal friendships have lightened the burden of authorship along the way. James Forse first initiated me into the study of medieval history as a professional discipline; his continued friendship has been a constant source of encouragement. Bruce Woll has listened to endless conversations about the book and read chapters with unflagging interest. Gerson probably would have frowned on such curiosity, but I found it refreshing and stimulating. David Bachrach, Christine Caldwell Ames, Lezlie Knox, and James Mixson made numerous tangible and intangible contributions to the book. Chapter 7 benefited from the comments of medievalists at Northwestern University and at the Ohio Medieval Colloquium. Jim Bartholomew, Rita Copeland, Alan Farmer, James Forse, Maarten Hoenen, Howard Kaminsky, Ethan Knapp, Deborah McGrady, John Ott, Mircea Platon, Diane Reilly, David Staley, Kathleen Tonry, and Lori Walters all helped me improve individual chapters. Otto Bohlmann and Noreen O'Connor-Abel at Penn Press gave expert attention to the manuscript, and Jerry Singerman guided the work through the publishing cycle. A sincere thank you to all of them!

Early in my writing, Robert Lerner provided a wonderful forum for me to talk about Gerson at the Intellectual History Seminar at the Newberry Library in Chicago. He then responded to my article in the *American Historical Review* with a detailed, helpful, and encouraging letter. I also benefited greatly from the comments of William Courtenay, who revealed his identity as an outside reader during the review process. Maureen Boulton first encouraged my interest in Gerson, gave expert advice on his French works, and communicated to me her love for manuscripts. Many insights followed from conversations with Kent Emery, who also helped me think through the technical problems and issues dealing with Gerson's manuscripts early on and gave helpful feedback on several chapters at a late stage. Besides offering much encouragement, Tom Noble helped to clarify the stakes of the project. John Van Engen engaged and invested heavily in my work from beginning to end, and deserves my deep gratitude for his personal kindness and material generosity. What this book offers as a history of late medieval culture owes most to him. David Mengel and Rachel Koopmans each read multiple drafts of every chapter, at great expense of time and labor; clarity always resulted. Writing a book can be a lonely task, but their friendship and encouragement have made it much less so. My deepest thanks to them both for going with me on this journey, and for enriching it.

Les and Mildred Hobbins, my parents, filled my world with stability and love, made deep sacrifices for my education, and never failed to encourage and trust me. I dedicate this book to them, with love and gratefulness.

*   *   *

An earlier version of Chapter 5 was published in the *American Historical Review* 108:5 (2003): 1308–37. The revised version appears here by permission.